Creativity of
POWER

Creativity of POWER

Cosmology and Action in African Societies

Edited by W. Arens and Ivan Karp

Smithsonian Institution Press
Washington and London

Coeditors
Nancy L. Benco and Benjamin D. Reiss

Designer
Lisa Buck Vann

Cover Illustration
Magical figure (*nkisi*).
Southern Savannah, Lower Zaire River region, Kongo, Zaire.
The Stanley Collection, University of Iowa Museum of Art

Library of Congress Cataloging-in-Publication Data

Creativity of power : Cosmology and action in African societies / edited by W. Arens and Ivan Karp.
p. cm.
Includes bibliographies.
ISBN 0-87474-617-5
1. Ethnology—Africa.
2. Power (Social sciences)
3. Political anthropology—Africa.
4. Africa—Social life and customs.
I. Arens, W., 1940– .
II. Karp, Ivan.
GN645.C73 1989 303.3—dc20 89-32176
British Library Cataloguing-in-Publication Data available

∞ The paper used in this publication meets the minimum requirements of the American National Standard for Permanence of Paper for Printed Library Materials Z39.48—1984.

Printed in the United States of America

2 4 6 8 10 9 7 5 3 1
90 92 94 96 98 97 95 93 91 89

Dedicated to the memory of Meyer Fortes

with grateful thanks for his continuing inspiration

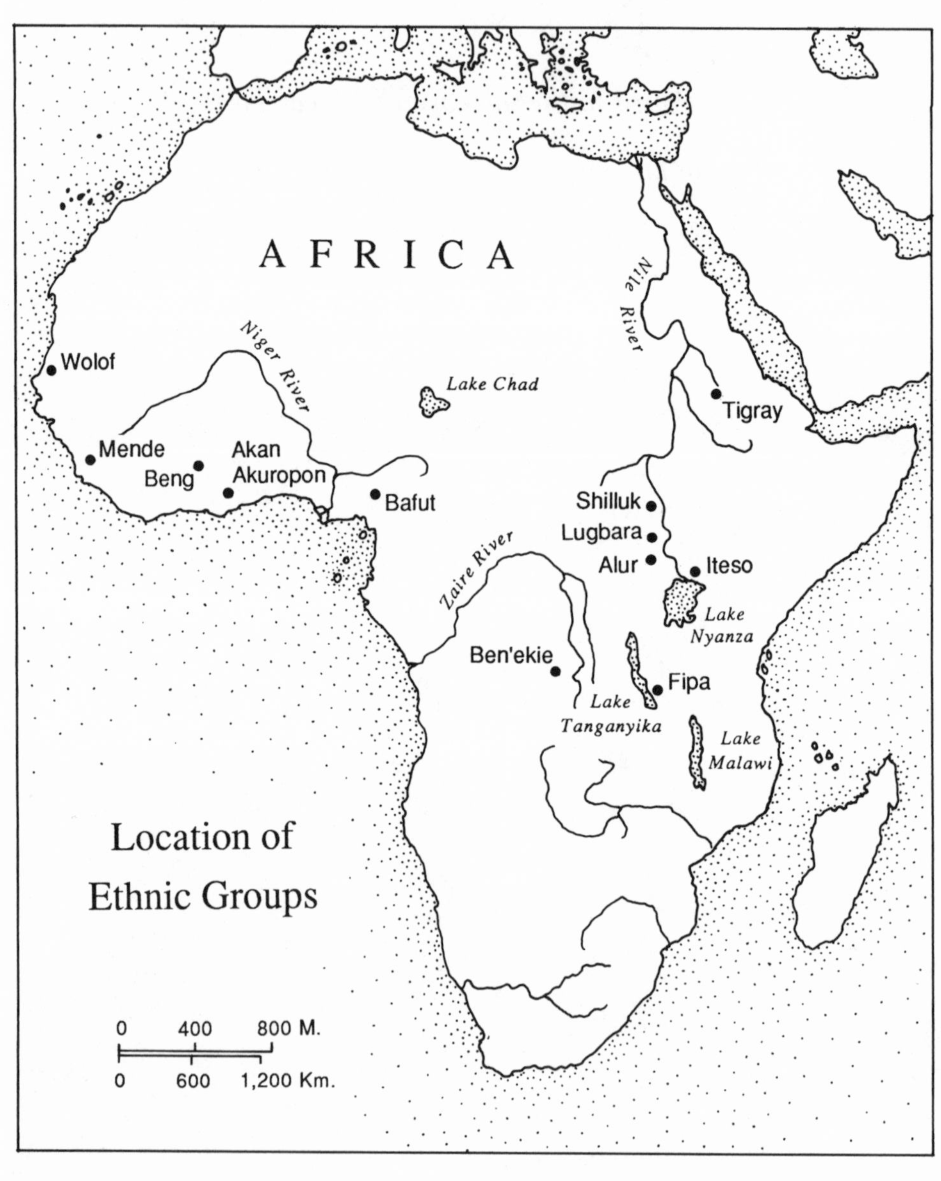
A F R I C A
Nile River
Niger River
Wolof
Lake Chad
Tigray
Mende
Beng
Akan
Akuropon
Bafut
Shilluk
Lugbara
Alur
Iteso
Zaire River
Lake
Nyanza
Ben'ekie
Fipa
Lake
Tanganyika
Lake
Malawi
Location of
Ethnic Groups
0 400 800 M.
0 600 1,200 Km.

Contents

W. Arens and Ivan Karp

Introduction

The essays in this volume explore the seemingly familiar concepts of power, action, and human agency in African social systems and cosmologies.[1] Unfortunately, the simplicity and adequacy of this statement is immediately cancelled by the fact that the average English-language dictionary offers a dozen or more definitions of the meaning of power. These move uneasily between the mechanical and the spiritual implications of the word. Moreover, there is a considerable literature devoted to the specific sociological analysis and application of the concept. Yet, as one prominent sociological commentator has remarked, no consensus on the definition of power has ever been achieved. Hence each discussion begins anew with a preliminary clarification of the intended usage (Dahrendorf 1959:166).

A frequent response to this situation is influenced by the model of analysis found in ordinary language philosophy. This orientation assumes that clear a priori definitions are neither useful nor necessary and that meaning can be sought in patterns of use. Furthermore, it assumes that the quest for a clear and concise definition of any concept is both naive and distorting, as there is no correspondence in the external world to match the multiple significances of utterances (Clegg 1975:8). The danger here is that neither *definition* nor *use* will be carefully examined and power will be taken to be a common sense, transparently clear, concept.

This line of reasoning is taken by the editors of a recent volume of essays on power in a cross-cultural perspective who conveniently dismiss the problem by concluding that the term power is an "intellectual catch-all" (Fogelson and Adams 1977:xi). This is undoubtedly the case in cross-cultural studies of "power," but disarming the issue in such a manner fails to address adequately the problem of how this has come to be the case. It is not unreasonable to ask why the concept of power should lend itself so easily to a variety of situations and interpretations, instead of producing a uniform and comparable literature.

This question has not gone unanswered, and in an authoritative essay that reviews the intellectual history of the concept, the sociologist Steven Lukes convincingly argues that embracing a particular view of power "arises out of and operates within a particular moral and political perspective" (1978:26). Citing the philosopher Gallie, he refers to power as "an essentially contested concept" which "inevitably involves endless disputes about their proper uses on the part of the users" (Gallie 1955–56:169). Lukes concludes, therefore, that the attempt to define power is in itself a subtle form of intellectual politics, a rhetorical gesture. The act of definition implies a particular view of the nature of society, political institutions, the goals of action, and the means used to achieve them. Lukes does not add, as we would, that the semantic equivalents of "power" in different languages and cultures embody as much a view of society and human action as they do in the Western social sciences.

This observation is directed toward what we think is the significance of this volume. The concept of "power" as it is used by all peoples encodes ideas about the nature of the world, social relations, and the effects of actions in and on the world and the entities that inhabit it.[2] We explicitly argue that power must be viewed in part as an artifact of the imagination and a facet of human creativity, and as such a fertile field of investigation for social anthropology. The essays in this volume show how choosing this perspective produces greater insights into the conceptual problems involved; they also broaden the intellectual horizons of scholarship by confronting the indigenous definitions of the social scientists with the different ways in which power is thought to be generated and put to use in social life by other locals. Yet even this statement begs the question of the way in which the idea of power is understood and employed by the social scientists in this volume to confront the others whose concepts of power they describe and analyze.

Any consideration of the notion of power must surely begin with reference to the work of Max Weber, whose ideas, so dominant and influential in the other social sciences, have been largely ignored in social anthropology.[3] As many of the essays in this volume attest, however, Weber's ideas lead to valuable insights into the nature of domestic and public political activities in the sense of the quest of one social actor to gain influence over others.

If Weber's typology of political systems has been generally unused by anthropologists, his definition of power has been accepted and used by almost all social scientists. According to Weber, "power (*Macht*) is the probability that one actor within a social relationship will be in the position to carry out his own will despite resistance, regardless of the basis on which this probability rests" (1964:152). This famous definition often provides the basic premise for more extended and abstract discussions of power (see Parsons 1963), so it is worthwhile to consider some of its implications.[4]

First, Weber's view conceives of power as arising from relationships between social actors in a mutually acknowledged competitive or cooperative context. Power is exercised for the achievement of practical ends through the mechanisms of domination and submission. Furthermore, the focus is primarily on the pursuit of individual rather than collective goals, for it views power as the outcome and expression of dyadic relationships. This perspective fails to examine one of the oldest and most important problems in social theory, that is, the relationship between individual actions and collectively defined ends (Emmett 1972).

Second, this framework implies that the source of power is found in human agents who exercise their rationality to calculate the costs and returns of using different means in the pursuit of accepted ends. This is precisely how Weber distinguishes between power and authority. Power is rational and authority is accepted without reflection; that is, it is *legitimate*. In Weber's view, Western bureaucratized social systems elevate rational calculation to the status of a norm. This elevation is not universally shared by all peoples, as Weber explicitly recognized in his own typology of social systems.

The view of power as rational calculation emphasizes the exercise of power and the pursuit of goals, which raises the third problem. The framework fails to consider how concepts of power are used by agents to produce their actions or how those concepts are grounded in cultural resources. Most accounts of the exercise of power and political relationships presume that these are secularly based, even when religious activities are being described. The consequence is a twofold failure in analysis. First, many studies exhibit a tendency toward a universalizing stance, which many African philosophers have decried as ethnocentric (Hontoundji 1983; Mudimbe 1988). These accounts view the universal source and application of power relationships as almost always secular, unvarying in time and space. Second, many studies reveal a static view of both power relationships and culture. They fail to provide an account of how cultural resources are used in guiding actions, defining goals, interpreting the experience of such "power" relationships as domination and subordination, or even expressing legitimacy. As a result culture is only an aspect of power, usually called "political culture." We have little sense of how the actors make these beliefs and values relevant while they use these beliefs and values in pursuit of their interests.

A valuable alternative to Weber's approach has been articulated by David Parkin in his introduction to *Semantic Anthropology* (1982: xlvi): "Power rests not simply on the acquisition of land and material objects but rather derives from unequal access to semantic creativity, including the capacity to nominate others as equal or unequal, animate or inanimate, memorable or abject, discussor or discussed." This perspective moves us away from an exclusive emphasis on the exercise of power and provides room for examining the relationship between power and consciousness. It encompasses the subtle insights of Simmel (1950), for example, who remarked that domination "is not so much the exploitation of the other as much as the mere consciousness of the possibility" (p. 151).

We could even question whether assumptions about the culturally transparent nature of power make sense in the context of the Western industrialized and rationalized social systems so well-known to Weber and succeeding generations of sociologists and political scientists. Rationality as a norm is not often the defining principle of forms of social organization. Rationality as a process can be grounded in assumptions other than rational choice theory.[5] Yet the majority of anthropological studies of non-Western political systems and political action are restricted to this focus on the exercise of power as manifested in the form of influence and control over others' behavior, usually situated in its relationship to roles and institutional settings. In fact, few studies in political anthropology, considered to be one of the major subdisciplines, adopt what we would consider an anthropological perspective, which involves a conceptualization of power as it relates to other aspects of the encompassing cosmological system.[6] While this may not be surprising in sociology and political science, it is a striking ellipsis in anthropology, which asserts that cultural forms affect the structure of social action.

Anthropologists should therefore consider indigenous concepts carefully and recognize that the comprehensive study of power involves "all conceivable qualities of a person and all conceivable combinations of circumstances" (Weber 1947:153). This implies that the study of political relations involves more than the recognition that power is what power does. It also entails the recognition that power is how power means, and that interpretations may vary from place to place and time to time. Clastres (1987) made this point in stark terms when he observed that the model of political power usually used by social scientists is constituted within a Western cultural context, which then obscures the beliefs and experiences of those sought to be understood (p. 16).

As Adams (1977) notes, power can also be examined as an aspect of the locally defined cosmos in the form of an immanent force derived from some "extra-human" agency (p. 390). This view of power as a cultural construct leads to the conclusion that images of power entail ideas about the nature of society, the nature of nature itself, and the nature of human actions. It also leads to a definition of human social and personal potential, as these may be contrasted with the capacities of other causal agents. The general failure among anthropologists to consider power in this ideational capacity has meant that some of the more interesting comparative insights into the operation of power in society remain unexplored. One such comparison might be drawn between ideas about power and the means through which power is inscribed in relationships. Another comparison might be made between societies that possess writing as a means of asserting and storing differences in power and those that reproduce power and conflict in ritual and symbol formation.[7] We suggest that a necessary feature of any investigation into the exercise of control, or the resistance to control, should be an analysis of the cultural premises that give meaning to such behavior. Power may always involve the exercise of an individual's will over another's, but the rationale and basis for domination, acquiescence, and resistance may vary considerably from one cultural setting to another.

An ethnography of domination should identify the cultural notions that compel the group to accept the direction of a few—or suffer the presumed consequences. This is a question about legitimacy and suggests that power takes varied ideological forms. It should be of paramount concern to an anthropological inquiry, in contrast to a one-sided concentration on the mechanisms for exercising power. Sources of legitimacy need not be secular and rational. We can not presume that they are derived from the resolution of disputes among human agents or that they only emerge out of considerations of political purpose. The idea that what is defined as legitimate is the natural outcome of rational decision-making is a classic instance of the hegemonic extension of an ideology over increasingly large sectors of peoples' lives. Debates over definition and ontological considerations cannot be reduced to questions of practicality. Even a brief consideration of recent history suggests that social systems, including ours, are not systematic and coherent. They are composed of groups and individuals who continually define their lives in contraposition to seemingly accepted norms. This is the stuff of which resistance is sometimes made (Scott 1985). Perhaps resistance is too strong a concept. The point is that power does not emanate from a single source and social formations are composed of centers and epicenters of power in dynamic relationship with one another. Domination and subordination operate on both sides of all relationships, even between two persons, since dependence and control are shared unequally among the actors. The key question is not how power is centralized; it isn't. The key question is how the illusion that power organizes a social formation composed of a center and a periphery emerges and acts in society.

This illusion implies that power emanates from a single or central source. This idea has obvious affinities with the rise of the modern state. It brings us to the concept of authority, to those concepts and processes that legitimize the exercise of power. As Lukes (1978:639) informs us, definitions of authority tend to be two-tiered. They place the exercise of power in the public arena, where the state claims hegemony over social action and defines the rights of persons. There is also a second tier; it defines not the *where* of power but the *who*. Lukes reminds us that authority entails an appeal to legitimizing values and not to practical reason. He identifies three types of justifications that underpin ideologies of authority: belief or faith, convention, and imposition (Lukes 1978). Foucault (1978) argues in a similar vein that "power is tolerable only on condition it mask a substantial part of itself. Its success is proportional to its ability to hide its own mechanisms" (p. 6).

The utility of the distinction between power and authority is apparent in many of the conclusions drawn by the contributions to this volume, which show that power is multicentered and, further, that the idea of a center may itself be produced through the ideology of power. The essays avoid a common problem encountered in political anthropology—a movement from a concern with how power and authority interact and are experienced in society to a conclusion that power is both rational and real and authority is simply mystifying. This is the notion behind Maurice Bloch's unfortunate attempts to argue that ritual embodies the false claims of authority over the real exercise of power.[8]

In this context, we believe that the African societies analyzed in the following pages do more than merely "mask" the exercise of power with a more emphatic concern for the relationship between this and the other world. Members of these societies assert that the source of power resides in the interaction between natural, social, and supernatural realms. This contrasts with the ideal image of Western political systems. Arrangements in the liberal social democratic tradition typically draw attention to the common good and the consent of the governed as paramount ideological features, in order to obfuscate the potential exercise of power for the achievement of the political ends of a particular segment of society. In many African social systems, however, the exercise of political influence derives from access to and work upon the natural and supernatural spheres, both as the source of power to control others and as the legitimization for actions. As a consequence, power in itself has a different cultural foundation, since it involves several domains ordinarily separated in experience and practice.

Thus, Fortes and Evans-Pritchard (1940) remarked some time ago that "an African ruler is not to his people merely a person who can enforce his will on them. He is the axis of their political relations, the symbol of their unity and exclusiveness, and the embodiment of their essential values" (p. 17). The programmatic implications of this statement, which pointed to the cultural significance of such offices and their incumbents as symbolic mediators, was by and large ignored for some time in political anthropology. An interest in this approach was revived primarily by Beidelman's re-analyses of the role of priests and prophets among the acephalous Nuer of the Nilotic Sudan (1971) and the Incwala ceremony of the Swazi of Southern Africa (1966). In the latter ceremony, Beidelman not only demonstrated that the Swazi king is a figure who mediates between the normally opposed spheres of the indigenous cosmology, but, more significantly from the present perspective, he is thought to annually regenerate the cosmos itself by his actions. Thus "the pathos" and power of the Swazi king is demonstrated at the moment that he "takes the filth of the nation on himself" (Beidelman, 1966:396; Lienhardt 1961). These and subsequent insights, which also focus on regeneration, draw our attention to the use of different cultural idioms in the attempt to comprehend widespread conceptions of the essence of power and its practitioners in Africa (see Kopytoff 1980, Packard 1982, and Vaughan 1980).

First among these is the recognition of the role of ritual, especially in the context of royal installation or renewal ceremonies, which set in motion the attempt to tap the inherent forces of the universe. These studies illustrate how the human imagination creates systems of transformation that channel creative forces into their own lives. Such activities, which are now well understood from the existing literature, involve symbolic activities that bring together domains normally viewed as best kept apart. The ritual behavior creates danger for those most intimately involved, and as such they demonstrate their control over such situations and emerge as sources of power themselves. In the course of the rituals indigenous conceptions of power undergo permutations, as they are transformed into capacities which are characteristic of the office and its incumbent. This process of redefinition becomes a feature of political ideology in the form of legitimization.

Anthropologists have customarily viewed social life as a process, and have recognized politics in particular as a series of purposefully related activities (see Swartz, Turner and Tuden 1966). Such interpretations also involve the recognition of social transformations, such as the interaction between economic and political systems, in which one type of control is converted into another. We suggest here a similar orientation toward the construction of power, which would be consistent with the conceptualization of the exercise of control in its behavioral context. According to this perspective, power takes on various forms in both the cultural and social domains. As Russell (1938) argued, a legitimate concern of social science is to recognize and explore the paths of such transformations in the cultural universe (pp. 13–14). This view not only provides a broader spectrum of analysis, but it also offers a more encompassing grasp of the definition of power in the many senses it takes in English usage. Power thus becomes a series of ideas linked with actions, which have an effect on other ideas and actions, rather than merely a characteristic of isolated situations of social interaction.

Interpreting power in this polymorphic and dynamic fashion also draws attention to contrasting definitions of human and supernatural capacities in other cosmological systems. In those instances where an office-holder is seen as a source of transformed power, the continued viability of the social system is consistent with his abilities. In addition, a number of societies considered in the essays, which are representative of others in Africa and elsewhere, more explicitly recognize the fragility of their social universe and suspect, rather than assume, the condition of continued viability. The cultural energy which maintains their social forms is not taken for granted, nor is this attitude unreasonable, in light of a very recent past, experienced with a comparatively simple technology in an often threatening human and natural environment. Members of these societies do not presume that progress is automatic and nature can be altered at will. This is a stance that the West might seek to emulate in our own era of acid rain and global warming. Natural disasters are generally attributed either to the action of human malevolent powers or the failure to take the necessary ritual precautions (Douglas 1966; Karp 1986a). In these circumstances it is necessary to resort to measures that require people with special powers and knowledge.

Communal ceremonies accentuate the themes of renewal in a universe with a constant potential for failure. This entropic view of the cosmos demands a resort to the immanent and personal powers to create and recreate the social conditions of existence. Foucault (1977) remarked that in the West we tend to view power in negative terms. We emphasize its one-dimensional capacity to exclude, repress, subjugate, and censor, while ignoring the possibility of power (from whatever culturally-defined source) to produce and reproduce "objects" and "truth" (p. 194). The societies considered here, by their recognition of the tenuous nature of their existence, place an undisguised emphasis on power as a means to forestall both the demise of extant social arrangements and create new forms of experience and activity. Communal rituals, which aim to convert power from one form to another, are therefore collective expressions of the human imagination. These ritual circumstances seek to establish orderly control over social life (Moore and Myerhoff 1977: 3), but it is possible to recognize even further that in some instances they are concerned with symbolizing the creation of order itself. This is especially apparent in those instances of royal installation or renewal, in which the constituent elements of what is to be society perform their assigned tasks in the creation of successive monarchs who serve as the symbols of their social system.

As the preceding argument suggests, and the following essays document, it is insufficient to conceive of power as many different but unrelated ideas or activities. Nor is it reasonable to divorce the notion of power from its cultural component by reducing it to an abstract feature of social relationships. Admittedly, the idea of power takes on many forms. However, it also involves indigenous concepts that, through a series of ritual occasions, draw attention to the recognition of particular aspects of cosmology as cultural processes involving not only shifting contexts but also "transformations in experience, identities and action" (Kapferer 1979:3).

Transformation is the key to understanding concepts of power in African societies. A central cultural theme in the essays is that the powers agents have allow them to transform the world. "Transformative capacity" is a key element in people's understanding of power, as much as it is the link between actions and agency in social theory (Giddens 1979). Precisely because our actions have effects on and in the world, we are able to produce form and fashion something out of nature. The concepts of power described in this book are, in effect, theories about the workings of people on nature, in society, and in interaction with other powers.[9]

Underlying much of the ritual and cosmology described in these essays is a sense of power derived from different capacities and used to act on the world. The ideal demonstration of this conclusion would be by means of a systematic survey of the semantics of power in African languages. Problems of translation and the biases inherent in most published dictionaries make that an impossible task. Some evidence is provided in our essays. Among the Iteso the word used to translate "power" is *apedor,* whose primary meaning is ability or capacity. This can be contrasted with *agogong,* meaning physical strength, or in some contexts *abeikin,* meaning to comply, but not having any sense of ability. There is no word for authority and duly constituted government authorities are referred to by some of the words for control. A similar semantic is found among the linguistically related Maasai, for whom *aider* means ability and who separate out physical strength and control (Naomi Kipury, personal communication, 1987). Among the Nilotic Luo the root word for ability is *timo,* which can also mean action. A noun form of *timo, tim,* has come to mean culture (E. S. Atieno-Odhiambo, personal communication, 1987). The papers in this volume on the Akan-speaking peoples demonstrate a similar semantic structure. Among the Mande-speaking Loma of Liberia, the word for ability is *ghaabaa,* which contrasts with the term for physical strength. *Ghaabaa* enables people to engage in ritual actions such as divination (Robert Leopold, personal communication, 1989).

Once we incorporate semantics, cosmology, and action, power can be understood as something significantly more subtle and meaningful than sovereignty or domination isolated at one single point in time or place. Rather, it is recognized as a pervasive social resource, which provides the ideological bases for various domestic and public relationships in Africa and elsewhere. This emphasis on the cultural basis of agency does not deny the material base which has been explored in other approaches to the subject. However, it is also necessary to recognize and explore power as a feature of the intriguing and often opaque world of cultural symbols, expressive performances, arcane knowledge, and ambiguous statuses which impart meaning to social action.

Power and agency are themes that can be discerned in much of the literature on African systems of thought. What one of us argued for in an earlier publication holds equally well for this collection of essays:

> A different view of power is exhibited in African societies than in Western social science. The stress in Africa is not on the element of control but on the more dynamic aspect of energy and the capacity to use it. . . . African ideas of power . . . have to do with engaging power and creating or at least containing the world. They may allow for the possibility of transformations in a way that Western social science concepts of power do not (Karp 1986a).

We have divided the essays in this volume into three sections, *Creating Power, Forms of Power,* and *Circulating Centers of Power.* As with many collection of this type, the essays in each section could easily have fit into another. Our division emphasizes themes that cut across each author's concerns and which express the cultural forms of the peoples described in the essays.

Section I, *Creating Power,* is directly related to our concern with agency and personhood. The essays describe different powers and effects that actors can produce. They show how power is acquired and examine the dilemmas and nightmares in the imagination of power.

In the first essay, W. Arens describes incest in the installation of the Shilluk *reth*. In this classic case, the violation of a primordial norm is used to create the power of a ritual office. Disorder is put in the service of order. Donald Cosentino's account of Mende stories about Musa Wo explore the "underside" (Karp 1980) of the exercise of power, as does the essay on the Tigray by Dan Bauer. Where Arens shows how the violations of norms create order, Cosentino describes the Mende portrayal of a world in which order becomes impossible and where power rules in its most chaotic and unmanageable form. Arens describes the successful creation of power, while Cosentino shows how a power's inherent dangers are imagined, as well as how entertaining such danger can be.

Bonnie Wright moves more explicitly to the theme of power, agency, and personhood. Her essay argues that occupational differentiation (commonly called "caste" in West Africa) is based on a cultural theory that distinguishes among the powers held by categories of persons and makes them interdependent. This interdependence affects the exercise of power. Domination by the "nobles" is countered by their dependence on the Griot. Subordination is affected by the powers of speech that only the Griot have but that the nobles require.

No such set of social distinctions affect the exercise of power in Akuropom. There, power can be created by anyone, but only at great personal cost. Michelle Gilbert describes in exquisite detail how power is acquired through the making of a thing, a so-called "fetish". This study demonstrates how cosmology is a resource-in-action that is used to create power. At the same time, she shows that manipulation of categories and things for the purpose of making power overflows the boundaries of the very categories used and becomes a potent source of danger.

Finally, Ivan Karp examines the acquisition of power through affliction. In rites of possession Iteso women become more powerful and act against the sources of jural power. Iteso society is characterized by the jural subordination of women, but this essay clearly shows how jural domination is only one center, and that the creation of power can constitute other, partially opposed, centers. Karp suggests that a clearer awareness of a cultural formation's idioms of power leads to a better understanding of its modes of resistance.

Section II, *Forms of Power,* describes the complex relationships that exist between power and different spheres of activity. Power is not only created and controlled in separate domains, but it acts upon those domains as well. The essays in this section demonstrate the importance of fine grained ethnographic descriptions in accounting for the meaning and exercise of power. In the first essay, Roy Willis describes forms of mutual commensality among the Fipa of Tanzania. Willis shows how domesticity is related to productive relations, which in themselves influence domestic relations. He describes a reticulum of cause and effect in which the changing distribution of power affects the etiquette of everyday life, while the etiquette of everyday life authorizes shifts in power relations.

Ron Engard examines dance and constitutional politics in Bafut. His analysis shows how power is manifested through public ritual and dance, which express duly constituted power. Although much has been written on art and power in Africa and elsewhere, Engard shows how far-reaching an analysis can be when the understanding of the political system equals the researcher's understanding of the art form.

John Middleton's essay provides a metaphoric choreography of images of power. Middleton describes how Lugbara ritual and symbolic classification orchestrate not only attitudes towards the mystical and practical danger of exercising power, but also the ambiguous attitudes Lugbara hold towards the right to do so. Middleton's concern with ambiguity joins with Michelle Gilbert's demonstration of the ambiguity inherent in the fashioning of a power object.

Aidan Southall takes the most systematically materialist stance in the book. Southall is concerned to situate the idioms of power manifested in rite and symbol in the "necessities" of appropriating nature and social and physical reproduction. His regional perspective takes the *longue durée* to show how systemic potentialities develop over time and space. His analysis may appear to be less concerned with the theme of agency that animates the other articles in the book, since agency tends to disappear as the temporal frame of analysis grows larger. Yet his interest in how identity is constructed shows that Southall is no vulgar determinist. Identity, power, and sanctity are the cultural material neighboring peoples use to construct boundaries between ethnic groups. They are a fundamental source of authority and a means of social reproduction. The papers by Southall and Karp provide interesting parallels. Southall examines the symbolic means by which group identity is reproduced despite their vivid sense of the frailty of the world in which they live. Karp relates spirit possession to the frailty inherent in internal physical and social reproduction. Southall and Karp approach similar problems from two different perspectives: Southall's is the more Olympian point of view, while Karp's is concerned with reproduction in the shortest period of time.

The struggle against the statist bias of social political thought, which has been a central concern of political anthropology from Fortes and Evans-Pritchard to the present, is revived in the final section of our volume. Section III, *Circulating Centers of Power,* attacks the illusion of a centralized authority discussed in the first section of the introduction. The essays in this section make a real advance by showing how social formation are composed of competing epicenters of power whose relative strength may change over different spans of time. These may include not only long-term political change and social transformation, but also the moments in repetitive social processes when duly constituted authorities leave the center stage to the seemingly powerless.

Dan Bauer examines the common cultural resources used by the high-prestige priests and disreputable diviners among the Tigray of highland Christian Ethiopia. He shows how spatial categories, training, and key symbols are shared among the two, but manipulated differently. Power is derived from the same source although its practitioners act in different arenas and compete with one another. The epicenters in this case share a common culture but compete for scarce resources and status.

Alma Gottlieb explores the "underside" of a duly constituted authority among the Beng. While Bauer's Tigray case shows how low-status figures use the same sources of power as high-status sources, Gottlieb's material reverses this relationship. She demonstrates that the highest Beng authority is perceived as deriving his power from the most illicit source, witchcraft. In this case we have a figure who acts in two epicenters of power that are opposed in ordinary discourse. The theme of ambiguity is also nicely illustrated.

More than any other paper, Victoria Ebin's takes as its theme competition between epicenters of power in an Akan-speaking chiefdom. She shows how power moves between priesthood and chieftancy. For her the most important element is the context of crisis which may produce interdependence when competition is more frequent and normal. Her point is not that social order is reproduced by crisis—although it may be—but rather that power is redistributed because of crisis, and that the sense of a hierarchical ordering of power relations is belied by the background knowledgeable people have of how crises can alter power relations.

Finally, Nancy Fairley takes a historical perspective to competition between competing epicenters of power. Her essay describes the shifts of power that have taken place between secular authorities and secret societies among the Ben'Ekie of Zaire. This paper invokes the contexts of interethnic relations, warfare, and conquest to show how the larger regional arenas can affect the balance among competing centers of power, as well as create new epicenters.

Taken together, the essays in this volume move beyond the identification and description of how power is exercised and acquired in different social settings. The perspective of this volume examines power as an essential element in the cultural resources used to produce structure and action. The essays explore the culturally and historically specific imagery of power more than its exercise or the legitimate basis for its application. This definition of problem has led us to describe such aspects of power relationships as images of generation, systems of transformation, and ideas about the capacities of persons. The organization of power relations is viewed less as emanating from a center than as shifting among domains at different levels of interaction.

Power is not often manifested in simple or transparent fashion. The following discussions struggle with elaborate and necessarily imprecise images of creativity, domination, and subordination. We see power as an artifact of the creative faculty of the moral imagination.

Notes

1. Most of the essays were presented at a symposium organized by the editors at the annual meetings of the African Studies Association in 1982. Others were solicited and one is reprinted. We thank Christine Mullen Kreamer and Robert Leopold for their help in preparing the manuscript for publication and Nancy Benco and Benjamin Reiss for skillfully editing so many diverse styles and attitudes into something approaching consistency.

2. The examination of how actions produce effects is a central theme in our essays. As a result, we are also fundamentally concerned with the theme of human agency, a consideration of how action affects people society and nature. This is a concern of much recent thinking in social theory (Karp 1986b). Our essays may provide an instance of the convergence of anthropological thinking and cultural beliefs. We believe that taken as a whole the essays demonstrate that the production of effects and the problems inherent in doing so are a critical theme of the African systems of thought examined here. The idea of paradoxes of agency is examined in Karp 1987.

3. A persistent historical puzzle has been the general neglect of Weber's work by anthropologists, particularly in research on political and legal systems. Beidelman (1966, 1971, 1982) and Fallers (1956) stand out as exceptions in Africanist research. Perhaps one reason for this state of affairs is the perception that Weberian theory applies more to bureaucratic social systems than those he called "patrimonial." This is an error that fails to recognize that Weber's typologies were "ideal," not "real." He formulated them in order to exhibit tendencies in social action, not to describe naturally occurring systems. From a Weberian point of view "real" systems should have elements of more than one ideal-typical system in them. The analytical and historical problem is to demonstrate how these tendencies operate in the production of action. In any of the papers in this volume, for example, a Weberian approach to political systems would be to show not only how epicenters of power charismatically challenge the center, but also to examine whether there are processes of institutionalization and bureaucratization in the epicenter as well as the center.

4. We leave aside for the moment the nineteenth-century mechanistic physics of force and resistance on which it is based. The history of physics in the nineteenth century underwent a conceptual shift yet to appear in the social sciences, in which the definition of "power" moved from force to energy (Elkana 1974). A

number of the papers in the volume, notably Gilbert and Karp, argue that the underlying notion of power in the cultural forms they describe is "energy."

5. Marx (1965) noted this problem when he stated that Jeremy Bentham's Utilitarianism "elevated the mentality of the English shopkeeper to a universal principle of human behavior."

6. See, for example, such standards as Balandier (1970), Banton (1965), Bailey (1965), Cohen (1974), Gluckman (1965), Swartz (1968), Swartz, Turner and Tuden (1966).

7. This comparison might make an additional test of Goody's conclusions (1977) about the superior storage capacity of the written over the oral word. Comparative research that is internal to social formations is also possible on this topic. One might take a perspective derived from Bakhtin (1984), for example, and show how the "carnivalization" of official culture is an assault using oral cultural forms on the claims of the technology of literacy (Karp 1987).

8. See especially the Introduction to Bloch and Parry (1982), where death rituals are reduced to ideology and then claimed to "deny" the world through their status as a "device for the creation of ideology and political domination" (p. 42) These assertions can only be made by ignoring the "semantic creativity" referred to in the quote by Parkin (1982) above. Underlying them is the assumption that power is universal and the cultural grounds for action examined in the essays in this volume are simply part of the ideological veneer masking differences in the distribution of power.

9. We use the concept of "powers" here much as Lienhardt does in *Divinity and Experience* (1961), as a way of describing supernatural entities whose actions affect the human world.

References

Adams, Richard N.

1977 Power in Human Societies: A Synthesis. *In* The Anthropology of Power. Raymond D. Fogelson and Richard N. Adams, eds., pp. 387–410. New York: Academic Press.

Bailey, F. G.

1969 Stratagems and Spoils: A Social Anthropology of Politics. Oxford: Basil Blackwell.

Bakhtin, Mihkail

1984 Rabelais and His World. Helene Iswolsky, transl. Bloomington: Indiana University Press.

Balandier, Georges

1970 Political Anthropology. A. M. Sheridan Smith, transl. New York: Vintage Books.

Banton, Michael (ed.)

1965 Political Systems and the Distribution of Power. London: Tavistock Publications.

Beidelman, T.O.
1966 Swazi Royal Ritual. Africa 36:373–405.
1971 Nuer Priests and Prophets. *In* The Translation of Culture, T. O. Beidelman, ed., pp. 375–415. London: Tavistock Publications.
1982 Colonial Evangelism: A Socio-Historical Study of An East African Mission at the Grassroots. Bloomington: Indiana University Press.

Bloch, Maurice and Jonathan Parry (eds.)
1982 Death and The Regeneration of Life. Cambridge: Cambridge University Press.

Clastres, Pierre
1987 Society Against the State. New York: Zone Books.

Clegg, Stuart
1975 Power, Rule and Domination. London: Routledge and Kegan Paul.

Cohen, Abner
1974 Two-Dimensional Man. Berkeley and Los Angeles: University of California Press.

Dahrendorf, Ralf
1959 Class and Class Conflict in Industrial Society. London: Routledge and Kegan Paul.

Douglas, Mary
1966 Purity and Danger. London: Routledge and Kegan Paul.

Elkana, Yehudi
1974 Discovery of the Conservation of Energy. Cambridge: Harvard University Press.

Emmett, Dorothy
1972 Function, Purpose, and Powers. London: Macmillan.

Fallers, Lloyd
1956 Bantu Bureaucracy: A Century of Political Evolution among the Basoga of Uganda. Chicago: University of Chicago Press.

Fogelson, Raymond D. and Richard N. Adams (eds.)
1977 The Anthropology of Power. New York: Academic Press.

Fortes, Meyer and E. E. Evans-Pritchard
1940 African Political Systems. London: Oxford University Press.

Foucault, Michel
1977 Discipline and Punish. New York: Pantheon Books.
1978 The History of Sexuality. Vol. 1. New York: Pantheon Books.

Gallie, W. B.
1955–56 Essentially Contested Concepts. Proceedings of the Aristotelian Society 56:167–98.

Giddens, Anthony

1979 Central Problems in Social Theory: Action, Structure and Contradiction in Social Analysis. Berkeley and Los Angeles: University of California Press.

Gluckman, Max

1965 Politics, Law and Ritual in Tribal Society. Oxford: Blackwell.

Goody, Jack

1977 The Domestication of the Savage Mind. Cambridge University Press.

Hontoundji, Paulin

1983 On African Philosophy. Bloomington: Indiana University Press.

Kapferer, Bruce

1979 Introduction: Ritual Process and the Transformation of Context. Social Analysis 1:3–19.

Karp, Ivan

1980 Beer Drinking and Social Experience in an African Society. *In* Explorations in African Systems of Thought, C. S. Bird and Ivan Karp, eds., pp. 83–119. Bloomington: Indiana University Press.

1986a African Systems of Thought. *In* Africa. Second Edition, P. O'Meara and P. Martin, eds., pp. 199–212. Bloomington: Indiana University Press.

1986b Agency and Social Theory: A Review of Three Books by Anthony Giddens. American Ethnologist 13(1):131–38.

1987 Laughter at Marriage: Subversion in Performance. *In* The Transformation of African Marriage, D. Parkin and D. Nyamwaya, eds., pp. 137–55. Manchester: Manchester University Press for the International African Institute.

Kopytoff, Igor

1980 Revitalization and the Genesis of Cults in Pragmatic Religion. *In* Explorations in African Systems of Thought, C. S. Bird and I. Karp, eds., pp. 183–212. Bloomington: Indiana University Press.

Lienhardt, Godfrey

1961 Divinity and Experience: The Religion of the Dinka. Oxford: Oxford University Press.

Lukes, Steven

1978 Power and Authority. *In* A History of Sociological Analysis, T. Bottomore and R. Nisbet, eds., pp. 633–76. New York: Basic Books.

Marx, Karl

1965 Pre-Capitalist Economic Formations. With an introduction by Eric J. Hobsbawm. New York: International Publishers.

Moore, Sally Falk and Barbara G. Myerhoff (eds.)
1977 Secular Ritual. Assen: Van Gorcum.

Mudimbe, V. Y.
1988 The Invention of Africa: Gnosis, Philosophy, and the Order of Knowledge. Bloomington: Indiana University Press.

Packard, Randall
1982 Chiefship and Cosmology. Bloomington: Indiana University Press.

Parkin, David
1982 Semantic Anthropology. New York: Academic Press.

Parsons, Talcott
1963 On the Concept of Power. Proceedings of the American Philosophical Society 107:232–62.

Russell, Bertrand
1938 Power. New York: W W. Norton and Co.

Scott, James C.
1985 Weapons of the Weak: Everyday Forms of Peasant Resistance. New Haven: Yale University Press.

Simmel, Georg
1950 The Sociology of Georg Simmel. Kurt H. Wolff, transl. and ed. New York: The Free Press.

Swartz, Marc J. (ed.)
1968 Local-Level Politics. Chicago: Aldine Publishing Co.

Swartz, Marc J., Victor W. Turner and Arthur Tuden (eds.)
1966 Political Anthropology. Chicago: Aldine Publishing Co.

Vaughan, James H.
1980 A Reconsideration of Divine Kingship. *In* Explorations in African Systems of Thought, C. S. Bird and I. Karp, eds., pp. 120–42. Bloomington: Indiana University Press.

Weber, Max
1947 The Theory of Social and Economic Organization. New York: The Free Press.

Wilson, Monica
1951 Divine Kings and the 'Breath of Men.' The Frazer Lecture for 1959. Cambridge: Cambridge University Press.

Part One

Creating Power

W. Arens

The Power of Incest

Speculation on what is usually referred to as the "incest taboo" is a staple of western social thought. Consequently, the literature is so vast and familiar as to belie either summary or novelty. However, the same cannot be said for the related, indeed precisely opposite concept of incest: the act itself. Depending on the context of occurrence, such behavior is typically relegated in history and social science to either ethnographic oddity or psychosocial deviance. As such, the interpretations of incestuous episodes strain to account for a particular moral failure or peculiar abnegation of an assumed cultural universal. Thus, even when incest occurs, it subsequently tends to be ignored in favor of a refocus on the prohibition, albeit its failure, which is the positive feature of the social complex. As a consequence of this inclination to avoid incest, we know comparatively little about its cultural function or meaning in a particular time or place.

This is surprising, since we are well aware that incest occurs in a variety of cultural settings as an antisocial violation of a specific prohibition or, quite the opposite, as socially sanctioned behavior in ritualized form. Instances of the latter especially demand exploration, for they present an ethnographic curiosity and cultural paradox of some significance for the cultures involved. Instead of reconsidering the incest taboo in yet another cultural context, in this paper I will offer an interpretation of an incestuous episode that takes place during the installation ceremony of the king (*reth,* pl. *ror*) of the Shilluk of southern Sudan.

The theme of incest is often encountered in the myth and ritual of traditional monarchial systems in Africa (de Heusch 1958, 1981, 1982; Beattie 1959) and other parts of the world. This inquiry attempts to elicit some of the more common ideas concerning indigenous concepts of power and the definition of the right to rule. However, before exploring Shilluk ideas on this subject, the meaning of both incest and taboo in our cultural system must be recounted.

Some years ago Needham (1974:63–64) confronted this very issue, and in doing so characterized incest prohibitions as "in part moral injunctions" and "indigenous ethical doctrines" which "have particular cultural meanings which no attempt at explanation can reasonably neglect." Following this line of reasoning he points out that, in its derivation from the Latin, the English word connotes "impurity," which is not directly comparable to the meaning of the term for the same act even in related Germanic languages which focus on the notion of "bloodshame" (p. 63). He further remarks on the notions of "disorder," conveyed by the word in Chinese, and "improper" or "repugnant" in Indonesian (p. 64). In light of these linguistic distinctions, Needham concludes that "incest prohibitions do not compose a class of homogenous social phenomena" (p. 64). Although they should not be classed together in this formal sense, a recognizable connotation of negativity characterizes the various ideas we translate into English as incest (see also Heritier 1982).

Needham has done the characteristic service of drawing attention to the cultural variability of the terms often mechanically glossed as "incest" in the literature. Moreover, he reports that there are some societies that, although they deem the act illicit, do not have a prohibition in the sense of an explicit rule against it, nor is there a common emotional response to its occurrence (Needham 1974:66–67). This suggests that there may well be some societies with no actual cultural experience of the deed we refer to as incest. In a sense, they lack the very concept or potential concepts implied.

If this were insufficient reason for caution, the second half of the phrase "incest taboo" suffers from even greater misunderstanding, since "tabu" does not mean prohibited in a absolute sense. According to the *Oxford English Dictionary,* the word, borrowed from the Tongan, means "set apart for or consecrated to a special purpose: restricted to the use of a god, a king or chiefs, while forbidden to general use." Therefore, taboo in this sense is not universal, if for no other reason than some societies prohibit the deed entirely. Putting it the other way around, an incest taboo exists only where some individuals are allowed or enjoined to have sexual relations with close kin while the same behavior is forbidden to others. Thus, it would seem best to reserve the phrase "incest taboo" for those particular ethnographic instances, and employ the more applicable phrase "pattern of sexual avoidance" for the general problem.

In recognition of the various facets of the topic, the following discussion will be restricted to the analysis of particular features of the Shilluk royal installation ceremony, which entails at a crucial juncture a ritualized sexual confrontation between the initiate to the office and his half-sister.[1] The act may take place only at this one time, and it would be deemed unacceptable behavior for all other Shilluk. If it were to occur in other contexts, the Shilluk refer to it as *dwalo,* a concept implying misfortune or disease—which is also the case in related Nilotic languages.

The Shilluk are the northernmost Nilotes of southern Sudan, located in a series of almost continuous residential clusters stretching for approximately 110 miles along the western bank of the Nile. They are distinguished from related ethnic groups, such as the Nuer and Dinka, by a variety of characteristics. The most immediately apparent is the Shilluk reliance on agriculture rather than on pastoralism. More pertinently, they stand in strong contrast to their neighbors in their possession of a complex hierarchical political system.

A number of hamlets, each occupied by distinct groups of patrilineal kinsmen, are joined together to form a recognized settlement under the authority of a chief (*jago*), who is normally a member of the dominant lineage associated with the original occupation of the area. Thus, although lineage and territory are not coterminous, the descent system provides the conceptual framework for the political system. A number of these units are recognized as making up one of the eleven named divisions of Shillukland ruled over by the settlement chiefs.

These divisions are in turn grouped together to form two overarching provinces representing a division of the country into northern and southern halves. The geographical boundary between this major territorial dichotomy is a watercourse located just south of Fashoda, the capital of the country. Each half of Shillukland is represented, in ritual and other matters, by one of the division chiefs. The chief of the district just to the south of Fashoda occupies one such office, while his counterpart from the immediately northern district occupies the other. This structural system of territorial oppositions culminates with the office of the *reth*.

In addition to these territorial arrangements, the Shilluk are also socially subdivided in a corresponding fashion to the political system. The great majority of the commoner population, grouped into exogamous clans, is referred to as *colo,* which is also the Shilluk name for themselves. Distinguished from this conglomeration are the *ororo,* a particular clan descended from a former ruler, whose members no longer have the right to exercise a royal claim but retain certain privileges. They in turn are preceded in the social hierarchy by the *kwareth,* members of the royal clan. Another recognized group, known as the *bang reth,* form the band of retainers attached to a reigning *reth*. Their distinction is based on a personal relationship to the officeholder rather than on descent, which is the prominent feature of all other social categories. Those counted among the *bang reth* serve the monarch in a variety of capacities during his lifetime, and after his death they and their descendants maintain his burial shrine, located in the village from which he ruled. Thus, the countryside is dotted both with shrines to a former *reth* and the associated communities of *bang reth,* who no longer maintain a principal identity with a descent group. Finally, at the apex of the social system stands the *reth* himself, occupying a position corresponding to his political one.

In this dual hierarchical capacity, the *reth* of the Shilluk has been referred to since Frazer's time as a classic example of an extant "divine kingship."[2] At a general level, this is a vaguely defined and disputed type of centralized political system (Young 1966). Moreover, there has been some controversy over a definition of the traditional political role of this particular officeholder for the Shilluk. Some early ethnographers, such as the Seligmans (1932), portrayed him as omnipotent in political affairs; later, in a very influential essay, Evans-Pritchard (1962) vehemently argued that the *reth*'s function was politically insignificant in contrast to his sacred role.

As I have suggested elsewhere (Arens 1979), the historical reality most likely lay somewhere in between these two extreme positions, due to the association of any one *reth* with a particular territory (from which he drew his primary political support and where he maintained his personal capital) in contrast to the ceremonial capital at Fashoda. In the former he had a strong political base while in the latter the fortunes of any particular *reth* waxed and waned. Regardless of their orientation on these secular matters, it is possible to state with confidence that the Shilluk reflected and continue to reflect a regnal idiom, in the sense that this peculiar institution informs their perception of the past and offers an interpretation of the present in a variety of the most significant social contexts. The position of *reth* is, as has so often been mentioned, the center of their cosmological system (Lienhardt 1954:150). This crucial cultural concern of the Shilluk as they ponder their existence as a distinct people is of primary interest here.

This notion of the *reth*'s centrality requires some elaboration, since the Shilluk, as with other Nilotes, conceive of the representation of divinity in a number of different contexts (Burton 1981; Evans-Pritchard 1950; Lienhardt 1961). In one capacity, *Juok,* as an immanent being, created the first humans and animals in a distant land at an unspecified point in the past. Removed in time and space, *Juok* is a figure who plays little part in Shilluk daily religious activities in contrast to *Nyikang,* one of the first human beings. According to Shilluk tradition, *Nyikang* led a band of followers from a lake area in the south to their present homeland along the Nile. In the process, he gathered other peoples encountered along the way and incorporated them into his entourage. Upon arriving at their present location, the invaders subdued the existing inhabitants and allocated the conquered territory by district to specific followers for administration under *Nyikang*'s rule. This series of events entailed the incorporation of the autochthonous residents into the new social order based upon historical distinctions that are maintained today. Thus *Nyikang,* as the Shilluk culture hero and first *reth,* is responsible for the creation of society as the Shilluk now experience it. In this capacity as the originator of the social order, *Nyikang* is a more immanent figure, who is evoked in prayer and ritual by the Shilluk in daily activities as *juok piny* (God below). Each successive *reth* assumes the responsibility of insuring the social order by his presence, while his demise indicates the potential for dissolution and eventual decay.

The incestuous act to be considered here takes place in the course of an elaborate and drawn-out installation ceremony set in motion by the death of the prior incumbent (Arens 1984). The death and burial of one *reth* and the installation of another are phases of a single ritual process. However, little will be said about the mortuary stage, except to note that, with the expiration of the reigning officeholder, his spirit is said to depart, taking up residence in the northernmost district of Shillukland at a major shrine to *Nyikang* in an effigy of this mythical figure. This is significant, since each successive officeholder is believed to incorporate *Nyikang*'s spiritual essence upon taking the throne. The association with *Nyikang,* who for the Shilluk never died, gives support to the idea of the divine nature of each *reth* who succeeds to the position. It should also be mentioned that, with the death of the *reth,* the Shilluk say, "there is no land" (Howell and Thomson 1946:18), drawing attention to the correspondence between the extant officeholder and the existence of society itself, in the sense that there cannot be one without the other.

In the context of this ideological framework, the nominated successor, who was informed of his election with the phrase "You are our Dinka slave; we want to kill you" (Howell 1944), indicating his demise as a mortal, is brought to Fashoda to prepare for his installation. During this time he remains in seclusion, which involves avoiding his predecessor's mortuary ceremony, until the liminal stage of the installation process is initiated by a different series of ritual events. At this point, the would-be *reth* is ensconced in a sacred enclosure on a rise in Fashoda, the capital and approximate geographical center of Shillukland. After a few days of residence, he is informed that an effigy containing the spirit of *Nyikang,* and similar representations of Dak and Cal, his sons and succeeding kings of the Shilluk, are marching on Fashoda with supporters from the northern districts of the country. Their intent is to confront and formally engage in battle with the candidate and his entourage, who have gathered from the south. As they close in on the capital, the nominee crosses the stream that separates Shillukland into two parts and retreats southward for a short distance to another village to prepare for the coming encounter with divinity in the form of *Nyikang*'s effigy.

At this time and place he spends the night with his half-sister and actually consummates, or possibly only fictionalizes, the act of incest—all we know is that they are together for this period (Howell 1953). On the following morning, other Shilluk males who have committed actual sexual offenses during their lifetimes gather at the site and are absolved of their deeds by the candidate as he confronts them en masse.

This episode is doubly significant for the female involved. As a *nyireth* (child of a *reth*), she is too exalted to become a suitable marriage partner for a commoner and is prohibited by rules of exogamy from marrying another member of the royal clan. As a consequence, daughters of previous *ror* are not allowed to marry, though in practice it has been reported that they may enter into unsanctioned sexual relationships with men during their lifetimes (Howell 1953). Thus, for the particular *nyireth* involved, this one incestuous liaison is ironically her only culturally sanctioned sexual encounter.

To return to the ritual process, the soon-to-be *reth* then recrosses the stream bed with his "army" and engages in a mock, but nonetheless physical, melee with the opposite forces of *Nyikang,* who have also arrived on the scene. The candidate loses this first encounter by being taken prisoner, along with an unrelated young girl who has been presented to him earlier in the ceremonial process as a wife of the throne. He is then escorted back up the hill at Fashoda to an enclosed shrine dedicated to *Nyikang,* where the stool of the *reth* awaits. First, the effigy is placed on the stool, only to be removed at once; then the prospective *reth* takes its place, and in sitting down shudders as the spirit of *Nyikang* enters him. Having now been fused with *Nyikang,* he is finally the *reth,* though still a prisoner of the effigy.

He spends the same evening at the capital, this time in the company of three *ororo* women, members of the debased royal lineage. Their status and that of their kin was earned by their ancestor, an early *reth* who, according to local lore, brought political ruin and disgrace to the Shilluk people during his reign. As mentioned earlier, although the male members of this descent group are now barred from succession, their representatives accept the polluting responsibility for handling and burying a dead king. Thus, the newly anointed *reth* encounters in their presence the historical image of failure and disgrace, as well as the contemporary impurity of death, which he had previously avoided as a candidate to the throne by absenting himself from the mortuary activities held in honor of his predecessor.

There are two further noteworthy elements in this second sexual encounter. First, although the *reth* may marry women of the *ororo* clan, there is at the same time another hint of incest, since they have a recognized distant common royal ancestor. Second, it is customary for a *reth* to take an *ororo* wife or wives during his reign. Traditionally they are said to have the responsibility for smothering him when aged or infirmed, which accords with this clan's close ritual association with both kingship and death. Moreover, the *reth*'s liaison with them during the installation procedure is a further suggestion of his ability to confront and control dangerous elements inherent in the cultural system by overcoming disease and decay.

On the following morning, the new *reth* descends from Fashoda, and in a second but this time triumphant clash with the contingent associated with the effigy, he reclaims the young girl, who was separated from him, and returns to Fashoda with her. The effigy, now under the *reth*'s control, makes a peaceful appearance with its retainers, who then depart for the northern shrine where the effigy remains until the demise of the newly installed *reth.* The succeeding phase of the installation ceremony involves secular events initiating the political activities of the new *reth,* and have little relevance to the preceding ritual events.

As to the symbolic meaning of the activities just summarized, a number of now obvious interpretations come to mind. Among them are, first, the recognition that the liminal stage of the installation ceremony involves a series of conjunctions between categories normally kept apart in Shilluk cosmology. These include the merger of the northern and southern halves of the country, with the combat at the center of Shillukland; the joining of the secular and sacred domains represented by the candidate and effigy, which are fused at the moment of enthronement; the physical coming together of the candidate with his half-sister, in contradiction to a prohibition intended to segregate close relatives sexually; and finally, the intimate liaison between the candidate who stands for vitality and order with women representing death and decay. The nominated successor's subjection to these episodes and his ability to surmount them confirms his right to succeed.

The symbolic implications of these activities are now standard anthropological fare, and are readily appreciated since the appearance of Beidelman's influential reanalysis of the Swazi *Incawala* ceremony (1966). In this pioneering interpretation of royal ritual in Africa, Beidelman convincingly argues that employing the notion of "cosmetics," in the sense of making something orderly, is essential to an understanding of these national ritual occasions. According to him (1966: 389), "the royal rites involve a dangerous but potent process of increasing animation, a combination of various symbolic attributes (in terms of the king) not normally together." The Shilluk example, which thrusts the candidate for the throne into such a position of centrality and thus of categorical mediation, confirms this insight.

However, the second major integral and recurring theme of the installation ceremony, which involves sexual activity and its potential meaning, has received less consideration in the comparable literature. The acts described in this context involve the sexual activity of the principal figure with, in turn, a prohibited female relative, women symbolizing historical and contemporary pollution, and a young girl free of any social stigma.

It is always at least somewhat mechanical and arbitrary to impose conceptual boundary lines in distinguishing the various stages of a ritual process in the fashion of Van Gennep (1960) and Turner (1967). Yet, it seems reasonable to follow their lead here and suggest that the first two sexual liaisons characterize the transitional or liminal stage of the installation, since they involve both a confrontation with and fusion of the "building blocks of culture," and enjoin those passing through it to reflect on the basic nature of the cosmos (Turner 1967:105). By combining what should be, and regularly is, kept separate, the actor—in this case, the candidate—encounters the danger of losing his own distinctiveness in the form of a separate social identity. Specifically, this involves the candidate's overcoming the basic social dichotomy between We and They in the sense of not distinguishing between legitimate and nonlegitimate sexual partners. Moreover, this is achieved by an act that Leach characterizes as blurring the sensory distinction between self and other (1976:62). Perhaps it is not too fanciful to state that, at least in terms of the way the Shilluk interpret the situation, the *reth*-elect metaphorically becomes one with the universe, and through this physical act recreates and unifies the entropic cosmos, which has failed with the death of the prior king.

In addition, the *reth*-elect, by engaging in actual or implied sexual relations with both his half-sister and the three other women, confronts and absorbs potential sources of pollution. As Beidelman (1966:396) puts it, "the king himself assumes the filth of the nation, and though endangered by this, gains power." The second half of this observation is particularly relevant here, for in a variety of ways already noted the nominee legitimizes his succession to the position by exercising his ability to control dangerous moments. These activities confirm Franz Steiner's observation (1956:20) that taboo is concerned with "the sociology of danger." In each instance, in Shakespeare's words, the *reth* has demonstrated that "nice customs curtsy to great kings." By this single prohibited act, the *reth* overcomes common social barriers with an exercise in physical creation. In addition, it is noteworthy that, in this particular instance of liminal ritual behavior, the protagonist does more than passively confront the danger of pollution, which is the common cultural context of most ritual situations. Instead, he actively creates the danger with his own person and capabilities. As a consequence, his own body becomes the source of power.

The *reth* becomes the creator of danger by bridging the normally inviolate categories of We and They, so that he has no social identity in contrast to all other members of society who must abide by this prohibition, as well as by merging the cultural categories of purity and pollution (Leach 1969). However, at the same time he becomes a potential victim of his own forces. In effect, as a candidate for the throne he simultaneously generates power and overcomes its inherent danger by his actions. This is not at all surprising in light of the definition of his cosmological function, the nature of the occasion, and the political system that contains little material support for this office. To complete the cycle, it is necessary to note that the recapture of the pure girl takes place after the candidate has become *reth,* which signals the end of this phase of the ceremony. Thus, for a time at least, the officeholder is no longer required to express divinity by his actions. The entire sequence of events is encapsulated then by the dual aspects of royal incest, which simultaneously involves both separation and conjunction, and the recreation of the cosmos with the advent of a new *reth,* so that for the Shilluk once more there is a "land" with the regeneration of *juok piny* (God below).

The association drawn in Shilluk ritual and cosmology between power as an ability to recreate the social order and the incestuous act as a variation of the theme of sexual potency has been demonstrated to have widespread applicability. In our own mythical literature, Oedipus achieves kingship in a similar incestuous fashion (Yamaguchi 1977), while as Leach (1969) has demonstrated, the thematic continuity in Genesis concerned with the process of creation, destruction, and recreation is achieved by resort to incest. A more exact parallel is offered by the politically centralized Lovedu of southern Africa, who rationalize the recreation of their social order after a period of chaos under the cultural domination of females, rather than males, by royal father-daughter sexual relations (Krige and Krige 1943:308).

This cursory review of other cultural contexts indicates that power and incest are often inseparable notions and activities in human affairs. In such cultural systems, power is conceived of as infinitely more than mere control or influence over others. This western theoretical conception of power as coercion typically draws on the pioneering influence of Weber, but only in a most restricted utilization of his ideas. In anthropology, this curtailed interpretation rarely involves more than a glancing reference to Weber's often cited distinction between power and authority in a secular context (Gerth and Mills 1958). This is a misguided limitation, for this well-known dichotomy was only one element of Weber's ideas on the subject. To his thinking, power was more than the ability of a political leader to enforce his will through resort to bureaucratic machinery and personnel. The idea of power was also generated and displayed in exotic cultural forms and behavior.

According to one contemporary interpretation, Weber's interest in power and authority were features of his more general concern with "the processes of institution building, social transformation, and cultural creativity" (Eisenstadt 1968:xvi). Thus Weber identified "charisma" as a particular form of authority which, as a type of political legitimization, relied heavily on an understanding of the indigenous cultural construction of power. Unlike the narrow interpretation of power alluded to above, this Weberian concept of charisma has experienced a vastly different intellectual fate by its application to an extremely diverse set of social settings. As Geertz (1983:122) points out, charisma "presently has an elusive and uncertain referent except for a vaguely perceived psychological quality of an individual." He suggests avoiding such a prevalent form of reductionism by returning to the arena of cultural dynamics, an effort that involves determining the reasons that prompt others to recognize the "transcendency" of particular individuals (p. 122). According to Geertz's interpretation, charisma entails a symbolic value emerging from an individual's involvement in what he refers to as "the active centers of the social order," which take their form in "concentrated loci of serious acts" (p. 122). In other words, socially significant acts at culturally important places and times are essential to generating indigenous ideas of power.

The symbolic significance of the idea of "centrality" as the focal point of charismatic legitimization in the interpretation of traditional political systems, such as the one offered by the Shilluk, deserves close attention. In his reevaluation of Weber's concept of charisma, Shils (1965:205) has suggested that "great power" is a cultural concept best understood and most readily recognized by intense and infrequent activities intimately related to what is conceived of as the center of social and value systems. From this perspective, power is the simultaneous capacity of an ordained individual to discover, create, maintain, or destroy existing social forms (p. 205). As such, this definition of power is closely related to the human conceptual need for the recognition of an ordered framework of experience. Following from this, the apex of power is often envisioned as a divine creator in nonbureaucratic political systems such as that of the Shilluk, who cast their monarch in just this light.

The concern of Geertz and Shils for a more classic and yet, at the same time, expanded interpretation of the aura of charisma is well taken. Weber's initial definition of charisma implied not only a psychological quality of an individual, but also involvement in cultural performances, so that an individual could "prove" himself as a result of "personal experience" (1968:20–24). Thus the psychological component of charisma, which is not denied, should be understood as deriving from a particular encounter with existing social forms. Moreover, for Weber (1964:361–63) these occasions are often contradictory to social experience, for charismatic authority is "foreign to all rules" and "foreign to routine structures." This form of legitimization stands in illuminating contrast to the routine, the traditional, and the rational. More relevant to the interpretation of the particular political system and the meaning of incest considered here, charisma tends toward the antisocial.

This characterization implies that the display of charismatic quality demands an assault on what is sacred and a denial of what is true and proper, so that in part the quality and context take the form of sacrilege (Eisenstadt 1968:xix). According to this perspective, charismatic fervor has the added quality of defining society by drawing attention to its moral limits, while concomitantly redefining the individual involved in such a performance by his breach of these strictures on behavior.

As a consequence, the royal incestuous episode considered here conveys with it the social and psychological aspects of charisma. Both society and the individual have been redefined in the ritual process of kingmaking. In this sense, charisma is displayed in Geertz's words as "a sign, not of popular appeal or inventive craziness, but of being near the heart of things" (1983:123). For the Shilluk, this ritual process encompasses an exercise in antisocial behavior, a turning inward of potential sexual and social energies at a time when the various elements of the social system are fixated on the literal center of their land during the installation process. This context implies that the *reth* is transformed into more than a mediator between opposed realms of the Shilluk cosmos (de Heusch 1982); he is also conceived of as a source of individual power to create and destroy the rules which govern others. In this sense the *reth* then becomes the figurative center of the social system.

The preceding ethnographic facts and their interpretation suggest that the Shilluk possess a political system Weber (1968:25–27) would characterize as an instance of "charismatic kingship," which is defined primarily by ambiguous rules governing succession to high office. In such a political arena, the legitimacy of any given candidate is always somewhat suspect in the minds of others. This ambiguity has clearly been the case for the Shilluk, whose dynastic system ideally involves the rotation of kingship among three distinct royal lines whose members often contest the arrangement during the period of crisis generated by the death of an incumbent. Moreover, each lineage of the royal clan produces a number of viable candidates for office, in different sections of the country, supported by different sets of maternal kin who seek to raise their own offspring to the throne. Historically, the new *reth* has been only one of a number of acceptable candidates for what was and remains a tremulous throne often subsequently beset by rebellion and civil war.

Therefore, the charisma of the successor is a hereditary aspect of the position, rather than a personal quality. Indeed, the most acceptable candidate indicates himself to the selectors, who are the division chiefs, by his social conformity and ideal individual comportment to this point in his career. Having drawn little attention to himself by his personal behavior, the son of a previous *reth* is marked as an acceptable candidate for investiture. From a purely secular perspective, such an individual appeals to the electors as a judicious political choice as they assume that the nominee's future behavior as *reth* would be an extension of these conforming tendencies. As the holder of what is, in part, a political office they expect that he will continue to act with reason and constraint in the exercise of administrative power. This expectation appeals to those charged with this responsibility, for after making their decision theoretically they become his political subordinates at the local level.

At the same time, however, an individual conceived of in this mundane manner would experience a profound redefinition of self in the eyes of others as he was subjected to the rituals of investiture, which are expected to convert an idealized human being into divinity on earth. With an eye on the sacred components of the office, the individual invested would be transformed in the most dramatic and complete fashion possible. Thus, a further significant aspect of incest emerges, for the Shilluk recognize the act as an antisocial one, and as such it signifies a reordering of their perception of the chosen individual in light of his previous tendencies.

The transformation of a candidate into a *reth,* and all that this entails in an ideological sense, is dependent upon the transmission of qualities of office from one incumbent to another through ritual encounters. The charisma, or transcendent quality of a *reth* involves, then, a conception of legitimacy as an objective, transferable force, perceived of by the Shilluk as a form of power. For the Shilluk, a successful candidate for the position of *reth* must demonstrate an indigenous cultural definition of charisma, which entails the production of individual antisocial tendencies and the ability to survive these encounters as befits their definition of a political leader.

The particular cultural problem which besets the Shilluk political system as it prepares to confirm a new leader is the need to demonstrate that the candidate has charisma in the sense of the ability to overcome extraordinary situations. However, crises which allow for a demonstration of personal power are neither predictable nor regular in the course of events. As a consequence, the cultural moments are created by the Shilluk in the form of rituals (Elias 1983:121–26). Without them, there can be no charisma and thus no validation of the right to rule. Such a demonstration of charisma involves the power of sexuality to engage in dangerous antithetical social forms, and in this context to confront the cultural negativity associated with historical and social decay.

This interpretation does not exhaust the potential meanings of sexuality, incest, centrality, and power as themes of political ideologies for other parts of Africa. The assumption is that the indigenous cultural constructs discussed here have widespread applicability for the understanding of centralized political systems on the continent, where the subject of incest as a form of sexuality is often associated with kingship. As de Heusch has noted (1981 : 102), engaging in such behavior clearly defines the individual as being above society in some symbolic political sense. However, the incestuous deed also entails the notion of representing what society is by drawing attention to both its perimeters and center, and, as a corollary, engaging in recreating the conditions of social existence. The manner in which these themes are portrayed, elaborated, and interpreted in each era for the Shilluk as it invests a new *reth* draws attention to profound levels of human experience inherent in political ideology and ritual.

The Shilluk rituals of kingship also draw attention to the variety of meanings that may be assigned to the commission of incest, rather than assuming cross-cultural uniformity of response and interpretation. For the Shilluk, this "incestuous solitude" (de Heusch 1981 : 102) relates to a particular political form and corresponding ideology concerned with the definition of transcendent power. The ethnographic data also affirm the importance of recognizing the concept of taboo as a type of restriction on human behavior, rather than absolute prohibition. In this society, incest has greater social meaning in its performance than in its absence, for it defines the conditions of the existence of the Shilluk as a distinct people.

Notes

1. Preliminary field and archival research among the Shilluk was carried out over three months in 1978 while I served as a Research Associate of the Institute of Asian and African Studies, University of Khartoum; it was supported by a grant from the Social Science Research Council. The interpretation of Shilluk royal burial and installation ceremonies is made possible by the pioneering ethnography and publications of Munro (1918), Howell (1944, 1952, 1953), and Howell and Thomson (1946). My thanks to Diana Antos Arens, John Burton,

Gretchen Gwynne, David Hicks, Ivan Karp, and Kathy Yunger for their comments and editorial assistance.

2. The institution continues to flourish in the contemporary southern Sudan under the aegis of His Excellency, *Reth* Ayang Aney Kur Nyidhok, the thirty-third recorded king of the Shilluk.

References

Arens, W.

1979 The Divine Kingship of the Shilluk. Ethnos 44:167–81.

1984 The Demise of Kings and the Meaning of Kingship. Anthropos 19:355–67.

Beattie, J.

1959 Rituals of Nyoro Kingship. Africa 29:134–44.

Beidelman, T. O.

1966 Swazi Royal Ritual. Africa 36:373–405.

Burton, John W.

1981 God's Ants. St. Augustine: Anthropos Institute.

Eisenstadt, S. N.

1968 Editor's Introduction. *In* Max Weber on Charisma and Institution Building. S. N. Eisenstadt, ed. pp. ix–lvi. Chicago: University of Chicago Press.

Elias, Norbert

1983 The Court Society. New York: Pantheon Books.

Evans-Pritchard, E. E.

1962 The Divine Kingship of the Shilluk of the Nilotic Sudan. *In* Social Anthropology and Other Essays. pp. 192–212. London: Faber.

1950 Nuer Religion. Oxford: Claredon Press.

Geertz, Clifford

1983 Local Knowledge. New York: Basic Books.

Gerth, H. H. and C. Wright Mills (eds.)

1958 From Max Weber. New York: Oxford University Press.

Heritier, Francoise

1982 The Symbolics of Incest and its Prohibition. *In* Between Belief and Transgression. Michael Izard and Pierre Smith, eds. pp. 152–79. Chicago: University of Chicago Press.

de Heusch, Luc

1958 Essais sur le symbolisme de l'inceste royal en Afrique. Brussels: Université Libre de Bruxelles.

1981 Why Marry Her? Cambridge: Cambridge University Press.
1982 The Drunken King, or the Origin of the State. Bloomington: Indiana University Press.

Howell, P. P.
1944 The Installation of the Shilluk King. Man 44:146–47.
1952 The Death of Reth Dak Wad Fadiet and the Installation of His Successor. Man 52:102–104.
1953 The Election and Installation of Reth Kur Wad Fafiti of the Shilluk. Sudan Notes and Records 34:189–203.

Howell, P. P. and Thomson, W. P. G.
1946 The Death of a Reth of the Shilluk and the Installation of his Successor. Sudan Notes and Records 27:5–35.

Krige, E. Jensen and J. D. Krige
1943 The Realm of a Rain Queen. London: Oxford University Press.

Leach, Edmund
1969 Genesis as Myth and Other Essays. London: Jonathan Cape.
1976 Culture and Communication. Cambridge: Cambridge University Press.

Leach, Edmund and D. Alan Aycock
1983 Structuralist Interpretations of Biblical Myth. Cambridge: Cambridge University Press.

Lienhardt, Godfrey
1954 The Shilluk of the Upper Nile. *In* African Worlds. Daryll Forde, ed. pp. 138–63. London: Oxford University Press.
1961 Divinity and Experience. Oxford: Clarendon Press.

Munro, P.
1918 Installation of the Ret of the Chol (King of the Shilluks). Sudan Notes and Records 1:145–52.

Needham, Rodney
1974 Remarks and Inventions. London: Tavistock Publications.

Seligman, C. G. and Seligman, Brenda Z.
1932 Pagan Tribes of the Nilotic Sudan. London: Routledge and Kegan Paul.

Shils, Edward
1965 Charisma, Order and Status. American Sociological Review 30: 199–213.

Steiner, Franz
1956 Taboo. London: Cohen and West.

Thomson, W. P. G.
1948 Further Notes on the Death of a Reth of the Shilluk (1945). Sudan Notes and Records 29:151–60.

Turner, Victor
1967 The Forest of Symbols. Ithaca: Cornell University Press.

Van Gennep, Arnold
1960 The Rites of Passage. Chicago: University of Chicago Press.

Weber, Max
1964 The Theory of Social and Economic Organizations. New York: The Free Press.
1968 On Charisma and Institution Building. Chicago: University of Chicago Press.

Yamaguchi, Masao
1977 Kingship, Theatricality, and Marginal Reality in Japan. *In* Text and Context. Ravindra K. Jain, ed. pp. 151–79. Philadelphia: Institute for the Study of Human Issues.

Young, Michael W.
1966 The Divine Kingship of the Jukun. Africa 36:135–53.

Donald J. Cosentino

Midnight Charters: Musa Wo and Mende Myths of Chaos

Lo! thy dread Empire, CHAOS! is restored;
Light dies before thy uncreating word;
Thy hand, great Anarch! lets the curtain fall,
And universal Darkness buries All.
—Alexander Pope

Le myth capture l'univers et rêve la société.
—Luc de Heusch

The comparative analysis of . . . nightmares is one of the keys to the understanding of society.
—Monica Wilson

Mende oral tradition presents students of myth with a unique and perplexing hero. He is called Musa Wo (Little Moses) and is the protagonist of six long, fragmented oral narratives that I collected in Sierra Leone in 1974. In both form and content, these narratives differ from other *domeisia* (Märchen) of Mende tradition whose themes reflect the society's emphasis on the maintenance or restoration of precarious social balances. In form and plot structure, Musa Wo narratives are analogous to other long, elaborate oral compositions about the achievements and events in the careers of African royal heroes (Chief Mwindo, Emperor Sundiata), which critics have described as epics. But whereas the heroes of those acclaimed epics are transformed from abused and willful miscreants into beneficent rulers, Musa Wo begins as an *enfant terrible* and descends to the level of a relentless, obscene, and amoral monster. His actions are the obverse of all the delicate balances that scholars such as Little (1967), MacCormack (1975) and Cosentino (1982) have discerned in Mende social order. He seems to represent the dark side of Mende social ideals, in the sense implied by Bobby Kennedy when he said that Dick Nixon represented the dark side of the American dream. There is a dreadful contrarious quality to his narratives, as if, while smiling at the antics of "Dennis the Menace," one were suddenly yanked into the grossest reels of *The Texas Chainsaw Massacre*.

I use these bizarre, far-flung comparisons deliberately, for I believe that the genesis of the character is heterogeneous. And I believe that Mende narrators seek to realize this heterogeneous character and the multiplicity of lessons he carries for the culture by deliberately yoking together the most bizarre and disparate images available from the repertoire of their oral tradition. Musa Wo is a *bricoleur*'s delight, and to appreciate him we must become *bricoleurs* too. So inspired, I propose using tools of comparative mythology and folklore, philosophy, literary criticism, cultural anthropology, and even the warring psychoanalytic concepts of Freud and Jung to analyze this character. But I won't forget that the Mende say that a Musa Wo tale can never be ended. Since their hero-trickster is himself open to endless permutations, with no final resolution of plot or theme possible (or desirable?), all analyses are perforce prolegomena, and all hypotheses must remain as such.

With these caveats proclaimed, and with diverse methodological tools in hand, the mythologist may confront the conundrums of Musa Wo. What is the genesis of this peculiar mythological figure? Why do the Mende choose such a perverse character as the protagonist of their only epic? What elements in the culture and society sustain, and are sustained by, this myth? Why does the image of Musa Wo seem to be expanding from oral tradition to contemporary popular culture, and how does it relate to analogous figures in West Africa and the West Atlantic diaspora?

To pursue these broad folkloristic and anthropological questions, one must first appreciate Musa Wo as he exists in his proper narrative environment. The most finely articulated of his narratives that I recorded was performed by Mama Ngembe, an old woman of great authority from the Mende-Krim border town of Pujehun, near Liberia. I have edited the following variant of the myth she performed on the night of May 24, 1974, in the meeting place of the old town, before an audience of twenty adults:

MUSA WO

There was a fellow long ago who married many wives. They were all giving birth to these children. One woman remained pregnant for forty years. So the man drove her from town.

She had only one machete and she cut the bush with it. Then she built a small hut there. She was there for one full year. One day she went to cut wood in order to cook and eat cassava. Then the child in her stomach said, "Mother, don't split the wood. Drop the machete on your knee."

So this woman dropped the machete on her knee, and a boy jumped out. He was completely grown, and he had a beard. She asked, "Hey, child, what's your name?"

"My name is Musa Wo."

On the very day he was born he built a house for his mother, because he could understand the language of the animals. He daubed it with mud and roofed it, and they were living there now.

Then he asked, "Mother, where is my father?"

She replied, "Your father is in the town."

So he said, "I'll chop some wood and carry it to him."

And the woman replied, "*Kpoo* child, do you want to kill me? All my co-wives and I became pregnant together. Their grandchildren now have children. So, if you go and say that man is your father, won't he kill you—and kill me too?"

"Oh ya, Mother," he said, "I'm going anyways." So he chopped a wood pile. He came and dropped it in the town, and it broke three houses.

After the child came with the wood, the man's senior wife said, "Father, this child who comes to greet you is your own child. He is a great rascal. Therefore, let's make a plan to kill him!"

He asked, "How will we kill him?"

She said, "Let's tell him to come tomorrow and carry away the raffia bundles that they've cut and stored at the entrance to the bush."

So the child returned to his mother and said, "Father told me to come tomorrow and carry his raffia to him."

She said, "The thing that I warned you about yesterday is beginning."

He said, "Mother, don't worry about it. I'll carry the raffia."

Before dawn broke, an ant came to him and said, "They've hidden riflemen in the raffia to kill you."

He made a spear with three heads. Two miles before he reached the raffia, he shouted, "My father called me to carry the raffia. I'll throw my spear, and if it hits anyone, it will kill him at once." Then those riflemen scattered from that raffia. So he did that, and carried the raffia to town.

Then that woman said, "This is what I've been saying: he is your murder-child. How did he know the riflemen were in the raffia? But this is what you must do to kill him. I have the bile duct of the crocodile that they killed recently. Let's cook food tomorrow. And to make sure, we'll dig a hole. We'll set the food on it. Then you call him to come and eat the food."

So that very night the crocodile went and told him.

At dawn, the chief sent someone to call him. He came and washed his hands. The woman was there with her own child. She mixed the rice and put the crocodile's duct in his portion. After she put that sauce on his rice, he switched the plates. She cried, "Child, don't kill my child!"

He answered, "Oh, but you want me to die today?" So her plan came to nothing.

So again she said, "Father, you said we should kill this child. Let's get the best of him. Let's tell him to go to the foot bathing place. Say that your sacrifice ring, that *very* ring, has fallen off your finger at the foot bathing place. Say you will die if it is lost. Then the crocodiles will kill him!"

Then the crocodile's own huge mother went that night and told him the plan. So he told his mother and she said, "Oh, I told you not to go into town, and you said you would go. Now you must die."

"No mother," he said, "I won't die."

So the child went and met the crocodile. It was the very crocodile they dropped the ring on. So the crocodile gave it to him. He stayed there one full week, and the woman said, "The child is dead now."

Long ago, when that child came back from the water, he brought many clothes for that woman. He gave that man's ring back to him and said, "Father, they told me you must sacrifice a jealous woman. You must throw her in the ocean. If you don't do that, you will die tomorrow."

So the man said, "That's it, lady."

Then the woman said, "Am I a jealous woman?"

And he said, "*Koo* . . . Yes!"

At dawn they performed the sacrifice. They tied her tightly and threw her in the water. At once the crocodiles ate her.

There they are now. The child and his father. They are going about as comrades. Then something came into his heart, and he said he wouldn't stay there. So he went out into the world.

Just after he went into the world he found a turtle on the road. He said, "*Kokoko,* I found my turtle. I'll roast it and eat it with cassava."

Then the turtle said, "Don't eat me. I will save you."

As he was going along he discovered a chief's wife who had died. They were bewailing her. So he said, "*Kieeee,* why are you bewailing her?"

They said, "The chief's love-wife is dead."

He said, "*Kieeee,* I killed her!"

Then they grabbed him and tied him up. He said, "Leave me alone. I will save her."

They asked, "How will you save her?"

He swore many oaths, with his turtle in hand. He said, "Surround the meeting place with country cloths. Put her there. She and I will go there."

After they went to the meeting place, he told them to set a fire. Then he leaned four sticks beside the fire and he said to the turtle, "You told me I shouldn't eat you and you'd save me. Save me now!"

"*Kuo,*" said the turtle, "how can I save you? You came and said you killed this so-and-so's child, and now you say I should save you?"

He answered, "Yes! You *will* bring her back to life."

So this turtle said, "Lower me down to her nose." He lowered him down to her nose and he farted: *kakaka*. She shook: *foyo foyo foyo,* and she sneezed: *bo*. Then she got up: *saa,* and she was sitting—this person who was dead!

The people exclaimed: "*Kpooo.*" He said, "Bring water so she might bathe completely." So they came with water and she washed. And so she was saved.

Then they divided the town down the middle and gave half to him. But that didn't satisfy him. He brought his mother's children there, and they stayed. But he left again, and reached another chief who was boundlessly rich. The only thing he lacked was a Troublemaker. He had complained for a long time that he had no Troublemaker so God brought him this one—the One who Spoils the Insides.

There were cows in this chief's village. There were slaves but they couldn't eat these cows. The Troublemaker went to visit them and said, "Since these cows are here, why not eat them?"

They answered, "*Kuooo,* if we eat the cows the chief will kill us."

He said, "That's a lie. With so many cows, how would the man know?"

So at dawn he came and brought the cows and they killed them. They cooked them and ate them. The cows which had been plentiful were becoming scarce.

So he went to the chief and said, "You are sitting? Those slaves you put in charge of the cows have eaten them up!"

"*Koo,*" said the chief, "Is this true?"

"Yes. If you think it's a lie, go tomorrow and you'll see it." So he got up and went and saw it. The cows were few. So he drove the slaves out.

Things went on like that. Then a fellow chief had his daughter initiated in the Sande Society [the Mende women's secret society] and gave her to him. The night she arrived and joined the man in his house, the Troublemaker came again. He said, "I've just had your future divined. It is said that you should sacrifice a Sande initiate. They say that will prolong your life."

"Aah," he said, "but how will we do it?"

He said, "They say that once you have killed her you should bury her in your own house. You should set a red bucket at the head of her grave." So the Troublemaker provoked this and they killed the child.

That very night he walked back to visit the girl's father. He told him, "Your child whom you recently initiated into Sande—the one you gave to this man—this very night, just after they had lain together, he killed her! He buried her in the house and set a red bucket at the head of the grave. She's there. She died there."

So this chief rose up. He and all his followers were coming there. As they were coming, Troublemaker once again said to this man, "Father, I've once again cast the stones and they divine that the chief who gave you his daughter is coming here. Therefore, the only thing that will save you is to get out of this country."

The man prepared a small bundle. He who had had a great following then prepared a small bundle. So he travelled far from his country. He kept on going long ago, and trouble fell upon him. . . .

I heard that little story, and I've told it.

In plot outline, Mama Ngembe's narrative agrees with the other variants I recorded from Kamara and Ernest Koba of Batema, Sherrifu of Njayehun, and Bobadeen Goba of Mattru (Cosentino 1976: 385–540). Each performer used the struggle between the father and son as the core conflict, but after settling that original score, each performer developed the excesses of Musa Wo in his or her own way. Considered together, these narratives constitute a sort of mythic indictment of the prince-miscreant from which this hypothetical police blotter might be constructed:

Name: Musa Wo (M. W.) Also known among Mende as "Gbabango" and "Kongomakanya." May be living disguised among the Krio as "Hab Sens Pas Chif" and among the Kuranko as "Gbentoworo" (Jackson 1982). Alias list provisional and may stretch eastward to the Mande (where he goes by "Sundiata"), and across the Atlantic (according to provisional reports on Afro-American characters such as Stagolee and Shine).

Age: Adolescent from birth. Seems to have suffered a peculiar period of gestation in utero. Disparate reports of mother's term of pregnancy range from seven to forty years. Parthenogenetic birth from thumb or knee. Goba variant reports M. W. swallowed and gave birth to his own mother, negating any further filial obligations. Postpartum behavior indicates arrested development.

Physical Features: Peculiar gestation rumors confirmed by neonatal beard and/or spikes on chest. Reputed to know animal language. Has special relationship with crocodile who acted as unindicted coconspirator in hoax that led father's subjects to drown in vain search for underwater riches. Also reputed to travel with magic turtle whose farts revivify the dead. Turtle captured after reviving M. W., who had fallen to death from the back of hawk. M. W. dumped for taunting hawk's "stinky wings." M. W. seized flatulent amphibian, and under threat of death by roasting, regularly forces turtle to fart into victims' noses as part of elaborate extortion bilk perpetrated on rich and/or powerful dupes.

Family Background: Unwanted son of chief and battered wife. Raised in single-parent family. Record of constant hostility with father's senior wife. Physically precocious: uprooted trees for firewood; built house for mother on day of birth. Indications of Islamic background: one report claims he made hadj with mother's blessing; obtained talisman in Arabia later used in criminal scheme. Goba asserts royal lineage claims bogus. He reports M. W. a twin with latent incestuous feelings for sister, and homicidal hatred for brother. For roasting and immolating siblings, M. W. banished from home. Lives by marauding on road.

Criminal Record: Accused of fratricide, patricide, genocide, mutilation, mayhem, conduct regardless of human life, incitement to murder, criminal fraud, and political destabilization. Unindictable offenses include depraved incivility, vagrancy, gross deception. Specific charges:

1. Organizing mass suicide of father's subjects.
2. Inciting brother to assist in mass murder of chief's wives.
3. Urinating on head of mourning chief from overhanging branch.
4. Shooting lizard who attempted to save brothers hiding in tree from irate chief and townspeople.
5. Castrating Father Deer with his own poker, and then taunting animal friends with the mutilation. . . .

The list goes on, but in the same vein. Mass murder tends to blur, like multiple fornications, and narratives about both kinds of pornographic activity run downhill toward exhaustion after the first exhilarating climaxes. This entropy of pornographic violence is why, perhaps, Mende narrators always say that a Musa Wo story can never be ended.

One might observe from Mama Ngembe's performance and the police blotter summary above that the character of Musa Wo shows signs of acute narrative schizophrenia. Our protagonist at first demonstrates the traditional heroic hallmarks outlined by Lord Raglan (1934). He is a deposed royal aspirant. He is miraculous in birth and abilities, and full of righteous indignation and plans of revenge, both for the sake of his wronged mother and in pursuit of his rightful place in the succession. But in achieving these ends he becomes an amoral monster, an unrestrained psychopath who murders his own creations. He is Hero and Trickster.

There is no analogue to Musa Wo in Mende oral tradition. But he does relate to the most extreme category of social rebel that Hobsbawm (1959) locates in the archetypal bad man of Afro-American lore, Stagolee, who murders, rapes and smashes anything which constrains him, determined to be a devil if he cannot be a man. Hobsbawm has described such rebels as "avengers:" "Thus, in the romances of the oppressed, to assert power, any power, is itself a triumph. . . . Killing and torture is the most primitive and personal assertion of ultimate power, and the weaker the rebel feels himself to be at bottom, the greater, we may suppose, the temptation to assert it" (p. 56). In the desperation of our own times, we need not look to oral tradition to find parallel examples of the Trickster Hero. On the political level we have the antics and mayhem of Adolf Hitler, Pol Pot, and Macias Nguema. And with a more particular horror, because he operates on a domestic level, we read of Richard Speck, the Reverend Jim Jones and Charles Manson. All these docu-demons tell us the great message that Mende performers embed in their myths of Musa Wo: a man may be very brave, and no damn good.

The tools of psychoanalysis may help explain the genetic pathology of the avenging Trickster Hero. One might easily discern in Musa Wo's neurotic relationship with his parents: his mother dependence and the obsessive hatred he projects on his father, the primal mythic conflict described by Freud in *Totem and Taboo* (1950). There are other examples of Oedipal conflict in African myths (though less so in folktales). Mwindo, Trickster Hero of the Nyanga epic, emerges from the same sort of mother-dependent/father-rival matrix (Biebuyck and Mateene 1969). Surface elements in the Musa Wo myths I collected, however, point to a more immediate myth source. Frequent allusions to Islamic tradition, the manner of his birth and the nature of his prodigies, the consuming hatred between his parents, and later between Musa Wo and his father—all narrative elements otherwise absent from Mende *domeisia*—point to the Northeast, to Mande and the epics of Emperor Sundiata, as a source. Considering the history of migrations into the western Sudan, it is not difficult to imagine the Sundiata myth being swept into Mende culture on the tides of the Mande invasions (Rodney 1970: 58–59). Like other cultural elements brought by the invaders, however, the epic hero underwent a sea change. The superego qualities of the warrior king were lost as the youthful Sundiata was twisted into the grotesque shape of the avenging Musa Wo.

The Sundiata epics (Niane 1965; Johnson 1986) seem to serve the fringe areas of the old Mande empire in the same manner that Freud (1952) described the unconscious manifesting images for the selecting ego to transform into encoded dreams (pp. 40–114). From a wealth of stored images, the dreamer and the mythmaker seek out those most latent with meaning, distorting or displacing original meanings and thereby revealing their individual preoccupations. Thus from a borrowed and ingested heroic myth, the Mende extract images of the trickster—Sundiata refusing to learn how to walk, Sundiata uprooting the baobab tree to provide firewood for his mother—and from those images they construct their idiosyncratic hero. The character they construct is not predetermined by the material they have borrowed. The Kuranko, to the north of the Mende, clearly borrow from the same Mande trove, but their hero Gbentoworo concentrates on resolving the problems of intergenerational succession (Jackson 1982). Krio speakers in Freetown narrate yet another version of this same character, whom they call Hab Sens Pas Chif, but for them he personifies the primacy of wit over ascribed power. Each of these groups treats Mande mythology as a free-floating international currency which can be exchanged into local coin with a culture-specific value.

So, if by rummaging through historical accounts, analogous traditions, and some Freudian analyses, we can come up with a mechanical theory for the genesis of this Trickster Hero, we must still ask what it is in Mende culture, or perhaps in the Mende psyche, which compels them to dwell on the anarchic qualities of their epic figure to the exclusion of any positive heroic quality. Sundiata creates and sustains a great empire; Mwindo learns the nature of perfect chieftaincy; but Musa Wo destroys the very institutions of office and state.

The hallmark of all Musa Wo's actions is volition unrestrained by social consideration. His narratives are set in opposition to the rest of Mende oral tradition and social structure, which are predicated on the maintenance of careful balances (Cosentino 1982:23–52). A curious parallel exists between this Mende expression of narrative anarchy within a tightly wound social order and that celebrated by German intellectuals—most famously by Nietzsche, but most concisely by his forebear and mentor G. W. F. Hegel: "[Heroes] are individuals who undertake and accomplish a complete enterprise in consistent reliance upon their personal resources and initiative, and with whom it is consequently a purely arbitrary act of their own when they execute anything within the moral principle" (p. 189). Hegel (1969, in Brombert) stresses above all else the absolute quality of the untrammeled will as essential to the hero:

> The validity of the ethical principle derives its support from individuals, men who make for themselves a great place in the arena of life through the activity of exceptional volitional power and inherent greatness and effectiveness of their character. With such, right is simply that which they choose to accept as such, and if that which is essentially moral is compromised by their action, there is no all-constraining public might which brings them to judgment and exacts punishment, but only the right of that inner voice of necessity, which accentuates itself as vital in particular character and through external circumstance and condition and only thus is actually existent. (p. 189)

Like Hegel and his German followers, Mende narrators bind their world view to a rigorous system of dialectics. It is perhaps not surprising then that in the creation of the hero, they too would seek the *Übermensch*—someone who transcends or even smashes the careful constructs of the social world to proclaim himself the absolute hub of his own moral universe. If the thesis of Mende social life is the balance of discrete social units, then its antithesis must be sought in the continuous and the unbalanced, which precisely describes the structure and narrative content of a Musa Wo tale.

Mama Ngembe's narrative performance revealed a most acute consciousness of this Manichean concept of the hero. She also demonstrated a willingness to play with that conception which marked the dandyism of her work as an artist and an intellectual. In her performance, images from the extreme poles of the Trickster-Hero axis are fused into a single narrative which succeeds in examining both the Sundiata and Hobsbawm's "avenger" modes of heroism by holding them in simultaneous juxtaposition. Aside from minor narrative details (*e.g.*, the length of pregnancy, the mode of birth), the initial images of her account jibe with those of the other performances mentioned in the police blotter summary. Her resolution of the conflict between Musa Wo, his father, and the senior wife, however, diverges from those other mythic accounts. Musa Wo deliberately spares his father from the act of revenge. Instead, he vents his wrath on the senior wife, who is tricked into becoming the propitiatory sacrifice to the crocodile. Mama Ngembe prepared her audience for this dénouement by focusing on the machinations of the senior wife, and resolving the conflict between her and the boy through a series of tricks and countertricks. After the senior wife's death, father and son are reconciled in a resolution that underscores the integrity of Musa Wo's actions and demonstrates the reestablishment of a proper order and balance that ultimately flows from so restrained a revenge. Mama Ngembe deliberately tampered with the conventional carnage employed by most Mende narrators to resolve the crisis within the royal family in order to create a hero more recognizably human than the usual Musa Wo—one who would contrast more sharply with the capricious moral monster she now intended to create.

The transition between the poles of her narrative is abrupt and effective: "There they are now: the child and his father. They are going about as intimates. Then something came into his heart and he said he wasn't going to stay there. So he went into the world." Musa Wo II immediately acquires the farting turtle, which he uses—just as he used his innate magic in the first images—to overturn a kingdom. The distance between these narrative events may be measured by the purposes to which his revolutionary acts are put: the first reestablishes an order broken by the unjust treatment of his mother and the usurpation of the senior wife, the second institutionalizes chaos. Musa Wo barters the turtle's miraculous farts for half a kingdom, which he then gives to his sister. And so he is free to continue down the road, duping villagers into killing their chief's cows, and then reporting the slaughter to the chief who orders their banishment. Having depopulated the country, Musa Wo dupes the chief into murdering his new bride. He then reports the murder to the royal in-laws who chase the chief from his throne. In the final image the chiefdom is returned to nature, without inhabitants or rulers. Musa Wo has succeeded in recreating the sort of zero ground that always marks his intrusion into the ordered affairs of society.

Mama Ngembe emphasized the character extremes of this dangerous man-child, augmenting his moral purpose in the first part of the narrative and accentuating his gratuitousness in the second. In that juxtaposition she plainly revealed the contradictory potential for creation and for chaos inherent in the Trickster Hero.

What does this anarchic hero offer such a balanced society? Perhaps he offers the narcotic of nihilism—the antidote to endless social rigor. In place of the entropic stasis represented by the union of the father with the son, Musa Wo's peripatetic violence promises relief—the relief of the tabula rasa. There may even be positive psychic value to the actions of Musa Wo. The very abandon of this bad boy rushes past the self-conscious posturing of a Zarathustra to offer Mende audiences the sensation of a liberated new world beyond their seemingly immutable social order. Norman Mailer's visionary description of the *White Negro* (1957) during the social rigidities of the American 1950s may offer, *mutatis mutandis,* an unexpected gloss to the actions of Musa Wo and his analogues, and a clue to their persistence in the transformed urban cultures of contemporary African and diaspora cultures:

> Truth is no more nor less than what one feels at each instant in the perpetual climax of the present . . . what is consequent therefore is the divorce of man from his values, the liberation of the self from the superego of society. The only hip morality is to do what one feels whenever and wherever it is possible, and to be engaged in one primal battle: to open the limits of the possible for oneself, for oneself alone because that is one's need. Yet in widening the arena of the possible one widens it reciprocally for others as well, so that the nihilistic fulfillment of each man's desire contains its antithesis of human cooperation. (pp. 14–15)

It may be that in framing these hypotheses I am proving no more than Levi-Strauss's assertion that myth holds up a mirror to the mythologist. To what extent were the images I saw in these Mende performances self-reflections? How anomalous are these visions? Are they shared by the audiences of Mama Ngembe, Bobadeen Goba, and the other performers I witnessed? I returned to Sierra Leone in 1983, as coleader of a research team, to investigate contemporary manifestations of the hero in oral narrative tradition and in popular culture. Team members recorded variants of the key Musa Wo myth from Krio, Kuranko, Temne, and Mende performers in Freetown, villages in the Western Province, and in Mattru, our original research site. We found that the myths I had collected from three Mende villages in 1974 had counterparts throughout the country. Each group had snatched from the manifest Mande myth its own figure of a rebellious youth overturning some sacrosanct ancestral construct in pursuit of some personal sweet latent in the inherited mosaic of images. This archetype of the willful child had moved from its premier place in the oral epic tradition to dominant roles in contemporary media, but the semantic value of that shift has yet to be understood.

Predications of a "Child Archetype," which persists in related cultures across epochs and media, evoke the work of Carl Jung and his grab bag of latter-day disciples. Jungian theories are rightly suspect among scholars who note their tropism for the fuzzy mysticisms of Mme. Blavatsky or Rudolf Steiner. In particular, scholars of African mythology must reject Jung's naive distinction between the conscious and preconscious mind in oral-traditional and "civilized" societies. But given his historical limitations, Jung's description (1963) of archetypes as "the myth-forming structural elements present in the unconscious psyche [which] personify certain instinctive data of the psyche, the real but invisible roots of consciousness" (p. 79), still offers a powerful mechanical hypothesis for the widespread distribution of the naughty-boy image in African oral tradition and its emergence into contemporary popular culture.

Jung's explication of the significance of the "Child" also remains compelling:

> It represents the strongest, the most ineluctable urge in every being, namely the urge to realize itself. It is, as it were, an incarnation of the *inability to do otherwise,* equipped with all the powers of nature and instinct, whereas the conscious mind is always getting caught up in its supposed ability to do otherwise. The urge and compulsion to self-realization is a law of nature and thus of invincible power, even though its effect, at the start, is insignificant and improbable. Its power is revealed in the miraculous deeds of the child hero (pp. 89–90).

Jung's intuition was in fact more powerful than his evidence. None of the examples he adduces fits the ineluctable willfulness of this "Child" with as much force and persistence as Musa Wo. Whether the archetype is precultural, as Jung claims, need not concern us here. Rather, we might reexamine the hypothetical existence of a "Child Archetype" with the fresh evidence offered by Mende oral tradition, and by the startling transformations being wrought upon the figure by the changing cultures of West Africa and the West Atlantic diaspora.

In 1983, the most important medium for the transformation of Musa Wo in urban Sierra Leone was pop music, particularly Jamaican reggae and Afro-American soul. The absorption of this music in West Africa already makes McLuhan's vision of a global village real for the Atlantic diaspora. Pirated tapes are available everywhere, and street corners are knotted with youths dancing to the blare of speakers from record shops that do not sell the discs, but rent them to patrons who copy them onto fake Sony tapes from Hong Kong or Taiwan. Hanging over Kissy Street in Freetown was a banner advertising a local group called the Heroes playing at one of the night clubs. And painted everywhere—on shop doors, bar walls, in provision shops and private homes—were images of a new demi-pantheon: Peter Tosh, Eddy Grant, Eric Donaldson, La Toya Jackson, José Feliciano, Michael Jackson—as well as their local imitators in sound and look. Alone, apart, and above all others, reigning as the Holy Family of this juvenile iconostasis, were the images of Bob and Rita Marley—the king and queen of "natty dread."

There is more than the celebration of musical youth in these ubiquitous icons. They make their appearance in juxtaposition to the images of age and authority, suggesting the persistence of the primal struggle between the overbearing father and rebellious son that is at the heart of the travails of Musa Wo, Mande myth, and *Totem and Taboo*. When we queried a Freetown youth on the identity of the maharishi pictured on the ads for Transcendental Meditation, we were told, "Na Bob Marley, im Papa," meaning that the maharishi was Bob Marley's father. We watched the construction and parading of a float depicting the Anglo-Jamaican reggae group, Musical Youth, for the post-Ramadan Lantern Parade, and then saw it juxtaposed in performance with a float depicting the venerable Imam of Foulah Town Mosque and banners celebrating the Ayatollah Khomeini. Everywhere were images of youth—now appearing as physically outrageous as Musa Wo is morally outrageous—held in check by images of senescent power. On the level most analogous to the plot of the myth, one read and heard of the audacious youth who had smashed into the political scene in the neighboring Sudanic fringe states of Ghana and Burkina Faso. One also noted that the most popular T-shirts were stamped with the image of the post-teen commander and chief in Liberia,

Sgt. Doe, who had engineered the ferocious overthrow of the ancient Americo-Liberian oligarchy (and who had himself embarked on a series of public outrages reminiscent of Musa Wo). But even those Doe T-shirts were worn by lorry drivers whose vehicles were painted with banners proclaiming, "We love you, Pa." Siaka "Pa" Stevens, the octogenerian president, was still in power then, but the memory of the post-teen sergeants whose coup had preceded his accession to power was still powerful, and was a harbinger of the youthful military officer, Jo Momoh, who would follow. Clearly the jury was split on the question of Musa Wo's quest for power.

The struggle between a youthful will to power and established (paternal) authority is not always limited to icons. We visited a youth club called Texas, which was located between the rock outcroppings at the foot of Mt. Aureole, the site of Fourah Bay College. The main enterprise of Texas was the growing, processing, sale, and consumption of marijuana. A barracoon in the middle of the fields of ganja served as the Texas "parliament," where a byzantine code of laws insured that the many infractions would be met by the purchase and distribution of more joints to parliament members and visitors alike. The visitors sitting and smoking in the barracoon racks included well-dressed Freetownians, presumably from nearby offices, and at least one policeman. One "parliamentarian" informed us that aside from their agricultural activities, members of Texas also worked as auxiliaries for the political party whose good offices in turn kept Texas free from any official harrassment; a visit from a Mercedes Benz seemed to confirm reports of official party linkage. But it was also apparent that the heart of the enterprise lay in this shed of dreams, where in the smoke of ganja, and to the beat of Marley—through their "inability to do otherwise"—this Parliament of Youth sat in perpetual fulfillment of all the adolescent wishes of Musa Wo. His myth had become their "Midnight Charter"—a dispensation for Freetown youth to play Child Triumpant in a world turned upside-down and made over in their vision. Their social drama recalled other images: 60s youth, in berets and "Che Lives" T-shirts, playing with Trotskyism, or today's Armani-suited yuppies playing robber barons of a resurgent capitalism.

Popular culture in Sierra Leone in those early days of the 80s seemed engaged in the same mythic activity as traditional society, though the process was a step further removed from the source and thus vaguer in outline and darker in purpose. The ancient Sudanic coin was exchanged for fake Sony tapes; the manifest myth of a tyrannical king disowning a magical prince mined for the latent image of an octogenerian president suppressing rebellious, ganja-blowing youth for the dubious spoils of a dissolving state. And like all true myths, the diachronic values were always bursting into synchronic realities. A few months after our research, we read in letters and news reports that the students at Fourah Bay College had taken to the road in riot, overturning rice pots on college administrators, and marching to the state house to demand that government-contracted helicopters be exchanged for a more substantial portion of Saturday's cassava fufu.

Musa Wo and his avatars surely do not inspire confidence in a stable or predictable future for Sierra Leone, Africa, or the world. He reminds one of the vacant-eyed but determined little teenage murderer of Hector Babenco's film, *Pixote,* berefit of any social context and moving along down the rail line, coming at us, mean and small. That young street actor, unsuccessful in gaining any further film roles, was himself killed in Brazil in 1987—the role he played and the life he was forced to live converging so quickly in a police shoot out. His route also belongs to Stagolee, to Gbentoworo, Hab Sens Pas Chif, the *White Negro,* Bob Marley, and all the parliamentarians of Texas. All these characters have perceived a massive and unresolved generational contradiction at the heart of their societies. Musa Wo is an archetypal expression of that unresolved conflict: the wild longing for free expression in a tightly constructed society. Neither his performers nor his audience knows where he is going. His myth has no ending, and cannot be ended. But his persistence on the road may express what Samuel Beckett has called mankind's pernicious optimism—the dark hope for a happy, if unknowable, end to the adventure.

References

Biebuyck, D. and K. C. Mateene

1969 The Mwindo Epic from the Banyanga. Berkeley: University of California Press.

Cosentino, D.

1976 *Patterns in Domeisia: The Dialectics of Mende Narrative Performance.* Ph.D. dissertation, Department of African Languages and Literature, University of Wisconsin-Madison.

1982 Defiant Maids and Stubborn Farmers. Cambridge: Cambridge University Press.

Freud, Sigmund

1950 Totem and Taboo. New York: W. W. Norton & Co.

1952 On Dreams. New York: W. W. Norton & Co.

Hegel, G. W. F.

1969 The Philosophy of Fine Art. F. P. B. Osmaston, trans. *In* The Hero in Literature. Victor Brombert, ed. Greenwich, Connecticut: Fawcett Premier.

Hobsbawm, Eric

1959 Social Bandits. Glencoe: Free Press.

Jackson, Michael

1982 Allegories of the Wilderness: Ethics and Ambiguity in Kuranko Narrative. Bloomington: Indiana University Press.

Johnson, John William

1986 The Epic of Son-Java. Bloomington: Indiana University Press.

Jung, Carl and Kerenyi, Karl

1963 Essays on a Science of Mythology: The Myths of the Divine Child and the Mysteries of Eleusis. Princeton: Princeton University Press.

Little, Kenneth

1967 The Mende of Sierra Leone. New York: Humanities Press.

MacCormack, Carol

1975 Sande Women and Political Power in Sierra Leone. West African Journal of Sociology and Political Science. 1(1):42–50.

Mailer, Norman

1957 The White Negro. San Francisco: City Lights Press.

Niane, D. T.

1965 Sundiata: An Epic of Old Mali. G. D. Pickett, transl. London: Longmans.

Raglan, Lord

1934 The Hero of Tradition. Folklore 43:212–31.

Rodney, Walter

1970 A History of the Upper Guinea Coast. 1545–1800. Oxford: Clarendon Press.

Bonnie L. Wright

The Power of Articulation

> Human plurality, the basic condition of both action and speech, has the twofold character of equality and distinction. If men were not equal, they could neither understand each other and those who came before them nor plan for the future and foresee the needs of those who will come after them. If men were not distinct, each human being distinguished from any other who is, was, or will ever be, they would need neither speech nor action to make themselves understood . . . Action and speech are so closely related because the primordial and specifically human act must at the same time contain the answer to the question asked of every newcomer: "Who are you?" (Arendt 1958: 175–6, 178)

In the quotation above, Arendt has highlighted two areas fundamental to any examination of the caste system of the West African savannah: a distinction between speech and action, and the importance of speech and action in the identification of oneself and others.[1] Just as the European philosophical tradition commonly distinguishes between speech and action, so do these West African societies. This similarity is obscured, however, by a third cultural element that radically transforms the speech/action dichotomy.

The question "Who are you?" when posed in the Western Sahel cannot be answered solely on the basis of the speech and action of the individual interrogated—it can only be answered when speech and action are joined to identity, and identity in the Western Sahel is inextricably tied to caste. Further, speech and action themselves are colored by caste: *action* is ideologically allocated to one caste and *speech* to another. In other words, the speech of one caste differs in essence from the speech of another, as does the quality of action. The dilemma is, of course, that speech and action constitute the media of *all* human beings, regardless of caste, a fact recognized as fully in West Africa as it is in the West. But while we share a common set of analytical distinctions, we have a different ontology, a different notion of precisely how to answer the question "Who are you?"

In the following pages, I will explore the Wolof ideology of caste identity through this prism. Wolof society is divided by caste, yet joined again through the interdependence of its segments and through the culturally defined capacities—the power—of each segment. The focus of this exploration is the bard, the one whose capacity or power is that of speech. For the Wolof, as for the Mande, Fulbe, Serer, Lebu, and Tukolor, the bard is the articulator of action, the memory, the mediator, the one who "identifies" the other. His action *is* speech. He is the identifier, the witness, the vitalizer, the judge—in short the sole means of tempering death with something like immortality. The ambiguity of the English word *articulation* is precisely analogous to the role of the bard in West Africa; that is, the articulation of the bard is both that of speech and that of the joining of the segments ordained by the caste system.

A profound study of caste in West Africa has been hampered by a number of factors; foremost among them is that the term *caste* itself derives from the study of Indian social organization[2]—some definitions are applicable to West Africa and others are not. Because of this difficulty, anthropologists have been divided in their opinions about the advisability of applying the term to West African societies; some use it, but others opt for *class* (not a happy choice), others for *occupational specialization groups* (unwieldy and incomplete), and still others avoid the problem altogether by not labelling these social segments at all.

Furthermore, even when a definition which suits both West Africa and India can be agreed upon, the cultural emphasis on particular elements of the system in one part of the world may not accurately reflect the system as it functions elsewhere. An illustration of this problem is the scholarly response to Dumont's classic work *Homo Hierarchicus* (1970). This work was intended at least in part as a contribution to the then-flourishing debate about the extent to which the term *caste* could be applied to non-Indian societies. Following Bouglé, Dumont began with a working definition of caste which could be applied to West African societies as well as to India:

> The caste system divides the whole society into a large number of hereditary groups, distinguished from one another and connected together by three characteristics: *separation* in matters of marriage and contact. . . ; *division of labor,* each group having, in theory or by tradition, a profession from which their members can depart only within certain limits; and finally *hierarchy,* which ranks the groups as relatively superior or inferior to one another. (p. 21; italics mine)

As the title of his work indicates, hierarchy is for Dumont the crucial characteristic and one he considers too long neglected by scholars and sociologists. To support this claim, he argues that to the working definition must be added the ideological principle of opposition between ritual purity and impurity (pp. 59–61, 212). This argument, however, does not emerge from a truly comparative framework but only from his study of Indian social organization; by raising what others may consider a culturally idiosyncratic emphasis (purity/impurity) to structural equivalence with separation, division of labor, and hierarchy, he effectively denies the applicability of the term *caste* to any but Indian society. This criticism has been made by others, among them the West Africanists Hamès (1969) and Diop (1981). Dumont, anticipating the charge, sought to divert it thus:

> It may be objected that if we insist on speaking of caste only in the presence of this configuration, we make it impossible to use the term for the classification of social groups. Some would even say that we are confining ourselves to Indology and making comparison impossible. To this it may be replied that there is no absolute need for purposes of classification to use a concrete term like *caste,* and that abstract terms or neologisms should be used as paradigms rather than impoverish the content of the term "caste" by extending its use in an arbitrary manner. (p. 201)

Dumont also criticized the indiscriminate use of the term *caste* to describe social stratification in the American South (*e.g.*, Berreman 1960), medieval Europe and Japan (Kroeber 1931), and elsewhere. (Significantly, he did not mention West Africa.) But although his reaction to such a diminution of an important sociological term is understandable, and his remarkable analysis of the Indian caste system laudable, his argument that there is no middle ground between reserving the term for India and "extending its use in an arbitrary manner" is not convincing. (Even its applicability to India has been questioned, both because of its hierarchical emphasis and its holistic approach [Appadurai 1986].)

Furthermore, although the emphasis upon hierarchy, the pure/impure opposition, and ritual status are useful to an understanding of the Indian caste system, their overuse in West African studies has greatly impaired the understanding of African caste systems, as it has for caste systems elsewhere in the world. Some, such as Pollet and Winter (1971), Vaughan (1973; 1977), and more recently Richter (1980) and Abdoulaye-Bara Diop (1981), have tempered this hierarchical orientation by taking into account the groups' interdependence—a precondition as well as a result of the caste system. Others, however (Hamès 1969; Irvine 1973, 1974, 1978; Boyer 1983), have continued to assume that hierarchy is the most fundamental characteristic of African caste systems. The greatest problem facing those who define the system in terms of hierarchy is to find a plausible explanation of the ideological and material power of the "low-ranking" castes. This problem is especially apparent in discussions of the bard caste: how is it possible for a group so low-ranking and "despised" also to be described as shameless parasites upon and exploiters of the higher-ranking group? If they are so despised, why should the higher rank support them, and what is the nature of the bards' power such that others fear to disappoint them? Clearly, there is a great deal more involved here than hierarchy.[3]

I will argue that the West African caste system, rather than being composed of hierarchically ranked groups, is really best understood as a set of groups differentiated by innate capacity or power sources. The inequalities of the system are less matters of rank than of culturally defined realms of power, and the conjunction of all these realms constitutes the social universe. To *action* and *speech* may be added the realms of *transformation* (the other occupational castes) and *servitude* (slaves).[4] The labels of such realms of power are neither immutable nor arbitrary; caste, as I will show, is but one framework among many for defining power and identity. Other frameworks include descent (double descent in the past, patrilineal today), ethnic group (Wolof, Tukolor, Serer, Bambara, etc.), gender, and place of origin (often a region or village in the precolonial empire where the individual may, in fact, never have been). I will discuss these other frameworks and their interrelationship below. Although hierarchy is intrinsic to all of these frameworks, it does not carry one very far toward an understanding of how West African societies are organized, either at the ideological or the jural level. In this, West Africa presents a very different sociological picture from that of India. Yet one must retain Dumont's usage of the term *caste,* because these societies are composed of endogamous specialized groups which inherit their professional capacities genealogically. The ethnic group upon whom I shall base my argument is the Wolof of Sénégal, and the caste that will best serve to focus the terms of the argument is the *gewel* (bard) caste, the articulators of experience for all individuals, *gewel* and non-*gewel* alike.

Before colonization by the French in the nineteenth century, the territory that is now Sénégal was composed of a group of states or kingdoms; the states north of the Gambia River were joined temporarily in an empire, each state owing allegiance and paying tribute to the kingdom of Jolof. The relations among the states fluctuated a great deal, and probably at no time was the empire very stable. The states are usually distinguished roughly along ethnic lines (Tukolor, Wolof, Serer, Lebu, Manding), but there was considerable intermarriage, at least among the political and religious aristocracy, and movement, marriage, and communication between and among the various states seems always to have been common. The importance of this point will become apparent below in the discussion of ethnic identity, descent and place of origin, in conjunction with caste, as parameters of individual identity.

The Wolof are the largest ethnic group in Sénégal and the Wolof language the most commonly spoken. Islam arrived in the area very early, via the pre-empire state of Tekrur, probably in the eleventh century. The Wolof today are nearly all Muslim (see Colvin 1974).

The caste system is the most striking characteristic of Wolof social organization: all people are born into one of two broad castes, the first being *geer* (roughly translated as noble, freeborn, or gentry and including farmers as well as descendants of royalty); the second *ñeño,* which includes blacksmiths and jewellers (*tëgg*), bards or griots (*gewel*), and leatherworkers (*ude*). Each broad group is endogamous and dependent upon the other groups for the products of their labor. Each group and subgroup has its own quarter or quarters in each town and village, even in such an international metropolis as Dakar. This caste system also is characteristic of the other major ethnic groups of the region, which include the Fulbe, Tukolor, Mande, and Serer; and intermarriage between ethnic groups within the same caste is still easier and more prone to be forgotten or assimilated in succeeding generations than is marriage within the ethnic group but across caste boundaries.

The descent system of the Wolof today is patrilineal, but the historical record shows ample evidence of a double descent system in existence before the colonial period (see Rousseau 1929; Ames 1956; Diop 1970; Niang 1972). Of the six major precolonial states north of the Gambia River, four chose their rulers from both patrilineal and matrilineal royal clans, one from only patrilineal royal clans, and one from only matrilineal royal clans. The Wolof had four specific linguistic terms for both lineal and lateral patrikin and matrikin:

	Patri-	Matri-
Lineal	*geño*	*meen*
Lateral	*gir*	*xet*

Today, both the terms *gir* (patrilateral kin) and *xet* (matrilateral kin) have other meanings important to a discussion of Wolof identity; *xet,* for example, can now mean nationality or animal species. Both terms may even be synonymous in certain contexts: the question "*gan gir/wan xet n'ga?*" ("what *gir/xet* are you?") can elicit a response of ethnic identity ("*man, olof laa,*" "I am Wolof"), place of origin ("*Jolof-jolof laa,*" "I am from Jolof") or caste ("*gewel laa,*" "I am a bard"). Bards at least retain the words *xet, meen, gir* and *geño* in their more precise kinship meanings, though it usually requires some elaboration on the questioner's part for them to give these particular meanings.

Today the Wolof descent system can only be considered patrilineal, but it retains a strong emphasis on matrifiliation. This emphasis is evident in: (1) the Wolof belief that a child's character and fortune in adulthood are more influenced by his mother's behavior and nature than by his father's;[5] (2) the joking relationship (*kal*), in which the matrilateral cross cousin is one's "master" (*surga*) and one's patrilateral cross cousin is one's "slave" (*jam*); (3) the notion of birthplace, or place of origin, which is often, if not usually, the place of one's mother's birth, because a woman nearing childbirth often returns to her mother's home for the event; (4) a marked preference of adult men to return to their mothers' homes for the traditional Muslim holidays (Tabaski and Korité, especially) rather than to their fathers' homes (it is not uncommon for married women to maintain households separate from their husbands'); (5) the preference to rear orphans by the mothers' kin rather than by the fathers'; (6) matrilineal inheritance of witchcraft: if one's father is a sorcerer, one may inherit a gift of sight, or divinatory capability, but one cannot be a sorcerer oneself unless one's mother is one also; and (7) a marked matrilateral tendency in the inheritance of *rab* (personal spirits), which are said to participate in and mirror the lives of their hosts (see Zempleni 1977).

Ethnic identity in Sénégal is highly manipulable within bounds; for instance, intermarriage across ethnic lines is fairly common, and, at least for the aristocracy, has always been so. This flexibility exists because people are free to identify themselves as members of either their mothers' or fathers' ethnic groups. Because identity is so negotiable, and because many of the markers traditionally used to identify a person as a member of a particular ethnic group (*e.g.*, language or surname) are not always reliable, any discussion of ethnic identity for Sénégal must be complex. Conjoining the principle of ethnic identity are three principles of social identity: caste, descent, and place of origin.

A useful assumption to make upon meeting someone for the first time is that patronymics indicate both caste and ethnic origin, so that Fal, Jop, and Njaay indicate Wolof and *geer* (nobility); Mbaay, Mbup, and Samb indicate Wolof and *gewel* (bard), and so on. But in fact the name without the place of origin (commonly an ancient village or particular region in the old kingdoms, where the person may actually never have been), indicates no such thing. Here, the common intermarriage between ethnic groups (*e.g.*, a Serer man and a Wolof woman), together with the tendency for a person to evoke his mother's birthplace as his own place of origin, shows that a man of a Wolof mother with a Serer surname such as Saar may consider himself Wolof, particularly if he believes his mother's lineage or place of origin to be more important than his father's or if he happens to visit or reside in a predominantly Wolof region.

Furthermore, at least in the past, a person of *ñeño* caste (blacksmiths, bards, or leatherworkers) whose family was formally linked by patronage to a family of *geer* caste would sometimes adopt the patronymic of the *geer* family, so that there are today noble Njaays and *ñeño* Njaays (especially *gewel*). Whenever a bard meets someone and seeks to "place" or "identify" that person, he always asks about the personal name and the place of origin. He may then ask the mother's and father's names, but often the first two are sufficient for identification. When bards in performance discuss specific patrilineal clans, they always distinguish lineages of the same patronymic by giving the place of origin. This implicitly indicates the caste identity and ethnic origin of the particular clan as well.

A similar method of identifying clans of the same name can be seen in the following excerpt of an interview with El Hadj Mamadou Samb, a direct descendant of the last Fara Jungjung (royal bard) of Mbul (recorded in Thiès on June 5, 1979). Clans here are differentiated both by the offices they were entitled to hold in the precolonial kingdoms and by their places of origin:

> The bards who served the damel [king of Kajoor]: Fara Jungjung and Bëc Ngewel of Mbul; at Ngocen those named Seen chose Amari Ngone [the first independent damel], and the Fara Lamb [royal blacksmith] from Mbelgor. The Fara Lamb and the Fara Jungjung were closer to the damel than any other. These five bards: those named Seen, companions of Amari Ngone; those named Samb, Fara Jungjung; and those named Cam, Fara Lamb; for Muse Mbore the bards were named Jeng and Samb [these Samb were not the same clan as the Fara Jungjung Samb], who came from Caraxen. There are many bard clans at Sugeer—Mbaay, Sal, Juf and Samb—and each had a precise role in the administration of the damel. Those named Samb were with the Jeng clan at Kër Muse Mbore, where they held the office of Jaraf Buntu Kër. Those named Sal were the bards of the Fal clan, both of whom were from Sugeer. Those named Mbaay were the bards of the Fal clan of Njemel; these Fal were the descendants of Daw Jere [*i.e.*, Daw Demba Fal, a seventeenth century damel], and of Damel Biram Yasin Bubu Fal. They didn't live in Mbul but in Njewen. There are also Fals descended from Muse Ndumbe at Kafrin, but these are different from the Fals of Njewen. At Mbul, there are the Mbup clan who could be the bards of the sons of the damel, and the Jop clan of Kër Pate Fari, and the Njaay clan of Gati Ndongo.

A second aspect of the personal name which links it with ethnic origin and place of origin is the joking relationship. This is not precisely identical with the joking relationship between cross cousins (*i.e.*, it does not entail ritual duties of any kind) but it takes a similar form of good-natured ridicule, and Wolof call it by the same name, *kal*. The relationship cuts across caste identity (*e.g.*, Niang-Jeng-Fal, who joke together regardless of caste, ethnic identity, or place of origin). It also exists between ethnic groups (such as the Serer and the Tukolor), between villages, and between regions. The banter usually takes the form of a stereotypic statement about the other, such as "the Mbaays eat a lot of rice," or an invitation to the other to change his patronymic to one's own, since the latter is "better." People say that this bantering relationship, far from indicating hostility, is really a mechanism for incorporation, indicating a close role relationship dating from an event in antiquity and which facilitates cohesion. Thus, it is said, a Tukolor would have an easier time moving into an unknown Serer village than into a Wolof one; he would be more graciously accepted and more quickly assimilated by the group.

A third aspect of the personal name which links it with ethnic identity is the equivalence of names of different ethnic origin. Njaay (Wolof) is said to be equivalent to and interchangeable with Jaata (Serer), Fal (Wolof) is equivalent to Kulibaly (Manding), and Geey (Wolof) is equivalent to Sisoko (Bambara). So a Serer man named Jaata, for example, visiting a Wolof village may well introduce himself as Njaay.

There is no single word in Wolof which means *caste* as opposed to *ethnic group;* only the social context resolves the ambiguity of the question "*wan xet/gan gir n'ga?*" ("Who are you?"). This merging of caste and ethnic group seems to be common to all societies which share this caste system, and it is often explained by positing a cause-effect relationship between the two. Caste and ethnic group are the same, because the castes (and here such scholars apparently only mean the *ñeño* castes) were of different ethnic and regional origin. Thus, much of the literature on the Western Sahelian populations speculates on the nonindigenous origins of the occupational castes (most recently in the published proceedings of the 1981 Séminaire internationale de l'Association SCOA [1984: 3–44]). And it is not at all uncommon for Mande scholars to distinguish between Bambara and *ñamakala* (or *ñeño*), thus implicitly asserting that bards, blacksmiths, etc., are somehow not "Bambara." The same opposition is evident in a major early work on the Wolof, in which Yoro Jaw, a regional canton chief, states that most of the *ñeño* castes are not Wolof by origin but Fulani (Gaden 1912: 121). Diouf (1981) responded to this "ideology of blood" (p. 34) by arguing that although some *ñeño* castes—for instance, *lawbe* (woodcarvers), *maabo* (weavers), and *gawlo* (bards)—are definitely of Fulani origin, they were only incorporated into the Wolof system in the eighteenth and nineteenth centuries, long after the system was firmly in place.

Although there is so much speculation about caste origins in the literature, I believe it strays from more interesting issues. I have spoken of caste and ethnic groups as merged, but they are only truly merged in certain contexts, as in general discussions about the stereotypic differences between *ñeño* and *geer* and the origins of the caste system—and even then never totally. Ethnic identity, as I have shown, is open to manipulation and change, but caste is immutable.

Marriage between ethnic groups is common and fairly easy; proscriptions of marriage between castes are rigidly maintained. The case of Y. F. illustrates the force of these proscriptions. Himself a *geer,* he was courting two women at the same time, one *geer* and one *gewel*. To everyone's surprise, he married the *gewel* woman, but on the day of this marriage, his mother went to the *geer* woman, married her to her son by proxy, and thereafter asserted that the *geer* woman was his first wife (*awo*) and the *gewel* woman his second wife. It is perhaps noteworthy that Y. F. was of royal descent (*garmi*) on both his father's and mother's side; in precolonial times, *geer* men, especially *garmi,* were allowed, even encouraged, to marry *gewel* women (but only as third or fourth wives) "to bring happiness to the household." Offspring of such marriages were raised as *gewel*. The case of Y. F. illustrates the breaking of the caste endogamy rule, but it even more clearly shows how efforts are always made to prevent such violations. Further evidence for the continued strength of the marriage proscriptions is that violation of the marriage contract through subterfuge (one spouse lying about his or her caste identity in order to marry the other) is grounds for immediate annulment.

This background suggests for the West African caste system a rather more fruitful interpretation than that usually employed. First, caste should be seen as only one of many ways of identifying oneself or another. Other identification parameters include gender, age, ethnic group, place of origin, and genealogy; the last three factors are highly manipulable within certain constraints, but gender and caste are immutable. Although some seek to take advantage of the unreliability of surnames as indicators of caste and seek to "pass" as *geer,* such subterfuges never quite succeed, for place of origin and genealogy always expose the truth, at least to knowledgeable *gewel*.

Second, status is determined not only by these parameters, but also by such idiosyncratic characteristics as skill, knowledge, honor, loyalty, and generosity, all of which provide not only a means of identifying a person but also of describing a person's reputation. A *ñeño* may achieve high status, just as a *geer* may be brought low. However often Wolof rank the various castes (and there is seldom agreement about the relative ranking, for example, of the *ñeño* castes), they hesitate to rank individuals, and they never do so solely on the basis of caste. Status or hierarchy, therefore, do not sufficiently explain caste, nor are they necessary concomitants of caste identity.

What, then, does distinguish caste from other modes of identification, if hierarchy does not? An examination of the past and present roles and functions of the *gewel* caste can lead some way to a deeper understanding of the system as a whole. Bards among the Wolof, as among the Mande, Tukolor, Fulbe, and Serer, are musicians, dancers, poets, historians, genealogists, and praise singers; in the past they acted as intermediaries and ambassadors between states, between lineages, and between individuals; today they are often propagandists for politicians and religious leaders, and some have even become ministers in the national government and important religious leaders themselves. In the past, they raised the courage of warriors with their drums and praise songs, and they led them in battle, weaponless except for their speech and artistry. Today, they similarly encourage farmers at planting time, wrestlers, jockeys, and soccer teams. Many lead singers of popular bands, national and international merchants, and announcers on the radio are also of the bard caste.

Now, as in the past, their presence at all major life ceremonies (births, naming rituals, marriages, and funerals) is essential. On these occasions, they act both as performers and as witnesses—as participants in an important genealogical/historical event and as recorders of that event. Their role as performers involves music and dance and the recitation of genealogy to praise and to mark the event in relation to past and future social groupings. Normally, the principal *gewel* attendant at the particular celebration is lineally and/or customarily associated with the host family; other *gewel,* however, are nearly always present as well, often by invitation. To hold such an affair without the *gewel* present would be unthinkable. Were such events to go unrecorded by *gewel,* the persons involved, not only the living but the dead and the unborn as well, would suffer oblivion, itself a veritable death.

The people for whom the *gewel* perform reimburse them for their services, either in money or gifts. The size of the recompense is contingent upon the ability of the individual(s) to pay and upon the quality of the services rendered. A bard who feels that the gift is too small or that the patron has been parsimonious always has recourse to insult, which is greatly feared by all. The *gewel*'s tongue, after all, far more than the *geer*'s, is thought to have the power to ruin a person's reputation, and consequently his life and posterity. In this, *gewel* power is akin to sorcery, and indeed, of those suspected of being sorcerers, a large proportion are *ñeño,* especially *gewel.* It is possible that such suspicions and accusations of *ñeño* arise, at least partially, from the *geer*'s sense of victimization by *ñeño* in the public domain, as a kind of revenge. Another reason that *ñeño* often are accused of sorcery is provided by the beliefs surrounding the nature of sorcerers, or *dm.* Although sorcery is performed in private, Wolof people recognize *dm* not only by the illness or misfortune of their victims but also by the public characteristics and behavior of the *dm* themselves. In a social world in which reciprocity is highly valued, *dm* are egocentric, jealous, greedy for attention and goods, and never willing to reciprocate—the very antithesis of the social person. Persistent begging is one of the most common signs by which they are known. And *geer* often complain of *ñeño* (especially *gewel*) by saying that *ñeño* "demand too much," they are loud and uncontrolled, etc. *Dm* can use hair and nail clippings to cause physical or mental illness, and *gewel* can use stolen letters to cause social embarrassment or damage to one's reputation; both, therefore, are disposed of carefully.

The capacity for sorcery is inherited from one's mother; if only the father is a sorcerer, the child may inherit clairvoyance, the ability to detect the sorcery of others and force a perpetrator to release his or her victim through the threat of exposure or violence. *Dm* are thought to work either for themselves or for others, "eating" their victims—causing illness, madness, even death. A client who hires a *dm* (*e.g.*, to ensure the former's success in a particular endeavor or his rise in power and/or wealth) is required to "pay" for the *dm*'s services—I was often told that many of the rich and powerful were missing one or more joints of the little finger. While this kind of sorcery is in some respects very like the activities of marabouts or imams, it differs from these in several important respects. A marabout does not increase another's power by attacking that person's opponents, but by protecting the person from the harm that others may intend; payment for these services is of a far more socially acceptable kind; and the medium of the marabout's power is the word of the Koran. Indeed, if one suspects that he or she may be the victim of a sorcerer, it is the marabout who makes the amulets (which commonly consist of passages from the Koran encased in leather to be worn or carried) to protect the person from *dm*.

At the level of myth and legend, this conjunction of bard and sorcerer is a recurrent theme. A Fulani and Wolof myth about the origin of the bard caste is illustrative. Two brothers are wandering in the drought-stricken bush, and the younger says he will die if he doesn't eat something soon. The elder brother hides himself and cuts off a piece of his own leg, cooks it, and gives it to the younger, who eats it (which refers to the *dm*, who figuratively "eat" their victims). When the latter notices how his brother limps, he discovers the source of the meat he has eaten, is overcome with awe and gratitude, and declares that from that day forward he will be his brother's bard (Zemp 1966: 632). A variant of the Sunjata epic collected in the Gambia contains the same motif, in this case Sunjata feeding his bard Musa (Sidibe 1980: 30).

Another legend, also attributed to the Fulbe, relates a similar bodily sacrifice. A poverty-stricken young man is approached by some bards, who are probably looking for money or gifts. The young man's relatives offer the bards cloth and cattle, but they refuse. To escape the shame of having nothing worthy to offer, he goes into his hut, cuts off his finger, and offers it to the bards (Smith 1973: 479). The similarity between this and the payment exacted by *dm* for their services is obvious.

At a more ideological level, *dm* and *gewel* share the ability to transform people, the former in secrecy, the latter in full view of the world. Sorcery, therefore, may be interpreted as the illegitimate use of a power to which *gewel* are the legitimate heirs. This proposition explains the tendency to conflate *gewel* and *dm;* it also points to their differences. Whereas *dm* use their power to diminish a person, *gewel* use theirs to aggrandize; *dm* work in private and appear publicly as normal beings, but *gewel* work in public and in private are indistinguishable from *geer.*

The arena of *gewel* power is the most public of arenas, in which people are most exposed to societal scrutiny and most vulnerable to humiliation. It is also the arena in which praise is most likely to occur. When *gewel* praise someone, they recount that person's genealogy and selected actions performed by the person's ancestors (male and female); the pride one feels in hearing his or her praises sung in public is thought to inspire the person to perform deeds equally great or honorable. If this indeed happens and if the praiser is treated well, the beneficiary of *gewel* praise is assured of having his or her own name remembered and recited in the genealogies of descendants, perhaps for centuries to come, provided that the descendants also act well and reward their praisers.

Another form the *gewel*'s praise may take is in musical performance. To perform well is to gladden and strengthen all those who hear and see the performance, to vitalize and validate the community at large. To perform poorly is an insult, especially if it is deliberate.

In addition to performing the more modern roles of merchant, radio broadcasters, and political propagandist, *gewel* continue to mediate disputes and marriage contracts, relay messages between important personages, and act as counselors and trusted confidants, as they always have. In these capacities the *gewel* is more clearly the intermediary—between buyer and seller, between bride and groom, between politician and electorate. More generally, however, bards in all their roles both praise and mediate, praise here being interpreted as that particular form of mediation between the person and his or her reputation, hence between the person and his or her past, present, and future social world.

It is appropriate at this point to ponder the significance of the bard's own complex reputation. *Geer* commonly describe *gewel* in general as parasitic, lascivious, loud, and uncontrolled; they often suspect them of being sorcerers and liars. Such statements, however, are rarely if ever applied to specific individuals; furthermore, these statements are intended to describe *gewel* public behavior, not private. This stereotypic public reputation may be interpreted as a metaphor of social distance from *geer* in the public arena. Similar metaphors of social distance exist for other mediators of experience; the Wolof also consider women and children, for example, to be morally unreliable and more closely allied to "things of the bush" (such as sorcery) than are adult males.

On the other hand, a potentially more useful explanation for the *gewel*'s reputation sheds light not only on the *gewel,* but on the whole of West African caste systems. Although people provide the raw materials for their own reputations, it is the bard who articulates, interprets, and perpetuates those reputations. I have often seen Wolof tear personal letters, however innocuous, into tiny fragments before disposal "because *gewel* are everywhere," and may read and use them to reveal private information. The bard is not only in the position to know, but also in the position to say. The *gewel*'s power is that of the presenter of social identity for *all* persons. It is not surprising, therefore, that bards are maligned, in a vain effort to call that power into question by attributing unsavory qualities to them. *Gewel* themselves lend credence to their stereotype; in public performance they present themselves as loud, mischievous, and provocative, while in private they display the same range of personality traits as the members of any other caste. *Gewel* power derives from their capacities as ever-present witnesses and public, even vociferous, commentators. *Geer* may claim to be victimized, but however they protest and deny, they continue to fear and to pay.

By a circuitous route, this leads back to Arendt's dichotomy between speech and action discussed earlier. We of the West European tradition, as well as the Wolof, separate *speech* from *action,* even as we, and the Wolof, know that speech *is* action. Were this not so, the speech of *gewel* would be as valueless and unintimidating as the speech of *geer* and would go equally unrecompensed. Because the power of speech and the memory of action are granted to *gewel,* the *geer* are deprived; and because the power of action is granted to *geer,* the *gewel* are deprived. But both groups, as human beings, retain both capacities, and it is only by an elegant cultural investiture that the speech/action dichotomy can be expressed in this particular way. Analysts may differentiate *geer* from *ñeño* by saying that *ñeño* are transformers of matter and deed—blacksmiths transform ore into iron or gold, leatherworkers transform animals into skins, weavers transform plants into cloth, and bards transform action into identity. But *geer*—rulers, farmers, "actors"—do they not transform as well? The farmer transforms seeds into food and the ruler transforms a population into a polity; it is difficult to see how these transformations differ from those of *ñeño*. These questions are perhaps unanswerable by anyone seeking a purely logical position in the social sphere. No matter what profession the modern *ñeño* may choose to follow—veterinarian, teacher, foreign policy advisor, publisher—that profession can always be accommodated within the existing caste system and never threaten that system's existence. Rebellious acts which might truly confound the system (*e.g.*, marriage between castes) are still met with vigorous resistance from interested parties.

These inherited differences in capacity, therefore, are an elaborate mechanism whereby the use of the speech/action dichotomy may work for society; given a low ranking in the field of action, *gewel* excel in freedom and speech. *Gewel* can withhold their speech, required for social immortality, at will. When the bard speaks for good, and speaks well, he is indeed bestowing gifts. When he speaks for ill, it is a moral judgment upon the one of whom he speaks, and the responsibility lies with the person judged rather than with the speaker. This effectively insulates the bard from charges of evil intent (except perhaps surrepticiously, through accusations of sorcery), and so from responsibility for his actions, since they do not constitute conventional "action," and since a bard would not deliberately alienate his patron, or rather his subject, without good cause.

That inimical difference between speech and action is determined by descent—a bard, even if his personality is retiring, his speech halting, and his profession not obviously one which bards are "supposed" to follow, is still a bard, as his children will be. He still has inherited the power to articulate, even when he cannot exercise it.

Descent for the Wolof is the keystone of identity formation and is elaborated not only in the descent pattern (double descent in the past, patrilineal descent with matrifiliation now), but also in the caste system, the options people have in identifying their ethnic identity and their place of origin. The spirit world of the Wolof and Lebu corresponds exactly to these systems of descent: personal spirits (*rab*) and the spirits of places and lineages (*rab* or *tuur*) may be inherited, may have "personalities" as widely varied as humans have, may have caste, ethnic and origin identities.

In the past, dual descent and the caste system defined the politico-jural domain. The continuation of the caste system has tempered the changes brought by the rise in Islamic political power, the fall of the precolonial states, and the imposition of colonial rule, despite predictions that it would disappear under the forces of modernization. *Gewel* in particular have contributed a strong hand in the system's conservation; as the articulators of personal identity and experience, they have upheld the ancient rules of identification within which all manner of social changes may be accommodated—except perhaps those which would call into question the existence of *gewel,* the speech/action dichotomy and the descent idiom.

Having thus peered through a Western European statement about speech, action and identity at the caste system of a West African society, one perceives, perhaps darkly, an alternative to the traditional emphasis on hierarchy as the system's dominant characteristic. Bouglé's original definition of social organization as characterized by separation, division of labor, and hierarchy is as applicable to Western Sahelian societies as it is to Indian. The ideological basis of the system, or the network of philosophical tenets of the nature of human identity, together with the cultural emphases and expressions of human differences, varies from society to society and within each with the passage of time. Endowed with the power of speech, the Wolof bard articulates the basis upon which the caste system as a whole can be fruitfully explored: the question "Who are you?" is meaningless without the questions where and of whom were you born.

Notes

1. The field research on which this paper is based was conducted in Sénégal in 1978–79, and was funded by a Fulbright-Hays predoctoral research grant. A preliminary version of this essay was presented at the African Studies Association meetings, Bloomington, Indiana, on October 23, 1981.

2. The Oxford English Dictionary states that the term *caste* is an adaptation of the Spanish and Portuguese *casta,* meaning race, lineage, or breed. In its modern sense, it was originally applied by the Portuguese to India in about the middle of the sixteenth century.

3. For example, while Irvine's description (1974) of Wolof greeting patterns has the merit of demonstrating the importance of status manipulation in everyday social interaction, the importance of the expectation of reciprocity in greetings is omitted. Wolof, whether *geer, ñeño,* or *jam,* all expect that the respondent to a greeting will at some point become the initiator. Respondents who systematically fail to initiate in normal contexts are thought to be snobbish, if not actually rude.

4. I follow Diop (1981) in excluding *jam* (slaves in the past, and descendants of slaves today) from the caste system. Diop argued that there are in reality two different systems in operation; one of castes (*geer/ñeño*), and one of political orders (*geer/jam*).

5. Sylla (1978: 94) cited two Wolof proverbs which express the importance of the mother's behavior for the success of the child: *Wurusu manding, teela xey du ko meye, yaay ju ligeey-a koy meye.* (To find gold, it is not enough to wake up, you must have a mother who has worked for you.) *Liggeeyu ndey añu doom.* (It is the mother's work which feeds the child.)

References

Ames, David

1956 The Selection of Mates, Courtship and Marriage among the Wolof. Bulletin de l'Institut fondamental de l'Afrique noire sér. B (18): 156–68.

Appadurai, Arjun

1986 Is Homo hierarchicus? American Ethnologist, 13 (4): 745–61.

Arendt, Hannah

1958 The Human Condition. Chicago: University of Chicago Press.

Berreman, Gerald D.

1960 Caste in India and the United States. The American Journal of Sociology, LXVI: 120–27.

Boyer, Pascal

1983 Le status des forgerons et ses justifications symboliques: une hypothèse cognitive. Africa 53 (1): 44–63.

Colvin, Lucie G.

1974 Islam and the State of Kajoor: A Case of Successful Resistance to Jihad. Journal of African History, 15(4): 587–606.

Diop, Abdoulaye-Bara

1970 Parenté et famille wolof en milieu rural. Bulletin de l'IFAN sér. B, (32): 216–29,

1981 La société wolof: tradition et changement: les systèmes d'inégalité et de domination. Paris: Karthala.

Diouf, Mamadou

1981 Le problème des castes dans la société wolof. Revue sénégalaise d'Histoire 2 (1): 25–37.

Dumont, Louis

1970 Homo Hierarchicus: The Caste System and its Implications. Chicago: University of Chicago Press.

Gaden, Henri

1912 Légendes et coutumes sénégalaises: cahiers de Yoro Dyao. Revue d'Ethnographie et de Sociologie, 3(3–4): 119–37.

Hamès, Constant

1969 La société amure ou le système des castes hors de l'Inde. Cahiers internationaux de Sociologie (Paris), 46: 163–77.

Irvine, Judith T.

1973 Caste and Communication in a Wolof Village. PhD dissertation, Anthropology Department, University of Pennsylvania.

1974 Strategies of Status Manipulation in the Wolof Greeting. *In* Explorations in the Ethnography of Speaking. Richard Bauman and Joel Sherzer, eds. Cambridge: Cambridge University Press.

1978 Wolof Noun Classification: The Social Setting of Divergent Change. Language and Society 7: 37–64.

Kroeber, Alfred

1931 Caste. *In* Encyclopaedia of the Social Sciences, Volume 3, New York: Macmillan and Co.

Niang, Mamadou

1972 La notion de parenté chez les Wolof du Sénégal. Bulletin de l'IFAN, sér. B(34): 802–25.

Pollet, Eric and Grace Winter

1971 La société soninké. Bruxelles: Ed. de l'Institut de Sociologie de l'Université libre de Bruxelles.

Richter, Dolores

1980 Further Considerations of Caste in West Africa: The Senufo. Africa 50(1): 37–54.

Rousseau, R.

1929 La Sénégal d'autrefois. Etude sur le Oualo. Cahiers de Yoro Dyâo. Bulletin du Comité d'Etudes historiques et scientifiques de l'AOF, 12 (1–2): 133–211.

Séminaire internationale de l'Association SCOA (ler : 1981 : Niamey, Niger)

1984 Actes du séminaire: rapport du Moyen Niger avec le Ghana ancien. Paris: Association SCOA.

Sidibe, Bakary K.

1980 Sunjata. Banjul, Oral History and Antiquities Division, Vice-President's Office, Old National Library.

Smith, Pierre

1973 Principes de la personne et catégories sociales. *In* La notion de personne en Afrique noire. Paris: Centre National de la Recherche Scientifique.

Sylla, Assane
1978 La philosophie morale des Wolof. Dakar: Sankoré.

Vaughan, James H.
1973 Ngkagu as Artists in Marghi Society. *In* The Traditional Artist in African Societies. W. L. d'Azevedo, ed. Bloomington: Indiana University Press.
1977 Mafakur: A Limbic Institution of the Margi (Nigeria). *In* Slavery in Africa: Historical and Anthropological Perspectives. Suzanne Miers and Igor Kopytoff, eds. Madison: University of Wisconsin Press.

Zemp, Hugo
1966 La légende des griots malinké. Cahiers d'Etudes africaines 6(4): 611–42.

Zempleni, Andras
1977 From Symptom to Sacrifice: The Story of Khady Fall. *In* Case Studies in Spirit Possession. Vincent Crapanzano and Vivian Garrison, eds. New York: John Wiley and Sons.

Michelle Gilbert

Sources of Power in Akuropon-Akuapem: Ambiguity in Classification

In the old days, if people tried to get hold of a chief in times of war or crisis, he could turn himself into a tree so that people would pass him by. The chief was powerful: because they believed it, it became true. . . . Many chiefs could turn into cats. One could touch a wall with his body and then you would see him behind the house. A very old chief in Amanokrom could do that: if he wanted to run away, he just leaned against the wall. . . . In those days, if you wanted to go to the king and were arrogant or came with an air of pride, he would put his foot on the ground and say: "Behold, what are you doing?" and then you would fall down. Today, this kind of belief has gone away. In the old days, the palace was a fearful and a wonderful place.

In the old days, if someone fired a gun all you would see was water coming out of the gun. People could collect the bullets with their right or left hand. In those days, you could cut someone with a cutlass and the cutlass would break into pieces. In the old days, things happened which were fearful and wonderful.

—An Akuropon elder[1]

Things Which Are Fearful and Wonderful

In the Ghanaian town of Akuropon-Akuapem, things which are fearful and wonderful are thought to be brought about through the action of gods and ancestors. This paper is about the indigenous concept of power and its sources and how these notions are used by the people of this town.[2] The categories of this belief system, although generally agreed upon, are constantly redefined in use. What should be kept in mind throughout is the ambiguity of this power, which can be used for good or bad, but which is always dangerous (*cf.* Douglas 1966: 114–36).

The Akuropon world view is reasonably clear cut with respect to the various kinds of supernatural entities in the system. Everyone agrees upon the terminology, that some types of entities are more powerful than others, and that this ranking may change. Akuropon people thus provide themselves with an easily understood cosmology whose elements form a single conceptual and ritual whole. In practice, however, the situation is often less tidy. Specific supernatural entities may be allocated at different times (or by different persons at the same time) to different places in the hierarchy, depending on social and historical conditions and the individual's position in the society.

In practice there may be no apparent relationship between the particular entities and the kinds of power and rank allocated to them (*cf.* Middleton 1960: 25). I hope to show that the construction of the shrines in which power is believed to reside reveals the interlinking and at times overlapping of the seemingly discrete popular categories. I shall relate the logic of ritual practice to people's beliefs concerning fearful and wonderful things, that is, to how they represent the effects of power in their everyday world. Consistency is not necessarily to be expected. Indeed, it is through the at first sight seemingly unpatterned ways in which elements in the system are categorized that power and authority are seen to be exerted and maintained. Yet there is a pattern: it is the people's ability to define the categories in different ways according to their own advantage that allows the system to work. Nonetheless, the actual workings of power and their sometimes unintended effects on innocent people are frightening, as is the danger of close proximity to it. Akuropon people see the world as a dangerous and fearful place.

Akuropon is the capital of the southeastern Akan kingdom of Akuapem, which was founded in 1733 by members of the Asona clan from Akyem Abuakwa who came to help the indigenous Guan overthrow their Akwamu overlords; therefore the Asona are the royal clan in this kingdom. The people of Akuropon are Twi-speaking and matrilineal. Many features of their political and religious organization are similar to those of other Akan peoples, but others are specific to Akuapem. The rest of this heterogeneous kingdom of Akuapem includes mostly Guan-speaking patrilineal peoples, with some Twi-speaking groups of Akwamu origin. The kingdom comprises seventeen traditional towns scattered along a high ridge and many villages in the plains beneath; its population is about 70,000, and that of Akuropon is some 6,000. The people of the capital town are mostly food crop and cocoa farmers, and there are also many teachers and civil servants, for the population is highly educated.

Between two-thirds and three-quarters of Akuropon people are Christian, either converted as school children or later attracted by the promise of a prestigious funeral with burial in the Christian cemetery. Even though most people are at least nominally Christian, beliefs in the powers of ancestors and non-Christian deities are fundamental aspects of Akuropon interpretations of experience, as are healing and purification rites and some jural procedures in which these same powers are invoked. Beliefs about mystical powers and the sources of that power continue to be widely held, despite the Christian influence. Many Christians in the late 1970s would have agreed with the elder who said to me:

> Society, property, moral conduct are safer with "fetishes."[3] You have fear to do wrong. If you do wrong, you will be punished immediately. This is the competition for Christianity. Christianity has no morality. You can do wrong forever. God punishes you later.

Rather than competing with Christianity, such beliefs in fact constitute a set of explanations which complement those of Christian doctrine. Hence the introduction of Christianity has merely widened the range of categories which can be invoked or chosen in the ever-changing interplay between category and practice.

Used as a verb, the Twi word for power (*tumi*)[4] simply means "to be able." The major sources of power held to be effective in people's everyday lives include the Supreme Being (Onyame) and the Goddess of the Earth (Asase Yaa), ancestors (*asaman,* whose power is localized in Black Stools, *nkongua*), "large" and "small" gods or deities (*abosom* and *asuman* respectively), and "medicines" (*nnuru*). There are also believed to be tiny forest beings with backward feet, called *mmoatia,* who steal little children and are versed in the construction of *asuman,* and a giant with long hair called Sasabonsam, who is said to be dangerous and "very fond of" *asuman*.

There are other sources of power as well. These include unusually traumatic historical events, places where these events occurred, certain objects of royal regalia, and witches. Anything unusual is said to have power. Thus twins and albinos (and the first missionaries) are all likened to *abosom*. Even the status of seemingly ordinary human beings may be seen as ambiguous, for by attaining elderhood they take on certain ancestral attributes—both elders and ancestors are addressed as *nana*. A father may give some of his food to his child and thereby give him a bit of his power; an elder may sip palm wine and spray it breathily towards someone as a blessing.

The people of Akuropon see the human and the spirit worlds in similar ways, using the same metaphors for both; and they see man as a microcosm of the whole, as a part of the total cosmology that gives that whole pattern and comprehensibility. There are three kinds of spiritual power in society: the ancestors, associated with the matrilineal descent group (*abusua*); the deities, associated in many ways with the group of patrifiliation or "father's deity" (*agyabosom*); and the soul (*kra*) that is given to an individual directly by God (Onyame) and has no direct association with any particular social group or category. The first two mystical elements mediate between the living and God and are usually given shrines; the *kra* has no shrine. I will discuss here ancestors and deities, but not the *kra,* which is of a different order.

The power of the ancestors and deities are seen as distinct, even incompatible:

> Stools [ancestral shrines] are not deities [*obosom*], they are power [*tumi*].
>
> What is found in the *obosomfie* [deity house] should not be in the *nkonguafie* [stool house].

In practice, however, just as ancestors and elders are difficult to separate, so too, on another level, are ancestors and deities. Akuropon powers are in practice neither as discrete nor as tidily categorized as one might assume from the different terms applied to them in the formal system of categorization. An example is the deity called Akonedi.

Akonedi, variously spelled Akonnedi or Akon(n)odi, is a female deity with a famous and well-attended shrine in the Akuapem town of Late (or Larteh) and a number of lesser "branches" of the shrine in other

Akuapem towns and elsewhere in Ghana (see Brokensha 1966:158, 173–80). People from all over southern Ghana come to consult Akonedi about the reasons for their illnesses and misfortunes and to seek her remedies. People from other Akuapem towns, including Akuropon, also swear oaths on Akonedi to assert that what they have said is the truth or to declare their innocence of a particular charge, such as stealing. They may call upon Akonedi to kill themselves or someone else, or they may simply place themselves under her protection. Although no one disputes the success and popularity of Akonedi, there is considerable disagreement about what kind of deity she is—that is, about her status and rank. Most of Akonedi's adherents in Late and elsewhere consider her to be a strong and active *obosom.* In the Akuapem town of Abiriw, where there is a "branch" of Akonedi that is weak in influence compared to the main town deity called Bosompra, most people declare Akonedi to be merely a *suman* (small god, pl. *asuman*). In Akuropon some elders go so far as to assert that because Akonedi is believed to be the spirit (*sunsum*) of a woman who died in pregnancy or in childbirth, she is really an ancestor (*asaman*), not an *obosom.* As if to clinch the argument, they note disparagingly that she is a relatively new deity, implying her weakness by analogy to the weakness of those "stools" (ancestral shrines) made in recent years; the latter being created with sheep's blood rather than the now-illegal but traditional human blood, are not considered to be very powerful.

This example is not unique. In principle *abosom* are ranked from higher to lower until they reach the level of *asuman* (*cf.* Rattray 1923:86), but in practice a fluidity exists between the categories of *obosom* and *suman.* Thus as a *suman* increases in power, it may come to be considered an *obosom,* and vice versa. This fluidity or negotiability also allows people to make distinctions reflecting their own power and status in the community: individual ranking can be manipulated for purely political reasons.

Because of the overwhelming importance of the kingship, it is not surprising that Akuropon people often speak about the relationship of various *abosom* and *asuman* to one another as if they were palace officials. The latter are members in another ranked structure in which there is always room for negotiation, with the possibility of old positions being eliminated or redefined and new positions being created. Although ranks are nominally fixed relative to one another, such manipulation is as widespread as it is in Akuropon society generally, where political patronage is a key institution. The capacity for accommodation likewise exists in certain aspects of the descent system, when decisions may be made in spheres which the local people formally state are invariant—for example, deciding who should perform a funeral or in whose lineage house one should live. Negotiation of the same kind is also seen in the choice of to whom one appeals for the jural resolution of oaths. In the past, flexibility was even manifest in practice, though not in formal belief, in defining the status of free and slave.

In brief, both ancestors and deities form a single system in which their domains are constantly being readjusted. In Akuropon verbal discourse the domains are kept separate, whereas in practice the distinctions disappear: the systems are complementary rather than contradictory. Akuropon elders are aware of this:

> Deities and ancestors are one and the same, because both are invisible and yet can do wonders. They determine individual fate and societal fate; fertility, greatness, and so on come from them. If not, and if they are offended and vengeful, then that too is social and spreads to the community. They are difficult to separate—if deities are offended then ancestors may appear to say why. . . . If the dead ancestors are offended and do harm, then one may go to an *okomfo* [a person who can be possessed by deities] and he communicates with the ancestors.
>
> Deities know about the land of the ancestors because they are spirits. Some deities can say things about the ancestors. They will say: "Your mother greets you, your father greets you, do this, do that."

In rites of propitiation roughly the same type of offerings are given to both gods and ancestors, and the sacred space of shrines for both is demarcated by placing the same type of leaves on the ground to prevent evil from crossing. Even the expression to describe the anointing of ancestral shrines is the same as that used to describe anointing the shrines of deities: *due obosom*. So although there are different words for ancestors and for gods, from another perspective the differences dissolve.

The Sources of Spiritual Power and the Construction of Shrines

On every important social and ritual occasion libations are poured to make contact with all the supernatural powers and to inform them of the impending event.[5] A typical prayer accompanying such a libation in the palace begins:

> Oh, Onyankopon Kwame [Great God, born on Saturday], Asase Yaa [Earth, born on Thursday] come and take wine to drink; *Nana* Mpeni the Great [the shade tree in the central town plaza which is also an *obosom* and whose roots proverbially stretch under every house in Akuropon], drink; *ahum ne aham* [*Microgramma owariensis,* a fern which grows on trees, and which metaphorically implies all the leaves in the firmament], drink; *abosom* from Berekusu to Apirede [from the southernmost town of Akuapem to the northernmost], drink. . . . *Nana Asonafo nsamanfo* [ancestors of the Asona people]. . . . *Nananom* [lit. grandparents], drink oh, *nananom* drink oh, *nananom* drink oh [*nananom* here refers to ancestors].

I turn now to an examination of the beings invoked in this prayer—God, Earth Goddess, deities and ancestors—and of the construction of shrines for ancestors and gods. In order for supernatural beings to be worshipped and so contacted, they generally need to have a locus. There are several types of shrines. Their construction involves the mingling of contrasting elements (all of which in themselves have some power) into a single bounded space, which is then said to contain power (*tumi*) in a new and greater form. The components used to make shrines for gods and ancestors differ, but as I will show, in each case the basic process of construction is similar. I was told how the shrines were actually made in response to my very open-ended queries as to the nature of ancestors and gods.[6] It should be stressed, however, that this is a local expert's explanation, which reflects only how Akuropon ritual specialists understand the sources of supernatural power; indeed it is how they themselves create power. Most laymen know merely that the shrines are ritually established in some way or other. Finally, I will look at the powers of leaves, trees, and "medicines"—plants are of central importance in the Akuropon belief system, and Akuropon people do not separate "medicines" very clearly in ritual practice from deities. My material shows that the same features underlie the whole system and also that the people differentiate these entities into a hierarchy. I will argue that the cosmological categories and ritual practices do not simply complement one another, rather that the latter make meaningful the seeming vagueness of the former.

The Supreme Being. The Supreme Being, variously known as Onyame, Onyankopon, and Odomankama, is said to be omniscient, omnipotent, and the giver of rain and sunshine. He is the creator of all the world: plants, animals, forest, hills, and streams, and is appealed to in all prayers. But both he and Asase Yaa, the Goddess of the Earth, are too high and remote to be approached directly.[7] In most rituals, people appeal to their ancestors and to the deities because it is they who mediate between God and men (*cf.* Kilson 1969 on the Ga).

The Ancestors. Ancestors (sing. *osaman,* pl. *asamanfo* or *asaman*) are said to live beyond a high mountain or across a river in a place called Asaman.[8] The world of the ancestors is inhabited by kings and commoners, just like places on earth. It is believed that the ancestors can not only see what the living do on earth, but they may send help to the deserving and punish wrongdoers by causing illness or even death. Libations are poured daily to the ancestors (only respectable and honourable ones are named), who are informed of important issues and problems.

Blackened stools are used as shrines that may temporarily be occupied by the ancestral spirits of a particular lineage (*cf.* Rattray 1923 : 145); they symbolize and indeed hold ancestral power. In Akuropon are a dozen or so important lineages, each of which has a blackened stool, generally only one. The royal Asona lineage has seven Black Stools for former kings of Akuapem.[9] The royal and nonroyal blackened stools are the same in appearance and in function, but the former are considered both more sacred and more powerful, as they represent former kings and are the source of the present king's authority over the holders of nonroyal stools.

Knowing how Black Stools are created allows one better to understand the source of their power. Traditionally, a new stool was blackened with the blood of a human being who had to be an important member of the matrilineage concerned. Other materials were also used.

> The Black Stool has power (*tumi*), but you must get that power from a relative who is important to you. You do not just take any man from anywhere to make a Black Stool. It must be a fellow lineage member. His head is cut off to make the stool. . . . You use gun powder and spider's web and mix it with the blood. . . . You use an executioner's knife to pierce the neck and the blood comes out and is poured onto the stool. You put the head on the stool, and the heart and sex organs, you put them on the stool for a while. Then power has come into the stool.

Formerly, during the periodic *adae* rite or the annual Odwira celebration, a man was killed and his blood used to anoint the blackened stools anew.[10] In this case the man was rarely if ever a lineage member, and seems generally to have been a slave. This use of human beings ceased around the turn of the century, and today castrated rams, considered to be symbolically clean and peaceful, are used for sacrifice instead.[11] It is likely that recent stools in Akuropon have been "created" with the blood of sheep, but many people do not consider such stools to be sufficiently strong; I was repeatedly told that "you cannot make stools without the blood of human beings."

The Black Stool belongs to the matrilineage and is created with blood (*mogya*) from the matrilineage (*abusua*); but although the names of the matrilineal ancestors are called when libations and sacrifices are made, it is generally the "spirit" of the original stool occupant which is derived from the group of patrifiliation (*agyabosom*)[12] that is specifically addressed (Kyerematen 1969:1–2). The Black Stool thus represents the two complementary and necessary components of a "person:" blood derived from the matriline and "character" derived from the patriline (Gilbert 1987).

Besides blood, gunpowder and spider's web are used in making stools. Gunpowder is powerful and is associated with men who in the past went to war together with fellow members of their *agyabosom*. Spider's web alludes to the mythical trickster, Ananse, and its reputed wisdom is a link by means of the kitchen to women (and their knowledge of members of the *abusua*). In Asante, stools are blackened with eggs or the yolk of eggs mixed with soot (Rattray 1923:92; Sarpong 1971). The soot, according to Sarpong, "is formed in the kitchen from the web of the spider and smoke from the fire" (p. 43). In Akuropon the "old women" (*mmerewatia*) of the matrilineage are considered to be the repositories of wisdom, to possess the important knowledge that pertains to genealogical identities of the legitimate heirs of the matrilineage. They are said to be the ones "who know." The components contained in a Black Stool may be expressed schematically as:

male	female
war (gunpowder)	wisdom (spider's web)
patriline (*agyabosom*)	matriline (*abusua*)
"character"	"blood"

The Deities. There are two main kinds of deities, known as *abosom* and *asuman*. The former are said to be "large" and personalized, the latter "small" and not given personality. Even though the terms are linguistically different, the categories should not be separated too rigidly. *Abosom* and *asuman* are essentially the same kinds of power, and they bring about the same kinds of effects, such as death, serious illness, failure or success in economic or political activities, protection from poisons, and so on. Even though in practice deities and ancestors are similar in the ways I set out above, both conceptually and in composition *abosom* and *asuman* are even closer to one another, and so differentiated as a single category from ancestors.

The power of the deities is grounded in natural phenomena from the wild, whereas ancestors gain their power from human beings and the domestic sphere. Both, however, mediate between Onyame and man and both can generally be contacted at shrines made by the living. The shrines for the deities themselves vary in composition. Some consist of objects placed in brass pans; others consist of black clay pots of water; yet others take the form of bundles suspended from walls, and of similar objects placed on the ground. In general, brass pan shrines and those suspended from walls are given masculine attributes; water pot shrines and those placed on the ground are said to be feminine. Some deities are said to have both male and female aspects.

In what follows, I will examine these shrines and the powers that reside in them to show that the overlapping attributes of the different types of powers make it possible for the people to vary the deities' rankings to their own advantage. I do not, however, wish to give the impression that Akuropon people are no more than confident and cynical manipulators. They tend to see the world as a dangerous and fearful place—for them power manifests itself in deities and ancestors. This power can be used for one's advantage, but also to cause harm. The experience of power is fundamentally ambiguous, and people's attitude toward it is also ambiguous. Power is feared. It is dangerous. To swear an oath on an *obosom* or a *suman* is not something one does lightly. A protective deity placed in a field to stop thieves is effective because people fear the consequences if they do not take heed.

The Deities Called *Abosom*. *Abosom* (sing. *obosom*) number in the hundreds and may be invoked as a group (*abosompem ne abosommagua;* lit. "thousands of *abosom* and assembly of *abosom*") or individually by name. Since they are closer to man than God is, they act as intermediaries between the two. It is through *abosom* that God and man are made known to each other. *Abosom* are said to be the "children of the skies," the "children of God," and "God's messengers."[13]

Abosom are not manmade objects, but are spirits identified with specific lakes, rivers, streams, rocks, trees, or other natural objects. More precisely, most rivers and streams are *abosom,*[14] as are some, but not all trees:

> The *odum* [*Chlorophora excelsa* or *C. regia*] is the greatest of all trees. It is very strong and very hard; therefore we can see there is power in it. It is an *obosom*. We can fell an *odum* tree, yet we fear it. Other trees are medicinal. We put an egg or coin before we use them, that is, we buy them; we don't take them free. But they are not *abosom*.
>
> Strong animals are feared. Big ones, such as the leopard, elephant, bush cow are *abosom;* they have power to kill humans; we give them reverence.

McLeod (1981) wrote that in Asante, "In general, *abosom* were associated with the bush and the wild; and they are still believed to come from outside human society" (p. 62). In Akuropon it is the same; those *abosom* not associated with specific things of nature are said to be simply deities who descended from the sky. *Abosom* in general are free-ranging and, although not omnipresent, they can travel quickly and be in more than one place at any time; most can be localized temporarily in shrines in the form of clay pots filled with water, or brass pans.

While *abosom* are thought to be benign and protective, they also punish wrongdoers and are considered greedy and capricious, eager for food or sacrificial offerings, and likely to break off contact with men at any time. They are considered useful but also very dangerous to deal with.

> They do good and bad. Because their ways are different from ours, "fetishes" are good and dangerous at the same time.
>
> *Obosom,* being a spirit, will know the guilty person and start to cause death in the family—it is always a quick death, such as from an accident or snake bite, or an illness that lasts one or two days only. The innocent will be affected, not necessarily the guilty.
>
> Deities can declare a person innocent or guilty by punishment of death. If you call a deity to prove your innocence, it is said the guilty one will become ill and confess before he dies, or confess and be told to do certain things before he will become well again.
>
> These deities, anytime you call them, whether you are right or wrong, they will do what you bid them to do. If you swear on a deity to search for your stolen cloth, whoever owns it will be affected. It is direct. It is not the thief who is caught, but the one to whom the thief sold it.

According to some informants, the degree of specialization of *abosom* is not marked. I was once told, rather impatiently, that *abosom* are not like hospitals with specialists: herbalists (*adunsinfo*) may specialize, but not owners of *abosom* and *asuman*. Nevertheless, in practice, certain *abosom* and *asuman* do establish a reputation for having destructive powers, for curing diseases, or for helping those who are barren and want children. The *obosom* priests (*osofo*) say that the deities do not compete—each has his own duties and people can go to whichever they wish.

All the *abosom* active in Akuropon were brought from outside. It is said that in the past, when a particularly powerful deity became known, the king would announce that any subject who wished to be apprenticed to it could do so, and would then be free to introduce it into Akuapem. When the new worshipper had paid a fee to the main shrine, then a "branch" of that shrine could be established in Akuropon, and thereafter a percentage of the fees accruing to the "branch" from the local adherents would be sent annually to the main shrine.

Akuropon people often express the relationship between "branches" of a deity in a kinship idiom. Ntoa, the main *obosom* for the town of Akuropon, is said to have been brought from Nkoransa in Brong-Ahafo for *Omanhene* Fianko Betuafo (died c. 1742). The one at Brong-Ahafo is reported to live in the forest where there is a big cave and rocks. He is senior; the one at Akuropon is considered to be his "son;" and there is another in the Akuapem town of Aburi who is said to be his "daughter." Similarily in the Guan town of Abiriw, Bosompra is said to be the husband of Topre, another *obosom* in the town of Mamfe, some five miles away. An Abiriw elder told me:

> Bosompra's wife is Topre of Mamfe. . . . All the rest are perhaps his sons, but we cannot really know their proper relationship to one another because they are deities.

Other deities in Akuropon, such as *obosom* Gyamfi and the *asuman* Amanfo and Adade, are said to be related as soldiers are to their king. They are perceived as the "strong medicines" following the stool to war.

> Gyamfi is a war *obosom*. And Amanfo and Adade are *asuman* for war. Gyamfi came from Asante. Since it helped in fighting wars, it is a strong *obosom*. Because it succeeded in winning wars, the state adopted it. When there is any doubt about what someone says, people swear on Gyamfi. If what they said is not true, Gyamfi will kill him immediately. . . . Amanfo is a warrior. Adade is a warrior too. Adade is not Gyamfi's son, but Gyamfi is like a king and Adade his soldier.

It is said of those deities presently in Akuropon that "they came and stayed and are not returning." But if the religious official in charge of a deity dies and is not replaced, or if a deity does not produce results, there will be a loss of patrons and the shrine may be termed "dry;" then it will be said that the *obosom* has gone away. The rise and fall in popularity of a deity generally is attributed to the fluctuating power of the deity itself.

> The god Buruku was originally at Late, it was a Guan god. Then it was taken to Kwawu, then to Yendi on the Togo border. When a deity is dissatisfied with the people it moves away. The Yendi chief brought it to help him in war. Now the Dagomba worship it.

People can transfer their allegiance at will from one deity to another. Worshippers of a particular *obosom* may belong to different lineages, towns, or even ethnic and language groups.

> Certain deities do cures, reveal secrets, reveal witches, and so on. Every deity has its specialty. They cannot all do everything. Every deity has its own powers. We wanted to communicate with a particular dead person, therefore we went to Nkonya, Ntonda, beyond Hohoe where there was a clairvoyant. She took a brass pan with cowries.
>
> (an Abiriw elder)

The *Obosom* House and Its Shrines: To illustrate some of the ambiguity of the supernatural beings which emerges in ritual practice and to show how both the ancestors and deities share features in one ritual system, I turn now to a description of one of the *obosom* houses or temples in Akuropon. It is said that the *abosom* and *asuman* work independently. On occasion one may swear an oath or appeal to only a single deity to witness the truth of an event, but at other times one may appeal to several *abosom* and/or *asuman* simultaneously. In practice a number of deities tend to be linked together into a single system, either literally (as in the following case, in which they are "housed" together) or simply in the sense that people are generally possessed first by lesser "attendant" gods and then by the main deity (much as a king, when entering the palace, is preceded by his attendants).

The deity house (*ebuw*) for the *abosom* Wontumi and Osraman is one of the few still in active use in the town of Akuropon.[15] Inside the Wontumi and Osraman deity house, on a raised platform[16] are two large brass pans (*ayowa*), each of which contains a pounded conglomerate mass of sacred ingredients. These represent the two *abosom*. Each of the brass pan shrines rests on a small wooden stool, further separating them from the profane ground. Black balls of earth said to be Wontumi's children surround the mound in the pan for Wontumi and they are anointed with blood annually. (These brass pan shrines, each filled with a mound of pounded "medicines," are similar to shrines for the Tano River deities in other Akan societies.)[17] Also on the raised platform are three black terracotta pots referred to as *denkyedenkye* (swamp, marsh), which contain river water and certain leaves. Here, it is said, other *abosom* come when called. Lizards or crocodiles (*adenkyem*), symbolically anomalous animals which live in caves in rivers and breathe air, often are said to come to these *obosom* pot shrines. There are also six highly schematized black terracotta heads (sing. *abaduaba,* pl. *mmaduaba,* lit. child-tree-child[18]) representing unnamed deities said to be the "children" of the *abosom* or executioners and soldiers (*abrafo*) who watch over Wontumi and Osraman. One special stool for both Wontumi and Osraman is anointed periodically with omentum, fat skin from the peritoneum of sheep, in much the same manner as are the ancestral Black Stools in the palace and elsewhere—although without using blood. In addition, there are three iron swords for the *abosom*. The layout of the deity house is similar to that of the royal ancestral stool house, and the repeated use of symbolic elements inside the temple refer both to kingship and to the ancestors (iron swords, stools). These express the interlinking, indeed overlapping, in practice of the linguistically discrete categories of ancestors and the gods called *abosom*.

The Deities Called *Asuman*. I turn now to the other, "lesser," kind of deity, which is lexically differentiated and in formal cosmology accorded a lower rank than *abosom*. Akuropon people say that *asuman* (sing. *suman*) are "small" deities—they can be held in one's hands (in contrast to *abosom*). *Asuman* are "fetishes" in the proper sense of the word, manmade objects in which mystical power resides. They may be bought, sold, or reproduced by their owners. In practice, *asuman* range from small nonpersonalized charms and amulets to much more personalized ones with cults resembling *abosom* cults. And in practice, as I have said, an *obosom* perceived to be weak may come to be classified as a *suman,* and conversely an increasingly powerful *suman* may come to be called an *obosom*.

In general, however, *asuman* are lower in the hierarchy of deities than *abosom*. They are the messengers or spokesmen (*akyeame*) of the *abosom,* sent to perform their errands, and they are the executioners (*abrafo*) sent to punish a man if he offends a deity.

> So for day-to-day activities we approach the *asuman,* rather than *abosom.* Except on very special occasions when *abosom* possess someone to tell us something, curses, help, disputes are done by *asuman.* All day-to-day problems are solved by *asuman.* Something on a national scale goes to the gods, to *abosom.*
>
> God is too far above us to approach. Therefore we speak to him through our *abosom,* who represent God for us here. And the *abosom* direct us what to do. The *abosom* tell us, Don't steal, don't kill, don't commit adultery . . . all our rules. And the *abosom* have messengers who are *asuman* and who they send to perform their errands.

Just as *asuman* are not equal in rank to *abosom,* so the officials who care for the deities reflect the same hierarchy. All the prayers and rites for *abosom* are performed by *osofo,* the priests who are hereditary "owners" of the deities; *asuman* generally do not have *osofo.* Both *asuman* and *abosom* usually have *akomfo* (sing. *okomfo*), mediums, or people who become possessed. It is said that the *akomfo* do not choose to be possessed, but that the *obosom* or *suman* catches and then "marries" them.

> Not everyone can be possessed . . . but any deity that is about can possess you if it is in your nature. One "fetish" can possess you, then another and then another, in succession. Each has its own language and action, characteristics and behavior. Adade, Akonide [*suman*] and also ancestors possess *okomfo.* Also rivers, mountains, springs [*abosom*] can possess you, and each one has a different language and action. Some have specific duties, such as maternity cases, sores, fractures, fevers, foretelling the future. But always and only through being possessed. A linguist is not always necessary; as soon as they are possessed, they will say, "I am so-and-so, this is why I came. Do such-and-such a thing." Then he [the deity] will go away, and the person comes back.
>
> Every deity and *suman* has an *okomfo* because it is through the *okomfo* that they speak to us. They are deities and we are mortal. Special people are possessed.

The *akomfo* formerly had a great deal of power as the spokesmen of the gods. Today people are not as inclined to serve the deities as before, and many deities have no *okomfo.*

Asuman may be protective or destructive. Their powers are said to be more specific than those of *abosom.* Protective ones may help a person to absorb bullets, give effective blows, disappear, or prevent the effects of evil and witches; destructive ones may cause illness or even death.

> Protective amulets—copper rings, bracelets of twisted different metals, and so on—are specific according to the *suman* which protects you from particular things. You go to someone with a *suman* who knows. You are told to bring certain leaves and are washed with the herbs for several days and you drink or eat certain things and then he anoints the ring and gives it to you. This protects you from poisoned drinks, for example, so if you are given a glass in which someone has put poison, then the glass will break in your hand.

Kunkuma is a general term for those *asuman* that destroy the effects of evil. *Kum* means to kill. In the old days, *kunkuma* (said to be made of various leaves) were placed at the entrances to the palace and to private houses and kept in pots of water, generally with an egg. Visitors sprinkled themselves with the water before entering, and if they were witches or had evil intentions the *suman* would protect the occupants from harmful effects. Other *suman* were destructive.[19]

> One *suman* was called Asanan. When a pregnant woman wished someone to help her lift water at the Adami River, the person assisting might have had Asanan on her fingers. When her fingers touched the water, the *suman* got in and when the pregnant woman drank, the baby in her stomach was affected and became sick and the mother too might die. There was a lot of this. Sometimes people put black powder across the path; if you stepped on it, your leg would swell, or you might fall. Some bad people had *asuman;* these people were called *adutofo* [sing. *odutofo*]. The poison was not always in the body. Sometimes it went through the air or by other means.

In the old days there were many *asuman*. They were brought with *abosom* from elsewhere in Ghana because the chiefs thought such supernatural powers would help them "to live peacefully and to win wars." Today, there are no longer many *asuman* in Akuropon, although they have by no means entirely disappeared. The growing influence of Christianity has reduced participation in *abosom* and *asuman* cults, which have faded with the deaths of older practitioners. There has also been active opposition for some time by Christian-educated kings, especially toward those *asuman* used for destructive purposes. Many people still wear protective amulets. Some also still swear oaths calling on the deities, but this now requires previous permission from the town chief, and promiscuous use of these oaths has been legally restricted.

The king and chiefs are thought to be particularly vulnerable to certain kinds of dangers and thus tend carefully to protect themselves with a myriad of *asuman*. They cannot be Christians because of their office. The main *suman* which protects the king of Akuapem is called Oboaman, and can only be summarily described here. A composite object containing, among other things, male eagle feathers, gold-covered ram horns, and leopard skin over the bones of a human skull are all shaped into the form of a headdress[20] that is worn by the king's "soul child" (*okra*).[21] This is the male aspect of Oboaman. The female aspect of the same *suman* consists of a bundle that hangs from the top of the king's double umbrella or is placed in the central support (neck) of the stool upon which he sits. Both guard the king. Although Oboaman is almost always said to be a *suman*, the same people may also refer to it as the king's *obosom* because it is said to protect the state.

The persistent and pervasive ambiguity in actual use of these lexically discrete categories of deities reappears again in the above example. A person may refer almost simultaneously to a single entity using the two different terms that generally have implications of rank. To explicate further both the interplay between category and practice, I turn now to a more detailed examination of the nature of deities (*abosom* and *asuman*), to their relationship to medicine (*aduru*), and to the actual sources of their power in trees and leaves—elements of the wilderness.

Those Who Hear the Language of the Leaves

The Twi language is filled with allusions to trees and leaves. Some of these are simple analogies to obvious external properties of particular plants; for example one may say of a person's sour expression: "his face is like *kankuwa*" (*Afraegle paniculata*, a sour-tasting herb used to cure arthritis); or one may say that a king or a chief is like *nsasono* (*Tragia volubilis*), a species of nettle which irritates the skin, implying that if the king touches you, you will be "hot." Dozens of proverbs similarly relate obvious external properties of plants or trees to human relationships.

As in Asante, shady trees are associated with the concept of kingship and with the spiritual "coolness" or peace of the town. The tree, as McLeod says (1981), is "part of the town's moral state" (pp. 29–30). "A large tree has fallen" is a common euphemism for the death of a king. Each Akuapem town has, or formerly had, a large shady tree in its central plaza; this is usually a *Ficus leprieuri*. The shady tree in Akuropon is called the Mpeni, and is considered to be an *obosom*. Generically, these trees are known as *amangyedua* (lit. "tree that receives states" or "tree that gives shade for the people," who meet under it for "durbars,"[22] as the great public assemblies are called). In Akuapem, as in Asante, the shade of a king's state umbrella is likened to the shade these trees give to the people.

Leaves themselves are used in specific ritual contexts. In former days, cutting a fresh leaf from the Mpeni shade tree was an indirect way to curse the king. Even today, at funerals of important chiefs, townspeople adorn themselves with elements of the wilderness: they wear leaves intertwined around their heads and necks and even beehives as hats as a sign of disorder, the confusion of the social and natural spheres, and the powers associated with the latter.

The esoteric meaning of some leaves is known and recognizable immediately to virtually all in Akuropon. Thus, fibers from the young leaves of a raffia palm, called *adobe* (*Raphia vinifera,* a wild tree that grows near rivers where there are thought to be *abosom*), are used for skirts or girdles worn by the *okomfo;* the wine from this palm is used for drinking, but never for libation. The cultivated palm called *abe* (*Elaeis guineensis*), in contrast, provides palm wine for both drinking and libations, and palm oil; and the young leaves from this palm (*mmerenkensono*) formerly were put around the neck of a person to be sacrificed for the ancestral stools. Not all leaves are known to the general populace, however; some are used only by ritual specialists and others only by herbalists.

Medicines. *Aduru* (pl. *nnuru*) refers both to Western medicines and to herbal remedies. No offerings are made to *aduru,* nor are any taboos attached to their use. Those with the knowledge of herbs and roots used for curing are called *adunsinfo* (sing. *odunsinni*). In former times, *adunsinfo, akomfo* and *abosomfo* were often the same people. For this reason, the missionaries did not want the Christians to go to African doctors to consult about herbal remedies—they feared that the black powders rubbed into cuts were "fetishes." These prohibitions seem to have had little lasting impact on most people.

The relationship between *abosom* and *nnuru* is in practice rather ambiguous, as the following example illustrates. The Aberewa antiwitchcraft cult was prominent in Asante in 1906 (see McLeod 1975) and was very popular in Akuropon between 1912 and 1915, coming from Wa in the north through Obo in Kwawu. The cult is now well-remembered, but no longer present in Akuapem, having been superseded in recent years by the cult of Tigare (also of northern origin). The *obosom* variously was called Aberewa (lit. Old Woman) or Nanuro in its female aspect, and

Nsakra in its male aspect. Nsakra, as the husband, was said to be strong, like a executioner or soldier. The female one was placed on the ground; the male one hung in a bag or pouch on the wall of the compound. As a physical object, it was called medicine (*aduru*).

> It is medicine which one drinks and which cures and reveals witches: this is Nanuro.
>
> But Nanuro is also an *obosom*. It does the work of *abosom* as well as *nnuru*. The whole thing is called *aduru,* although it does the work of *obosom,* it cures and exposes. . . . The medicine has killed him—but we think of the *obosom*.

This seems to imply that the major difference between medicine (*aduru*) and *obosom* is that the latter is personalized.

The close and ambiguous relationship between these entities may also be seen in what is said of a person who has taken *aduru: waben* ("he is hardened or cooked"); the same is said of a person who has been protected by *asuman*.

> Just as yam on fire is well cooked, so too you can say a man is cooked: *waben*. He is burnt in fire, so he is so powerful nothing can harm him. The man is cooked, *waben,* protected from bullets, for example. It is said of him, *Wadi aduru:* he has taken [lit. eaten] *aduru* [medicine]. But he is not necessarily an *okomfo;* and the man who prepares it is not an *okomfo*. He may have medicine to hear the speech of the *suman*. The man who makes it is one who has medicine [*owo aduru*]: he has *suman; waben* [he is cooked].

I asked, therefore, whether one could say that all *suman* were also *aduru,* and was told:

> It depends on the work it does. If it protects from evil, gives power to fight or disappear, then you can call it *aduru*. And the *suman* may be there. But it is the leaves of the *suman* that when taken by you will do that work. . . . The *suman* tells you "take this leaf, put it on fire, stir, burn it black, cut three marks, and so on. Put in gin, drink it, and then nothing will happen to [harm] you." Therefore we call it medicine [*aduru*].

This seeming vagueness and confusion of the words *aduru* and *suman* or *obosom* arise because these are questions which Akuropon people do not need to ask. Here again is a classification of three discrete words— medicine (*aduru*) and deities (both *obosom* and *suman*); yet in practice, in actual use, this clear classification seems to dissolve. To understand the situation better, one needs to know more about how leaves are used in ritual contexts and how a *suman* is made and of what it is composed.

To understand more about trees and leaves, knowledge of their external superficial characteristics is not sufficient. One must also examine the concept of *sunsum,* the essence or "activating principle" of an object or being (Hagan 1964:24; Minkus 1980:182). It is the "spiritual" as opposed to the "material" aspect of an object or being. Akuropon people say, for example, that when an offering of meat or mashed yam is given to the ancestors or to an *obosom,* the supernatural being eats the *sunsum* of the meat, while what is visible is left for the ritual specialists to eat; the latter thereby gain power from the spirits.

Every being and object has *sunsum* specific to its type, and some *sunsum* are stronger than others. As Minkus stated (1980:183), God, *abosom, asuman* and the ancestors "are" *sunsum* (*ye sunsum*)—their whole being consists of *sunsum*—whereas men, animals, plants, rocks, streams and other objects "have" *sunsum* (*wo sunsum*) as their essential component. I have found that although usually one cannot say that a particular herb is for a specific remedy, it is clear that every leaf has its own "power" (*tumi*) or *sunsum,* which becomes qualitatively more effective when mingled with or added to the *sunsum* of other leaves. This is consistent with the belief that although a *suman* or *obosom* may be rendered ineffective if brought into contact with that which is taboo or "hateful" to it, it may be purified or renewed by a combination of leaves, each of which in itself has different and minor powers (see Appendix II).

The following description of the construction of a particular *suman* shows how objects that "have" *sunsum* (both leaves and animals) are combined into something more powerful, something which "is" *sunsum.* It also provides a way to appreciate how those who deal professionally with *suman* and *aduru* tend to think about such things—the narrator was an eighty-seven-year-old palace elder who was still consulted for herbal medicines and who formerly owned several *asuman.* The description of the creation of a *suman* relates to the earlier discussion of the process of making an ancestral stool and illustrates the manner in which the two entities (deities and ancestors) form a single system. Finally, in this example the similarities between the sources of power of the deities and of the ancestors and the implications of other similarities between the categories of *abosom* and *asuman* force one once again to confront the problem of the relationship between formal lexical categorization and practice.

The Making of a Suman

Get some feathers of *akoo* [*Psitaccus,* parrot with red feathers at the tail]; some feathers of *obereku* [Senegal coucal with red eyes and a black beak, reported by Christaller (1933 : 17) to be an ancestor and fortuneteller]; the hide of a leopard [considered to be the king of the animal world]; and the hide of one other wild feline animal. Put these together. Bind them with *mmofuma* [*Ficus glumosa,* a tree used to make cord or rope].

Then collect a number of leaves:

onunum [*Ocimum gratissimum,* an aromatic plant with white flowers, a type of basil]

eme [*Ocimum canum,* a type of basil with white flowers]

apeabaa [*Hyptis pectinata,* a plant which grows in water near river banks]

tofabeng [*Amaranthus viridis,* a plant with reddish leaves and flowers and red veins]

nyankomiretire [*Scoparia dulis,* a small plant with white flowers]

abam ha [?]

odum bark [*Chlorophora excelsa* or *C. regia,* a very large tree with white latex and bright red roots]

adesaa roots and leaves [*Chrysophyllum albidum,* a tree with white latex and yellow-red fruit which is sour-sweet in taste]

ofeferaa or *fra* [*Lonchocarpus sericeus,* a small tree with purple flowers]

Get both the roots and leaves of all these and put them together. Get a brass bowl, a small one. Put the bundle of feathers and hide bound together with the leaves and roots in the brass bowl. Put a stone [*opemmo,* pl. *apemmo*] in the brass bowl. [See *apembo* in Appendix I.] And put in an egg, whole (raw, not cooked). Get *krow* [the red pith from the *odwen* tree (*Baphia nitide,* camwood), a very hard tree which is believed to have the power to fight anything or to stop anything] and white clay [*hyirew*].

Do not put the brass bowl on the ground. Collect *nyinya* [*Momordica charantia,* a strongly scented climber with tendrils] into a pad [like a head-carrying pad], and use the fresh middle leaves [*mmerenkensono*] of the palm tree to bind the pad. Then put it on the ground, and put the brass bowl with the "fetish" in it on top.

Break the egg and use it to smear the stone. Then smear the stone with the red pith [*krow*] and the white clay [*hyirew*]; so one part of the stone is white and one part is red.

The main *suman,* the one which is bound [feathers and hide], is put on the stone, and the red pith and white clay is put on this. Then smear the *suman* with another egg. Kill a fowl and put the blood on the *suman*. Then scrape the roots and pound the leaves and mix them together . . . and put the bound bundle [*suman*] on it.

You can put some of the leaf-root mixture into a small pot with water and an egg and the blood from a fowl. That is another *suman* to assist the main *suman*. So you have: (1) The small brass bowl with the medicine, stone, and the bound bundle, which is a powerful *suman*. And you also have: (2) The small *suman* in the black pot into which you put the water. Here you also add *ahum ne aham* [*Microgramma owariensis*] bound together with the heart of *Sasabonsam kyew* (lit. Sasabonsam's or the Giant's hat) [*Platycerium elephantote,* the staghorn fern. These two ferns grow as parasites on the palm tree].

Then whatever you want it to do for you, it will do. It is now a *suman*. The one in the pot alone is a *suman,* a powerful one, and the other one is too. One is male and one is female. The male one is in the brass bowl. You can even put a knife in it. The female one is in the small black pot—it is just leaves and roots. You tell both the same problems, you pour libation on both. Having put them in the pot, some people hear what the leaves say to you. The point at which it begins to speak is when all is completed. You pour libation, and put blood on it [sheep, fowl, or goat, according to the taste of the particular *suman*]; then you ring a small bell and call the deity. And those who hear the language of the leaves can hear what they say. Those who can hear the talk, know it is powerful. If it is not good, there are some who will know that too. If you do not treat it well, it will not do what you want it to do for you. It will not wear out. If you like it, you celebrate it annually and put medicine anew on it. The one who made it before tells you what it likes. If you make it on your own, you decide which animal [to sacrifice]. Goats are capricious, strong, they can even kill. Fowls are powerful.

[I asked, Does it have a name?]

You name it Bonngae [an Ewe name].

One thing was quite explicit in the narrative: the brass pan for the *suman* called Bonngae is male, whereas the clay pot with water is for the *suman*'s female aspect. Since brass pans are generally said to have descended from the heavens, this may be an oblique reference to Onyame, the Supreme God. By analogy, the clay pot of water, which is like a cooking pot, is made from the earth and may indirectly allude to Asase Yaa, the Earth Goddess. Looking at the form of shrine, however, suggests further ambiguities about the categories *abosom* and *asuman*. In the course of this paper, I have described in varying contexts a number of deities and their shrines. These include:

1. *abosom* Wontumi and Osraman, which only reside in brass pan shrines;
2. *obosom* Ntoa, which only resides in a clay pot of water;
3. *obosom* Aberewa has two aspects: male, Nanuru, a leather pouch on the wall, and female, Nsakra, a bag or pot on the ground;
4. Oboaman, variously referred to as a *suman* or *obosom,* which has two aspects: male, a feather headdress, and female, a bundle hung from umbrella and kept in the king's stool;
5. *suman* Bonngae, which has two aspects: male, a brass pan shrine, and female, a water pot shrine.

The brass pan shrines in Akuropon were brought from Asante or Bono-Techiman. Representing or localizing deities in pots of water in Akuropon may have originated with the Guan, indigenous to the Akuapem hills.[23] Regardless of the historical explanation for the different types of shrines, by relating these deities called variously *abosom* and *asuman* to the forms of shrines to which they are associated, we find that once again we need to explain the overlapping system of classification. Despite clear linguistic differences between *abosom* and *asuman,* and despite assertions of their hierarchical ranking, they are approached for nearly identical reasons, in much the same manner, and their shrines are constructed in virtually identical fashions. It is this which permits people to juggle their rank order.

In constructing a Black Stool, the shrine for the ancestors, the main ingredients traditionally came from human beings. In contrast, in making a *suman,* the main ingredients come from nature—from wild animals (feathers and hide) and from wild plants (leaves and roots). The stone which is used (*apembo*) is somewhat problematic. Since such rocks are said to prevent evil from passing and are the place for pouring libation as well as for sacrifice, it is likely the *apembo* symbolizes a mediatory position between God and man, just as the egg, with which it is juxtaposed in the narrative, is transitional between life and nonlife. Eggs, it should be noted, are often smashed to the ground or eaten raw by *okomfo* when they are possessed, which is another period of transition or liminality. Eggs, generally, are considered peaceful and delicate, as they are boneless. They are also complete in the sense that they are both white and "red" (the yellow of the yolk). The colors red and white are used repeatedly in Akuropon rituals and everyday life. They are the only "real" colors other than black (see Bartle 1983). In some contexts, such as clothing, white stands for joy, victory, and purity; whereas red stands for danger and seriousness, as in the cloth worn for important funerals. Yam is considered to be the only "real" food, and the main offering to both ancestors and deities is mashed yam (*oto*), half of which is always left white, and the other half of which is mixed with palm oil and is therefore "red." Akuropon elders offer no explanation for this. However, red pith (from inside a tree) is analogous to blood, and white clay may refer to semen, thus giving the two elements deemed necessary for conception: blood of the mother and semen of the father. At the same time, the same two elements refer to the blood of the matrilineage (*abusua*) and the spirit of the group of patrifiliation (*agyabosom*). The narrative thus gives three complementary pairs of materials:

feathers and hides	leaves and roots	animal and plant kingdoms
stone	eggs	transition and mediation
red pith	white clay	human society

Conclusion

I have described the indigenous concept of power and its sources and how these dangerous, fearful, and wonderful notions are used in the town of Akuropon. In so doing, I have considered some aspects of the ambiguity of this power. I hope to have shown that decoding the symbolism of the elements that compose the shrines of ancestors and different types of deities in Akuropon, although interesting in itself and illustrative of other known features of Akuropon culture, does not explain adequately the inconsistent and contradictory ways in which these entities are invoked in practice. When the *abosom* are examined closely, one sees a deity house or temple surrounded by ancestral imagery. Indeed, it would appear that Akuropon people only think about their deities by means of the imagery of the ancestors and of the kingship. Thus, deities are referred to as royal messengers, linguists or soldiers; their shrines rest on stools; and they are said to possess swords and even stools, which themselves are anointed in much the same manner as are the ancestral Black Stools. When, similarly, the ancestors are examined carefully, one sees virtually identical means of worship as for the deities, down to the use of the same expression for anointing them: *due obosom*. In an admittedly extreme case, different people referred to the same supernatural entity variously as ancestor or deity. In another example the same deity was referred to by the same people alternately as *obosom* or *suman;* another example illustrated differing uses of the terms *aduru, obosom* or *suman* for the same entity. In order better to grasp the origin of power of these entities, one may look at how shrines are fashioned. There too one sees an overlapping of types of shrines for supernatural beings for which there are ranked lexical differences. This vagueness of categorization cannot be explained away by saying that the Akan people of Akuropon-Akuapem simply do not think very tidily or logically. On the contrary, if one examines the relationship of cosmology to ritual practice, it becomes apparent that the ambiguity is a positive feature, because it allows the concepts of "ancestor" and "deity" to be differently conceived in different contexts and at the same time to be negotiated in an ever-changing system of power.

Appendix I

According to Christaller (1933), the word *obosom* "is supposed to come from *obo* and *som*" (p. 43) to serve or worship stones. While it is indisputable that this is what the word literally means, in a general sense I could never confirm it, and I suspect that part of my difficulty arose from the fact that educated (*i.e.*, Christian) Akuapem people feel that this interpretation has derogatory overtones of animism. Certainly some but not all rocks are considered to be sacred. Furthermore, sacrifices and libations are poured on certain rocks which are called *apembo* or *apemmo;* it is said that an evil person cannot then pass and that any evil thought will stop there. Christaller (1933:385) noted that *apembo* is a heavy kind of stone containing iron ore or consisting of gravel or pebbles conglomerated or cemented together.[24] But according to local etymology, the word means a stone which you have to knock yourself against and even then cannot push (*apem bo—oko pem abo*). So, it is said, if any enemy attempts to cross your line, he cannot. A few Akuropon people wear a small reddish pebble (containing iron ore) around their necks or carry one in their pockets for protection from evil; one sees this most often at funerals. The word *abosen,* according to Christaller (1933), refers to the "hanging up of stones to avert a threatened evil" (p. 42). B. S. Akuffo (1950:85), in a passage which seems to refer to Akuropon, describes how when an oath is sworn a woman is given a pebble, which she throws to the ground upon its completion.

An *obosom* owned by the lineage of the chief known as the Benkum Kyeame house in Akuropon is of interest etymologically, and also because it illustrates once again the problematic relationship between category and practice: this is a god which is called an ancestor. As a material entity, this *obosom* consists of a smooth, slightly mottled greyish-white stone approximately five inches in diameter. It is referred to as *oboba kurukuruwa*. The term *oboba kurukuruwa* literally means a small round stone (*obo,* stone; *-ba,* small); but it was exceedingly difficult to discover more about its meaning. In Akuropon puberty rites and marriage rites, one always wishes the girl to have thirty children (*i.e.*, many) and one *oboba kurukuruwa*. One also finds the word used in appelations cited for twins. The stone used to tighten the top of the *atumpan* drums (the drums which "speak") is also called *oboba kurukuruwa*. Its principal meaning, however, is a pestle or grinding stone. There is, finally, a sacred stream near Obosomase (lit. "under the rock"), a Guan town south of Akuropon, called Osekyereso in Guan, where there are many round, polished stones, smooth, I was told, "like those used for grinding." Such stones are called *kokwabo* in Guan. It is possible that this is the origin of the word *oboba kurukuruwa:* two words meaning small stone in Twi and Guan respectively. (The process of incorporating and corrupting Guan words into Twi is not without precedent.)

The Benkum Kyeame's deity is of particular relevance because although it is regarded as an *obosom,* it is named Osamanpa, which means "Good Ancestor":

> There was a woman called Aberewa Kosi who gave birth to our ancestors. She had plenty of children [literally "thirty children"], and one *oboba kurukuruwa* is kept near our stool now. It is called Osamanpa [Good Ancestor]. If you have no children and pour libation on it [the stone], then you will get a child.

Once a year, after the annual purification ceremony in which the ancestors—that is, the Black Stools—are fed, the Benkum Kyeame offers food to Osamanpa. Those who wish can then ask Osamanpa for anything they need. If they want children, they eat the mashed yam (*oto*) or part of the fowl that was cooked and placed before Osamanpa, and by eating the food placed before the *obosom,* they receive some of the power or strength of the *obosom;* the *obosom* eats the "spirit" (*sunsum*) of the meat.

Appendix II

The following description of a defiled shrine and its purification shows explicitly how leaves, which in themselves have only a minor and specific power, when conjoined as ingredients become something which has greater power than the sum of its parts alone.

If a *suman* or *obosom* is exposed to that which is taboo to it, it may be rendered ineffective and purification or renewal will be necessary. Such was the case one day in 1977, when some goats entered the shrine of *obosom* Ntoa. The shrine was defiled because the goat is taboo to Ntoa. Some elders gathered and the woman who owned the goats was fined and told to offer sheep, palm wine, and certain other things so that libation could be poured to Ntoa and the shrine purified. The priest for *obosom* Ntoa then cleansed the shrine—he put white clay (*hyirew*) in a pot with water, a little blood (from the sheep), and certain leaves, then he sprinkled the water around the compound. The leaves that he used included the following:

> *Opete nton,* also called *ntomme* (*Dracaena manii,* a plant with long ensiform leaves used for plaiting mats; a kind of palm). Since it lives long and does not die easily, it is a plant often used for marking borders. It is sometimes referred to as the "sister" of *ahum ne aham* (below) and is used for making a head-carrying pad to put other medicines on; for this reason it is called "the carrier of all medicines;"
> *Ahum ne aham* (*Microgramma owariensis,* a fern which grows like a parasite on palm

trees). It is always used with *nno nno ne ha ha* (a creeper with white sap and large leaves), another parasite on palm trees. It is said that the "power" of the one comes into the other and that they are brought to the tree by the wind, *i.e.* by God; and so "fetish" people use them and make them work in the same way as the wind does. Thus, they are used for making black powder which can make people disappear if they are being chased or if someone wants to kill or beat them;
Nyankonnuru (*Tapinanthus species,* a parasite with red flowers and berries). It has no roots in the ground, and therefore it is believed that "it happened from God; Onyankopon fell suddenly onto the tree." It is used for the safe delivery of pregnant women;
Adwere, also called *adwennwere* (*Portulaca oleraceae*), is used frequently in rituals to sprinkle water for purification or otherwise take away uncleanness. It is also used as a medicine to promote suppuration (Christaller 1933:105), and for whitlow. It removes pain and makes the treated area very cool. It is said to have the power to cleanse and drive away evil spirits.

The *sunsum* of these herbs is deemed to be very strong or hard (*den*). Therefore, when all are joined together they make a powerful and effective remedy. In all cases, it should be noted, the leaves are chosen because of their supposed ritual efficacy, which can only be assessed by those with specialized knowledge of the particular *obosom* concerned.

Notes

1. All texts, unless otherwise attributed, were given to me verbatim by Akuropon informants, mostly elders of acknowledged reputation. The names have been withheld because some of the information was given on the condition that the informants' identities would not be made public. The phrase "things which are fearful and wonderful" is from Psalms 139; the speaker was a man of long Christian education and such biblical references are found in much of Akuropon everyday speech.

2. I discuss only the single town of Akuropon and not the socially and culturally diverse Akan people as a whole. A considerable amount of published material exists on Akan beliefs and rituals concerning deities and ancestors (especially among the Asante) from Bosman's early, albeit derisive, description of a shrine in 1705, through Rattray's extraordinarily extensive work in the 1920s, to more recent analytical work by Fortes, McLeod and others. That clarification is still needed in defining and translating these concepts points to the difficulties inherent in the task, difficulties of which Rattray himself was well aware.

I did fieldwork in Akuropon from 1976 to 1978. I wish to thank the School of Oriental and African Studies of the University of London for a postgraduate fellowship which made the research possible, the University of Cape Coast for providing sponsorship, and the National Endowment for the Humanities for grant #FA-24250(1984) during which time this paper was written. I wish to thank *nana* Addo Dankwa III, *Okuapehene, Nana* Boafo Ansah II, *Kurontihene,* my assistant Mr. B. E. Ofori, and those elders and friends who so generously helped me. Mr. D. K. Abbiw of the Legon Herbarium, University of Ghana, kindly identified the plants. I also thank John Beattie, T. O. Beidelman, Ivan Karp, and John Middleton for invaluable criticisms.

3. The term "fetish" was introduced by Christian missionaries and is used loosely by Ghanaians speaking English to refer to either of the indigenous categories of deities: *suman* or *abosom*. (See Note 12.)

4. Twi words in this chapter have been Anglicized without the use of diacritical marks.

5. Libations in Akuapem ritual are very similar to those in (non-Akan) Ga ritual. See Marion Kilson (1969, 1970) for an analysis of the latter. She suggested (1970) that "libation in Ga ritual is a form of sacrifice . . . basically to renew the moral contractual relations between gods and men" (p. 60).

6. Rattray (1923), working among the Asante, saw the value of such inquiry. He offered a general account of the making and consecration of a shrine for one of the Tano gods (*obosom*) in Asante: "When I first had time seriously to study Ashanti religious beliefs, it occurred to me that if one could know just what these miscalled fetishes . . . contained, and how they were made, and the rites in connection with the making, we might be approaching the solution of a very difficult and very little understood problem" (p. 146).

7. In many Akan states, and formerly in Akuapem, there were trees (*Onyame dua*) before many houses with pots of offerings for Onyame. A rarely performed ritual executed in times of crisis by the women of the town at night purports, it seems, to make contact with Asase Yaa.

8. See Gilbert (1987) for a more detailed description of ancestors and the Black Stools in Akuropon.

9. There are presently only six stools, but they are spoken of as if there were seven, since the latter is a symbolically propitious number. In other Akan kingdoms, apparently, Black Stools are made for every "good" king or chief and thus there may be many. Nowhere, however, is a stool blackened for a destooled king, nor for one who dies a bad death by sudden accident or unusual disease—such a king should not be commemorated.

10. *Adae* is a periodic ritual held every forty-two days which combines secular functions with honoring and feeding the ancestors. Odwira is the great annual purification rite of the kingship (Gilbert 1987).

11. In other Akan states, such as Kwawu, goats are used as substitutes for men in sacrifices, though sheep are used for ordinary offerings (Philip Bartle, personal communication, 1976). In Akuropon, goats are considered to be "trickish" and unreliable and thus would pollute the ancestral stools; they are sometimes used as sacrificial animals for certain *asuman* or *abosom* because of their reputed strength.

12. *Agyabosom* (lit. father's deity) is the group of patrifiliation; it is the same as *ntoro* in Asante and Kwawu, and as *nton* in Techniman-Bono.

13. The word *obosom* has usually been translated as "fetish," but this is not accurate. Rattray (1923) was concerned about the translation of these terms. "There is one term the indiscriminate use of which, I believe, has done infinite harm, the word 'fetish.' This term will confront and befog the inquirer who is ignorant of the vernacular, at every turn. It will appear as exactly to fit some aspects of Ashanti [variously spelled Asante] religious beliefs, as to be totally in-

applicable to others to which, however, it will be as commonly applied. . . . Broadly speaking, all those objects which we ourselves would loosely call charms, amulets, talismans, mascots, or fetishes, he [the Asante] calls *suman,* and I think the word 'fetish' should be rigidly confined to designate such only.

"His other category of non-human spirits, which he himself calls *abosom,* which he clearly distinguishes from the *suman* we should never call 'fetishes,' for it is a totally inappropriate and misleading term.

"The only correct word to use for the Ashanti word *abosom* is 'god,' or, when speaking of the brass pan itself, which is, the potential resting place of this non-human spirit, 'a shrine'. . ." (See Appendix I for the etymology of the word *obosom* and an example illustrating further classificatory ambiguities of the supernatural entities in Akuropon.)

14. Rattray (1923) noted that "waters in Ashanti . . . are all looked upon as containing the power or spirit of the divine Creator, and thus as being a great life-giving force" (pp. 145–46).

15. McLeod (1981) said that in Asante, temples for *abosom* "were often situated at the edges of villages, between human society and the wild, or isolated on river banks" (p. 62). It may be that this was so in Akuropon as well, and that in the past the larger shrines were located primarily in the villages in the plains outside the town proper, as they are today, though I have no evidence for this. The ancestral Black Stools, in contrast, are kept in the town (except during times of utmost political disorder, when departing families may take them with them into exile).

16. *Cf.* Swithenbank (1969) on Asante "fetish" architecture. The Black Stools in the Akuropon palace stool house are placed on a similar raised platform.

17. See Rattray's account mentioned above of the construction of a Tano River shrine in Asante (1923:146–50). Warren (1976) discussed such Atano shrines and their associated sculpture in Techiman-Bono. There are a number of differences between the shrines and shrine personnel found in Techiman-Bono and those found in Akuapem; most notable, perhaps, is the absence of deities localized in clay pots of water in Techiman-Bono. That both Ntoa and Aberewa are classified as witch-catching deities (*abosommerafoo*) in Techiman-Bono, whereas in Akuropon Aberewa was formerly a witch-catching deity, but Ntoa is presently an *obosom* localized in a pot of water and not associated with witch-catching at all, points to the difficulties in making comparisons between Akan kingdoms, especially since Ntoa was originally brought to Akuropon from the Techiman-Bono region.

18. *Abaduaba* literally means child-tree-child, but is loosely translated as woodcarving. This is one of several terms used to refer to the terracotta heads in Akuropon. The fact that they are made of terracotta but referred to as wood suggests that the medium does not matter here. Terracotta heads such as these have long been reported from differing parts of Ghana and the southeastern Ivory Coast. Most of the literature suggests that they have a common function throughout the Akar area—that they are funerary. The Akuropon material forces one to question these assumptions (Gilbert n.d.).

19. According to Christaller (1933) there was a type of *suman* known as *kabere,* which consisted "of a stick driven into the ground and wound round with string,

intended to keep off evil spirits from entering the towns and houses and to avert their influence from the inhabitants" (p. 219). I was told that such a *suman* could also be used for destructive purposes:

> Get short sticks with cowries attached to the sticks. Pour the blood of a fowl on it. Then say, "I'll kill so-and-so." Take the string and bind it around the stick seven times, saying so-and-so must die, then bury it in the ground and put a stone on it. In seven days, he will die.

20. Akuropon people think of the animal kingdom as parallel to the human one. Thus eagles are considered to be the king of the sky, and leopards the king of the forest. The ram is the domestic animal *par excellence* and is used in certain sacrifices to represent the king. While such feather headdresses are seen today in most other Akan states, Akuropon elders say theirs was captured from the Asante at the battle of Akantamansu in 1826; the skull is alleged to be that of an Asante king taken in that war.

21. The king's "soul child" (*okra*) is born on the same day of the week as the king was and symbolically shares the king's destiny.

22. "Durbar" is a term borrowed from India by British administrators for a large public assembly or meeting. The Twi equivalent is *egua*.

23. It should be noted, however, that the *kpele* gods of the neighbouring Ga in coastal Accra (who are not Akan, but are influenced by them in a number of ways) also have shrines which consist of a pot of water (see Kilson 1969:176).

24. In Benin, among the Fon, cults for Sagbata, the Earth deity, are identifiable by a number of small laterite stones or a slab of rock with a stippled surface that is half buried at the shrine entrance, always with a cactus growing near it (see Herskovits 1938, vol. 2:144,299). In Akuropon one always finds a certain cactus called *afare* (*egoro* in Akyem; *Kalanchoe crenata*) growing near the sacrificial stone (*apembo*). It is said that because *afare* is soft and watery, it has the power to soften things; thus if a case is difficult, *afare* will reduce its power and bring peace. The similarities are striking enough to suggest a wide West African distribution of these cultural traits. I am not suggesting a Ghanaian Sagbata cult in Akuapem; nor do I have direct evidence that the stone is identified with Asase Yaa.

References

Akuffo, B. S.

1950 Tete Akorae. Accra: Bureau of Ghana Languages.

Bartle, Philip F. W.

1983 The Universe Has Three Souls. Journal of Religion in Africa 14(2): 85–114.

Brokensha, David

1966 Social Change at Larteh, Ghana. London: Oxford: Clarendon Press.

Christaller, J. G.
1933 Dictionary of the Asante and Fante Language called Tshi (Twi), 2nd and revised ed. Basel: Basel Evangelical Missionary Society.

Douglas, Mary
1966 Purity and Danger. London: Routledge and Kegan Paul.

Gilbert, Michelle
1987 The Person of the King: Ritual and Power in a Ghanaian State. *In* Rituals of Royalty: Power and Ceremonial in Traditional Societies. David Cannadine and Simon Price, eds. Cambridge: Cambridge University Press.

Gilbert
n.d. "Akan Terra Cotta Heads: Gods or Ancestors." African Arts (forthcoming).

Hagan, George
1964 Some Aspects of Akan Philosophy. M.A. Thesis, Institute of African Studies, University of Ghana, Legon.

Herskovits, Melville J.
1938 Dahomey, an Ancient West African Kingdom. New York: J. J. Augustin.

Kilson, Marion
1969 Libation in Ga Ritual. Journal of Religion in Africa 2:161–78.

1970 Taxonomy and Form in Ga Ritual. Journal of Religion in Africa 3: 45–66.

Kyerematen, A.
1969 The Royal Stools of Ashanti. Africa 39(1): 1–9.

McLeod, M. D.
1975 On the Spread of Anti-witchcraft Cults in Modern Asante. *In* Changing Social Structure in Modern Ghana. J. Goody ed. London: International African Institute.

1981 The Asante. London: British Museum Publications.

Middleton, John
1960 Lugbara Religion: Ritual and Authority among an East African People. London: Oxford University Press for the International African Institute (1987, Smithsonian Institution Press).

Minkus, Helaine
1980 The Concept of Spirit in Akwapim Akan Philosophy. Africa 50(2): 182–92.

Rattray, R. S.
1923 Ashanti. Oxford: Clarendon Press.

Sarpong, Peter
1971 The Sacred Stools of the Akan. Accra-Tema: Ghana Publishing Corporation.

Swithenbank, M.
1969 Ashanti Fetish Houses. Accra: Ghana Universities Press.

Warren, D.
1976 Bono Shrine Art. African Arts 9(2): 28–34.

Ivan Karp

Power and Capacity in Rituals of Possession

Spirit possession must surely be one of the most written-about subjects in the subdiscipline known as "anthropology of religion." A single researcher would have difficulty in reviewing the literature on spirit possession in African societies alone.

This literature has been subjected to a number of interpretations and exhibits diverse perspectives. Lewis (1971) still has provided the most extensive summary. He considered possession to be a strategy used by the powerless to achieve goals when they lack access to legitimately available means and resources. Lewis' interpretation echoed Robert Merton's (1956) functionalist argument that actors pursue illegitimate means when they are otherwise blocked from achieving socially ascribed goals. The parallel is probably not intended but is instructive nonetheless.

Functionalist arguments animate the literature on spirit possession, even as scholars regularly attack functionalism as anthropological sin. I have no particular animus towards functionalist explanations as long as they account for the criteria by which agents produce their actions. Of course this is not easy in discussing phenomena such as spirit possession in Africa, in which the knowing subject is dispossessed by an other. Possession is by definition interpretatively opaque, but people do use culturally available ideas about possession, even when they cannot provide reports based on personal experience.

When explanations move immediately from cause to consequence without considering the intervening variables of culture, history, and society, problems arise. Even Wilson (1967), in his important critique of Lewis, accepted that one can explain the rate of possession without examining local concepts of person and action. Wilson replaced Lewis' idea that possession is the product of competition over household resources between husband and wife by positing competition between co-wives as the condition that explains possession. Neither scholar examined what possession means or how it fits with different historical conditions.

Those studies that do attempt to examine possession and meaning have their own flaws. They tend to reduce possession to individual needs, just as they deny that possession is one of the tactics of social life (Crapanzano and Garrison 1977). The difficulty is not that they lack a theory of meaning; they do see possession as a mechanism for responding to problems of meaning experienced by the actors. The meanings they unpack, however, are related to psychological and experiential dilemmas that are a result only of the social situation of the people involved. Thus, meaning is not as transparent and universal in these psychologically oriented studies as it is for those who interpret spirit possession as manifesting easily understood strategies. But meaning is still reduced to the relationships of individuals and situations. The meaning of possession is not related to world view or ontological concerns, such as how persons are defined and judged.

The most interesting set of studies remains Crapanzano and Garrison's edited volume, but their failure to examine possession in terms of the meaning it has for the agents has consequences. The first is that the authors do not seek to understand how the actors' definition of the structures of their natural and social world makes rituals of possession appear to them as the most effective course of action by which suffering can be alleviated. The question they do not ask is "How do local concepts of being lead to possession as a rational choice of action?" The problem here is also one of rationality. Possession can be shown to be a rational choice for action, but one must be careful to examine local rationalities. It is too easy to assume that the market-oriented criteria of western rationality are universal.

None of these studies acknowledges that possession phenomena have a history and may be responses to changing social and historical circumstances. Universal explanations of possession cannot possibly work across time and space. The studies of Fry (1976) and Lan (1986) are the results of a more historical perspective, in which possession phenomena are tied to changing political conditions. I have little doubt after reading Fry and Lan that possession can be related to resistance to the imposition of alien rule and a means of political assertion under conditions of domination.

I do not want to dismiss functionalism and its aftermath out of hand. All of these studies uncover an element that is critical for interpreting possession. They relate possession to considerations of power, whether this be domestic conflict or resistance to colonial and imperial domination. For me, the literature is a bit like an iceberg that only hints at the bulk beneath the sea. We know that possession is connected to ideas and relations of power, but we are unable to see sufficiently beneath the surface. How is possession, a form of action, related to local concepts of action and personhood, and what do these have to do with power? Lewis (1971) provided a hint. In those cults of possession that he classified as "peripheral," the act of becoming possessed can be directed against the powerful. What Fry and Lan showed in their Central African material was that the image of the powerful is not restricted just to such local agents as husbands and slave masters, but also to the suddenly visible representatives of imperialism and the world capitalist system.

Still, one need not assume that possession always takes on such a serious demeanor. Lambek's (1981) account of *tromba* spirits in the Comoros is a remarkable account of spirits as children and possession as play. Possession may still be a form of resistance, but the social organization is so thinly described in this study that it is difficult to discern precisely what is being resisted. I was left wondering why a society with such an egalitarian marriage system, with such small differences in social participation between men and women, has such a high rate of possession for women. Lambek's implicit explanation—that possession is fun—seems to run counter to his few descriptions of marital conflict, but it is attractive nonetheless.

This cursory summary indicates that I find most of the accounts of spirit possession in Africa that I have read plausible; some of them are even convincing for the specific formations that they describe. Possession can be resistance, a form of female assertion against males or competition with co-wives, play, or even relative deprivation. But these are all accounts of how possession can serve the interests and needs of the actors at a specific time and place. They are not what most accounts of possession claim to be: universal explanations.[1]

An element shared by almost all of this extensive literature is that the explanations of spirit possession in Africa implicitly invoke power as part of their explanatory account. Few of these studies, however, seek to examine power as it is understood by the society in which possession occurs. An honorable exception is an early essay by Grace Harris (1957) about possession among the Taita of Kenya, where female possession is shown to be part of a continuing debate between men and women over the controls that can be exercised over women's bodies. Harris' fundamental insight is that the idiom in which women articulate their conflict with men is an embodied one, that spirit possession is not just any means of conflict, but a means that has a specific bodily form. It is not just that Taita men and women compete. They compete for the right to women's bodies and labor.

In my account of spirit possession among the Iteso of Kenya I want to follow up on Harris' perception and explore how Iteso notions of power are part and parcel of beliefs about the attitudes toward possession, and then to explore the consequences of this approach for understanding power relations in general.[2]

Possession phenomena are fascinating both to the distanced scholar and the engaged native actor. Exhibited in possession are situated and condensed forms of primordial aspects of the human condition, such as the opacity of other minds to direct observation, the embodiment of self and its relationship to others, and the struggle between self and possessing spirit for control over body and personality; this last item seems to me to be an essential feature of power relationships and a clue to the dramatic appeal of power struggles as a spectator sport.

I take the lead here from a book by the philosopher Bruce Wiltshire, *Role Playing and Identity* (1984), in which the author argued that the manner in which social scientists incorporate aspects of life into their theories tends to impoverish our understanding of life. Wiltshire criticized Erving Goffman's dramaturgical orientation and emphasized the essential mimetic involvement with roles that reproduce our mimetic involvement with others offstage. Goffman (1956) seems not to have known that imitation is a serious business indeed, and he has made uninteresting what is most interesting to us as actors in society.

There have been a number of attempts to discover parallels between possession phenomena and drama (Firth 1967; Beattie 1969). These studies have been criticized on the grounds that possession is felt to be real by the people involved, whereas drama is feigned (Peel 1969). The most common view of drama is the common-sense one that the dramatic frame constitutes an event that is not "real" in some sense. Although this assumption is true enough for the modern Western definition of drama, it obscures the mimetic involvement of the participants that occurs both in drama and possession ritual and trance. There is a sense in which the experience of drama, possession, and even some categories of contemporary psychiatric nosology are experientially similar. Possession, drama, and multiple personalities, for example, are all experiences that raise epistemological dilemmas for actor and observer alike. In all three types of experience one body is host to competing personalities that exhibit different motivations and dispositions. In possession and multiple personalities, the knowing self is dispossessed by an other, and the self's reports of the experience are not possible (Karp 1986). Even some varieties of dramatic theory, such as method acting, blur the boundaries between the actors and the selves assumed by them.

The blurring of boundaries between self and others is not easy or automatic in possession, drama, or multiple personality disorders. One of the patients of the Boston psychiatrist Prince wrote to him that "You have induced a host of conflicting personalities in us and now have left us. What are we to do?" (Kenny 1986). All of these transformations tend to be accompanied by indices of struggle and described by those experiencing them as associated with violence and struggles for control.

All indigenous descriptions of possession with which I am familiar include references to its involuntary dispossession of the knowing self. Trance is accompanied by violent actions, erratic movements, and struggle over control of the host's body, at least in the initial stages of possession. Possession is initially defined in many societies as an illness, a source of discomfort. This is yet another indication of the element of conflict and struggle for control that is so much a part of the possession experience. Among the Iteso and in the other trance settings in which I have participated in East Africa, the afflicted "patients" are always surrounded by helpers who strive to keep them from hurting themselves or the people around them. The most flamboyant experience I had was in the home of the Iteso who had joined Dini Ya Msambwa, a reformist movement with Christian and anticolonial overtones. (Buijtenhuijs 1985). The adept in the cult seemed quite pleased at the alarm her guests experienced. I knew her well enough to sense that here was an instance of putting an anthropological voyeur in his place.

Metaphors of possession (such as the West African example of the spirit "riding" the host as a rider handles a horse) are commonly found in, for example, Bori possession among the Hausa (Besmer 1975). These metaphors may indicate the presence of elements of abrasion as well as struggle in the possession experience. Similar metaphors tend to dominate Iteso descriptions of their experience. The spirit is most often described as "sitting" on the head of the host body. The result is that individuals lose control of their bodies and are unable to guide their movements. They struggle, usually violently, to cast off the spirit that has taken over the cognitive functions. The head is the seat of knowledge, perception, and skill (*acoa*)—cumulative qualities, which tend to grow over time and enable individuals to manage both their affairs and themselves. Older people are said to be more controlled by the cool qualities of the accumulated knowledge situated in the head than the "hot" passions located in the heart. Mental illness and drunkenness are afflictions of the heart and are described as entailing loss of control over cognitive capacities.[3]

The association of possession with the experience of struggle and control is not accidental. It is related both to the phenomenology of the possession experience and to the distribution of power in society. (At least, my Iteso data has led me to this conclusion.) I may seem here to be arguing the case for the very studies I criticized earlier; but in those studies, power was left unexamined and undefined. Customarily, power is defined in anthropology and the social sciences in Weberian terms of access to and control over people and resources. This is clearly useful for understanding cults of possession in two ways. First, as many studies have shown, becoming possessed is a means of exercising controls under conditions of inequality. Taken less seriously, however, is the second type of political statement: members of cults also assert that they struggle for control with their spirits and sometimes that the spirits struggle among themselves. This is often one of the defining features of trance.

Access and control are only the surface features of power relations. The powers people have and how they exercise them are not defined in the same terms in all cultural formations. I am led to wonder how accounts might change if observers were to listen more seriously to the assertions and meanings enacted by their informants. Perhaps they would begin to examine a second dimension of power that involves differences in the capacity to exercise and create power.

Capacity need not refer only to naturally occurring abilities, to natural differences between persons. Capacity is socially defined and created, sought and lost in social process, and often expressed in those local idioms we call cosmologies. Research on kingship in African societies, for example, has shown that kings are mediators—ritual operators who tap the powers of disordered nature in order to create the conditions for the orderly reproduction of society. The nature of kingship cannot be understood as an automatic product of the confusion of categories.[4]

One can play here upon the two senses in which I use the word "power." In many African societies, world view is both cyclical and entropic (Kopytoff 1980), fundamentally concerned with physical and social reproduction. Reproduction is perceived as dependent upon human agency, including that form of practical activity translated as "ritual."

Many ritual forms are purposive; they tap the energy (power) of nature to turn it into a finished cultural product—whether this be a human adult or first fruits. Thus the power potentially available in nature is tapped through the activities of certain individuals who possess the "powers" to mediate between the potential energy of disorder and its dissipation in the material world of creation.

The place of women in cults of spirit possession provides an instructive case study because of its similarities and contrasts to divine kingship. In most African societies women, like kings, are mediators; they mediate among particular social units such as households, lineages, ethnic groups, and so on. These forms divide societies into parts; hence they relate parts to one another within social wholes.[5] They do not mediate, however, for a social whole, as do kings, prophets, and others who stand outside of particularity or social division.[6]

Another significant difference between women as mediators in possession and kings is that possession both involves involuntary affliction and is sought after, while kingship is (at least in ideology) a matter of entitlement. In possession, entrance to a cult is usually made through illness and suffering, but both in the ideology and practice of possession, an element of virtuosity exists that has been underestimated in the ethnographic literature. The Sotho speaking people of Natal, for example, associate possession with poetic inspiration, and the colors in which the possessed often describe possession would provide an interesting area for investigation, given their association with emotional states (Hilda Kuper, personal communication). The display of emotions seems, in any case, to be part of the aura that gives possession its specificity as an experience.

This mixing of voluntary and involuntary elements in cults of possession is one of their most interesting aspects. Lewis (1971) referred to this as the "apotheosis" of possession. Obviously, this is not a form of religiosity that is unusual in the historical and ethnographic record. The combination of the involuntary and the desired are characteristic of many types of ecstasy in the history of cults. There are many reasons for individuals to participate in ecstatic cults, and I am not particularly concerned with problems of individual motivation here. I have already argued that patterns of motivation are historically determined and extremely varied. Not only do they vary from society to society, but also over time and for different categories of persons at the same time. Among the Iteso, for example, possession was virtually an exclusively female experience in the late 1960s, and had always been so, as far as I can tell. In the mid-1970s, a small but significant portion of cult participants were men, and by 1985 possession appeared to be on the decline in the area in which I did most of my research.

Individual motivations are well-covered in the literature. I am primarily concerned here with the structure of experience and the relationships among three aspects of the possession experience: the definition of experience itself, beliefs about the capacity or powers of the actors to have effects on that experience, and the struggle for control between spirit and host. As I have argued above, the notion of power is central to an understanding of the possession experience. This is so because the notion of power is central to the cosmology of societies with cults of possession and to the situated practices in terms of which these societies mediate their experience of the world and the sense they make of that world.

I will turn now to a description of some aspects of rites of possession among the Iteso of Kenya. Possession was a recurrent feature of Iteso life[7]—from the second night of my fieldwork until its conclusion two years later, I was surrounded by the noises of possession ceremonies in my neighborhood. Women predominate in cults of possession as the main actors, although as an entertainment form possession is open to all persons, and children learn about possession and its effects from an early age. At the time of my first fieldwork period, 1969–71, 50 percent of the married women in the neighborhood where I lived had been treated for possession illness and 90 percent claimed to be afflicted. Rites of possession are open-ended; new ritual forms are continually being added and old ones discarded. Each adept has her own cult and particular set of rituals, and competition among cult groups can be keen. Possession itself is a regional phenomenon and incorporates elements from neighboring peoples. As with much of Iteso medicine, exotic cures have more prestige than locally known ones, a trait the Iteso share with my family.

There have been three cults of possession among the Iteso since the turn of the century, and there are two levels of possession spirits. The first level is the local spirits of the dead (*ipara*), who are to be found loitering around homes and at the heads of streams, and who possess out of greed. In what I like to call "deep possession," the possessing spirits are polyethnic in origin and always described as the *ipara* of strangers killed by Iteso in the past. They are the source of the exotic rites and songs that are a prominent part of the activity of the cults. These exotic spirits are named after rivers or spiritual entities found among the neighboring peoples. These include Malaba, a river that forms part of the border separating Kenya from Uganda, Sumba, a Kisoga spirit, Were, the Luo word for high god, and Awori, a spirit of the Abaluyia peoples. These spirits are usually male, but Sumba and Awori are sometimes said to be husband and wife.

Ipara afflict people through illness and misfortune. Possession illness (*emusebe*) is only one type of affliction. Even though cults of possession were very little in evidence in the mid-1980s, *ipara* are still believed to afflict people, and recourse to *akigolo ipara* (medicines and rituals to "block" the *ipara*) is the virtual second level of resort when serious illness strikes.[8] Very little in the way of serious illness or a continuing series of misfortunes is not attributed to *ipara*. They cause suffering not because of moral transgressions, but because of such base desires as greed for meat or revenge. Negative and childish emotional states are characteristic of spirits of the dead. As I mentioned above, Iteso distinguish two fundamental capacities in individuals, which stem from the regions of the heart and the head. The head is the seat of knowledge and the repository of experience. Evidence derived from the senses, but especially visual experience, is used to guide the individual in making decisions. The heart is the seat of the stronger emotions. While the capacities associated with the head change and can grow over the life course, the capacities of the heart remain static or even wane with age, as does physical strength, *agogong*.

The ideal to be sought is a balance in the actions of heart and head, and actions should be motivated by a combination of vitality, wisdom, and physical strength.

Unbalanced emotional dispositions are attributed to the capacity of the heart to overcome the head, as are character flaws such as systematic "bitterness" and unreasonable and disproportionate actions. The stronger negative emotions of anger and hate, as well as uncontrollable desires, are always attributed to a strong heart overcoming a weaker head.

Ipara are figures of primary desire. They are the id to the ego represented by the head. Even when they cause illness because of someone's desire for revenge, they are also said to attack their victims because of their unrestrained appetite and greed for meat and beer. Hence they often cause illness because their victims have failed to perform rituals, such as mortuary ceremonies, at which the *ipara* are fed. They can not be appealed to; they do not respond to reason or to positive sentiments and memory of past ties. They can only be appeased. Revenge is a frequently invoked motive for a spirit attack. Madness, for example, is always taken as a sign that the mad person killed someone whose spirit was taking revenge by destroying the capacity for reason, a faculty of the head. *Ipara* were often described as "*etau kijokis,*" ("all heart"). *Emusebe,* the affliction caused by possessing spirits, demonstrates the character of spirits. It is defined as a disease in which the spirit "sits" on the head of the patient. An entity that is "all heart" overcomes the capacities of the head.

Even the exotic spirits who brought *emusebe* to the Iteso are "all heart." They play an essential role in cults of possession. The local spirits act as guides and hosts to the spirits of external origins and lead them to Iteso homes, all speaking simultaneously, grumbling and quarreling as they proceed. The leaders in cults of possession form tutelary relationships with these exotic spirits and the apotheosis that Lewis describes is always with a non-Iteso figure. The spirits are always described as belonging to persons killed by the Iteso, but the main ones are tutelary spirits derived from the Bantu-speaking peoples surrounding the paranilotic speaking Iteso. The Iteso have no such pantheon of spirits and acknowledge the Bantu spirits only in possession ceremonies. Recently, European spirits have joined the pantheon. I have the impression that among the neighboring Bantu speaking neighbors of the Iteso, the pantheons of cults of possession are not comprised exclusively of exotic spirits.

The Iteso used to believe in a group of generalized nature spirits called *ajokin,* which are sometimes associated with exotic spirits. Church-going Christian Iteso sometimes associated *ajokin* with the devil. Even the line between *ipara* and *ajokin* has become blurred, and many of the attributes of one are now attributed to the other. The exotic nature of tutelary spirits in cults of possession makes up a virtual history of Iteso foreign relations.[9] It may be possible to reconstruct part of the history of interethnic relations by collecting the lists of exotic spirits and the events to which they are related; I have yet to do so.

Members became mediums through greater penetration into deep possession. The adept who leads the cult is "married" to her fellow cult members, who act as her "wives" in rites. Descriptions of the marriage are ambiguous, and it is difficult to tell whether the "wedding" is between the adept and her followers or between the spirit for whom the adept is medium and cult followers; elements of both exist. Customary polyandry is unknown in Africa. For the Iteso, however, an element of spiritual polyandry inverts the polygyny that is the statistically normal experience of women in marriage. While each household generally has at least two wives, women have second and third husbands in spiritual form in the possession experience.

Women move into and out of cults over a long period of time, and I know of one instance of rites of possession that were performed erratically over a thirty-year period. The impression I wish to give is of an open-ended and even labile quality to ritual in cults of possession, of a regional rather than society-specific system, one which incorporates change into its image. Even so, according to my informants, a core of ritual practice in cults has remained constant throughout the history of change and elaboration. This ritual core has three elements that are expository of the ideology and practice of power in possession, and they emerge in the central rite in which a local spirit is drawn into the cult by inducing trance in the afflicted patient. This curing ritual, found in all cult groups, is the central curing rite of possession cults and has remained constant over the years. The following three aspects of this rite are relevant to our account: (1) the paraphernalia associated with fertility and sexuality with which the patient is decorated during the rite; (2) the dramatic performance of productive labor, found also in domestic ritual and rites of twinship; and (3) the assumption of signs of male prerogative at the conclusion of the rite, the ritual inversion of gender identity.

Many of the objects used in the ritual that "block" or exorcise spirits occur in other rites. These paraphernalia are associated with sexuality and fertility and are central to domestic and life-cycle rituals, rituals of twinship, and possession rites. These include creepers such as star grass whose strength and tenacity is associated with successful fertility. *Emaniman,* a vine that twines around small shrubs, is also associated with twins. *Emaniman* unites with its host plant so that one is unable to tell where one begins and the other leaves off. Twins are perceived as having united two separate lineages through an act of procreation.

Other objects and materials with which the patient is festooned are associated with spirits of the dead, *Ipara*. These may include white clay taken from anthills, a favorite dwelling place of the dead. Fertility symbols all use the metaphor of sexual conjunction, with its associations of unity and division, mixing and separation. These ritual objects and their associations are found in rituals whose purpose is either to ensure regularity and orderly social and physical reproduction or (in the case of twinship) to celebrate it in the face of danger. Twins have a special association with rituals of spirit possession. The mother of twins and a woman cured of spirit possession can take shelter under a tree with each other during the rain. Ordinary persons must find shelter elsewhere.

The symbolic association here is not through a direct connection between twins and spirit possession, but between intimate association with *Ipara* on the part of both the parents of twins and women who have been possessed. Twins themselves are defined as spirit-like, and are regarded as having much the same erratic characters and dangerous potentials as spirits. The parents of twins are said to be exhorted with the following statement: "*Ikulepek akwap nes bon ejas k'apedori naka ainakin ijo idwe iyaare*" ("The owners of the earth [spirits of the dead] are the only ones who have the capacity [power] to give you two children"). Embodied in this assertion is the idea that power (*apedor*) emanates from association with the spirits of the dead.

The spirits themselves are preeminently creatures of wilderness (Karp and Karp 1979). Underlying the rituals of possession is an attitude to and conception of the bush as containing disordered potentiality, which is ordinarily kept separate from the home because of the danger of disorder but which must be brought into contact with order to revive a failing world. Iteso women share a ritual status with such mediating figures as the Swazi king (Beidelman 1966a) and the Mugwe of the Meru (Needham 1960; Bernardi 1959). They act in and join ordinarily opposed domains because their everyday activities—their work—bring them into association with nature. Women produce order out of potentiality; the result of sexual contact is procreation; and so on. Ritual is also defined as work for women, and in ritual work, their activities in the division of labor are dramatized. I like to think of agricultural tasks as productive labor and ritual as reproductive labor in the Iteso scheme of things. A primary purpose of rites of possession is to produce the conditions for orderly reproduction, stated dramatically in the climax of the most important rite for curing possession, in which women ritually feed their children.

I do not want to give the impression that the Iteso are unabashed nature lovers. If nature is a necessary source of energy or potentiality, it is a dangerous source as well. Boundedness and avoidance of inversion, except in situations of male violence, are characteristic of Iteso thought and practice. The struggle to control nature is continuous, and experience provides the Iteso with sufficient evidence that they live with failure. There is an element of desperation in Iteso ritual. Ritual is purposive behavior, and display is not a primary motive for their work.

In the great majority of Iteso domestic ritual, work is a focus of symbolic attention. Ritual is designed to ensure that labor is productive. An additional element added to rites of possession is the assumption of male paraphernalia by women. The successful performance of a ritual for the cure of possession culminates in a public display of male symbols by a cured woman. After the cure, the patient goes to the market on the next market day and is entitled to a small gift from anyone she chooses to accost, often five Kenyan cents or, from women, a product that is especially associated with fertility, such as finger millet or sesame seeds. In addition to the other paraphernalia of possession, women display male insignia such as spears, clubs, and the like. The only other situation in Iteso social life in which women exhibit male insignia, to the best of my knowledge, is at the death of a male twin, when the widows of the twin sit on his stool and display a male insignia, the spear. One man who was cured by the possession ritual was told that male regalia was unnecessary for him.

I wish, for purposes of advancing the neo-Freudian interpretation that I find possible here, that there were some act of thrusting and a general element of identification associated with the display of the spear, as among the Nuer (Beidelman 1966b). Unfortunately, there is not. There is no question, however, that maleness is associated with active mastery of natural forces in Iteso thought. In the great ceremonies of the age system, men became aggressive animals of the bush—the bush buck, the ground squirrel, and flying ants that emerge at dusk. Men tend to operate in one of two spheres—either nature or culture—while women mediate between the two. In the division of labor, men always weed on the left part of a row of workers, or towards the uncleared bush. The left is associated with the bush. Men are stronger, Iteso say, and better suited for acts such as clearing; but it is women whose work brings to fruition what men have tamed.

In possession, the assumption of male regalia indicates an element of active mastery not usually associated with women. This interpretation is supported by the element of violence and struggle associated with both the entry of the spirit into the body and the violent treatment of the scapegoat that is made to stand for the spirit in the curing ritual. The animal is thrown violently to the ground until it urinates, a sign of agreement by the spirit to cooperate with the cult. In Iteso society, men do public violence to other men, while women do public violence to themselves, usually in mortuary ceremonies associated with emotional display. Although men do not participate in rites of possession, participants display maleness. The interdependence associated with the sexual act is an essential element of the curing and apotheosis of the possession experience. Women take roles of both active mastery and of the more quiet realization associated with women. The result of a cure is that women acquire a status to which they would not otherwise be entitled.

When engaged in cult activities, women are not subject to the ordinary controls that govern their behavior in their fertile period. They can go in cult groups unaccompanied by a male guardian; in cult situations they do not observe the relatively subordinate forms of etiquette required in other public situations—sexual joking and play not otherwise found in Iteso life are permissible here. Finally, women cured of possession have the same rights to marks of respect as those given to mothers of twins.

Iteso tell the parents of twins that only spirits have the "power" to give them two children. About women who have gone through rituals of possession they say, "*Ejassi apedori*" (lit. "there is power there"). The word *apedor* has a definable semantic range when the Iteso use it—it refers to the ability and capacity to carry out an act or to produce an effect. To ask a person if he or she is able to do something, one would use the verb *apedor;* for a request that requires compliance, the verb *abeikin* is used. I was often corrected for using *apedor* instead of *abeikin.* Force is translated as *agogong,* physical strength. I found no easy equivalent in the Teso language for the notion of authority. When the Iteso describe the transformation that women have undergone in rituals of possession, they use a form of the verb *to be* that denotes location. Literally, they describe the body of the woman as the locus for powers that were not in place before the rituals. I was unable to get anyone to respond to my suggestion that this was so because in some sense the body was occupied by two identities, the woman and the spirit. Whatever the relationship of the powers, the Iteso describe a person as changed and possessing enhanced powers to produce consequences in the world.

An element of this change in the definition of the person, her rights, duties, and the attitudes displayed towards her, after undergoing the possession and curing rituals, is that the relationship of women to power has been altered. Possessed women have gone to the source and returned unharmed. They are better able to deal with the dangers of power because they became androgynous characters. They know both male active mastery and female techniques of growth. In this sense women cured of possession have more power over their lives because they are more powerful, have different capacities; they control an important resource, themselves, to a greater degree.

In the preceding paragraph I have played fast and loose with the concept of power, moving back and forth from power as capacity and agency to power as energy and potentiality to power as the more conventional ability to control people and resources. The American College Dictionary lists more than twenty definitions of *power.* I realize that dictionaries are dangerous for anthropologists to use, but they do indicate the richness of what Wittgenstein called the crooked streets of natural language. The straight paths of causal analysis pare away the background meanings in terms of which specific contextualized definitions emerge. The Iteso follow a more crooked, and I think more interesting way than the strategizing approach in political anthropology, for example. They understand power in several senses and do not separate them precisely. Possession is tied to Iteso concepts of power, which is acquired through activities Westerners find difficult to grasp because our own concepts are situated in the generally mechanistic cosmology in terms of which too many social scientific concepts are articulated.

The Iteso evidence indicates not only that power can be created in ritual, but that the power in Iteso society has a center and a periphery, to use terms borrowed from world system theory. A major difference is that the center and periphery are not wholly stable. The relations among these epicenters constantly change. Spirit possession provides a context in which women acquire and exercise power as they exclude men. Both men and women are fully aware of this. Female power is at the center of possession, and male power is the periphery. I have not discussed the considerable costs of this system in this paper. They include social costs, such as the legitimation of male symbols of power, and more economic and environmental ones, such as the relative cost of possession and the unhappy consequences when the healing of many illnesses is relegated to the possession context.

Notes

1. I exclude those explanations of possession that reduce it to somatic incapacity, such as nutritional imbalance or calcium deficiency. They are anthropological fantasies, totally lacking in evidence. Kehoe and Giletti (1981), for example, have argued that "the preponderance of women in possession cults is linked with the likelihood of deficiencies in thiamine, tryptophan-niacin, calcium and vitamin D in women in old world traditional societies in which poverty and/or sumptuary rules restrict women's nutrient intakes" (p. 549). This extraordinary statement would have to be supported by evidence that the onset of possession is correlated with periods when the deficiencies most affect women. Such evidence is totally absent from the accounts cited by Kehoe and Giletti. In addition, they constructed a category of "old world traditional societies" in which the status of women does not vary, not to mention that female nutritional intake appears to be the same regardless of such factors as social organization and mode of production.

2. In another publication (Karp and Karp 1979) we interpreted possession in situational terms as related to the life course of women afflicted and showed how the form of healing embodied in possession has affinities with ritual, healing, and gender symbolism among the Iteso. This is the sort of social psychological interpretation pursued in Crapanzano and Garrison's volume (1977). It can help to understand how rituals mediate specific situations and are related to suffering, but does not concern itself with seeking to know how the possessed see their ritual actions as effective.

3. The Iteso distinguish between mental illness and inebriated states such as drunkenness or getting high from bhang. Mental illness is often believed to be caused by the spirit of a homicide. However, they use one word to describe the experience of both, *amerit*. The difference is not in the experience, which they assert is not capable of discursive formulation, but in whether it is permanent (like mental illness) or temporary (like drunkenness). *Amerit* means to lose control of oneself.

4. This is the sort of claim that might be made by Mary Douglas (1975). What she tends to miss in her studies of cosmology is that confusion can be deliberate, that what is usually separate is often conjoined in order to be revived and separated again. Thus Beidelman has shown in his analysis of Swazi Royal Ritual (1966a) that the Swazi king takes filth and confusion on himself in order to revive a failing world (also Packard 1981). The twin problems of classification and confusion can only be properly understood if they are examined in conjunction with the concepts of agency that define persons and discriminate among those with the

capacity to mediate and those who are excluded from that process (happily for them). This is often an overt purpose of cults in Africa: the action of the cult's members fights against the entropy they perceive as an essential aspect of their natural world (Kopytoff 1980).

5. If they can mediate between two parts of the whole, they can also stand as elements that divide a greater whole. This is the essence of the notorious "Nuer paradox" in kinship studies (Evans-Pritchard 1951). The children of different mothers are potential points of division within lineages, even as they provide the potential for relating their husband's lineage to their brothers'. (This is obviously a patrilineal point of view.)

6. I do not mean to assert here that I am describing any pattern of belief that is distinctively African. Not all African societies are as obsessed with reproduction as the Iteso, and many societies in other parts of the world are as concerned with reproduction as those of the African continent. I think it is almost impossible to make any assertions about the relative "Africanness" of systems of thought. I use references to "Africa" to refer primarily to those societies about which I have read the most.

7. The Iteso are a paranilotic-speaking people living in Busia District, Kenya, and across the Kenya-Uganda border. I have described their social organization, belief system and ritual in Karp 1978, 1980, and 1987.

8. The first level is usually seeking a cure in one of the local dispensaries or a mission hospital or from physicians in the larger towns. One major reason for this is that Western medicine is usually less costly than major local cures.

9. The Iteso are not historically minded. They have little in the way of specialized roles related to oral traditions, and what historical sense they have tends to be related to the histories of lineages and subclans. Since their genealogies are shallow, historical events beyond two generations are not well remembered. The larger patterns of interethnic relations are presented in stereotypical form with little in the way of specific events represented. The primary forum for presenting the history of contact with other peoples may be the cult of possession. Possession is by definition an exotic phenomenon among the Iteso; almost all the songs and many of the rites are taken from neighboring peoples, and the more exotic the derivation, the greater the efficacy attributed to it as a cure. In possession ceremonies in which I have taken part, songs from the surrounding Nilotic- and Bantu-speaking peoples were freely mixed. Customs derived from the Baganda, acephalous Bantu peoples of Uganda and Western Kenya, and Luo and JoPadhola Nilotes were all intertwined and acknowledged as being of exotic origins.

References

Beattie, John

1969 Spirit Mediumship in Bunyoro. *In* Spirit Mediumship and Society in Africa. John Beattie and John Middleton, eds. pp. 159–70. London: Routledge and Kegan Paul.

Beidelman, T. O.

1966a Swazi Royal Ritual. Africa 36:373–405.

1966b The Ox and Nuer Sacrifice: Some Freudian Hypotheses about Nuer Symbolism. Man (n.s.) 1(4): 452–67.

Bernardi, B.

1959 *The Mugwe, A Failing Prophet.* London: Oxford University Press.

Buijtenhuijs, Robert

1985 Dini Ya Msambwa: Rural Rebellion or Counter Society? *In* Theoretical Explorations in African Religion. Wim van Binsbergen and Matthew Schoffleers, eds. London: Routledge and Kegan Paul.

Crapanzano, Vincent and Virginia Garrison, eds.

1977 Case Studies in Spirit Possession. New York: Wiley and Sons.

Douglas, Mary

1975 Natural Symbols. London: Routledge and Kegan Paul.

Evans-Pitchard, E. E.

1951 Kinship and Marriage among the Nuer. Oxford: Oxford University Press.

Firth, Raymond

1967 Individual Fantasy and Social Norms: Seances with Spirit Mediums. *In* Tikopia Ritual and Belief. pp. 293–329. Boston: Beacon Press.

Fry, Peter

1976 Spirits of Protest. Cambridge: Cambridge University Press.

Goffman, Erving

1956 The Presentation of Self in Everyday Life. New York: Anchor Books.

Harris, Grace

1957 "Possession Hysteria" in a Kenya Tribe. American Anthropologist 59:1146–66.

Karp, Ivan

1978 Fields of Change among the Iteso of Kenya. London: Routledge and Kegan Paul.

1980 Beer Drinking and Social Experience in an African Society. *In* Explorations in African Systems of Thought. I. Karp and C. S. Bird, eds. pp. 83–119. Bloomington: Indiana University Press.

1986 Deconstructing Culture-Bound Syndromes. Social Science and Medicine 21:221–28.

1987 Laughter at Marriage: Subversion in Performance. *In* The Transformation of African Marriage. D. Parkin and D. Nyamweya, eds. pp. 137–54. Manchester: Manchester University Press.

Karp, Ivan and Patricia Karp

1979 Living with the Spirits of the Dead. *In* African Therapeutic Systems. C. Adede et al., eds. pp. 22–25. Boston: Crossroads Press.

Kehoe, Alice and Dody Giletti

1981 Women's Preponderance in Possession Cults: The Calcium Deficiency Hypothesis Extended. American Anthropologist 83: 549–61.

Kenny, Michael

1986 The Passion of Ansel Bourne. Washington: Smithsonian Institution Press.

Kopytoff, Igor

1980 Revitalization and the Genesis of Cults in Pragmatic Religion: the Kita Rite of Passage among the Suku. *In* Explorations in African Systems of Thought. Ivan Karp and C. S. Bird, eds. pp. 183–212. Bloomington: Indiana University Press.

Lambek, Michael

1981 Human Spirits. Cambridge: Cambridge University Press.

Lan, David

1986 Guns and Rain. Manchester: Manchester University Press.

Lewis, I. M.

1971 Ecstatic Religion: An Anthropological Study of Spirit Possession and Shamanism. Middlesex: Penguin Books.

Merton, Robert K.

1956 Social Structure and Anomie. *In* Social Theory and Social Structure, pp. 131–60. Glencoe: The Free Press.

Needham, Rodney

1960 The Left Hand of the Mugwe: An Analytical Note on the Structure of Meru Symbolism. *Africa* 30: 20–33.

Packard, Randall

1981 Chiefship and Cosmology. Bloomington: Indiana University Press.

Peel, J. D. Y.

1969 Understanding Alien Belief Systems. British Journal of Sociology 20:69–84.

Wilson, Peter

1967 Status Ambiguity and Spirit Possession. *Man* (n.s.) 2(3): 366–78.

Wiltshire, Bruce

1984 Role Playing and Identity. Bloomington: Indiana University Press.

Part Two

Forms of Power

Roy Willis

Power Begins at Home: The Symbolism of Male-Female Commensality in Ufipa

. . . adult men and women virtually never eat together. The woman brings the bowl of porridge to the men and leaves them there to eat. The pattern is widespread in Africa . . .

—Jack Goody, *Cooking, Cuisine and Class,* 1982

Sur les hauts plateaux de l'Ufipa, tout le monde mange ensemble.

—J. M. Robert, *Tables d'Enquêtes sur les moeurs et coutumes indigènes,* 1951

Some put their hands into the dishes when they are scarcely seated, says Erasmus, wolves and gluttons do that.

—Norbert Elias, *The Civilising Process,* 1978

The Problem

This paper originated with a felt need to explain an apparent ethnographic anomaly, the custom in one society of East-Central Africa of bringing together adults of both sexes in domestic consumption of food and millet beer. (Boys and girls in this society also eat together, although they are separated from older people.) The custom was first reported in 1951 among the plateau Fipa of southwestern Tanzania by the French missionary and amateur ethnographer J. M. Robert (1951:260), although he noted that the Fipa of the adjacent Lake Tanganyika shore practiced sexual segregation during eating. As well as confirming these two observations by Robert during my field research in the 1960s, I was also able to observe the custom of male-female commensality among the Fipa of the Rukwa valley, located east of the plateau where the bulk of the 100,000 Fipa population live.[1]

Consideration of the commensal anomaly led me in turn to ponder the broader question of Fipa table manners, their symbolic significance, and their historical origin. In this inquiry I was considerably influenced by Norbert Elias's fascinating study (1978) of what he calls the "civilizing process" in European society, as reflected in eating and drinking behavior. In implicit opposition to Freud's pessimistic *Civilisation and its Discontents,* Elias sees the development of a civilized sensibility, for all the affective constraints it entails, as an essentially liberating process in terms of personal freedom. The Fipa evidence suggests that this nonliterate, tribal society has undergone a "civilizing process" analogous to that described by Elias for the great literate cultures of Europe and, although the main focus of his historical inquiry is European, for classical China. The same evidence also suggests that the crucial transformation among the Fipa, which involved a major redistribution of social power, occurred in the remarkably short time span of a few decades, compared with centuries in the corresponding European and Chinese cases. Before introducing evidence for this transformation, I will describe present-day commensal behavior in Fipa society.

Fipa Culture

The kind of relaxed yet, paradoxically, controlled conviviality that Elias asserts to be the outcome of the "civilizing process," a cultivated spontaneity made possible through a willing and shared acceptance of constraint, was the most salient characteristic of Fipa culture for this writer, as it had also been for earlier observers (Thomson 1881; Deutsche Kolonial-Lexikon 1923). It should be noted here that eating and drinking are for the Fipa, as for other African peoples, different social and symbolic occasions. This distinction, whose origin and significance remain to be adequately explained, appears to constitute a major difference between the cultures of Africa and Eurasia (Goody 1982:72). Nevertheless, in Ufipa there are broad similarities in the sociology and symbolism of communal eating and communal drinking of millet beer, even though the respective occasions are invariably separated in time. Let us first examine the code of manners affecting food consumption among the Fipa, since the physical act of eating necessitates the deployment of a more complex set of practices than beer drinking, and thus exhibits in finer detail the ideas and attitudes structuring this intimate encounter of nature and culture that constitutes the social enjoyment of physical refreshment.

The size of the commensal eating group in Ufipa is limited by the physical capacity of the woman doing the cooking to produce food in quantity and never, in my experience, exceeded a dozen persons. The average was less than half this figure. Typically it consisted of a husband and wife and perhaps their adolescent children and often one or more elderly brothers, sisters, or cousins of either spouse who might be temporary visitors or attached to the household as permanent dependants. In the case of a kindred head who, like my patron Magdalena Ntaalu Ngalawa, was an unusually wealthy householder, the social composition of the commensal group could be more varied, reflecting the ability of the head to attract cognatic followers from among a large pool of relatives. Thus those who regularly ate with my patron during the period of my field research were her brother Basileo, a widower who had not remarried; her sister Maristela Waakalipa, who was like Magdalena a free woman (insiimbe);[2] Basileo's daughters Mama Kifalo and Elisa, also free women; Beda, her mother's sister's grandson, an unmarried adolescent; and Luisa, her brother's granddaughter, also an unmarried adolescent. This core group was frequently enlarged by the temporary presence of visiting relatives and neighbors, and by the intermittent attendance of the anthropologist.

Magdalena appeared to do most of the cooking (*-eeleka*), although her two brother's daughters also took turns in providing meals.[3] On most days Magdalena was assisted by Luisa, who was herself assisted by Kadia, a girl of about eight who was given food separately, together with other children of both sexes.

Two main meals are customarily served in Ufipa, one at midday and another in early evening, but a snack called *imisuunko,* which usually consists of roasted sweet corn (*amakoonde*) or raw fruit (*iciinka*), is often taken on first rising, about 6 a.m. This auxiliary food may also be taken at other times of the day, although not during either of the two main meals when the food is never raw (*-iisi*) but is always either boiled or steamed. In addition, millet beer (*isuute*) may be consumed at any waking hour apart from the two principal mealtimes.

The serving of a main meal is signaled when the cook (*unnweelesi*) brings the central item, a porridge (*insima*) made of finger millet (*amaleesi*) or, more rarely and in wealthier households, of sweet corn, and places it on a mat in an open but sheltered space. In good weather the food is usually placed just outside the cook's hut, but in rainy or cold weather it is placed in the covered and central "public" section of the hut, apart from the cooking and sleeping areas.

When they see the main dish of porridge presented, those nearby begin to group themselves around it. The more exalted, such as the householder and kinsfolk or neighbors of elder status, sit on wooden stools, while others, such as married women of child-bearing age and unmarried adolescents of both sexes, sit or squat (primarily men) or recline with legs drawn up (primarily women) on mats. Meanwhile the cook brings relishes (*inyeenyi*) in smaller bowls and places them around the main dish. In poorer households, which means the majority in Ufipa, there is often only one relish: lima beans (*ifilaanda*). But in wealthier establishments, of which Magdalena's was certainly one, three or more relishes are regularly offered. These consist of meat (beef, mutton, or goat) or fish (dried lake fish or fresh, local river fish), and sometimes both meat and fish, together with vegetables of various kinds and combinations. Most commonly served are sweet potatoes (*ifisela*), various pumpkins (*insaalo*), and a glutinous, spinach-like vegetable, not botanically identified, called *inkwiila.* A mixed relish called *insimwa* combined *inkwiila,* onions (*ifituungu*), tomatoes (*impwaampwa*), and groundnuts (*imbalala*). The porridge served in Magdalena's household was invariably the high-status variant made of sweet corn flour rather than the plebeian millet porridge, the staple diet of the multitude.

These culinary differences are, of course, significant indicators of relative social rank in Ufipa. But the code of etiquette associated with eating and drinking is, in my experience, remarkably uniform throughout Fipa society. When everyone has taken their place around the array of dishes, the woman of the house, or her deputy, brings a calabash of warm water, which she pours over the extended right hands of the diners in order of rank, washing her own hand last. Soap (*icifwewe*) and a cloth for drying are frequently brought as well. Only when this cleaning ritual is completed does the senior person present give the signal to begin eating by saying "*Twaacile!*" ("Let us refresh ourselves!"). Those nearby say or mumble the standard response, "*Taata witu, kaleesa!*", which may be roughly translated as "Our father, God be praised!"

The senior patrons help themselves to the first morsels of food, followed by their juniors. This is done without haste. The appearance of relaxed enjoyment is normally heightened by lively conversation, which begins immediately and to which all present are expected to contribute.

It is noticeable that these leisurely and loquacious eaters take food only from the receptacles immediately within their reach, and each avoids intruding into the space of his neighbor. If something he wishes to eat is out of reach, however, he typically makes some chatty comment to his neighbor on a topic not directly connected with food, and afterwards indicates with his eyes the object of his gastronomic interest. The neighbor takes the hint and moves the receptacle within convenient range. Thus there is an exchange of information for food, all within the constraints of civility. I saw this done many times, although the actual exchange was usually less direct than this outline suggests and more often took the form of dishes passed in both directions accompanied by an exchange of conversational niceties.

The business of conveying food to the mouth, the evolution of which in European civilization is described at length by Elias (1978), was also highly mannered among the Fipa in the 1960s. The diner inserts the first three fingers and thumb of the right hand into the central pile of warm dry porridge (boiled and salted millet or maize flour) and retrieves a ball of this material up to two inches in diameter (*itoonji* or *itosii*). He uses the thumb to make a deep depression in this ball, producing an edible scoop or spoon which he then dips (*-koomba*) into one of the dishes of relish and sauce (*usuuni*). He raises the "spoon" and its contents to the mouth, which is quickly opened, and almost simultaneously flicks porridge and relish inside with a sharp movement of the fingers. The aim is first to avoid soiling the fingers with sauce or gravy, which Elias says was the principal rationale for the adoption of eating implements in European society (1978 : 126). A second object of this technique appears to be to conceal the opening of the mouth, which is masked by the raised fingers.

The meal is formally brought to an end in the same way it began—with the washing of the participants' hands in water brought by the same woman.

The overall impression created by a Fipa meal is of an obligatory natural function, *i.e.*, eating, being pressed into the service of a cultural end. Later I will seek to identify that end. The elaborate code of etiquette governing social interaction (Willis 1978: 14–20) suggests massive behavioral constraint, yet what I mostly recall as a frequent mealtime guest of the Fipa was an urbane sense of convivial enjoyment. This is analogous to Elias's observation that "there is a liberation from one form of constraint to another that is less burdensome. Thus the civilizing process, despite the transformation and increased constraint that it imposes on the emotions, goes hand in hand with liberations of the most diverse kinds" (Elias 1978: 185).

Certainly there could hardly be a greater contrast with Fipa custom than Audrey Richards's account of the eating habits of the neighboring and linguistically cognate Bemba people of northeast Zambia:

> To the casual observer the most characteristic feature of their [the Bemba] manner of eating is its speed and almost complete lack of ceremony. It is true that there is a certain amount of etiquette prescribed before the meal is actually started. Invitations must be issued respectfully, for instance, and water brought to wash the hands of the guests. But once the company, whether of men or women, is gathered, there is no further delay. The five or six eaters squat around the vessels of food, and bolt the meal silently and swiftly . . . Meals are not times for rest, or chat, or merriment. (Richards 1939:75)

Richards's description parallels Meyer and Sonia Fortes's observations on the Tallensi of northern Ghana, who, like the Bemba and the majority of Africans, eat in sexually segregated groups and for whom "eating is a serious business; there is no conversation at meal-times, as soon as a group has finished they [*sic*] disperse" (Fortes and Fortes 1936: 270).

Yet even among the seemingly easy-going Fipa there is substantial repression. In particular, any tendency to gluttony (*-laka*) is rigidly suppressed in children from an early age. One informant noted: "Our father would often sit watching us children eat, his staff of authority, *iluwaasi,* in his hand. Any child who 'ate badly' would get a crack on the head from the [rounded] end of this staff."[4]

Fipa children are also taught to keep their mouths closed while chewing. It is the general observance of this rule, combined with the cultural tendency to be loquacious, that makes Fipa meals rather leisurely affairs. A similar control is exercised over other bodily orifices. Breaking wind (*-nya imisusi*), like urination, defecation, and disposal of nasal mucus, are private acts.

Yet, as I have already mentioned, these numerous indications of a scrupulous control of natural functions in a social setting went along with what other earlier observers of the Fipa described as an apparently carefree and even exuberant style of behavior. The Scottish explorer Joseph Thomson reported in 1880 "merriment and light-hearted laughter" at the queen mother's court; a late nineteenth-century French missionary recorded in his mission diary that the Fipa were "gais et ont l'esprit ouvert"; and the Deutsches Kolonial-Lexikon observed that "Sie [the Fipa] sind von . . . angenehmen Gesichtszugen, gutmutig und frohsinnig"—a remarkable convergence in the independent views of three Europeans from diverse national and cultural backgrounds.[5]

What has been said about the management of eating in Ufipa applies to that other major occasion of communal refreshment, the social consumption of millet beer (*isuute*). Beer is brewed in substantial quantities and its preparation takes about a week. Since it will go bad unless quickly consumed, the number of people present at a drinking party is typically much greater and the social range represented much wider than at a communal meal. As well as the core domestic group, there will normally be other kinsfolk and non-kin neighbors at a drinking party. But there will be the same commingling of adults of both sexes as at a typical meal. At a drinking party given by a wealthy householder the participants may be so numerous that several ephemeral subgroups, sometimes occupying the public areas of different huts, may be formed.

The formalities of drinking are also different, although marked by the same concern for civility that reigns over communal eating. Millet beer is either drunk warm from a common pot, through reeds, the traditional method (called *-sweela*), or taken cold in an enamel or tin bowl that is passed around the group, a modern innovation. Since the fingers should not come into contact with the beer, there is no hand-washing ritual. But drinking is inaugurated by the senior person present in the same way as a meal, by uttering the expression "*Twaacile!*" and then repeating the customary response to this invitation. As with eating, there is also care to avoid an appearance of selfish greed (*-laka*) and an emphasis on sharing. Reeds and bowls circulate in a clockwise direction, so that a drinker receives from his right in the circle and gives to his left. It is mandatory to offer and receive a bowl with both hands, signifying involvement of the whole self in the transaction. It is also polite, though not invariably done, to pass the reed with the right hand while holding the upper right arm with the left hand, a gesture that has a similar significance.

Since a beer-drinking party may last for many hours, it becomes necessary from time to time for drinkers to go outside to relieve themselves. This unavoidable intrusion of nature into the cultural circle is mediated by an elaborate exchange of stereotyped verbal formulas (Willis 1978:18). The person obliged to withdraw says "I am going to the bush" ("*Nayo uku'umwiiswa*"), and the others acknowledge with the standard response "*Taata witu, Kaleesa!*" ("Our father, God be praised!"). On going out to urinate, men turn to the right of the hut entrance, women to the left. Defecation necessitates a longer detour. On returning, the individual claps his hands and says "*Mpaali, ta!*" ("I was here, sirs!") and, on resuming his seat, "*Twamsaana, ta!*" ("We are all met together, sirs!"). He [or she] is received with the words "*Mwaweela, ta!*" ("You have returned, sir!") and "*Tuteesi, ta!*" ("We are established, sir!") and "*Taata witu, Kaleesa!*"

These elaborate forms of courtesy tend to be maintained even into advanced states of alcoholic intoxication. Even more remarkable, in view of alcohol's well-known disinhibiting effect, is that during hundreds of participatory hours in Fipa beer-drinking parties, I never saw anyone resort to violence, nor did I ever hear of any such incident. Elias (1978) devotes a long and engrossing chapter to the gradual control achieved by European man over his impulses to aggressive violence. What can be reconstructed of Fipa precolonial history suggests a roughly comparable transformation from bellicosity to the notably pacific order of society commented on by early explorers and later colonial administrators.[6]

Mixed drinking parties make ideal occasions for initiating sexual liaisons and are often used for this purpose in Ufipa. But here again behavior is carefully managed to avoid offense. Potential lovers communicate through an elaborate code compounded of covert gestures (the verbs are *-sinisya* and *-palisya*), particularly eye movements, intonation, and resourceful exploitation of the rich potential of the Fipa language for significant ambiguity and innuendo; I was told several times that it resembled English in that respect. These techniques appeared to be successful in maintaining the desired secrecy or at least preventing loss of face by a "deceived" spouse or lover. Although I lack quantitative evidence, my impression was that Fipa marriages tended to endure, an impression supported by Robert's assertion that "les divorces sont rares" (1951:198).

What has been said so far might seem to suggest a Utopian state of affairs but, of course, there is another side to the mannered surface of Fipa culture, what Ivan Karp in his perceptive study of Teso beer drinking has called, after Erving Goffman, the "underlife" (Karp 1980:109). There flourish the familiar human emotions of fear, anger, jealousy, and hatred, ugly emotions that the Fipa are supremely concerned to conceal. Interlineage conflict generates such negative feelings among the Teso (Karp 1980:112). Fipa society is structured differently, and may be summarily described as a "big man" (and occasionally "big woman") system geared to a centralized, hierarchical organization with a high degree of individual mobility. I learned early how fierce is the competition for followers waged by the elective heads of the cognatic kindreds. One day after returning from a protracted stroll around the village, during which I had accepted the hospitality of a number of Fipa householders, I was suddenly confronted with the towering figure of my patron and kindred head Magdalena Ntaalu Ngalawa. She informed me with manifest anger that, if I continued to consort with such people (referring to two influential members of rival kindreds who had given me millet beer), I would be afflicted with a fatal sickness. I would, in her (translated) words, be unable to piss or shit, my belly would swell enormously, and in this pitiable state I would die an agonizing death. I never again saw my patron so moved. I prudently mended my ways and avoided the dire fate she had threatened me with. (I also took the precaution of investing in antipoisoning medicine.)

The Fipa see poisoning as a constant danger attending communal refreshment, particularly beer drinking, when relatively large numbers of people come together and socialize for long periods (Willis 1968). It is obligatory for anyone offering a bowl of beer to take a sip first, to show the beer is not poisoned. But it is said that a skilled sorcerer-poisoner may nevertheless conceal poison under his (or her) thumbnail, which he covertly dips in the beer as he hands it to his guest. The only defense against such methods is one of the several kinds of antipoisoning medicine that can be obtained from indigenous doctors. But the ever–present danger of poisoning no more prevents Fipa from enjoying convivial occasions than the road accident statistics in our society stop people from driving automobiles.

Economics, Symbolism, and History

The culinary domain, as Lévi–Strauss (1970, 1978) has demonstrated, is universally charged with fundamental symbolic values. The cooking and (in Africa) brewing processes by which natural resources are converted into cultural ones (*i.e.*, food and beer[7]), and the consequent and associated processes in which obligatory natural functions (eating and drinking) are orchestrated for cultural ends, implicitly evoke the core symbolic ideas of the Fipa cosmology. These have to do with the domestication of wild nature, the control and conversion of the energies of the lower body (the Loins) by the intellectual powers of the upper body (the Head), and the social incorporation of incoming strangers. These are perceived as analogous processes (Willis 1981 : 189–93), and their intimate involvement in the economic business of food and beer production and consumption is apparent. Although like many other nonindustrial societies the Fipa perceive their world as structured by conceptual dualities (or binary oppositions), the cultural emphasis in Ufipa is on the integrating process of interaction between the structural dualities, rather than on the idea of duality, opposition, and separation (Willis 1981). This cultural bias towards the processual and integrative is also apparent in the culinary domain. An instructive contrast exists with the cosmology and sociology of another African people, the Iteso of western Kenya. This people, who practice commensal segregation of the sexes, perceive an association between women, the boiling of food, the home, and domesticity, a cluster of concepts opposed in Teso thought to the domain of men, which is associated with roasting, wild nature, and the external world of politics. This cosmological duality correlates with a social conflict between the economic interests of individual household subsistence and those of exchange between households (Karp and Karp 1977).

In Ufipa, although there is a strict and complementary division of labor between men and women in economic production (Willis 1981 : 105–13), the emphasis in the cooking and eating of foods is on integration rather than on opposition and separation. Whereas Teso men roast and eat meat only in the bush or in the courtyard of the household, the Fipa roast only sweet corn, a marginal or "snack" food, which is eaten at home by both males and females. Members of both sexes, likewise, jointly consume the products of boiling and steaming, the most "cultural" methods of cooking, around or near the domestic hearth.[8] The commensal symbolism is consistent with a social order that had achieved a notable integration of domestic and political domains in the late precolonial epoch (Willis 1981 : 178–79).

This integration was made possible by rapid economic growth. From the 1850s onwards, there was a massive increase in the volume and variety of vegetable foodstuffs available to the Fipa, associated with an unprecedented period, in the later nineteenth century, of relative peace and economic growth (Willis 1981). New species of vegetables imported mainly by Islamic merchants from central Tanzania and the coast included two varieties of potato, sweet potato (*ifisela*) and "European" potato (*ifisela Ulaya*); onions (*ifituungu*); tomatoes (*impwaampwa*); groundnuts (*imbalala*); and sweet corn (*amakoonde*). In return Ufipa exported indigenous cloth, iron implements, grain, ivory, and slaves.

This novel abundance of foodstuffs likely stimulated in Ufipa an increased cultural concern with culinary techniques, a concern probably reflected in the rather large number of terms denoting various stages in the cooking (*-eeleka*) process. A probable nineteenth-century innovation was the substitution of steaming for boiling as the preferred method of cooking relishes. Under this new method, a large cooking pot (*inyiingu*) containing some water is set on the three small earthenware pillars or stones (*amasiiko*), which contain the cooking fire (*umooto* or *unswaakanwa*). A smaller and shallower pot called *ulweeso luteele,* which contains the relishes and a small quantity of salted water, is placed on the large pot. This pot is never directly exposed to the fire and should not be polluted with soot. This cooking technique is considered especially appropriate when food is offered to distinguished guests (an activity denoted by a special verb, *-imula*).[9] Steaming took more of the cook's time than boiling but, by subjecting the raw materials to a more diffused and longer heating process, it produced foods that were easier to handle and digest. Presumably the social benefits were believed to outweigh the greater economic cost.

As I have argued elsewhere (Willis 1981), the precolonial nineteenth century also saw radical changes in the wider economic and political structure of Fipa society. A fundamentally ascriptive "conical clan" system associated with unilineal descent appears to have been succeeded by a much more fluid system based on competing cognative kindreds that were integrated at a higher level of early state organization into a unitary network in which the principal good transacted was political office, which was bought and sold according to market principles (see Willis 1981). Control over biological reproduction, the dominant social concern in lineage-based African societies (Meillassoux 1975), was downgraded in favor of material production. A significant change in the social status of women seems to be indicated by the emergence of an ethnographically rare, and possibly unique, separation of state power into two complementary structures: a predominantly male organization concerned with the management of economic production and exchange, and a female-run apparatus responsible for coercive social control (Willis 1981).

This complex of fundamental changes, which could be called a social revolution without exaggeration, is celebrated in a Fipa myth. In the myth incoming female strangers, after a symbolic usurpation of sovereignty from the aboriginal king, transact a mutually beneficial exchange of powers with the king in a contract that establishes the present social order.

It seems reasonable to infer that the peace, economic prosperity, and maximized individual mobility that characterized late precolonial Ufipa also encouraged the development of an elaborate code of social etiquette, particularly in the area of table manners. Goody (1982:77) attributes the custom of hand-washing before meals in the Gonja kingdom of northern Ghana to Islamic influence, and it seems likely that the present and comparable Fipa custom was originally introduced by the same Islamic merchants, who probably brought in the new food crops and who constituted a high-status immigrant community in late precolonial Ufipa. But cultural adoption was selective; not every Islamic custom became part of the Fipa cultural repertoire. Only along the Lake Tanganyika shore, where Zanzibari influence in Ufipa was strongest, were traditional African usage and Islamic doctrine combined to maintain commensal segregation of males and females. Elsewhere in Ufipa there was a further cultural innovation that overturned tradition and made the Fipa an anomaly both in Africa as a whole and in respect to their neighbors, the Mambwe and the Lungu.[10] This innovation was the establishment of normative male-female commensality, both in eating and beer drinking.

The "social revolution" in late precolonial Ufipa provided individuals with unprecedented autonomy, within certain limits, to better themselves. In fact, it imposed self-betterment as a norm.[11] But the associated norms of nonviolence made advancement largely dependent on the mastery of peacemaking social skills, particularly the arts of rhetoric and persuasion (Willis 1974, 1978). The twice-daily enjoyment of communal refreshment by men and women together, supplemented by periodic beer-drinking sessions, seems appropriate commemoration of an historic liberation, the social effects of which were in some important respects analogous to those of Elias's "civilizing process." The novel accession of women to the feast was "over-determined" in Ufipa by both history and cosmology. Their enhanced status after the complex precolonial transformation was combined with their symbolic equivalence to the mythological strangers, the bearers of wealth-producing labor power who, according to the myth-sanctioned ideology, should be ever welcomed—and incorporated.

Conclusions

This paper began with an attempt to solve an ethnographic puzzle: the apparent anomaly of male-female commensality in Ufipa. I cannot claim to have solved that puzzle. Indeed, by exploring territory that is yet foreign to the orthodoxies of both anthropology and history, the mystery would seem to have acquired new dimensions of strangeness. The most I could hope to have achieved is to have established a significant convergence between present social behavior and the collective decisions of a body of anonymous actors in the substantially undocumented past of this African society. In this endeavor I have been inspired by Elias's magisterial study (1978), particularly his conclusions that "the 'civilization' which we are accustomed to regard as a possession that comes to us apparently readymade, without our asking how we came to possess it, is a process or part of a process in which we are ourselves involved" (p. 59).

As an ethnographer, I was able to observe the corresponding cultural "possession" of the Fipa. In this paper, I have surveyed the phenomenon of Fipa "table manners," including evidence of incipient economic stratification and the apparent beginnings of an elite "cuisine," in Goody's terms (1982).[12] The various parallels cited between Fipa practice and Elias's account of earlier European custom point to a further extension of the "measure of commonality" Goody has noted between the European, Indian, and Chinese codes of etiquette, a commonality that he finds "surprising" (1982:144).

In the second part of this paper I brought together various strands of evidence pointing to a far-reaching transformation in the Fipa relations of production in late precolonial times, associated with the emergence of a commercially oriented early state. This transformation also appears to have involved changes in the status of the individual and his or her self-conception that are recorded symbolically in myth and social ideology. I conclude that history and sociology alike are condensed in the complex forms of Fipa sociality and are written there in a script that we are only just beginning to decipher.

Notes

1. Field research in Ufipa was supported by a grant from the Emslie Horniman Anthropological Scholarship Fund and a three-month return trip in 1966 was made possible by the generosity of the Wenner-Gren Foundation for Anthropo-

logical Research. I am enduringly grateful to both of these granting agencies. The present paper was originally presented at a symposium on The Symbolism of Power Relations, chaired by W. Arens and I. Karp, at the American Anthropological Association meetings in Washington, D.C., in November 1982. Subsequent versions were presented at the State University of New York at Stony Brook and the universities of Edinburgh, Scotland, and Birmingham, England. Among many helpful critics I would particularly mention, with grateful thanks, are Ivan Karp and Richard Fardon.

2. *insiimbe* is a woman whose marriage has ended and who has, usually by deliberate choice, become an independent householder.

3. There is no Fipa equivalent of the word "meal"; the nearest terms are *icakulya* (food) and *ifiliwa* (that which is eaten).

4. Statement by R. Ntwenya. When a young man is about to marry, he is given an *iluwaasi* staff by his father, signifying that he (the son) has come of age and is fit to be a householder in his own right. This is expressed by the phrases "*Taata waamp' iluwaasi*" (Father has given me a staff") and "*Nakulaaa!*" ("I am grown up-o!").

5. Thomson 1882, vol. I:221; Kirando Mission Diary 1894–1906:12; *Deutsches Kolonial-Lexikon* 1923, vol. III:652. The anonymous author of the German report would seem to have been, on internal evidence, the ethnographer Paul Fromm.

6. Notably Joseph Thomson, E. C. Hore, and Paul Reichard are among the early European visitors (cf. Willis 1981:95–97).

7. The term "beer" is rather misleading. As Karp has observed of the Teso product, African millet beer "might more properly be called an alcoholic, nourishing gruel" (1980:85). Fipa often asserted to me, with justice, that their *isuute* was a food. Some claimed to be able to subsist on millet beer alone for several days at a time.

8. There was one formal occasion, in precolonial times, when food was consumed outside the home and village. This was the celebration of New Year, when beans were boiled and eaten together by household members in the cultivated area called *amakoka* that surrounded every village (Willis 1981:115).

9. I neglected to discover whether there is a specific Fipa verb meaning "to steam," though it seems likely. I do not know either if modification of the Lévi-Straussian "culinary triangle" (1978:490) of roasted, smoked, and boiled was an independent Fipa invention or an introduced cultural trait. But see de Heusch (1980:39–40) on the cosmological significance of steaming among the Thonga.

10. Both of these peoples practice commensal segregation of the sexes (W. Watson personal communication, 1982).

11. A further social innovation in late precolonial Ufipa was an unusual and complex naming system (Willis 1982).

12. The major culinary distinction appears to be the marked preference for sweet corn flour as the raw material of the central porridge in the twice-daily menu of the wealthier Fipa elite, in contrast to the millet flour used by the poorer majority. A further difference is the proliferation of relishes, including a combination of vegetables in one dish, which is found among the wealthier house-

holds. Among the poorer majority a single relish, lima beans, is most commonly served. It could be significant that the root *-laanda* (meaning beans) is the same as the root of *ulaanda* (meaning poverty).

References

Deutsche Kolonial-Lexikon
1923 Leipzig: Spamer.

Elias, Norbert
1978 The Civilizing Process: The History of Manners. Edmund Jephcott, transl. Oxford: Basil Blackwell.

Fortes, M. and S. L. Fortes
1936 Food in the Domestic Economy of the Tallensi. Africa 9:237–76.

Goody, Jack
1982 Cooking, Cuisine and Class: A Study in Comparative Sociology. Cambridge: Cambridge University Press.

de Heusch, Luc
1980 Heat, Physiology, and Cosmogony: *rites de passage* among the Thonga. *In* Explorations in African Systems of Thought. Ivan Karp and Charles S. Bird, eds. pp. 27–43. Bloomington: Indiana University Press.

Karp, Ivan
1980 Beer Drinking and Social Experience in an African Society: An Essay in Formal Sociology. *In* Explorations in African Systems of Thought. Ivan Karp and Charles S. Bird, eds. pp. 83–119. Bloomington: Indiana University Press.

Karp, Ivan and Patricia Karp
1977 Social Aspects of Iteso Cookery. *In* The Anthropologists' Cookbook. Jessica Kuper, ed. pp. 101–106. London: Routledge and Kegan Paul.

Kirando (Ufipa) Mission Diaries, 1894–1906. Rome: Library of the White Fathers (Padri Bianchi).

Lévi-Strauss, Claude
1970 The Raw and the Cooked. J. and B. Weightman, transl. London: Jonathan Cape.
1978 The Origin of Table Manners. J. and B. Weightman, transl. London: Jonathan Cape.

Meillassoux, C.
1975 Femmes, greniers et capitaux. Paris: Maspéro.

Richards, A. I.
1939 Land, Labor, and Diet among the Bemba. London: International African Institute.

Robert, J. M
1951 Table d'Enquètes sur les moeurs et coutumes indigènes. Karema: mimeographed document (copy in Library of the White Fathers, Rome).

Thomson, Joseph
1881 To the Central African Lakes and Back. 2 vols. London: Cass.

Willis, R. G.
1968 Changes in Mystical Concepts and Practices among the Fipa. Ethnology 7(2): 139–57.
1974 Man and Beast. London: Hart-Davis MacGibbon.
1978 There Was a Certain Man: Spoken Art of the Fipa. Oxford: Oxford University Press.
1981 A State in the Making: Myth, History, and Social Transformation in Pre-Colonial Ufipa. Bloomington: Indiana University Press.
1982 On a Mental Sausage Machine and Other Nominal Problems. *In* Semantic Anthropology. D. J. Parkin, ed. pp. 224–40. London: Academic Press.
1985 Do the Fipa Have a Word for It? *In* The Anthropology of Evil. D. J. Parkin, ed. pp. 209–23. Oxford: Basil Blackwell.

Ronald K. Engard

Dance and Power in Bafut (Cameroon)

Introduction

Dance performances are a prominent feature of Bafut political life. The climactic moment of the annual ritual cycle—the death and rebirth of the year—is the *fon*'s (sacred chief's) Dance: Abin Lela (the Dance of the Flutes). Many subchiefs and other important nobles within the kingdom also possess their own Dance (Abin) or dance societies (*muko*). Indeed, the right to hold the Dance is an important constituting element of the legitimacy of chiefship (*nufoa*). As with the death and rebirth of the year, so with celebrations of the death and succession of individuals—dance is prominently featured. Here, in addition to honoring the dead, dance, display, and feasting also redound to the credit of the successor and his lineage.

The Annual Dance in Bafut is an essential act of constitutional politics, and Bafut dance in general is part of a strategy for converting material wealth into symbolic capital (Bourdieu 1977) within a political economy of prestige. In giving a political interpretation to these "artistic" events, I do not thereby eschew an aesthetic perception of them. Rather, I will try to show that for the Bafut (as, for instance, for the Gola of Liberia) we are dealing with what d'Azevedo (1979) has called "the asthetics of power and obedience." Two related sets of concepts which recur in the aesthetic evaluation of Bafut Dance and dance performances are strength (*teuh*) or power (*mbang*) and control (*bu'u*) on the one hand, and authenticity (*jwe-jwe*) on the other. Not far behind these "aesthetic" concepts lurk their sociological counterparts, operational and constitutional politics (Ruel 1969): the day-to-day acquisition and exercise of power, and its annually due constitution as legitimate authority. The Bafut case also suggests that although the concept of performativity (see below) may not be useful in the analysis of ritual per se (see Gardner 1983), it can be useful in analyzing events whose preconditions are ritually established.

Ethnological Background

In their oral traditions (as in those of many kingdoms of the Cameroon Grassfields) the Bafut claim to have come from the upper Mbam River, the region of a sacred lake usually referred to as Kimi or Rifum, where the present-day Tikar proper live. Because so many kingdoms share this common myth of migration from the East, the peoples of the Western Grassfields have traditionally been lumped together ethnographically as the Bamenda Tikar (McCulloch *et al.* 1954).

As with many traditions of successive waves of migration from a single center of diffusion, the myth of Tikar origins has gradually come to be seen as a charter borrowed by each group to assert the validity of a widely diffused set of political institutions surrounding sacred chiefship: queen mothers, a division of the population into royals, nobles, and commoners, an elaborate system of ranked titles, the development of powerful secret regulatory societies, and the like (Kaberry and Chilver 1971). This is not to say that it is only institutions and not people that have moved, but that the movement of populations has been the endemic movement of fragments in all directions, rather than the monolithic movement of groups in a single direction (Warnier 1975; Warnier and Nkwi 1982; Kopytoff 1981).

Several structural factors contributed to the constant reshuffling of the Grassfields population. Perhaps the most important of these was the uneven distribution of resources and products in the region and the resultant development of local and regional trade. Palm oil and iron were the major items in complementary distribution on the plateau or between the plateau and surrounding lowlands, but a variety of other goods were traded in conjunction with or in exchange for these primary items. In general, oil, salt, cloth, and guns moved against iron, foodstuffs, craft items, and slaves (see Warnier and Nkwi 1982; Warnier 1985). Those kingdoms that had the manpower to produce and transport agricultural and craft surpluses and to establish and defend markets and trade routes between the strategic mountain passes competed for control over the increasingly lucrative trade in the region. Thus the desirability of creating and maintaining alliances and trade partnerships in neighboring kingdoms or of occupying interstitial positions between oil- and iron-producing areas provided an impetus to movement and admixture on the plateau.

The "winner-take-all" system of positional succession[1] and inheritance practiced over much of the Grassfields also tended to encourage relocation, as disinherited brothers and half-brothers sought elsewhere for opportunities denied them in their natal kingdoms (*c.f.*, Brain 1972; Hurault 1962; Tardits 1960). Finally, reports of the rich Grassfields trade attracted the attention first of the Ba'ani (Chamba) and later of Fulani slave raiders from the north. The pressure exerted by these groups and their local partners on the plateau greatly exacerbated the processes of movement and admixture, as populations decimated or displaced by repeated raids sought the protection of better situated or more powerful chiefs.

By the end of the nineteenth century there were four relatively large petty conquest states (Nso, Kom, Bafut, and Bali-Nyonga) on the Bamenda Plateau. Smaller chiefdoms, if they wished to protect their interests in the regional trade, had to form loose, shifting confederations. Failing this, they could only retreat to more defensible locations in the vastness of the surrounding escarpment, or run the risk of incorporation into one of the larger kingdoms. Elsewhere (Engard 1988), I have suggested that this tripartite scheme—small chiefdoms, confederations, large kingdoms—which Warnier (1975) read synchronically, as a description of the "strategic ensemble" of the Western Grassfields at the moment of colonial contact, may also be read diachronically as a history of a particular kingdom, such as Bafut. Bafut, in the equally schematic form of myth, view their history as a passage through three such stages or movements. I will now summarize their myth to show how the Bafut conceptualize their own part in these regional processes and to introduce the reader to several key players whose successors, many generations later, are still involved in a carefully choreographed struggle around which this analysis is built.[2]

The Myth

Arriving in the Bafut area, Agha'anjoo and his people found the ridges on either side of the central depression, or *mumala'a* (the inside of the country), already occupied. On the Ntara Ridge, to the west of the depression, were the Mbebeli, the supposed original settlers of the area, and the Bawum, who had arrived only a generation or two earlier. To the east, in the hills overlooking the upper Menchum River valley, were the Buwe, also recently arrived, and perhaps by this time their neighbors the Bukari as well. Agha'anjoo deferred initially to Neba'atsi, chief of the Mbebeli, and received permission to settle his people on the Ntara Ridge. A loose confederation between Mbebeli, Bawum, and Agha'anjoo's people was established, with Neba'atsi as *primus inter pares*.

Neba'atsi, however, proved to be a very close-fisted ruler. He did not entertain his nobles in a manner befitting their status, and he gradually lost respect and support among his people. It is said that the Mu Tikali ("the child of Tikar"), Agha'anjoo, on the other hand, was very generous and he used to invite the nobles of the country to his own compound when they left Neba'atsi's court hungry and thirsty. There he entertained them lavishly. Eventually, the nobles of the three chiefdoms hatched a plot whereby Agha'anjoo "stepped on the foot"[3] of Neba'atsi during the performance of the latter's Annual Dance, thereby deposing him. Neba'atsi, his sacred person defiled, hung himself, placing the earth in a dangerous state of ritual pollution (*atsawbuh*).

In a subsequent episode of the myth, a woman of the Mbebeli royal compound, Ndieu-ala'a (lit. "to show the country"), leaves the palace to fish in a nearby stream. Crossing the stream that divides the Ntara Ridge from the central depression (*mumala'a*), she climbs a low hill and discovers a broad, flat plain—the site of the present Bafut palace—which she realizes would make an ideal location for a new palace. Ndieu-ala'a duly reports her finding the *fon*'s council, and a delegation is sent out to survey the site. Ultimately, a new palace is built there.

But Ndieu-ala'a becomes haughty, demanding special considerations for herself and her family in return for her service. The councilors decide that her grumbling is dangerous and cannot be tolerated. She is lured to a throne placed near the new palace, where the daily market now stands. Unaware that the throne is poised above a deep pit, she sits in it and falls to her death (a death that recalls at once the burial of *fons* and the trapping of leopards, their familiars).

The Myth as Structural History

The myth is an accurate, if schematic, representation of the basic elements and processes of Bafut state formation. Bafut is a congeries of ethnically diverse groups. Over the past two centuries or so, a dozen previously independent small chiefdoms gradually have been incorporated, by force or guile, into the kingdom. Another twenty quarters have been built up by peaceful expansion from the older, central areas of the kingdom, and by incorporation of refugee lineage segments and slaves from outside the kingdom. All comers were welcomed by a powerful royal house seeking the agricultural labor and porterage upon which their trade in palm oil and foodstuffs was based, while seeking to undercut the authority of those previously independent chiefs in the area with claims to aboriginal status or historical primacy (see Warnier 1985 for a wider, regional interpretation of this process).

But this process of the building of the kingdom is perhaps most graphically revealed in the forms that are planted, buried, and built in the central dance grounds (*nsaa 'bin*) of each fully constituted quarter and subchiefdom within the kingdom. There, in the cleared space that is the ritual and political focus of the polity, stands a wild rubber tree (*wum*) whose health, growth, and bifurcation are synonymous with those of the quarter and its subdivisions, or *euyung* (branches).

The *wum* tree is said to have been ritually planted by the lineage heads of the earliest settlers of the quarter. In expansion quarters, the tree has usually been planted in an area previously set aside as the hunting grounds or thatching grass hills of a particular subchief but now officially open for permanent settlement by those who have been encroaching on the land to make bush farms. In this process, temporary shelters gradually become more numerous and substantial, until finally the emerging community requires recognition and representation as a polity in its own right. The size of the trees thus serves as a rough index of the age of these subchiefdoms and quarters, and of the order in which they have been either incorporated into or constituted within the kingdom.

When the time comes to constitute an expansion area as a fully recognized quarter, the princes of the royal regulatory society (*takumbung*) are called in to construct a small, doorless, and windowless thatched shrine or "house," called *nduruh,* after the slit-gong or calling drum which sometimes sits on its stoop. This "house," constructed to one side of the dance ground, has become the icon of the princes' fraternity, even though the original form of the shrine comes from Buwe. Buwe is a small, formerly independent subchiefdom on the periphery of the kingdom, and it harbors (along with Mbebeli) a claim to historical primacy, or at least to very early settlement in the area. At Buwe, the *nduruh* was the symbol of a local antiwitchcraft society (*mbabo*) with regulatory functions. When Buwe was subjugated, the palace incorporated the shrine form and other symbols of the society into the sacra, or sacred items which are the "voice" of the royal regulatory society.

In such cases, the palace does not actually disband preexisting regulatory institutions, dismantle their shrines, or take all of their sacra. In theory, they need only acquire a single item or instrument of sacra: a long laurel leaf spear blade (*nukang*) for *mbabo;* an iron double gong (*ngkuh*) for *kwifon* (the main commoner regulatory society); a two-tone bamboo flute (*luruh*) for certain prince's societies (*e.g., baguhlum*); or the masquerade of the herald of any such society (see below). The item is then added to the sacra of the palace society, which becomes, by royal dogma, the "parent" society. The local society of the subjugated polity continues to operate, but its sphere of operations is reduced. It can "come out" only during daylight hours, whereas the palace society comes out at night. The local society becomes an affiliated branch of its palace counterpart, and the palace society in turn is incorporated into one or the other of the main palace regulatory societies (*takumbung* or *kwifon*) as an internal subsociety or "house," each with its own particular function. This is, in a somewhat simplified form, how many of the plethora of regulatory, medicine, mortuary, and entertainment societies come to be housed within the palace.

This gradual incorporation is also part and parcel of the process in which the influence of the older, formerly independent chiefdoms and important descent group heads within the kingdom has eroded gradually, as that of immigrants has increased. To the spears, gongs, flutes and masquerades of the older chiefdoms have been added those brought by important princes who left neighboring chiefdoms for Bafut after the disputed succession of a brother. (In fact, the present *primus inter pares* of the inner circle of Bafut *kwifon* is the second generation descendant of such an immigrant prince.) Thus the orchestra or "voice" of palace *kwifon* is composed of half a dozen or so large double gongs and a number of smaller ones, each, in theory, identifiable with a particular subchiefdom or group of immigrants within the kingdom. But although *kwifon* members readily divulge this fact, they refuse to identify specific instruments with their polities of origin, as this would defeat the unifying purpose of their combination.

All of these symbols of authority—including the small thatched shrine (*nduruh*) which stands beside the dance ground of each fully constituted polity in the kingdom—fall into the general category of "king things," (*njoo nufoa* or *njoo nto'o,* lit. "things of chiefship" or "things of the palace"). The most important of these symbols is the right to hold an Annual Dance, usually symbolized or embodied by an ensemble of two-tone bamboo flutes (*luruh*) which give the Dance its name, Lela or Abin Luruh (Dance of the Flutes). The choreographed positions of the dancers indicate their political relations to the *fon* and to each other. It is highly significant that the myth represents the beginning of the shift from confederacy to kingdom as Agha'anjoo "stepping on the foot" of Neba'atsi *within the context of* his Annual Dance.

It is also highly significant that precisely at this point the third confederate, the *ntoh* (subchief, lit. "go-between") of Bawum, drops out of the events of the myth, to be replaced by a group of nobles or councilors. (I will return to the *ntoh,* or rather to his present day successor, in the case study below.) It is the councilors who, responding to the close-fisted behavior of Neba'atsi and the pointedly opposed generosity of Agha'anjoo, choreograph the demise of the autochthonous ruler and his replacement by the stranger. Neba'atsi's place in the plot is taken, in turn, by Ndieu-ala'a ("a woman of the palace"), whose action of relocating the palace from the Ntara Ridge to the central depression represents the completion of the transformation of the confederation into a centralized kingdom. This action subtly represents a shift from a relation between more or less autonomous federated chiefdoms toward the current tripartite internal organization of a fully constituted Grassfields kingdom (on the model of Tikar): the *fon* (king), his "council" (representing the estate of the commoners, and their regulatory society, *kwifon*), and Ndieu-ala'a (representing the royal estate).[4]

The personal rebellion represented in these episodes, Agha'anjoo's usurpation of Neba'atsi's place within the confederation, actually represents a revolution—that is, a fundamental change in the order of sociopolitical relations and in the dominant pattern of economic relations. A loose confederation of more or less autonomous small chiefdoms becomes a centralized kingdom; relations ordered largely by membership in descent groups become increasingly territorially based. At the same time, the scale and character of relations of production and distribution is transformed.

Bafut, under the old order, was an economic microcosm—and still is an ecological microcosm—of the region. Before the putative arrival of Agha'anjoo in the Bafut area perhaps two centuries ago, the economy was fueled by the exchange of the complementary primary products between the people occupying the hills on either side of the then empty central depression: Buwe-Bukari palm oil for Mbebeli iron implements. The relocation of the palace turned the old order "outside-in," as it were. Thereafter, the previously autonomous small groups in the area become increasingly subservient to and dependent upon the emerging central authority—Agha'anjoo and his people (the so-called Feurlu dynasty). In their myth, the Bafut represent these incorporated strangers as generous, or as knowing the civilizing virtues of reciprocity. They transform Bafut from a scattered, inward-looking collection of small polities exchanging goods only among themselves, to an outward-looking unity exchanging across the region.

"Cooling the Earth"

So much for the Dance as it appears within the context of the myth. In life, the Dance can only occur as part of an elaborate ritual cycle spanning the length of the dry season. Beginning with the laying of specially medicated ropes across all roads entering the kingdom, the stages of the annual cycle close, step by step, inward—from the boundaries of the kingdom and its various quarters and subchiefdoms to the dance grounds of each of these internal polities, to the streams which surround the seven quarters of the central depression, and finally to the palace dance ground and the palace compound itself. Space limitations preclude a full description of the entire cycle here (see Engard 1986), but enough must be said to establish clearly the character and effect of the rites. Most important are the divinatory offerings (*ma'a bunwi,* "to give to the gods") made at the sacred pools (*euchum*) where the deceased *fon*s are said to dwell. Successful conclusion of these rites (often referred to as "going to get the Dance") culminates in the sacrifice of a black ram (*baw 'bin,* "to mold the

Dance") at the palace dance ground, immediately preceding the beginning of the first evening of the Dance (described below).

The ritual cycle is concerned first with closing the kingdom off from the outside world. Concomitant with this process is the idea of fertility and increase. All rites of protection (*ma'a bunwi*) against or exorcism (*mfee nu,* lit. "to untie the thing") of witches are also attempts to procure witchcraft's opposites: health, strength, vitality, fertility, growth, good fortune, and increase in general. Usually the mimetic acts and incantations of the rites refer explicitly to both aspects.

In the first phase of the *takumbung* rites (*mfee nu*) performed at each quarter's dance ground, a bundle of ashes taken from the hearth of the quarter's first settlement is distributed among participants and collectively dispersed by blowing it downwind. Immediately following this mimetic dispersal of evil and proliferation of children, red camwood powder (representing blood, strength, and the continuity of descent groups) and a salty, white clay powder, *mborasuh*—from *mboruh* (peace), are placed on the basalt monolith (*neuba'a* or *ntseu,* from the verb "to establish") which stands amid the roots of the *wum* tree planted by the founders of the quarter and marks the original *takumbung* sacrifices made at the time of the formal constitution of the quarter.[5] White palm wine (representing semen) is poured over the stone and into the (female) earth, amid requests that the coming year be prosperous, that crops should grow, women bear children, and the regulatory institutions (the secret societies) of the country remain strong.

The Bafut interpret the cumulative effects of all of these offerings (particularly the blood of the black ram) as "cooling the earth" (*sugutuh nsie*). *Nsuguh* (the infinitive of *sugutuh*) literally means "to go down," and by extension, "to reduce" or "diminish." Cooling, here as elsewhere, such as in offering drink to a visitor, implies a reduction of tension, the establishment of peace and harmony. White things especially have this quality: outside the sacrificial context, the white clay powder (*mborasuh*) is often given to sick children to quiet their crying so that they may sleep peacefully, and palm wine is offered to anyone showing signs of agitation, hurry, or anger "to cool his heart," to make it "go down."

Red things, by contrast, relate to heat, which is associated with exertion, strength, and power—except for the blood of the black ram (*mbii njuruh*), which is pointedly opposed, in the context of the *baw 'bin* sacrifice, to that of the goat (*mbii ndong*). (Black ram's blood—coolness—is sacrificed during the climax of the ritual in peacetime; goat's blood—

heat—is sacrificed during wartime.) The white man is called *mu bang* or *ngu bang* ("red child" or "red person") not because of his complexion, but because of the technical mastery he displays in subjugating native peoples and the bounds of space and time.

At the same time that peace and power are invested in the earth through the rituals of the state cult, a similar set of rituals, also called *mfee nu* ("to untie the thing"), occurs within the context of descent groups, and is accomplished with a similar array of symbols. The essential act of the lineage practice of *mfee nu* is the discussion and adjudication of any disputes which may have developed between lineage members over the course of the year. Once all grievances have been thoroughly aired, and consensus has been achieved among members on each issue, all present, and especially the disputants, drink sweet palm wine from the drinking horn (*ndongnuh*) of the lineage head while he proclaims the new state of affairs. The Annual Dance is thus ideally a time when all those who have been outside the kingdom return to renew their relations. It is also the time for contracting marriage alliances and performing marriage ceremonies, and for the ritual exchange of visits and gifts of food between in-laws.

The argument I am developing here is that the Annual Dance is best understood as a particular kind of "performative utterance" on the model offered by Austin (1962) and his followers, especially Searle (1969, 1979). As Gardner (1983) has convincingly demonstrated, however, this is a claim that, although frequently made—particularly in the case of ritual—has often done a certain amount of violence to the concept. It will therefore be necessary to take a brief look at this deceptively simple idea before returning to the Dance.

On the Performativity of Performance

A *performative utterance,* far from merely describing an existing state of affairs, actually brings that state into being, as, in the most often cited example: "I do thee wed," and "I now pronounce you man and wife." Within any utterance, three separate acts may be distinguished. The term *locutionary act* describes the act of producing the utterance itself. The central term, *illocutionary act,* describes the particular "speech act" accomplished by that utterance. Thus, in the example above, "I do thee wed" is a "commissive" speech act; *I now pronounce you man and wife* is a "declaration." Finally, the term "perlocutionary act" describes the reaction (intended or otherwise) evoked in the hearer by the speaker's illocutionary act.

Austin's original insight is a simple one: performative utterances ("I hereby . . .") cannot be adequately analyzed as sayings—that is, in terms of whether the propositions they contain are true or false—but must instead be understood as actions, or in terms of what they *do*. To many students of ritual and spoken art engaged in the analysis of what have long been understood as "expressive acts" (actions understood as *sayings*), this insight seemed to offer a possible solution, or at least an escape from the problem of the supposed "prelogical mentality" of magical acts. Thus rituals could be viewed not in terms of the efficacy of their acts, grounded in the truth or falsity of underlying notions of causation, but rather, somewhat on the model of the marriage ceremony, in terms of what is accomplished *by definition* in the performance of those acts.

Unfortunately, as Gardner correctly pointed out, in the rush to reformulate their material in the terms of this briefly fashionable concept, many analysts neglected a warning that Austin and Searle had taken considerable pains to make clear. For performative utterances (or acts) to achieve, by definition, the ends they are designed to achieve, there must be a preexisting set of social conventions setting forth the conditions within which the utterance or action may be said to accomplish those ends. Thus, following the matrimonial example, the officiant must be properly ordained or appointed, the participants must not be too close kin and must have acquired a license, there must be a witness, and so forth. If and only if these and other preparatory conditions have been fulfilled, the properly performed vows and pronouncements may be said to *constitute* the state of matrimony. Thus, for an act to be performative in the required sense, it must be *constitutive of* a new state of relationships.

Neglect of the necessary connections between performativity and preexisting conventions leads, in turn, to the conflation of the three basic concepts defined above, in particular to the assumption that the correct performance of an illocutionary act necessarily entails the appropriate or desired response from the hearer. However, as Gardner (1983) correctly observed, "the locutionary and illocutionary acts performed in the production of an utterance under particular circumstances is fixed by that utterance in a way that the perlocutionary act is not" (p. 348). One can specify the conditions under which, for example, a request or an order will be understood as such by properly socialized hearers; but one cannot so readily predict that properly formed requests will be complied with, or orders followed. (And such a formulation leaves aside the multitude of questions concerning the *manner* in which requests may be fulfilled, and orders followed, etc.—a concept that was richly explored in the "trans-linguistics" of V. N. Voloshinov 1973.) To return to the familiar example, the correctly performed vows and pronouncements of the wedding ceremony may in fact bring the state of matrimony into existence. But not all of the witnesses will react to the new state of affairs in the same way.

Between Ritual and Dance

In applying the notion of performativity to the Dance then, I should note that the Bafut make an important terminological distinction between the Dance itself and the ritual activities which bracket it. Conventional definitions of ritual as nontechnological activity and distinctions between ritual and ceremony by their reference to nonempirical beings (Goody 1961; Gluckman 1962; Turner 1967, etc.) are not helpful in understanding the Bafut distinction between ritual and the Dance. First, as Gardner (1983) pointed out, these definitions depend upon *our* assessment of what is or is not technological, and second, both the rituals and the Dance are grounded in mystical or nonempirical relations—to ancestors, witches, and gods in the ritual, the *fon* and royal cult ancestors in the Dance.

The rituals, whether of propitiation and divination (*ma'a bunwi,* "to give to the gods") or of prophylaxis and exorcism (*mfee nu,* "to untie the thing") are material attempts to establish desired states. As Gardner reminded us, that the agencies involved in the ritual are nonempirical and that some of the links in the causal chain of rites and their supposed effects are unobservable do not make these acts performative in Austin or Searle's sense (*cf.* Tambiah 1973). The ends of Bafut ritual (making peace and conferring power) are not established automatically through the mere act of properly performing the rites. The clearest indication of this is that the rites of the annual cycle sometimes fail to establish the propitious conditions—the divinatory aspect of the *ma'a bunwi* offerings at the pools, where the priests go to propose a date for the Dance to the Gods, means that the acceptance of the offerings is not a foregone conclusion. The priests can return from the pools without the (confirmed date for the) Dance.

In the dry season of 1982–83, the Annual Dance of Babanki Tungo was not held, as it has not been held for some years now, because the *fon* was still a minor and had not as yet produced children of his own. No amount of ritual action could change his (and, by extension, the earth's) infertile state or define it out of existence. Similarly, in Bali-Nyonga in the same year, an untimely boundary dispute with the neighboring chiefdom of Meta, reportedly involving the death of a young girl, demonstrated that the rituals, in progress for some weeks, had failed to achieve peace. The earth was not sufficiently "cool," and the Dance could not be held.

Ritual is thus a necessary but not in itself sufficient means of establishing the conditions under which the Dance may occur. At the same time that the rituals and the Dance are thus closely linked, they are also carefully separated. The essential act of *baw 'bin* ("to mold the Dance") is the blood sacrifice of the black ram. Before and during this sacrifice, the area around the palace dance ground is cleared and kept clear by the *fon*'s retainers, who place injunction signs across all roads entering the palace grounds. Only the initiated male nobles (*bukum*) of the kingdom may witness and participate in this event. Women, children, and the general public are strictly forbidden entry to the area, although they wait not far away for the Dance itself to begin.

Immediately upon conclusion of the sacrifice, even as the bleeding carcass of the animal is dragged from the dance ground, the drumming begins and a line of the *fon*'s wives file out of the palace and form the central spiral of the choreographic pattern of the Dance. The transition from the ritual to the Dance is in fact so swift that it would be almost imperceptible to a casual observer who had not witnessed these events before. And that is part of the point: there are no casual observers here. I was not permitted to witness these events in my first year of fieldwork and had to be initiated into and participate in them as a kind of honorary noble to be present at all during the second year. (Even then, I was expressly forbidden to film the events.) The rituals of the annual cycle are carefully bounded in time and space, and participation is restricted to narrowly defined categories of people; within the choreography of the Dance, ideally, a place is found for every member of the kingdom (and, as I shall describe below, part of the business of the Dance is precisely to establish those places).

The emic distinction between the rituals which bracket the Dance (*ma'a bunwi* or *mfee nu*) and the Dance itself (*abin*) is instructive. I must agree with Gardner that, in both the Mianmin and Bafut cases, ritual, however symbolic its means, is from the actors' perspective a direct attempt at material causation, and that, therefore, the concept of performativity does not apply to the ritual procedures. But I will argue that the Dance itself is *constitutive* of states of relationship in the politico-jural domain and is therefore performative.

The Constitutionality of Dance

Dance in Bafut is, as I have shown, constitutional in at least two senses. First, the fact of possession of an annual dance is no mere trapping of political office; along with the possession of regulatory societies, it is an essential element in the legitimate constitution of chiefship (*nufoa*): it is one of the "king things" (*njoo nufoa*). Second, the choreography of a legitimately held Annual Dance indexes the participants' political relations to the *fon,* chief, or subchief, and through him to each other. Yearly changes in these positions are the official recognition of the movements of individuals through the status hierarchy. This involves more than the representation of preexisting relations. In holding his Dance, the chief or subchief performs an illocutionary act; he proclaims, in effect, that for the coming year, this is the operational order of relations. This much is automatic (or conventional), and to take one's place in the widening spiral is to ratify the new (or renewed) state of affairs—to make a kind of collective New Year's resolution to uphold and act within the confines of this order.

A case that occurred during my fieldwork illustrates an important corollary to the manner in which the palace appropriates "king things" (such as the thatched shrine or *nduruh*) in the process of subjugating and incorporating peripheral polities into the expanding center. These "things of the palace," once co-opted, become available for redistribution to yet other polities, such as expansion quarters that are being elevated by the palace to subchiefdom status. For example, Mankwi, a quarter that had developed through expansion from older polities in the kingdom and immigration of "stranger" lineages from outside, had been elevated to subchiefdom only in one generation before my visit, by the father of the present *fon* of Bafut. A "Chapter" of *mbabo* (a regulatory society) was given to the new subchief, Talah Mankwi, at the time of his enstoolment.

Today, the polarity of Bafut is changing. The southeastern expansion quarters of the kingdom (esp. Nsem-Agyati), once opposed to the area around the palace as bush is to town, are emerging as the center of modern administration, while the palace remains the seat of traditional government. In the weeks before the Bafut Annual Dance of 1982–83, the *fon,* through his *kwifon,* announced his decision to elevate the quarter of Nsem to the status of subchiefdom. One of the quarter-heads of Nsem, a high-ranking national civil servant living outside the kingdom, was chosen to assume the title of subchief (*atangcho*). He was transferred promptly back to the Northwest Province, and in short order the princes of the royal regulatory society, *takumbung,* began the ritual activities that would constitute the quarter as a subchiefdom, and transform the quarter-head's compound into its palace.

They built the small, thatched shrine (*nduruh*) of *takumbung* and buried the appropriate sacrifices nearby. For their services they received fees (palm wine, fowls, goats, etc.) from the new subchief designate, and only when these had been distributed, amidst much drinking and feasting, was the last item, a small raffia bag, turned over by the ranking princes. It contained the sacra, the bamboo flutes and wicker rattles of Mandele, a Dance "owned" or held by the palace, which was henceforth to be the Annual Dance of the now *atangcho* (subchief) of Nsem. The princes instructed the new *atangcho*'s retainers in the correct sequencing and timing in which the two-tone flutes were to be played to produce the distinctive music of Mandele, and they practiced for the day in early December when the first Annual Dance of Nsem would be performed.

Although the *fon*'s Dance (Abin Mfo or Abin Lela) is generally conceived of in royal dogma as a composite form—an accumulation of parts "invented" by each succeeding *fon*—it contains elements appropriated from the dances of other subchiefs (which, by now, are remembered as always having been "things of the palace").[6] It happens that the new *atangcho*'s Dance, Mandele, was originally co-opted from Bawum, one of the old subchiefdoms of the Ntara Ridge, at the time that Bawum was incorporated into the kingdom. In the myth recounted above, one of the three original members of the confederation that was established at the time of the arrival of Agha'anjoo (the putative founder of the present dynasty) was none other than the *ntoh* (subchief) of Bawum. I interpreted the replacement of the *ntoh* of Bawum in the story by a group of nobles or a council as representing the transformation of the confederation into a centralized kingdom. One of the consequences of such a transformation is the reduction in status and the loss of autonomy of the previously independent petty chiefs, who become subchiefs under the new regime.

The decision that, in effect, gave the Dance of the *ntoh* of Bawum to the new *atangcho* (subchief) of Nsem must have been very pointed (although the *fon*, with a wry smile, will say only that Mandele has always been a favorite dance of his). The *ntoh* of Bawum has long been a thorn in the side of the *fon* of Bafut. He is known to have supported the *fon*'s chief rival for power during the contested succession of the late 1960s. He continues to press traditional claims to ownership of large sections of the quarters in the southeastern expansion area (Nso-Agyati-Nsem), even though the palace has constituted these areas as independent quarters. He hopes ultimately to regain these lost hunting lands and thatching grass hills (categories of land which are also *njoo nufoa,* "things of chiefship"), obtain recognition of Bawum as an independent chiefdom, and secede from Bafut altogether.

When Nsem, the emerging seat of modern administration, was elevated, undercutting the *ntoh* of Bawum's influence in the south, Ndifo, the *fon*'s titled elder brother and one-time chief rival for the throne, was also transferred back to Bafut from the coast, where he had been assigned as a teacher ever since the abdication and reinstallation of his brother, the present *fon*. Once back, Ndifo was made paramount quarter-head in Nso, further weakening *ntoh* Bawum's influence in the south of the kingdom. (As ranking prince in the royal regulatory society, Ndifo was also prominent in the ceremonies surrounding the enstoolment of the new *atangcho* of Nsem.) The *fon* had thus simultaneously consolidated his reign and carried out a modern reorganization of the kingdom, using his (now reconciled) former rival against his chief adversary in the bargain.

Further, this political maneuver was neatly timed to coincide with the presentation by the national government, through its district offices, of certificates of grade two chieftancy (the level of subchiefs within a kingdom) to the subchiefs of the larger Grassfield kingdoms, and to the chiefs of small independent chiefdoms. Thus Nsem received official recognition of its chiefship from the palace and the national government on the same day, the day of their first Annual Dance. A number of the other subchiefs of the kingdom were also on hand to receive their own certificates and to participate in the Dance that followed, thereby ratifying the implicit and explicit political statements being made; the *ntoh* of Bawum was conspicuously absent. He had, several days prior, contrived to bring the new district officer (a Bakweri man, who could not have known what he was walking into) to Bawum, where he presented the *ntoh* with his own certificate of chieftancy, which enabled him to avoid the events at Nsem described above. The pretext contrived by the *ntoh* was the performance of his own Annual Dance—Mandele!

The Dance of State

The fourth day of the Bafut Annual Dance (Bukwara Bumanjong)[7] is a great collective event in which the royalty, nobility, and honored guests of the kingdom array themselves on the palace dance ground like pieces at the start of a chess game. The military societies (*bumanjong*), once the militia of the kingdom, now voluntary associations engaged in its development, surround the field with their Dane guns (locally made flintlock rifles) awaiting the distribution of gunpowder from the palace stores. The general public, dressed in fine embroidered robes if they have them and tie-dyed tunics and shifts or modern dress if they do not, also fall in along the circumference of the dance ground, near their respective quarters' *manjongs* (military societies, now functioning mostly in ceremonial contexts).

Once the powder has been distributed and all available Dane guns are loaded, the *fon* signals the beginning of the climax of the Dance by striding to the middle of the field and firing the first shot. Great volleys of answering fire ensue as all *manjongs* and other citizens who have guns fire in unison, reload to advance upon the reviewing stand, and fire each in turn, dancing and posturing as though stalking some unseen enemy, waving salutes and presenting arms to the *fon*. When all *manjong* clubs have taken their turn, individuals and small groups of twos and threes come to fire and present before the *fon* in a great demonstration of strength of arms and fealty to the kingdom. Gradually the firing subsides and the day's dancing may begin.

The dancing literally revolves around a small group of princes and retainers who play the sacred blue and white beaded bamboo flutes (*luruh* or *lela*), which will later be laid, along with offerings of camwood, *mbo-rasuh* (white clay and salt), and palm wine, upon the graves of the deceased *fons*. They are accompanied by long, hourglass-shaped drums, pedestal drums, elephant tusk trumpets, wicker rattles, whistles, and the great slit-gong from the steps of the palace *takumbung* shrine. Around the orchestra, the *fon*'s wives form the central spiral, the tail of which is left open so that others may join on at the end, and so that the *fon* and his entourage of ranking nobles may enter. The *fon,* titled princes (Ndifo, Muma, Sama, Njoofor), the elders of *kwifon,* and important subchiefs enter the center of the widening spiral like offerings swirling into the vortex of the sacred whirlpools, while lesser notables join the lengthening eddy swirling outward behind the wives. The general public dance concentric rings counter-clockwise around this spiral.

When the climactic day of the 1982–83 Annual Dance arrived, Ndifo, the *fon*'s elder titled brother (and one-time rival) was, for the first time in years, in his proper place beside the *fon,* on his right hand. *Atangcho* Bonifor, the new subchief of Nsem, was at the head of the row of subchiefs to the *fon*'s left. The ranking princes and nobles of the regulatory societies, the Queen Mother, the *fon*'s wives, princesses, retainers, priests, military clubs, and commoners were all in their customary places, recreating in the Dance the ideal order of Bafut society. *Ntoh* Bawum was again conspicuously absent.

From Abin to Ko: The Society Heralds and Terror Masks

The use of both regulatory and dance societies as constituting elements of chiefship *njoo nufoa* ("king things") raises the question of the relationship between them. The Annual Dances (Abin) are great collective ceremonies with large numbers of participants, but another broad category of dance performance must also be considered here: the costume or masquerade dance societies called by the general term *muko,* rendered in pidgin throughout the Grassfields and beyond as "*ju-ju.*" This general category contains a wide variety of subtypes, including *musingkee* (the dances of pre-adolescent girls), many kinds of *njang* (the dances of adult women), *neulong* (the so-called string bands of men), mock military dances like *sambaa,* the various local versions of *kwa-kwa,* in which virtually all of the adult men of the community may join, and the masquerade dancers, who are the archetype for the term *muko.*

I will not give here a full description of the many exuberant masquerade dance societies now operating in Bafut. (Indeed, further research will be required to construct an adequate typology.) But several of the more important of these dances bear mentioning here, because they form a kind of transitional category between the Annual Dances (Abin), an element in the constitution of chiefship, and the common funerary or entertainment societies (*muko,* lit. "dancers"), which are not directly involved in the conferment of such status. (I say they are "not directly" involved, because, as I will show below, their possession and performances are part of the overall political economy of prestige that I am describing here.)

Bugwa'acho is a society owned and operated by the princes, a "thing of the palace." But in addition to the "chapter" that operates out of the palace, other *bugwa'acho* societies are owned by a half dozen other people in the kingdom, all of whom are either subchiefs or descendants of ranking titled princes. Thus it functions as the closest thing to an Annual

Dance of Mbaa, the subchief (*wangki*) of Mambu—one of the largest and oldest subchiefdoms on the southern Ntara Ridge. Another chapter is owned by Moses Asanji, who, as fourth generation successor to the Ndifo (titled elder brother and head of the royal lineage) of the *fon* Seulum, is a ranking member of the inner circle (*nda ngghura,* lit. "house of the sasswood ordeal") of *kwifon.* Although on some special occasions all seven existing *bugwa'acho* societies perform together at the palace, the Mambu claim to have acquired them originally from a distant Bamiléké group. It seems likely that this is another of those institutions (like the Buwe *nduruh* shrine or Bawum Mandele dance) that have been appropriated and redistributed as part of the process of constitutional politics outlined above.

It also seems likely that the present profusion of masquerades in Bafut is a historical outgrowth of the development and spread of strong regulatory societies to police the markets of the Grassfields (*cf.* Kaberry and Chilver 1968). Each of the two main palace regulatory societies may manifest itself in public (*mfe'e,* lit. "come out") on different occasions in the guise of one or another of its internal subsocieties, depending on the particular function being exercised. For instance, when six or seven members of *kwifon* go to the eight-day market to make public announcements (of levies of communal labor or materials by territorial quarter, for example) on behalf of the *fon* and the *kwifon,* they are accompanied by the herald Mubu'u. Members of the society "come out" to place injunctions (iconic notices of prohibitions or fines) against those who fail to meet communal obligations. The herald, *mbabo muwura* (*mbabo* of oil) leads them in this duty if the miscreant has failed to pay his palm oil tax, and *mbabo mulu'u* (*mbabo* of wine) leads in the confiscation of wine from local tappers to reward communal labor parties (members of the quarter called out by the palace or the quarter heads to provide free labor for public works projects).

The appearance of these heralds is generally uniform, although there are a number of variations. They usually wear a dirty brown, coarsely woven body shirt of raffia fiber with a hood which covers the entire head and face tightly, like a stocking mask. The hood is tight enough and the mesh loose enough to suggest the features of the human face without revealing the wearer's identity. The overall effect is one of menace. Any speculation as to who might be behind the mask is discouraged (though all present may in fact know). Most people maintain that despite the figure's bare arms and legs, the animating force is not human at all. This is to be expected, since an important function of society masquerades is to reduce or eliminate personal accountability in the exercise of power by interposing a supernatural barrier, or at least a veil of secrecy, between the people and their regulatory institutions (Nkwi, personal communication).

Each version of the costume of the herald incorporates its own identifying insignia. *Mbabo* carries a spear and a knife which it taps together rhythmically as it goes. Mubu'u has, in addition to a row of cowries sewn like buttons down the front of its body shirt, a wrought iron spear, the shaft of which connects a series of iron bells that jangle as it walks. Mabu'u, the usual herald of *kwifon* when the society comes out in full, wears a multicolored cape of layered feathers, and a bush cow or antelope helmet mask. *Takumbung*'s herald, "the running *ju-ju,*" carries two raffia staves, which it swings and beats together in irregular fashion. Other objects, such as bamboo or palm leaves, may be added to identify the dispatching agent and indicate the nature of the errand. All heralds have a whistle, held in the mouth, through which they "cry" softly and continuously. They never speak.

The appropriate attitude toward one of these masquerades is avoidance. In the case of Mabu'u, which heralds the approach of *kwifon,* women and children must seek shelter indoors, shuttering up and locking the house or shop they enter until well after the society, playing its sacred array of iron double gongs, has passed. As the single file of *kwifon* elder-announcers led by Mubu'u approaches the market, women and children move off the road or path into the tall grass or bush. They turn away and kneel, one hand upon the knee, the other cupped before the mouth. These are the attitudes appropriate to the appearance of *fon*s, subchiefs, and, in less extreme form, ranking princes and nobles. One of the eeriest sensations I remember from my time among the Bafut is the sudden hush that falls over the bustling market when Mubu'u enters for the weekly announcements (*nsa'a mitaa,* lit. "to rule the market"). Silence is strictly enforced at such times.

Finally, some maskers are said to have carried out the police functions of the regulatory societies in times past. The archetype of these "terror masks" is Ko. Ko still makes its appearance in Bafut at the death celebrations of very high-ranking members of *kwifon,* whose coercive powers it represents. Among the identifying features of Ko are a squarish head—much larger than normal human proportions, fashioned of a black woolly material—which accentuates the impression of bulk and strength. Its "eyes" and other features are only very vaguely suggested; its features are much less human than those of the heralds. Its body covering, reaching almost to the ground, is a thickly layered coat of raffia fiber, so that, as the figure whirls about, the head appears to rotate upon a large, churning haystack. It carries two long clubs, which it alternately walks upon and swings threateningly at its attendants. (Ko and its congeners are sometimes referred to as "the one that goes on all fours.")

Ko's attendants hold it, with much apparent difficulty, on long ropes, winding the masked figure up when they seem to be gaining control, only to have it escape again, leaving them hanging on to the ropes as best they can as Ko drags them helplessly about. Part of the drama consists in seeing how much minor structural damage will be done to whose compounds as this grotesque figure charges about uprooting plantain trees and knocking down fences, before the attendants finally manage to subdue it and control its erratic motions. Spectators alternately approach with caution and flee in fright, as everyone seeks a good vantage point for the spectacle, but they never get so close that they cannot escape if the creature should lunge in their direction. Those who come too near may be knocked down, or tangled in the attendants' ropes. The risk of minor injury is real; there is no "performer" who will be held publicly responsible for the creature's excesses (although some such accountability may exist within the society, outside the context of the performance).

I saw Ko only once in Bafut, at the death celebration of the father of the Queen Mother (*mamfo*)—the *fon*'s father-in-law. This man had been the highest-ranking member of *kwifon*'s inner circle and therefore the highest-ranking commoner in the kingdom. The *fon* was present at his death celebration, the only such public event I know him to have attended during my stay. At the climax of Ko's performance, when its keepers had finally managed to wind it up in its ropes and subdue it, it was brought, grunting softly, to kneel in submission before the *fon:* the wild, destructive, outside force domesticated in the service of royal authority.

Although this embodiment of all that is feared and powerful in otherness "belongs" to palace *kwifon* (*i.e.,* is a "thing of the palace"), other "lesser" versions of the terror mask are to be found among the old subchiefdoms of the Ntara Ridge. In fact, in the previously independent subchiefdoms of both Ntara and Bu'unti (the Menchum Valley) there is usually one such funerary or "entertainment" society consisting of a single dancer and his attendants. This type usually does not have carved wooden masks, but it may wear the bushy feather headdress typical of the dance costumes of the region. The figure of the lead dancer often carries an unsheathed cutlass or other weapon, and among its attendants may be one man, bound, hooded, and stripped to the waist, who plays the role of a prisoner about to be executed by the dancer. This dance generally consists of nothing more than the repeated miming of an execution. In fact, spectators say that (like Ko) such societies were once the agents of capital punishment operating under the aegis of the local regulatory society, but that their most extreme punitive functions have since been taken over, first by the coercive apparatus of the kingdom, then by the colonial and modern states.

The Aesthetics of Power and Obedience

All *muko* (dancers) share certain basic common features. They are usually clothed in the same dirty brown, coarsely woven raffia body shirts as the regulatory society heralds. A hood tightly shrouds the face, like a stocking mask. Often the body shirt serves as the mesh foundation for a cape of feathers—sometimes arranged in striking, multicolored layers—or for a patchwork of short, closely spaced tufts of hair that form a pattern (*nyaleu*) said to be in imitation of the leopard's spots . More rarely (in high prestige societies like *bugwa'acho*) rich, blue dyed trade cloth (Idoma or Jokun, named for their kingdoms of origin) from the Benue markets, or a wax print substitute, may be wound about the waist and loins of the dancer, or held in train by attendants. Some kind of headdress—frequently a bushy profusion of long parrot feathers sewn into a raffia skull cap, or something as simple as a young cocoyam or other leaf pinned with a pointed stick onto the top of the hood—is almost always a feature of the costume. The archetype is a beautifully carved wooden animal head (elephant, bush cow, or leopard) or human head mask (usually of royalty) pinned and held with one hand atop the dancer's head. The group usually consists of six to eight dancers.

Muko dance to the rhythms produced on one to three sets of four-key wooden xylophones (*njang*), which are usually accompanied by one or more long, hourglass-shaped drums, and a bass drone cut from a length of bamboo or polyvinyl chloride. The dancers wear loud ankle rattles—fashioned from bundles of large, flat, circular seed casings from a forest tree—which add to the musical texture. The dancing is often quite athletic, requiring the performer to move in a series of short, quick, tightly spaced steps to what is often the limit of his endurance (only males dance masquerade dances), or, alternately, to execute balletic leaps and turns. The choreography is not often intricate (except in the dances of children) and usually consists of the circling movements or oscillation of a line of dancers (which might be called the chorus), countered by the more free-style movements of one or more lead dancers. Part of the aesthetic objective is to keep the ankle rattles (*bu'u muko*) in time or in syncopation with the rapid staccato rhythms of the xylophones and drums.

Bafut societies range in size from a single dancer and his attendants and musicians up to groups of a dozen or more. The larger groups tend to have more elaborate costumes—fully feathered capes, and the like—added to the basic body shirt, as well as animal and human masks worn on top of the simple hood. And in general, the more elaborate the costume, the larger the groups of musicians playing faster accompaniments, and the more frenetic and intricate the dancing. The musical accompaniment of the single-dancer groups is usually slow and measured (like a death march), and the physical virtuosity of the dancer is not emphasized. But when many groups of varying types perform, spectators tend (when asked) to rate these smaller, simpler groups above (or apart from) the others, seeing them as "strong" (*teuh*) or "powerful" (*mbang*), "real" or "authentic" (*jwe-jwe*). Such groups are often referred to in the local pidgins as "bad *ju-ju*s." (Compare this with "bad!" in American English slang.)

Observation of spectator reactions bears these statements out. The groups whose performances spectators so evaluate also elicit the most noticeable and pronounced audience reactions, which consist of avoidance behavior of the sort I described in connection with regulatory society heralds, *fon*s, and subchiefs. Such reactions, in at least token measure, are appropriate to virtually all masked dancers, but they are most exaggerated, and even enforced by initiated adult males in the case of those dancers who most closely resemble (or are) the heralds and terror maskers of the regulatory societies (which, having lost their more coercive functions, are increasingly limited to funerary or entertainment functions).

The masquerade dancers of entertainment societies and the herald and terror maskers of the regulatory societies are called by the same vernacular term—*muko* (or *ju-ju* in the local pidgins). Although these two synonymous terms might today be rendered "masked dancer," it seems likely that the forms incorporated in and the attitudes displayed toward such "entertainment" societies are a historical elaboration upon the herald and terror maskers, the impersonal representations of the authority and coercive power of the regulatory societies.

Muko (or *ju-ju*) societies are thought to be derived from outside sources—either brought to the area by a particular *fon* or subchief, or purchased from a distant kingdom. (As I have shown, to think of them as indigenous would be an implicit recognition of the claims of the older internal polities of the kingdom to historical primacy in the area.) The rise of the regulatory societies was concomitant with an "implosion" of "strangers and bought men" into Bafut in the mid-to-latter part of the nineteenth century (Kaberry and Chilver 1968: 51; *cf.* Warnier 1985). These strangers, lacking the support of a full complement of kin, became wards and retainers of the *fon* and they eventually became the preferred agents for staffing the regulatory societies, which were the nascent administrative bureaucracy. Their growth coincided with the waning power of descent group heads and subchiefs.[8]

*Muko (*Ju-Ju*) as Metaphor for the Powerful Outsider*

The widely used term *muko* (or *ju-ju*) has many connotations—items of Western technology, for instance, are commonly referred to as "*ju-ju.*" When such items are demonstrated, one often hears exclamations such as, "the white man is terrible!"—meaning that the object is "powerful" (*mbang*) or "strong" (*teuh*), something to be held in awe or fear, something toward which avoidance behavior is appropriate. Like the dancers, it is also a thing to be purchased and possessed more or less exclusively by its owner, conferring status and the stamp of legitimacy upon him. But whether applied to a masked dancer or a VCR, a *ju-ju* is something otherworldly, something from the outside.

The dancer's face is never quite recognizably human, even though it vaguely, unsettlingly, suggests human features. It may have the head of a powerful and dangerous wild animal, capable of bringing destruction, disorder, and death into human society.[9] Its body may be covered in feathers, grass, leaves, or hair. It is the wild, natural, creative force domesticated, brought dangerously but beneficially into the social realm, and into the service of authority, and even plays a part in the very process of constituting legitimate authority. All the while, though, it retains its essential otherness in the familiar setting. In the case of imposed or imported technology, too, "*ju-ju*" is the outside, unknown, creative, and potentially destructive force brought in.

I have shown that an Annual Dance (Abin), itself an element in the constitution of legitimate authority, can, also, under certain ritually established conditions, serve as an instrument in the periodic redefinition of political relations within the kingdom or subchiefdom. If Abin falls to the constitutional side of Bafut politics, the *muko,* or *ju-ju*s, related to and probably derived from masquerades with regulatory or social control functions, belong to the operational side.

New Guinea Models in the Cameroon Grassfields

In the Bafut prestige economy, lineage heads and other "big men" (*ngu wé,* sing.) act as foci for the accumulation and redistribution of material goods (such as goats, fowl, oil, cooked foods, palm wine, and, increasingly, European beer and cash). It is a system of unabashed influence peddling, encouraging considerable movement within a hierarchy predicated upon entry and advancement in a succession of secret societies. The Bafut system nicely accommodates upward mobility through the status hierarchy by opposing to it a "four generation rule" whereby status automatically falls one level in each succeeding generation; thus a fourth generation prince reverts to commoner status, although he may retain titles (which also, however, decline in power) acquired in his royalty. Under the system of positional succession, one may, if chosen as his father's successor, inherit membership in all of his father's societies, but it is entry-level membership, and comes with the understanding that one will make every attempt to reattain, and, ideally, surpass the father's levels in each society.

Lineage authority and support begin to translate into territorially based political power at the first level of society membership—that of quarter politics. With the help of lineage mates and close friends, a man, particularly the head of a prominent lineage, may periodically amass the necessary wealth to pay fees (*tsyaa* lit. "to pass" to secret societies). In time, as he becomes a more effective go-between (*ntoh*) for those who follow, the group of matrilateral relatives, affines, and unrelated clients who seek his patronage grows, and the resources he can command from supporters increase. The system of quarter politics somewhat resembles that of the New Guinea Highlands, but it does not result in the simple dissipation of wealth, and cannot be analyzed as an egalitarian "leveling mechanism." Rather, it is best seen, following Bourdieu (1977), as an exercise in the creation of symbolic capital.

Conspicuous consumption and display are important elements of this system. A great public feast demonstrates the willingness and ability of a lineage head or other big man to supervise redistribution and to serve as a broker for his people. In more than a figurative sense, he sets himself up (like Agha'anjoo in the myth) as a "father" willing to "feed his children."[10] He says, in effect, that he has set the community's interests above his own, and pledges to work tirelessly and visibly to guarantee public values.

The most important redistributive occasions are the death celebrations of important men, or even of minor figures in important lineages. The feeding and housing of hundreds of guests for days at a time requires considerable wine, food, and labor. But for an important "die," the heaviest expense is payment of the fees of the societies that must come. All regulatory, entertainment, or mortuary societies to which the "die man" belonged in life must attend, and each must be "fed,"—literally provided with food for the duration of their stay and with fees for the performance of rituals or dances, to be divided among the membership both on site and at subsequent meetings. (If, on this occasion, the family wishes to present itself as Christian, then fees must be paid to these "pagan" societies to keep them from coming to the event!) In addition, the lineage will contract as many other mortuary and entertainment societies as they can afford for the event.

It would be a mistake to minimize the extent to which this expense—and the display it makes possible—is borne in order to honor the deceased. It is said that if a death celebration is not done in a style that does justice to the deceased, he may "walk aimlessly in circles" (*ngkarakuh*), visiting misfortune, infertility, disease, and death upon his descendants. But there is a harmony between belief and necessity here; fear of the ancestor's posthumous wrath is a constraint that enables his descendants to glorify themselves as well. For the death celebration (the "second" or "good die") is also the occasion for naming the successor (*jeu nda,* lit. "he who eats the house"), who will bear his father's name and full social persona. A successful death celebration—a great feast with many important societies in attendance, much dancing, many supporters bringing food and firing their Dane guns—is an advertisement. In sponsoring it, the lineage and its supporters announce their willingness to continue to support the successor—that he, like his predecessor, will serve as an effective "father"/broker to those who have supported the lineage in the past. The lineage (like the *fon* or subchief on the climactic day of his Annual Dance) puts on a ritual show of force, displaying its numbers, its unity, its wealth, even its military prowess.

In short, at a practical political level, the celebration of death and succession (whether of the year or the individual) is the occasion *par excellence* for the public demonstration of strength and solidarity, and provides both the foundation for the pursuit of ever-wider territorial power and the impetus to engage in this pursuit. It is within these contexts that dancers (*muko*) most frequently perform and Dances (Abin) are held, and so it is within these contexts that they must be understood.

Conclusion

I cannot claim to have demonstrated conclusively here that what Herzfeld (1987) calls "an aesthetic of the social order" is applicable to Bafut. But I think the pervasiveness of certain recurring terms and concepts in the evaluation of dance performances and performances of the Dance—the concern with "strength" or "power" and "control" (*teuh, mbang, bu'u*) on the one hand and with "authenticity" (*jwe-jwe*) on the other—strongly suggest such an aesthetic order. The reader may have noticed the frequent recurrence of the root *bu'u* (to control) in connection with the following: Bu'unti, the name for the Menchum Valley; recently assimilated Menchum Valley polities raided for slaves (*bu'u,* sing.) and for tribute in oil, and which were ultimately incorporated into the kingdom; Mabu'u ("mother of control") and Mubu'u ("child of control"), the important heralds of the commoner regulatory society (*kwifon*); Abu'umbi ("he who controls the world"), the name of the present *fon* and his grandfather; and *bu'u muko,* the ankle rattles of the dancers, and the aesthetic principle of their performance.

I first learned this verb in connection with the process of palm oil production; in this context it describes the vigorous circular stirring motion that separates the oil from the water in which the kernels are boiled and brings it to the top of the stone-lined pits found along the streams of the central depression. The regional trade patterns (and thus the wealth of the royal houses of the major trading kingdoms of Bamenda) are founded on the vertical trade of palm oil for iron rods or rings (*abu'u,* lit. "circles of ore,") (Crozier 1980) and implements. These rings or "manillas" once served as a form of currency in the region, and the current word for money (*ngkabuh*), whose original meaning was "slave rope," is also related (*cf.* Warnier 1975). The image of swirling oil also recalls the whirlpools in which divinatory sacrifices are made to the royal cult ancestors when the "fathers of the grave shrine" (*butaa bu nufum*) "go to get the Dance" (*ma'a bunwi*), as well as the central spiral of the choreographic pattern of the Dance itself. The noun "circle" (*abu'u*) also derives from this verb. Although some examples of the pervasiveness of this word and image may be dismissed as fortuitous, enough remain to indicate clearly the relation between concentric circles and spirals, centrifugal and centripetal motion, and the idea of encirclement, enclosure and control (*cf.* Bird and Kendall 1980; Jackson 1977 on *badenya* and *fadenya* in Mande cosmology).

In Bafut, power is acquired and enhanced by effective management of a redistributive network of kin and clients. Dance, in the context of the feasting and ceremony that surround death, is part of a strategy for the creation of symbolic capital—the obligations which may be built up over time and periodically collected and fed into the secret society system as fees for further redistribution there, further enhancement of status, the accumulation of still other obligations, and so on. But to be recognized as authentic, power must be duly constituted; newly acquired political positions especially must be performed within the choreography of the Annual Dance; or, if the aspirant is being elevated to a level of chiefship (*nufoa*), his status will be constituted in the possession and performance of his own Annual Dance, conferred by the *fon* through the royal regulatory society. To be legitimate, order must be performed in the annual act of recreation of the kingdom.

The archetype for this reordering of a hierarchy through internal movement is Agha'anjoo—the outsider who, in moving inside, turned the old order inside-out. He overcame his subordinate position in the first instance by "feeding" people through effective redistribution. But the generosity of the outsider, although beneficial for those he "feeds," may be dangerous to the superordinate insider, as it was for the old chief, Neba'atsi. And how was the outsider's succession of the autochthonous ruler imaged? He "stepped on his foot" at the Annual Dance, thereby violating his sacred person during the very performance which was to have reconstituted his authority and making himself chief.

And just as Dance (Abin) plays its part in the constitution of chiefship, so chiefs, in their turn, must constitute dance societies (*muko*). The first official public performance of a newly created dance society must be a command performance before the *fon,* and it must be held on Mumitaa, the "country Sunday" of the eight-day week, upon which all previous *fon*s are held to have died (or "got missing," as they say). Similarly, at the final month-long death celebration for a *fon,* every dance society in the kingdom must perform or be banned forever.

Finally, as the case study presented above (of the *ntoh* of Bawum loosing exclusive possession of his Dance, Mandele, to the new *atangcho* of Nsem) makes clear, the figures of the myth still walk the earth, in the form of the positional successors who reincarnate them. The ancient power struggle continues today, and even though the elements and forces of the modern regional and state administration have been added to the equation, the idiom of Dance possession and choreography still defines changing relations.

Acknowledgements

I would like to thank the National Institute of Mental Health (PHS F31 MH 08485-01) for generously providing funds for the research on which this study is based. I would also like to thank Ivan Karp, Michael Herzfeld, Tony Seeger, Drid Williams, William Arens, Susan Diduk and Chris Geary for reading and commenting on earlier drafts. I should also thank participants in the Indiana University Anthropology Department Colloquium Series for suffering the original oral version. A later version was also read to the Smithsonian Institution Fellowship Seminar Series.

Notes

1. Positional succession, or "perpetual kinship," (Cunnison 1956), as it is practiced in the Highlands, means that the son chosen to succeed his father assumes the full social identity of the father. He assumes membership in all of the associations to which his father belonged in life, inherits his father's wives (including, in theory, his own mother), and acquires control over an estate which is essentially indivisible (with the exception of a few minor adjutant titles and personality items of the deceased). His "mothers" become his "wives," his siblings and half-siblings become his "sons" and "daughters," and so on. In theory, his relations and responsibilities toward all kin and clients of his father are the same as they were with the deceased (although there is, of course, wide personal latitude in many of these relations, and it may take some time for the new office-holder to prove that he can fill his father's shoes).

In important Bafut lineages, the sociological identity of the father and his successor are beautifully demonstrated in a mass naming ceremony, which occurs at the palace during the second celebration of the father's death (the so-called "good die"). One by one, or in small groups, all theoretically eligible men in the lineage bow before the *fon* to undergo a brief communion-like rite (*miia mfo*), during which each one receives a new name from the *fon* and the right to address him without speaking through an intermediary. Only in the moment when, instead of a new name, one of the initiates receives his father's name, do all assembled realize the identity of the successor. Thereupon the crowd hoists him onto their shoulders and begins a ritual procession back to the compound he has now inherited. All along the route from the palace to the compound, groups of neighbors, kin, clients and friends stop the procession to sing spontaneously or formulaically composed stanzas, often ribald and jokingly abusive in character, memorializing the events of the young man's "previous life." The individual stanzas are frequently punctuated by the group refrain:

Crowd: "*A kwee!*" (He returns!)
Crowd: "*A kwee!*" (He returns!)
Caller: "*A laa, ka-a suh laa le?*" (He is clean, is he not clean?)
Crowd: "*A laa!*" (He is clean!)
Caller: "*A mwa'a, ka-a suh mwa'a nuh?*" (He shines, does he not shine?)
Crowd: "*A mwa'a!*" (He shines!)
"*A kwee!*" (He returns!) [Ululations]

2. I omit here the first episode of the myth, which brings the two princes, Agha'anjoo and Kedjeum (founder of the Babanki dynasty), from Tikar across the Ndop Plain and into the Bamenda Highlands. This episode, frequently omitted from recitations of the myth in Bafut (probably because of its recent, retrospective addition to the older episodes), describes a relationship between Babanki and Bafut that seems to reflect modern political alignments rather than actual ethnogenetic relations. Babanki and Bafut are administratively grouped together in the Tubah Rural Council, Mezam Division of the Northwest Province, and in the same subsection of the (then) Cameroon National Union, the only political party. This episode of the myth is probably an attempt to strengthen the Babanki assertion of autonomy from Kom suzerainty by pushing it into the mythical past (Nkwi, Diduk, personal communications 1981). The Bafut, for their part, are happy to support this version of events, as it provides a rationale for the eventual assimilation of Babanki, whom the Bafut already regard imperiously as a more or less subject population, often referring to them as "Bafut East."

3. This image is never explained, but is taken as self-evident by Bafut. The person of the *fon* is sacred, and in everyday life, elaborate protocol and security procedures ensure that no one will ever touch the *fon* in public. Indeed, usually only a few of his wives and retainers are permitted to get close enough to do so. "Stepping on the foot" here requires no act of imagination on our part to envision where the interlocutor would be. It simply means that the sanctity of the *fon*'s person is violated, just as it would be if one kept one's hat on or crossed one's legs in his presence. Such acts imply that the perpetrator is claiming equal or higher status than the *fon* himself. It is significant here, however, that I recorded this formula only in the context of this episode of the myth—that is within the context of the Annual Dance—and I believe it only makes sense in that context.

4. See Engard (1986, 1988) for more explicit formalization of the episodic structure of the myth.

5. The placing of the basalt crystal chronologically completes the complex of objects at dance grounds—*wum* tree and *nduruh* shrine—described in the previous section. In addition to its function and meaning within the system of constitutional politics, this complex of objects also is crucial to the construction of the Bafut sense of space; these forms, which provide the politico-ritual focus of territorial units, are derived from the domestic forms of house and hearth, and carry

the meanings of domestic relations into the politico-jural realm. Reproduced again in enlarged and elaborated form at the palace itself, these objects are ultimately projections of the human body. In a recent paper (1987), I explored the implications of this ritual replication of domestic forms ever further into politico-jural space, and of the body imaging on which it is ultimately based.

6. In emphasizing the internal aspects of this system of the circulation of instruments, shrines, dances, masquerades, and other "king things" within the prestige sphere of the Bafut multi-centric economy (*cf.* Bohannan 1959), I have ignored the fact that these things circulate between chiefdoms and kingdoms within the wider region as well. Dillon (1973) speculated plausibly that the Meta purchased the idea of kingship and certain chiefly titles from Bafut, and Kaberry and Chilver (1963) claimed that the more martial aspects of the Bafut Annual Dance, specifically the firing of guns by military societies on the climactic day of the Dance (Bukwara Bumanjong), were imported from Bali-Nyonga.

7. *Bukwara* is a compound of the plural prefix, *bu,* and the verb *wara* (to swear)—as in *wara ngkaa* (to swear an oath)—with a neutral consonant *k* interposed, apparently to prevent the plural form from sounding too much like the verb *bwara* (to scold) (Crozier 1980). The meaning of the name may thus be rendered, "the collective oath of the *manjong* [military] societies." Oathing or swearing falls into Searle's category of "commissive" speech acts (1979), akin to the paradigm case of performative utterance—promising (*cf.* Searle 1969). In the languages of the Grassfields, the "illocutionary force" of this speech act is, if anything, stronger than its English variants, since words here, as elsewhere in Africa, are thought to have a material or supernatural efficacy in systems of witchcraft and ritual conflict resolution (Dillon 1975), in addition to their grammatical meanings.

8. Another reason (perhaps the ritual expression of the sociological reason) that outsiders were desired as retainers of the regulatory societies, has to do with the Bafut concept of *atsawbuh* (ritual pollution). This condition results from (among other causes) the shedding of Bafut blood at the hands of another Bafut person. Ritual pollution, which enters the earth, dissipates over a period of four generations. Conversely, it takes four generations for an immigrant to attain full Bafut personhood—to become *jwe-jwe* ("real born"). Recent immigrants (including captured or bought slaves) were thought to be immune to the deleterious effects of *atsawbuh,* which would result from the execution and disposal of a Bafut man, and thus were obvious choices to perform the more extreme punitive functions of the regulatory societies.

9. The animals most often represented in dances—the leopard, elephant, bush cow, and occasionally the python—have constituting properties of their own. Throughout the Grassfields, as in the adjoining regions of the Mamfe Depression (see Ruel 1969; Dillon 1973), whoever is recognized as "chief" within the area of the kill is granted possession of the animals' bodies, and the rights to butcher and distribute the meat and to keep or display their pelts, tusks, teeth, whiskers, and certain internal organs. Hence the conferral of or failure to confer these animals upon one of those who lay sometimes conflicting claims to them may be taken as an act of fealty which recognizes and reconstitutes the authority of the receiver, or, alternately, as an act of rebellion or treason. I borrow the distinction between

constitutional and operational politics from Ruel's discussion of the working out of political relations among the Banyang in the idiom of "animals of the community" (in the Kenyang language, *naa etawk*).

10. The Bafut represent all relations of authority in a domestic idiom of "house" (*nda*), "father" (*taa*), and "child" (*mu*). Some titles of authority are *taa nduguh* (compound head), *taa 'tseu* (lineage head), *taa nukuruh* (quarter-head), *taa nda* (secret society retainer), *talah* (subchief [from *taa 'la'a,* lit. "father of the country"]). The *fon* sometimes refers to and addresses the *kwifon*—whose inner circle comprises the "kingmakers" responsible for carrying out the late *fon*'s oral will and installing his chosen successor, as well as looking out for the chastity of his premenopausal wives—as "my father." The anglicized form *kwifon* derives from the verb *kwi'i,* which means "to carry" or "hold," but is applied only to the carrying or holding of young children. The most common term of address for any man of equal or greater age or status than oneself is "*taa,*" and people often refer to men who act as their patrons as their "father." The extent to which people actually operate within this idiom gives them tremendous leeway in manipulating their genealogies, as they manipulate oral histories or myth (*cf.* Engard 1987).

References

Austin, John L.

1962 How to Do Things with Words. Oxford: Clarendon Press.

d'Azevedo, Warren

1979 Gola Socialization: the Aesthetics of Power and Obedience. Paper presented to the African Studies Seminar, Indiana University, Bloomington.

Bird, Charles and Martha Kendall

1980 The Mande Hero: Text and Context. *In* Explorations in African Systems of Thought. C. Bird and I. Karp, eds. Bloomington: Indiana University Press.

Bohannan, Paul

1959 The Impact of Money on an African Subsistence Economy. Journal of Economic History 19:491–503.

Bourdieu, Pierre

1977 Outline of a Theory of Practice. London: Cambridge University Press.

Brain, Robert

1972 Bangwa Kinship and Marriage. London: Cambridge University Press.

Crozier, David, et al.

1980 How to Read and Write the Bafut Language: An Experimental

Prepublication Edition. Yaoundé: S.I.L. and the Bafut Language Committee.

Cunnison, Ian
1956 Perpetual Kinship: A Political Institution of the Luapula. Rhodes-Livingstone Journal XX:28–48.

Dillon, Richard
1973 Ideology, Process and Change in Pre-Colonial Meta' Political Organization. Ph.D. dissertation, Anthropology Department, University of Pennsylvania.
1975 Limits to Ritual Resolution in Meta' Society. Paideuma 25:35–39.

Engard, Ronald K.
1986 Bringing the Outside In: Commensality and Incorporation in Bafut Myth, Ritual, Art and Social Organization. Ph.D. dissertation, Anthropology Department, Indiana University, Bloomington.
1987 A House Has Four Walls: Architectonics of the Body Politic. Paper presented at the African Studies Association, Denver.
1988 Myth and Political Economy in Bafut (Cameroon): The Structural History of an African Kingdom. *Paideuma* 34

Gardner, D. S.
1983 Performativity in Ritual: The Mianmin Case. Man. (N.S.) 18: 346–60.

Gluckman, Max
1962 Les rites de passage. *In* Essays on the Ritual of Social Relations. M. Gluckman, ed. Manchester: Manchester University Press.

Goody, Jack
1961 Religion and Ritual, the Definitional Problem. British Journal of Sociology 12:142–64.

Herzfeld, Michael
1987 For a Poetics of Social Life. *In* Cultural Anthropology. E. Schultz and R. Lavenda, eds. St. Paul: West Publishing.

Hurault, Jean
1962 La Structure Social des Bamiléké. Paris: Mouton.

Jackson, Michael
1977 The Kuranko. New York: St. Martin's Press.

Kaberry, P. M. and Chilver, E. M.
1963 Traditional Government in Bafut, West Cameroon. Nigerian Field 28:4–30.
1968 Traditional Bamenda: The Pre-Colonial History and Ethnography of the Bamenda Grassfields. Buea: Government Printing Office.
1971 The Tikar Problem: A Non-problem. Journal of African Languages 10:2.

Kopytoff, Igor
1981 Aghem Ethnogenesis and the Grassfields Ecumene. *In* The Contribution of Ethnological Research to the History of Cameroon Cultures, Vol. II. C. Tardits, ed. Paris: C.N.R.S.

McCulloch, Merran and Littlewood, Margaret, and Dugast, I.
1954 Peoples of the Central Cameroons. London: International African Institute.

Ruel, Malcolm
1969 Leopards and Leaders: Constitutional Politics among a Cross River People. London: Tavistock.

Searle, John R.
1969 Speech Acts: An Essay in the Philosophy of Language. London: Cambridge University Press.
1979 Expression and Meaning: Studies in the Theory of Speech Acts. London: Cambridge University Press.

Tambiah, S. J.
1973 The Form and Meaning of Magical Acts. *In* Modes of Thought. R. Finnegan and R. Horton, eds. London: Faber and Faber.

Tardits, Claude
1960 Contribution a l'Etude des Populations Dit Bamiléké de l'Ouest Cameroun. Paris: Berger-Levrault.

Turner, Victor W.
1967 The Forest of Symbols. Ithaca: Cornell University Press.

Voloshinov, V. N.
1973 Marxism and the Philosophy of Language. New York: Seminar Press.

Warnier, J. P.
1975 Pre-Colonial Mankon: The Development of a Cameroon Chiefdom in its Regional Setting. Ph.D. dissertation, Anthropology Department, University of Pennsylvania.
1985 Echanges, développement et hiérarchies dans le Bamenda précolonial (Cameroun). Wiesbaden: Franz Steiner Verlag.

Warnier, J. P. and Nkwi, Paul N.
1982 Elements for a History of the Western Grassfields. Yaoundé: Department of Sociology, University of Yaoundé.

John Middleton

Ritual and Ambiguity in Lugbara Society

Ritual and Ceremonial

This paper is mainly concerned with what have been called ritual and ceremonial. I see no point here in presenting an introductory discussion of past usages of these and similar terms, since it has been done excellently some years ago by Goody (1961). I will place this discussion in a particular ethnographic context, that of the Lugbara of Uganda, although I will be able to mention only a few of the many rites and ceremonies performed by this people.

When we speak of religious, ritual, ceremonial, and so on, this is usually to distinguish and define various types of social behavior. In my view this approach is too rigid and distorts what actually takes place. It would be more accurate, instead, to consider religious and nonreligious, or ritual, or ceremonial, rather as aspects of behavior. It would seem impossible to find any organized, conventional, or expected behavior in any society that does not contain some element of more than one of these aspects. Even the most technical behavior contains some touch of the ritual;

and even the most religious act some aspect of the technical. This is a commonplace but we do not always remember it. So if we see these as aspects of behavior rather than as types of behavior we can expect to make greater sense of the social reality before us. Besides seeing them as aspects of behavior, we should also regard these various types of behavior as representing positions on a continuum. We may see an item of behavior as being more or less ritual, or more or less ceremonial, instead of being qualitatively distinct. Some behavior is both ritual and ceremonial; some is ritual but with virtually no ceremonial; some is ceremonial but with virtually no ritual. Clearly, here I am using "ritual" as being essentially "religious" or at least as including a religious element.

The behavior among the Lugbara that I wish to consider is performed and/or controlled by persons whose roles are recognized and whose statuses are named and defined: rainmakers, prophets, chiefs, kinsmen, and so on. All their activities are formalized, in the sense of being conventional, normal, ceremonial, regular, or observant of form (*Oxford English Dictionary*). The terms "rite" and "ritual" refer to something very similar. The main distinction between rite and ceremony would seem to be that a rite is a performance that is not only ordered or formal but which also makes for or brings order in experience, and so in social organization. Again, according to the *Oxford English Dictionary,* there is nothing inherently religious about a rite, although a religious connotation has entered ordinary usage. Also we may generally accept that those who carry out a rite assume that it is effective by its performance. A ceremony, on the other hand, is rather a formal pattern of behavior that in itself does not "work," in the sense of making for order in experience, although it may express the desirability or assumed existence of order, and its performance may be effective in inculcating values in the minds of those taking part. Here we come to Gluckman's definition of the process of ritualization, which he sees as being central to ritual (Gluckman 1962:24).

On a rather different level it has usually been accepted that a crucial distinction between a religious and a nonreligious act, whether referred to as a rite or a ceremonial, is that the former involves occult or mystical powers, which are thought by the participants to make it effective, whereas the latter does not. To define behavior by reference to the occult is clearly difficult, since the definition of what is occult is bound to be ethnocentric and thus unsuitable for or difficult in comparative analysis. The often quoted definition from Evans-Pritchard's book on the Azande (1937), for example, refers to "supra-sensible qualities which . . . are not derived from observation or cannot be logically inferred from it, and which (the phenomena) do not possess" (p. 12). This definition is difficult to use, because the area of experience to be referred to will vary from one society to another. This variation is in itself, of course, significant, but it is then the variation that we need to analyze comparatively rather than the qualities themselves. But the main difficulty is who is to make the logical inference to which Evans-Pritchard refers, or who is to state that the phenomena do not possess these qualities.

In brief, the central problem is in the relationship between those forms of behavior that may be called "formal" or "ritual" or "ceremonial" on the one hand, and on the other a belief in the participation or intervention of spiritual forces or powers, since the existence of these powers cannot be accepted as an objective fact but is part of the belief system of any given people. We should perhaps try to get around this particular difficulty by taking as our criterion not the believed participation of a spiritual power but rather the particular item of behavior that is resorted to on formal, ritual, or ceremonial occasions to deal with or control the believed power: this behavior can be observed in a sense that is not true of the belief that is behind it. Power, in the sense of power without authority, is in all societies regarded as being dangerous to those who come into contact with it and who must therefore be protected from it. We come here to the notion of taboo, which would seem to offer a more workable criterion for the definition of the religious aspect of behavior. The observance of taboos marks off this aspect of behavior from other aspects and situations, although of course the symbolic details of the taboos will vary from one society to another. In brief, let us take the observance of a taboo as being critical rather than the belief in an exterior power against which the taboo is directed: the taboo can be analyzed comparatively whereas to do so with the content of a religious belief is more difficult and leads to confusion. In this paper I start from this notion in order to work out in a meaningful manner the significance of the distinction between religious and nonreligious (or more religious and less religious) behavior. It provides a useful starting point to my central approach, which is to analyze ritual and ceremonial behavior in its relationship to the inhibition and resolution of social ambiguity and conflict.

The main argument is a simple one and has three main parts. The first is that the event or period of formal behavior is marked off or bracketed by acts that bound it and so define and mark it. These marking items are given many forms: the observance of taboos; the use of particular forms of speech, gesture, attire, or ornament; the entry into particular spaces or areas; the exclusion of particular categories of people. The second is that these marking items are not equal in emphasis or degree of prescription; they may be invariable and stressed, slight and almost voluntary, but they always occur. The third point is the question of the factors that determine this variation. In Lugbara thought the main one would seem essentially to be the danger and strength of what external divine or spiritual powers are thought to participate in the main formal event. I think it credible and useful to regard this as a function of the kind and degree of conflict that the behavior is intended to resolve, and I therefore base my ethnographic materials on the types of conflict found in Lugbara and the means used to resolve them.

Lugbara Society

It is useful at this point to present certain features of Lugbara society (see Middleton 1965). The Lugbara are small-scale peasant farmers, lacking a king or traditional chiefs, although today they have administrative chiefs and headmen. The largest traditional political unit, the jural community, is the subtribe, formed around a subclan, the local core of a dispersed clan. A subtribe has an average population of about 4,000 persons. Each subtribe is segmented into from three to six levels of territorial section, the sections being formed around the lineages that are the segments of a subclan. The smallest section is the family cluster based upon a minimal lineage of some three to seven generations. The head of this small lineage, the elder, is also thereby the head of the family cluster. A feature of the Lugbara system is the low level of effective lineage authority, the elder being the only holder of authority in the lineage system (Middleton 1958).

Something should be said about Lugbara cosmological notions of the nature and relationship of men, spirits, and divinity. Divinity, a power outside the total understanding or control of men, omnipotent and everlasting, is experienced at three levels. These are the universe (*Adroa,* the Creator, the Divine Spirit, in the sky); the surface of the earth (*Adro,* the immanent aspect of divinity, in the bushland); and the individual psyche (*adro,* the source of idiosyncratic and antisocial behavior). Spirit is different from and opposed to the soul (the responsible element of a living man) and the ancestor or ghost (into which the soul is transformed at death). Throughout all Lugbara thought, whether overtly "religious" or not (a distinction that we may make but which is not made by the

Lugbara themselves), runs the basic differentiation between the two spheres of the "home" (*aku*) and the "outside" (*amve*). The former pertains to the social, moral, predictable, controllable, to authority, to men, and the lineage dead; the latter pertains to the asocial, amoral, unpredictable, uncontrollable, to power without authority, to women, and the world of spirits. For Lugbara, the "home" and the "outside" together form a conceptualization of the totality of human experience (see Middleton 1968). All societies have some such mode of conceptualizing experience (and may have others also) but the detailed criteria vary and the boundary between them varies from one society to another on the continuum from the social to the asocial, from the human to the divine or spiritual, or whatever terms we care to use.

Conflict and Contradiction

In this paper I essentially discuss means by which the members of this particular society cope with conflicts, contradictions, and ambiguities within their social structure and social experience, and with the inevitability of change and development within a system which is seen by its members as ideally unchanging. Despite this ideal, the Lugbara realize that they do have to accept change and underlying structural conflict that are brought about by ecological, demographic, and technological factors, and also by external causes such as Arab slavery, colonial rule, and national independence. These conflicts cannot easily be resolved by deliberate action by the Lugbara themselves, or at least they do not appear to have been so resolved in the past. Other, more everyday, conflicts are less radical and these the Lugbara know that they can deal with more easily by conventional and expected means, principally by ritual and ceremonial activities.

The terms conflict, dispute, and others refer to different levels and aspects of relationship and situation. We may clearly recognize and distinguish three as being distinct aspects of social relations. First, there are underlying structural conflicts which are essentially insoluble. Following Gluckman (1965: 109) I will refer to these as contradictions rather than as conflicts. These contradictions express the stresses that have arisen (in living memory, and we may assume there were earlier ones also throughout history) from changes in ecology and demography due to sudden and serious animal and human epidemics that largely changed the patterns of wealth, settlement, and political relations between territorial groups; and by changes in the patterns of money and labor that have brought changes in the traditional relations between men and women and between old and young. Secondly, we may distinguish recurrent struggles associated with the continual maturation of individuals and the cyclical development of groups. And thirdly, we distinguish disputes between individuals and groups over land and other resources, when they are not closely related and do not share close common ancestors.

We may, perhaps properly, argue that disputes are usually expressions of struggles, and that struggles are in their turn usually expressions of contradictions. But this is rather too rigid a view and it would be more accurate to say that they are aspects of all conflict rather than different types of conflict. In addition, the factor of social distance between the parties concerned in any level of conflict is highly significant, so that we may regard these three kinds or levels of conflict as being on a single continuum.

Among the Lugbara the various contradictions, struggles, and disputes are related to different levels of social grouping and networks of social relations, each of which is in a state of continual development, whether cyclical or not. Contradictions are found at the level of the jural community, the subtribe; essentially, these contradictions are insoluble, being an inherent quality of social structure at that level. Struggles are at the level of the lineage, especially of lower-level lineages. Disputes are found anywhere in the system, but here the crucial point is that the close lineage ties that characterize intralineage struggles are lacking, so that these disputes are either between individuals whose kin ties are temporarily irrelevant, or between lineages and neighborhoods more distantly related to each other than are the members of the minor or minimal lineage. I cannot discuss at any length either the different developmental cycles of different groups and fields of relationships, or the highly significant variations in these cycles found from one part of Lugbara to another. What I can do, however, is to discuss these levels of conflict from another viewpoint. I have so far mentioned them from that of an external observer and wish now to present them from that of the people themselves, one which is somewhat different.

The Lugbara see conflict as having two aspects. One is that of cosmological and categorical confusion and ambiguity; the other is that of actual physical dispute. The network of social relations—between kin, neighbors, affines, and others—within any one social grouping is regarded as having a proper form: relationships of respect and authority should be ordered, recognized, accepted, and maintained in behavior. When they are not so ordered and maintained, then ambiguity, uncertainty, and confusion appear. These are regarded as the manifestations of disorder from the sphere of the "outside" impinging upon and entering that of the "home." The group—in the persons of its senior authority-holders—then performs rites and ceremonies that are believed to remove disorder and to reinstall relations of order and certainty.

There are two points to be made in this regard. The first is that the sanctions for the maintenance of order are ultimately controlled by certain forces—Divinity, the dead, or the living, according to the identity of the group concerned. The second is that of the precise meaning for the Lugbara of "certainty," "ambiguity," and similar notions. It is convenient to discuss the second first, even though briefly. This point is essentially that of free will and choice in interpersonal behavior. I have described elsewhere Lugbara notions of soul and spirit (Middleton 1960). The soul is associated with responsibility and adherence to accepted norms; the spirit is associated with irresponsibility, the individualistic, the idiosyncratic, with evil, and the antisocial. The soul is part of the sphere of the "home," the spirit is linked with that of the "outside," as it were an extension of extra-social divine power into the person within the "home." When there is order, the soul is uppermost; when there is disorder, it is the spirit that takes control. This rather simplistic view of the situation is not a distortion. Another way of expressing this is to say that when there is order, there is no individual choice to be made, but that disorder is caused by the exercise of individual choice, particularly when irrational or irresponsible. I realize that these latter terms need lengthy analysis for which there is no space here, but I think that the general sense of the argument is clear enough. It leads to the fact that choice is a highly significant factor in the performance of rite and ceremony and that it is closely associated with the proper relationship between individuals and the remainder of their moral universe.

I will now return briefly to the first of the two points mentioned above, that of the ultimate sanctions behind ordered behavior—that is, behind the acceptance of the proper norms and the abandonment of the exercise of too great a degree of individual choice and self-definition. If for the moment we accept, for ease of discussion, the three levels of conflict that I have mentioned earlier—even though the boundaries between them cannot be made too rigid—we see that these ultimate sanctions rest in different areas in each case, and that each is associated with different categories whose confusion, disturbance, and uncertainty are seen by Lugbara as associated with different levels of conflict.

Religious Ritual

Among the Lugbara there are many holders of statuses and offices whose behavior is formalized and defined in space and in time by certain rules and taboos. Some of these appear as mainly secular or nonreligious persons: the chief, the headman, the market organizer, the shopkeeper, the kinsman, the neighbor, and the friend. As against these, using our own ethnocentric viewpoint, are personages whose behavior is more "religious," defined as being behavior directed to and/or controlled by presumed beings, forces, or powers that are either nonhuman (spirits) or transformed humans (ancestors). These include elders when sacrificing, rainmakers, diviners, prophets, and evangelists. This distinction is, of course, a situational one rather than one of basic social status.

I now wish to present examples of some rites and ceremonies performed by Lugbara in order to resolve the three categories of conflict mentioned, and I stress that these are areas of a continuum rather than distinct types of conflict. The first example has to do with conflict within the lineage, the type referred to above as struggle over the changing relationships between persons and between groups as part of their maturation and development.

The most noticeable and important ritual performances in Lugbara are the sacrifices made to the dead—to ghosts and ancestors. They are made mostly by members of the family cluster, the basic domestic, land-owning, and land-using unit. The minimal lineage on which it is based undergoes a cycle of development and segmentation that lasts on the average about twenty-five years. At the beginning of the cycle there is more or less congruence between the accepted genealogy of the group and its internal authority and status structure. The elder is accepted as effective head, and the senior men of constituent segments recognize both his overriding authority based on his being the representative of the dead members of the lineage, and their own respective relations of seniority and juniority as regards one another. As they and their dependent family members grow older, marry, die, move in and out of the cluster, and as they and their dependents' requirements in land, livestock, and wives change, so do tensions and struggles for authority and uncertainties and ambiguities in the accepted genealogical reckoning develop and increase.

Sacrifices are made as part of the process of settling internal struggles over the allocation and exercise of authority, to "purify the home," and to reestablish a properly recognized pattern of authority, sanctioned by genealogical statements, within the local group. The process begins with the sickness of a member of the lineage, who is shown by oracular consultation to have offended a senior lineage member. Sickness has been sent by the dead, usually after having been invoked by the senior member concerned, to "show" the offender his "sin." A beast is dedicated for sacrifice, which is performed when the offender has recovered. At the sacrifice living and dead share the oblation, the offender is purified, and the dispute is brought into open discussion in which participants must speak the truth, settled, and resolved. Either the past authority network or a revised one is affirmed and expressed at the sharing of the oblation. The central part of this process, the sacrifice itself, is marked by various defining signs: the presence of the sun or lack of rain and dark clouds; the formal exclusion of nonlineage kin and neighbors, including wives of lineage members in the area of the actual sacrifice; the use of sacred leaves at the ritual addresses; and speaking with solemn and measured voice and making slow and deliberate gestures and movements. The central act of sacrifice, the placing of meat and blood in the shrines, is marked by the sacrificing elder taking on symbolic attributes of inversion, mainly by his observing sexual taboos and using the left hand when at the shrines. The elder is at that time at least partially "outside," in contact not only with the dead, who are in the "home" as they are buried under the compound floor, but also with Divinity who is outside it altogether. (See Middleton 1960 and 1979 for a fuller account of these matters.)

There are several kinds of ancestral sacrifice but all share this basic form and follow the same pattern: the events leading up to the first ritual address which marks the formation of the congregation; the sacrifice proper at the shrines; then, following the second ritual address, the anointment and commensal sharing of sacrificial meat among lineage representatives. Any breach of the customary and proper is thought to be followed by the disapproval of Divinity, expressed in rain or dark clouds. The rite is then ineffective and regarded as void and must be performed again.

This behavior, associated with the "home," is obviously ritual behavior, with an essentially religious element. It reaffirms and reinforces an existing field of social relations. It takes place within a ritually defined place and time that represent the perpetual identity of the lineage. It expresses an unchanging pattern of lineage relations that transcends the patterns of relations of local neighborhood and interpersonal kinship that are in actuality continually changing. It makes for order within temporary disorder, the basic function of all ritual activity.

Secular Ritual

There are also occasions of formalized behavior which should not be regarded as religious ritual but perhaps, using the Gluckmans' terminology (1977:231), as ceremonious ritual, although some of them are as far as their function is concerned very close to the ancestral ritual I have just described. They comprise forms of intergroup hostility and fighting. I will discuss only one here; others, *e.g.*, death dances, show the same basic features and are described elsewhere (Middleton 1985). These occasions are all those of the resolution of disputes, in the sense used above, between groups not closely related in lineage terms.

The main form of ceremonious intergroup hostility is the feud. This no longer occurs but since older men have experienced it in the past (up to about 1930) they can still discuss it in detail; also they still try to set it in motion, to be stopped by the chiefs before it grows too serious. The feud is a jural mechanism, an expression in action of the segmentary lineage system. It is also a ceremonial performance, which is, of course, a central factor in its efficacy as a jural mechanism. (I have discussed some aspects of feud and warfare in Middleton 1958.)

The participants are men who are related by clanship but not by close lineage ties, and the form of a particular outbreak of feud is known and accepted (here I use the ethnographic present tense). The feud is typically part of a dispute over the allocation or use of productive resources, which have been the subject of tension, open quarreling, and some serious insult or injury which has led to demands for compensation or vengeance. Threats and warning of feud should be given by the injured group. It must be carried out in sunny weather and not in heavy rain or in darkness. The men of the group advance, uttering their *cere* (long falsetto whoops), the words and tone patterns each of which is "owned" by an individual man; to call a *cere* shows the caller's formal status and identity in a situation where these should be unequivocally stated. They carry weapons and fight along the intergroup boundary, each group standing apart making runs towards the other but not getting closer than the distance needed accurately to throw a spear or shoot an arrow. Great care is taken not to shoot at uterine kin on the other side, warnings being shouted to them to stand out of the way before a man shoots. A feud takes place only in the dry season, when there is no work to be done in the fields, when there are no crops in the fields and so visibility is easy, when there is still plenty of food and beer, and when the passing of time is regarded as coming almost to a standstill (I will return to this point below). At nighttime the warriors may wish to court the girls of the other side and they may then freely visit them. Women are not attacked and may pass openly from one side to another.

There are thus known rules which are strictly followed. Breach of them leads to purification after the feud, to continued fighting, to later suspicions of sorcery (those injured continue to fight by mystical means), or to curses by the subclan rainmaker. An important factor is that of the outcome in deaths and wounding, that is to say of choice within the content of the performance. In most feuds for which I have information, there are either no deaths or only one death, that of the original offender or his brother (men try to shoot their arrows at these men). But accidental deaths do occur, in which case the killer becomes a recognized homicide and requires purification after the feud is ended unless he is actually killed in retribution first. Until purification the killer is "outside," analogous to the hunter of animals in the bushland. Wounding occurs frequently and is usually accepted as a fit conclusion to the original dispute. Once it is agreed by the use of intermediaries (usually women) that the feud has achieved its main purpose, it is formally brought to an end by the subclan rainmaker who threatens to curse the participants with sterility if they continue to cross a boundary which he marks out between them. The rainmaker chooses his time so as to cause no loss of face or prestige on either side. After the feud is over, although there is no formal feasting to mark the resumption of clanship, there may be somewhat formal drinking between the two sides and displays of friendship and esteem made on the next occasion when they meet as participants in a lineage sacrifice.

These performances of feud (and of warfare, which has some similarities) clearly resemble games, although they are perhaps more clearly defined as to content and have a slight degree of mystical control. The resemblance to Classical Greek and Roman and American Indian games is close. For the Lugbara they may be regarded as containing much of the ceremonious and little of the religious aspect of ritual.

Today, the feud no longer takes place, its jural function as a means of settling what I have referred to as "disputes" being taken over by chiefs' courts. Much of the content persists, although the form is different. The form of court procedure is accepted in custom and behavior is highly formalized, including both periods of apparent argument and shouting (equivalent to the actual fighting in the feud), followed by periods of calm and dignified behavior by both chief and accused. As in the feud, the main aim is to bring about reconciliation between the parties and it is regarded as unseemly for anyone to win a case against another with too great a degree of success. After a decision both parties are expected to drink together at a beerhouse to show that ties have been restored. (For further information on courts and moots, see Middleton 1956.)

As far as the Lugbara are concerned, there is a significant distinction between the ritualization in the process of ancestral sacrifice and the statements about interlineage relations made in the feud and today in court actions. It is not merely that the former reaffirms and redefines a set of kinship relations. To say that is not perhaps to say very much. The former redefines genealogical statements about authority: it is for this reason that the intergenerational relationship between living and dead members of the lineage is restated. The dead exercise authority over the living, and the senior living exercise authority over their own juniors precisely because they are regarded as representatives of the dead. In the interlineage relations that are reaffirmed by feud, authority is irrelevant. The elder of the minimal lineage is genealogically the most senior man with lineage authority; the genealogical heads of minor and major lineages may act as representatives of those lineages at the rites performed by collateral lineages but they exercise no formal authority over anyone other than the members of their own minimal lineages. The point is that for Lugbara the process of ritualization has as its aim not to redefine and reaffirm networks of social relations as such, but more precisely to redefine specific relations of authority. Those social relationships that lack the content of authority are certainly redefined and reaffirmed, but by ceremonious performances that lack ritualization. With this difference goes another that is significant as far as the degree of religiosity is concerned. The sacrificial rite is defined by the observance of taboos by the main performer. There are no taboos observed in the feud or in court cases, although there is great formality. In place of an external power, from which participants are protected in sacrifices by the taboos observed by the elder, the power in the feud situation is that of the protagonists themselves. Only if they step outside this situation, by breaking the rules by killing outside the expected program of the feud, do they become liable to the effect of mystical powers and need to be purified later.

Prophets and Rainmakers

I come now to performances by two kinds of functionaries who are themselves clearly regarded as sacred: prophets and rainmakers (for longer accounts, see Middleton 1963, 1971, 1973 and 1978). They are significant in those situations in which what I have referred to above as "contradictions" become manifest.

The Lugbara prophets of whom we know anything first appeared at the turn of the century and were believed to have the power to remove the recently arrived Europeans and certain epidemic sicknesses, all of which were destructive to traditional Lugbara society. The greatest prophet was Rembe, a Kakwa, who lived in Lugbara for some months in 1916–17. His power was said to come directly from Divinity in the form of sacred water, drawn from a pool and dispensed to his followers. It gave them everlasting life and immunity to bullets. He introduced new forms of divination by which he revealed the "words" of Divinity to his followers. They were organized on an egalitarian basis, the principles of cult organization being radically opposed to those of traditional society based on descent, sex, and age. All of these principles were ignored according to the Divine instructions received by the prophet. The central part of his activities was the holding of meetings at which people gathered, drank the sacred water, danced irrespective of lineage affiliation, sex or age, and had sexual intercourse irrespective of clan or lineage affiliation. These performances were marked off from ordinary social activities not only by disobeying traditional principles of organization, but by being held in the bushland away from the settlements, at nighttime, under the influence of drugs, and by being led by a prophet who was given "inverted" attributes of many kinds. The performances symbolized the destruction of the contemporary political situation and the introduction of a "perfect" form of society, as it had been at the beginning of the world. By acting as though that society had come into being again it was in a sense brought into existence, even though only for short periods of time during the night and in the bushland and thus away from ordinary everyday life of lineage settlements.

The role of rainmaker is different from that of prophets and in certain ways more germane to this paper, so I will discuss it at greater length. The rainmaker is the genealogically senior man of his subclan and is given attributes that symbolically mark him off from other men. He is regarded as symbolically socially dead after his succession, as can be seen from his burial which is totally different and contrary in detail to those of ordinary people. He manipulates rainstones (which have features that symbolize their being of both sky and earth and which represent "all the words of men, those of yesterday, of today, and of tomorrow") inside his raingrove ("the vagina of the world"), a place kept secret to everyone except rainmakers. The more important attributes for our concern here are first, that he is the repository and the custodian of divine knowledge about the nature of society at the beginning of the world, as told in myth, before present-day society was formed. This knowledge is secret and he does not tell it to ordinary men (as does a prophet, who does not, however, understand the meaning of what he says and must therefore give it out in "tongues," as it is too dangerous to put into words). Secondly, his knowledge and his words are regarded as being totally true; ordinary men may think that they can speak the truth, at ancestral rites, but in fact their truth is only partial and incomplete. A rainmaker knows the absolute truth, "the words of Divinity," but he cannot tell it to ordinary people since it is so dangerous, its utterance being able to destroy and recreate all categories of experience. Thirdly, he stands outside the ordinary passing of time and he can both know of things in the past and in the future and also control the passing of time. Fourthly, he is associated with rain that links sky and earth and represents the fertility of land, livestock, and women; he can prevent death in feud and by acting as sanctuary for a homicide; he is himself above death.

His activities that have to do with rain are clearly central to his role. I have mentioned that the rainmaker "makes rain" in his raingrove; also he is said to have done so in the past by the killing of a captive alien. The latter was rare and a last and rather desperate resort, done at the end of a dry season that continued overlong. But the manipulation of rainstones with the raingrove is of a very different character, in two ways. One is that it is totally secret, as he does it alone out of the sight of ordinary people. It is said that he goes there to perform his "work" (*azi*). Azi means "work" and also "labor," but it also has in this context the connotation of "duty" or proper activity according to basic human and social conditions.

The other difference is the occasion for this "work." The rainmaker enters his grove at fairly regular intervals throughout the year. But there are two periods when people can expect him to do so more often and for greater lengths of time than usual. These are toward the end of the dry season, when anxiety is general about the advent of the main rains, the sign for planting crops, and toward the end of the growing season when people are waiting for crops to ripen for harvesting. Both depend on the weather being as expected and anxiety rises especially if the coming of the proper weather is late when measured against the rise and fall in the sky of certain constellations of stars and the rise and fall of the moon. If there is a discrepancy, it is a sign that "time" has become confused or "wrong."

The rainmaker does not really "make rain" except on very rare occasions. Rather he knows the true significance of rain, the link between heaven and earth. He controls time, change, fertility, and death. He does these things mainly by stating formally when planting and harvesting should be done, the two most crucial points in the agricultural calendar. He exercises little actual technical control or leadership, since each family can best judge exactly when to plant or harvest. The only thing that they cannot themselves ensure is peace. Planting and harvesting are the only occasions when open force cannot be permitted, and only the rainmaker can ensure this.

But there is more to it than that. The periods before planting and harvesting are both in a sense without time. These are the periods when shortages of land, grazing, and food or water all become the objects of disputes. There is then little farming work to be done, there is much mortality of both humans and livestock, and it is the time when feuding takes place. Being without certainty of time, they are occasions for weakening of ordered social relations and activities. Their termination is open to uncertainty. The signs are there: the climate, the position of stars, and the state of the crops and the ground. But these do not occur in perfect unison and the "work" of the rainmaker, who through his knowledge of the real truth can understand the relationship between these signs, is to decide what is the "true" time of their conjunction.

The rainmaker thus becomes a focus of conflict within the jural community, conflict which has been called contradiction. We must ask how this actually works—how does he purify his community of sin and trouble? Purification of the jural community caught up in dispute and unhealth is mainly done by his being blamed for them, since it is he who controls "time" and "knows the secret words of truth." Contradictions are focused on him precisely because they express ambiguities of purpose, uncertainties, events, and relations that are out of precision. His knowledge can destroy, create, and repair disorder or change, and he knows the ideal or true form and structure of society. Ordinary people can never know these things.

By using his secret and true divine knowledge he ensures the proper relationship between the rain, the moon, the stars, and men's behavior on earth. By doing this he controls the overt expression of conflict and tensions between groups on the land. And by inhibiting and controlling tensions he creates the "proper" or "true" relationship between the spheres of the "home" and the "outside." In many respects he is like a king: his role or his "work" is merely to be a rainmaker, to exist. He performs rituals continually in his raingrove, but in a sense his entire life is a single performance, marked off not only by temporary signs and taboos such as entering the grove, but also by his being symbolically dead and of almost a different nature from that of ordinary people.

Ritual and the Making of Social Order

Let me return to the questions of what the Lugbara are doing, and what they think they are doing when they perform these various rites and ceremonies, which are organized by various symbolic attributes that define their relationship to divine power, which lie along the continuum of religious to nonreligious ritual, and which have differing kinds and degrees of marking or bracketing from everyday activities. They are trying to resolve various levels of contradictions, struggles, and disputes, some of which are soluble by these means, at least temporarily, some of which are not. But the people themselves do not see the performances in these terms. They are, of course, perfectly well aware that disputes can be settled by taking an opponent to court or by wounding him with a spear. Yet they are also aware that to do so is still a kind of a game, a formal ceremony, and has other significance as well.

They regard what we may refer to as various levels and aspects of conflict in terms of areas of categorical ambiguity. I have mentioned the basic cosmological distinction between the spheres of the "home" and the "outside." The Lugbara hold two views of the ideally socially unambiguous: one is that of a social field in which the network of authority, which is stated and validated by genealogy, is completely accepted; the other is that of the mythical world, in time before the formation of society by the Heroes, in space on the "outside," and in detail unknown to ordinary men today. The first view, the Lugbara recognize explicitly, never lasts for very long even, indeed, if it ever actually occurs at all in everyday experience. The second view is hoped for at times of structural crisis, and Lugbara attempt to realize it through the activities of prophets. It is obvious that these ideal views are contradictory, but this is so only at first glance. They refer to different situations and to different levels of social organization. The first is the ideal organization of the jural community and its segments in the everyday world of the "home." The second is the ideal structure of an unchanging world under the authority of Divinity, as it was once and one day will be again when men have reacquired the secret knowledge that they lost when Divinity, who once lived with them, separated them from the sky and left them to their own devices on earth.

The Lugbara, like anyone else, wish to live in a condition of certainty and unambiguity of social categories. Yet they find that in actuality they cannot do so. They have two main recourses open to them—more accurately, their responsive behavior has two levels of aspects, distinguished largely by the identities of the leaders of the ritual performances.

The first is action taken to remove the ambiguity in relations of lineage and neighborhood, the former being those of authority and the latter lacking authority. This is the area of the everyday, in which categories are always somewhat unclear. But social life can continue despite these petty uncertainties that are due essentially to the vagaries of minor individual wishes, ambitions, and envies. In time these uncertainties increase due to the normal maturation of ordinary people. They lead to conflicts at two levels: struggles within the lineage over the exercise of authority, and disputes between lineages over the enjoyment of resources. The first is settled by the performance of ancestral rites, the latter by the performance of feud and the operation of courts. The latter are the more easily settled, in the sense that they in fact can be settled, and their religious content and degree of bracketing and the importance in them of taboos are all slight. The former are more deeply seated, due less to individual choice and idiosyncrasy and more to the necessary cycles of development of local groups, and can therefore never easily be settled for very long. Their religious content, degree of bracketing, and importance in them of taboos are all much greater.

The second level of recourse is more complex. It is attempted only when the underlying structural contradictions and tensions become so serious that the basic principles of organization become disturbed throughout the country, not merely at the local level. The general positions of old and young, men and women, wealthy and poor, powerful and weak, all become confused due to large-scale ecological and other factors that are both beyond the control and also the understanding of humans. Therefore they are seen as emanating from the "outside," the sphere of Divine power. Since Divinity is invisible and not comprehensible, the external power is regarded as a spiritual power associated with a particular historical force—Europeans (Rembe's cult) and in other cults that have occurred at various times, Azande (Mmua) and Baganda (Balokole)—which happen to be in evidence at the time but whose identity is in a sense fortuitous. Lugbara try to remove this total ambiguity and confusion by attempts to return to the only form of society that is known to them from their experience, that of the egalitarian society of the beginning of the world as recalled in myth. At that time Lugbara say that people lived together with Divinity in a state of changelessness in social relations, so they try to restore that ideal community by appealing to Divinity, by calling him into the sphere of the "home" from the "outside" in order to make the ambiguous and polluted sphere of the "home" vanish altogether. Men cannot actually call in Divinity since they cannot speak to him, so they call in prophets as his representatives. Prophets try to reestablish the egalitarian community but fail, Lugbara say, because they are merely mouthpieces of Divine secrets which they themselves do not actually understand, even though they utter them in "tongues." But the rainmakers do understand them and so take over the prophetic movements when these falter and also take on themselves the seasonal settlement of conflicts that erupt at timeless periods of agricultural stagnation and neighborhood tension. Because both prophets and rainmakers are of the "outside," they are given powerful bracketing attributes that symbolize their external and liminal status. Between them they know how to reorder social and cosmic categories: they have the dangerous secret truth to destroy and to reshuffle categories, in order to achieve the ideal society by re-creating order anew from the disorder they have found in society at a time of great crisis and turbulence. But because their experience of the world is limited historically and because these ideas are not clearly articulated, the reordering of categories has very much the same pattern as before, one which people have in fact been brought up to regard as normal and one which in any event they cannot change.

I should like to have made some comparisons between the Lugbara and other societies in respect to the points made above, but there is not the space to do so here. The Lugbara have no striking rites of initiation, and the only important rite marking change of status is at death, when mortuary rites may continue for up to a year after the burial (see Middleton 1982 and 1985). Their rites and ceremonies are performed almost entirely at periods of contradiction, struggle, and dispute within and between lineages and neighborhoods, with the exception of performances by rainmakers at certain points in the agricultural year. But these are also dependent largely on the eruption of intergroup tension and are called for by the people who do not themselves take part in or even witness the performances, the degree of bracketing to set them apart from the everyday being so extreme.

The significance of this is, of course, that at base the distributions along a continuum of the kinds of conflict I have mentioned, and of the degree of religious content of the performances made to resolve the conflicts, vary from one society to another. The Lugbara have a particular distribution that is unique to them. I use the word distribution advisedly, as it would seem that the nature of contradictions, struggles, and disputes is more or less invariable. The factors that are relevant here, basically those of ecology, demography, and history, are outside our immediate concern, although essential to any comparative analysis of the ways in which societies actually work. And I stress again the concept of distribution in the religiosity or otherwise of the performances: to state that there is some simple division between religious rituals and nonreligious rituals is to misunderstand the nature of social process entirely. We are dealing always with a continuum, a single complex, with aspects of behavior rather than with discrete bits of social activity. In one sense our problem is to be able to make comparisons from one social system to another, to show how the points on the continuum—which itself would seem to be common to all societies—vary, and identify the factors that are relevant to that variation. The problems faced by different societies are basically the same—how to ensure perpetuity and certainty of role–networks and how to accommodate insoluble conflicts and inevitable changes in organization and in structure. I have tried to separate out some of the key notions: conflict, authority, ambiguity, truth, defining by bracketing, and others, none of them very unusual. It is the ways in which they are grouped, differentiated, and used that merit our discussion, and which I have tried to analyze with regard to one particular society.

References

Evans-Pritchard, E. E.
1937 Witchcraft, Oracles and Magic Among the Azande. Oxford.

Gluckman, Max
1962 Essays on the Ritual of Social Relations. Manchester: Manchester University Press.
1965 Politics, Law and Ritual in Tribal Society. Chicago: Aldine.

Gluckman, Mary, and Gluckman, Max
1977 On Drama, and Games and Athletic Contests. *In* Secular Ritual. S. Moore and B. Myerhoff, eds. Assen/Amsterdam.

Goody, Jack
1961 Religion and Ritual, the Definitional Problem. British Journal of Sociology 12:142–64.

Middleton, John
1956 The Roles of Chiefs and Headmen in Lugbara. Journal of African Administration 8(1):32–38.
1958 The Political System of the Lugbara of the Nile-Congo Divide. *In* Tribes Without Rulers. J. Middleton and D. Tait, eds. pp. 203–29. London: Routledge and Kegan Paul.
1960 Lugbara Religion: Ritual and Authority Among an East African People. London: Oxford University Press for International African Institute. (Revised edition, Washington, Smithsonian Press, 1987.)
1963 The Yakan or Allah Water Cult Among the Lugbara. Journal of the Royal Anthropological Institute 93:80–108.
1965 The Lugbara of Uganda. New York: Holt, Rinehart and Winston.
1968 Some Categories of Dual Classification Among the Lugbara of Uganda. History of Religions 7(3):187–208.
1971 Prophets and Rainmakers: The Agents of Social Change Among the Lugbara. *In* Translation of Culture. T. O. Beidelman, ed. pp. 179–201. London: Tavistock Publications.
1973 Secrecy in Lugbara Religion. History of Religions 12(4):299–316.
1978 The Rainmaker Among the Lugbara of Uganda. *In* Systèm de Signes. M. Cartry, ed. pp. 377–88. Paris: Hermann.
1979 Rites of Sacrifice Among the Lugbara. *In* Systèmes de Pensée en Afrique Noire: Le Sacrifice III. Luc de Heusch, ed. pp. 175–92. Ivry: École Pratique des Hautes Études/CNRS.
1982 Lugbara Death. *In* Death and the Regeneration of Life. M. Bloch and J. Parry, eds. pp. 134–54. Cambridge: Cambridge University.
1985 The Dance Among the Lugbara of Uganda. *In* Society and the Dance. P. Spencer, ed. pp. 165–82. Cambridge: Cambridge University Press.

Aidan Southall

Power, Sanctity, and Symbolism in the Political Economy of the Nilotes

The Productive Relationship and Culture

Comparison is not a very fashionable current theme. For devotees of the interpretive turn, there is enough meaning in one moment or one place to keep us busy. Yet, after so much debate about Nilotic society and culture, it is important to attempt a provisional drawing together of common themes that, if not entirely original, have never been systematically integrated. Such a limited regional comparison of Alur, Acoli, Anuak, Col, Nath, and Jieng'[1] may reveal suggested relations between reported facts and theoretical interpretations, which can be confirmed or knocked down by more facts and more convincing interpretations, which is the only kind of objectivity and scientific program through validation or falsification open to anthropologists. This study will explore the limits of ecological and materialist interpretations, and the place of cultural and symbolic explanation in the formation of political economy in the Nile River valley.

I do not dispute Sahlins's argument that "the distinctive quality of man [is] not that he must live in a material world, circumstance he shares with all organisms, but that he does so according to a meaningful scheme of his own devising" (1976: viii). But I would contend that the meaningful scheme is devised, and always has been, within the general human context of the production relationship. Although Sahlins does not deny that "culture conforms to material constraints," he insists "that it does so according to a definite symbolic scheme which is never the only one possible" (1976: viii). He then adds "hence it is culture which *constitutes* utility," an apparent *non sequitur*. How extensive are the material constraints and how extensive are the alternative symbolic schemes? *Constitutes,* which has many meanings according to the Oxford English Dictionary, including "to determine," "to make a thing what it is," "to be the elements or material of which a thing consists," is far too sweeping a claim.

I prefer the way Marx put it in 1845. In describing how "the social structure and the state are continuously evolving out of the life process of definite individuals," Marx wrote:

> The production of ideas, of conceptions, of consciousness, is at first directly interwoven with the material activity and the material intercourse of men—the language of real life. Conceiving, thinking, the mental intercourse of men at this stage still appear as the direct efflux of their material behaviour. The same applies to mental production as expressed in the language of the politics, laws, morality, religion, metaphysics, etc. of a people. Men are the producers of their conceptions, ideas, etc.; that is, real, active men, as they are conditioned by a definite development of their productive forces and of the intercourse corresponding to these, up to its furthest forms. (Marx and Engels 1975: 36)

Sahlins quotes this passage, commenting that "this displacement of the conceptual order from production is the production of a disorder in men's conceptions" (1976: 135–36). But there is no such displacement. Sahlins has subverted his argument for the sake of a clever phrase. Marx's point is concretely confirmed by Evans-Pritchard's statement that "only a group of kinsmen can herd the cattle and from this necessity springs the solidarity of the kinship group" (1937: 211).

The Imperatives of Field Work and Comparison

The Nilotic peoples did not present themselves voluntarily for anthropological study. They were presented to the anthropologist through the distorting mirror of the colonialist presence. Who and what they really were is still being unraveled, fortunately no longer entirely by foreigners but with themselves to an increasing degree involved in the voyage of discovery.[2]

The glory of anthropological field work was that, as my mentors assured me, every stint of field research resulted in new insights for the discipline, regardless of the similarities of the group to its already studied neighbors. The assurance was usually borne out, but it always posed the danger of emphasizing differences rather than likenesses and of establishing and demarcating one's own distinctive ethnographic estate, with presumptively monopolistic property rights. The contemporary interest in regional comparisons and more specialized studies should help to reverse such tendencies and undo some of the harm inflicted by the exercise of such monopolistic property rights.

Of course, comparison necessarily involves the opposite process of stressing the like rather than the unlike, even to the point of speculation and conjecture. In looking back at the Nilotic ethnography, I am astonished at the extent to which I failed to realize the profundity of the similarities. They offer an excellent case study of the structural principles and idioms that are worked out in the long course of man's appropriation of nature with the ordering of spatial and successive transformations of both mechanical and statistical models until the point is reached at which the model itself has been transformed.

Here I try to combine the results of long-term field work with comparison and theory. I use the Alur as a kind of concrete paradigm to guide me, not for a scientific reason but for a personal historical one. I assume that any of the Nilotic peoples could have provided an adequate paradigm that would have led to the same conclusions, despite the fact that they arose within different contexts, just as any version of a myth is equally good.

The Symbolism of Ethnic Identities

When I first visited the Alur, I accepted the fact of their existence naively, as had the non-Alur informants who first told me about them. Since then I have puzzled over the meaning of the name Alur. At the time of my arrival, they had been under colonial administration for thirty years or more. They were accustomed to being called Alur and accepted the name. But they did not usually refer to themselves as Alur. My first informants, who were, inevitably by the nature of my introduction, members of dominant groups, referred to themselves as Lwo or Nyalwo and to other groups in the society as *lwak,* which I came to translate as commoners. Such distinctions between nobles and commoners or first settlers and later immigrants are widespread among the Western Nilotes. Unlike many current ethnic appellations, the name Alur is not without valid foundation, although it is obscure. It appears in the form of Loor, Lur, or Luri on the maps of early European travelers. In the 1870s Emin Pasha referred to the people living on the west bank of the Nile as Lur (Schweinfurth et al. 1883:522). A few years later Mounteney Jephson noted that "the people all round Wadelai (west bank) belong to the Loor race—Loor is pronounced very long. On the opposite side of the river between it and the hills is still the Loor race but beyond the hills are the Shulis . . ." (D. Middleton 1969:266). Many other early maps understandably show only local group (chiefdom) names and not any regional ethnic names, such as Loor (Alur), Shuli (Acoli), or Shifalu (Jopalwo). In more recent decades, however, these people have insisted that they are Junam, river people, not Alur, a term that has become associated with the larger populations occupying the highlands west of the Nile. Yet the old meaning lived on. When my highland Alur friends were visiting the lowlands, they would say that they were "going down to Alur."

When I arrived among the Ukuru in 1949, the name Alur, Aluuru, or Alulu appeared in the genealogy, which was acquiring Alur recognition, although it was already a genealogy affected by the thoughts and aspirations of western-educated people. In the genealogy, Alulu represented the primal ancestor of the Alur in contradistinction to Madia, the ancestor of the Madi; Lendini, the ancestor of the Lendu; Kebia, the ancestor of the Okebo; Adhola, the ancestor of the Jopadhola, and Silo (whom I could not identify). This part of the Alur genealogy reflected their recent broadened awareness of neighboring groups. But the Lendu and Okebu would certainly not have accepted Lendini and Kebia as their ancestors. These were fabrications by the Alur, and the Lendu (Bale) and Okebo (Ndo) did not even accept these latter terms as their proper designations. Nor is the appearance of Alulu here very convincing, for it is not widely known and lacks substantive content. Alulu appears more intriguingly in Crazzolara's genealogy of the Atyak chiefdom of Acoli, which was a Madi group until recently (Crazzolara 1951:297). In this genealogy Alulu appeared as the grandson of Atyak, who was the son of Baade. Crazzolara had envisaged, in a way that seemed wild then but turned out to be prophetic, a whole Madi Epoch (preceding a Lang'o

Epoch that was followed by the Lwo Epoch), in which the Madi occupied all of Alurland as well as Bunyoro (1954:346–50). Recent archaeological, as well as linguistic studies, have given substance to Crazzolara's view (Ehret 1982:23–26). The mysterious Aluuru also appears in Crazzolara's account of the origins of the Lugbara as the leper woman who became the consort of Dribidu (1954:359). If Aluuru was a common name, it would not be remarkable, but it is a name that apparently has not been used by the Alur in recent times. In Santandrea's account (1968: 28, 69), Alur, or Aluro, represents a territorial section of the Luo southeast of Wau, but the interpretations suggested for the name are quite foreign to the Alur. It also appears as the name of a river in Anuakland. More remarkably, Aluru appears as the designation of a territorial section of the Western Lugbara (Southall 1956:17). Whatever hidden connections may exist between these various occurrences, the name seems to denote—for the Alur of Uganda and Zaire—the emergence of a new society, or people from diverse elements after the proverbial crossing of the river, in this case from the east to the west side of the Nile (Southall 1954:148; Lienhardt 1961:195; Burton 1981:41).

The rulers of the numerous Alur polities and members of their noble lineages claim that they are Lwo, as opposed to Lendu, Okebo, Madi, or other foreign ethnic groups, large numbers of whom they have incorporated (Southall 1970:71–92). They also claim that they and all these peoples migrated together, or in succession, from the Sudan or Misri (Egypt) (Southall 1954:142–43). In the course of my research, I realized that this could hardly be the case, since many Madi seemed to have no connection with the Alur, and since many Lendu (Bale) and Okebo (Ndo) groups in Zaire had never had close ties with the Alur and probably had not come from east of the Nile. The royal tradition is obviously a symbolic statement that strengthens and legitimates the essential composition and structure of Alur society. It also presents Alur kingship and statecraft as an eternal fact of life, rather than a more recent development. It makes statecraft appear as a cause rather than a consequence of the present settlement organization of the Alur.

It took me a long while to discount this part of the migration story as unhistorical, however meaningful it was symbolically. I finally concluded as follows: the Alur Lwo were indeed descended from Lwo groups, who traveled south from the Sudan, arriving in what is now northern Uganda on the east bank of the Nile and crossing to the west, as well-known oral traditions recount (Bere 1947; Crazzolara 1950:62–65). This migration occurred quite separately from that of the Lendu, Okebo, and

Madi, whom the Lwo encountered only when they crossed the Nile to the west. (They may have encountered some Madi, Bantu, and others before this, but the major process of incorporation did not begin until they had crossed the Nile.) Indeed, it was the crossing of the Nile and the process of incorporation of other groups by the Lwo that constituted the emergence of a new, composite society, called Alur. It consisted of a number of descent groups, which became ruling lineages as a result of the incorporation process and which continued to segment and form new polities of a similar kind. The Alur identity, however, remained somewhat vague. It is difficult to say which polities recognized this identity before the European intrusion clearly crystallized it. Much firmer and more clear-cut, and more relevant to everyday life, were the identities of the main ruling clans, such as the Atyak or Ang'al. Even more sharply focused were the identities of individual kingdoms, principalities, and chiefdoms that shared this descent, such as the Ukuru, Panduru, Padea, Paidha, War, and others, all of whom were defined by their praise cry as Atyak (Southall 1956:352–54).

The Alur thus adopted an identity name with foreign, Madi connotations. In fact, the name Aluru seems to belong conceptually and territorially to more groups outside than inside the boundaries of contemporary Alur people. Even their major royal clan is distinguished only by the apparently Madi ancestral praise cry of *Atyaki!* Many polities seem to derive their identity from a cross or fusion between two groups who are foreign to each other. For example, the dominant element among the British is not British at all but Anglo-Saxon and, in the opposite sense, the language of the French is not Frankish. Thus everything is something else, and we are British, a language we do not know or speak.

If a single set of names were to be chosen to designate these Nilotic groups by outsiders, the individual polity names mentioned above would be the most accurate and authentic. Most of these polities, however, were too small, occasionally some too large, to fit the colonial demand for convenient administrative units. The same was true in Acoli and more widely throughout Africa. The term *Atyak,* as the praise cry of the ruling lineages in all five Alur polities mentioned above, could be used as the name of a segmented and dispersed ruling clan.

In the most authentic group designations of self identity, there is a buried hint of the Other, as already noted in the case of Alur. Neither Alur nor Atyak has any substantive meaning in the Alur language. In other such cases the use of a foreign praise cry may be explained as the name of an enemy group that was vanquished or successfully resisted, thereby providing an effective rallying cry for the in-group. However, *Atyaki!* also serves as the praise cry of the rulers of the Atyak polity in northern Acoli, which is thought to be of Madi origin. Perhaps more conclusively, it appears in the form *Utyaka,* as both ancestor and praise cry of a Madi group: "*wan wa Madi, Utyaka, kwaro mwa.* An Uyibo: *kwara, an. Uyibo ku Utyaka, gi Madi dyang (Arua).* Wapakire: *Uyibo! Wo pa ngu!*" (Vanneste 1949:28). ("We are Madi, Utyaka [is] our ancestor. I am Uyibo: ancestor, I. Uyibo and Utyaka, they are 'cattle' Madi (Arua). We praise ourselves: Uyibo! Son of the Lion.")

If the Alur express their ethnic identity through designations of foreign, Madi origin, the Madi reciprocate with an even more extreme phenomenon. The Lugbara, who were called Madi until the last quarter of the nineteenth century when Arab slave traders generalized this name from the small Lugbara clan southeast of Kakwa territory (Shiroya 1970: 2), recall two hero ancestors, Jaki and Dribidu (Middleton 1960:231; Dean 1978:30). Jaki came from Kakwa and was Kakwa- (Lui-, or Lu-) speaking (Shiroya 1971:1). Dribidu came from Acoli and was Lwo-speaking (Shiroya 1971:6). He found, cured, and married Aluuru, an ostracized leper woman by whom he begot the ancestors of many Lugbara clans. Both Jaki and Dribidu adopted the Lugbara (Madi) language. Thus we have a Western Nilotic (Lwo) speaker and an Eastern Nilotic (Kakwa-Bari) speaker as hero ancestors of the Eastern Sudanic-speaking Lugbara. In a hierarchical society, this might not be unexpected. In the egalitarian, segmentary society of the Lugbara, it is surprising.

It is common enough to find rulers with origins outside the areas they rule, or incorporate, as in the case of the Lwo rulers in Alur; but these rulers carry identity symbols that actually seem to place them outside their own most basic identity. On the other hand, in stateless, segmentary societies, such as Lugbara, it is common to expect their primal ancestry to emphasize a homogeneous agnatic structure, although one primal spouse can certainly be perceived as of mysterious, or foreign, origin. The Lugbara, however, not only trace their clan founders to the hero ancestors Jaki and Dribidu, both of whom come from outside Lugbara and are alien to one another, but the spouse by whom Dribidu begets the ancestors of Lugbara clans was the leper woman Aluuru, homonym of the Alur eponym (Crazzolara 1954:359). Thus a reciprocal symbolic interchange seems to exist at the deepest level of identity, wherein people in one place, however distinctive they feel themselves to be, conceive of themselves as derived from a fusion of other peoples coming from other places in opposite directions.

By an analogous symbolic reversal, the Col (Shilluk), as the vanguard of the confrontation of the Black Sudan with the White Sudan, accept their blackness as their most fundamental positive identity, but as their blackness is the reverse of their neighbors' whiteness, they made the blackness of other objects the reverse of the self subject (*col-loj*).[3]

It is as important for the anthropologist to understand the nature of the symbolic relation between the self-identities of individuals and collectivities whom he studies in the field, as it is to comprehend the identity of the anthropologist as it appears to those he studies in relation to the larger collectivities that he represents in their view. It could be argued, following Durkheim, that no sanctity is greater than that of the collective identity (1915:47). The symbolism of sanctity and power cannot be treated adequately except within the context of the symbolic meanings embodied in the representations of collective identities.

The Alur identity belongs more properly to the mass of commoners of diverse origin, since the nobles have their own distinctive Lwo identity. The same is true of Col, which socially belongs to the commoners, while the royal clan are *kwareth,* descendants of kings (Butt 1952:48–50). The cognate term *kwairwoth* is equally applicable to the Alur descendants of royal clans, although they more usually call themselves Lwo.

The message of these intricately involved complexities must be that we cannot naively continue to accept colonial ethnic identities at face value, like distinct and separate pieces moving on a chess board, but must look behind them. The factor of ecology, in the sense of man's place in, reaction with, and appropriation of nature, is a major influence in the formation, elaboration, and transformation of these identities, activated by the movement of innumerable groups in kaleidoscopic fissions, fusions, and recombinations, across the physical landscape in the course of their search for subsistence production and reproduction.

Ecological Variation

Three markedly distinctive ecological zones can be distinguished in Alurland: the Nile lowlands, the transitional midlands, and the plateau highlands. These zones are topographically more distinct in the northeastern part of Alurland in Uganda than in the southwestern part of Alurland in Zaire. In Uganda, it is relatively easy to distinguish between the three zones. In Zaire, however, the highlands fall so steeply along the northwestern shores of Lake Albert that the zones cannot be clearly distinguished. Each polity contains highly contrasted ecological zones, although there is a distinction between the shore polities, which also contain some highland areas, and the highland polities, which also usually contain low-lying valleys but no shore plains (Southall 1956:11, 16).

In Uganda, the lowland, midland, and highland distinctions coincide with a number of economic, political, and historical differences. The lowlands provided valuable fishing and hippo hunting, but relatively poor soil and rainfall (Southall 1956:13). The lowlands were subject to heavy helminthic infection, tsetse-borne sleeping sickness, and other diseases, which also limited the keeping of cattle. The lowlands were nearest geographically and by easy river communication to the powerful influence of Bunyoro. They were not settled and ruled by a single dominant group, but by a number of (mostly unrelated) ruling lines, some of whom claim to have drifted down the river from Bunyoro and Palwo on islands of sudd. Others came down from the Alur highlands and midlands or from Acoliland east of the Nile, or crossed Lake Albert from Bunyoro, all of them incorporating small groups of Bantu and Madi, whom they found already settled there. These movements created a series of small, parallel polities in the Nile valley, arranged spatially in strips at right angles to the river, inviting some comparison with the Col pattern of settlement on the Nile five hundred miles downstream to the north.

Beyond the lowlands was the midland belt with somewhat higher rainfall and better soil. Cattle could be kept, but with far less advantage than in the highlands. Here, too, small polities developed from the infiltration of potentially dominant groups. Some came inland from the Nile valley, but most migrated from the highlands. They incorporated small groups of foreigners, especially Madi and Okebo, and remnants and descendants of groups whose previous efforts at domination had failed. They lacked the parallel pattern imposed in the lowlands by exploitation of the river banks.

In the Nebi region of the midlands, there was a tendency for small polities to stagnate. The area received constant infusions of petty kingship, mainly of kings' sons from the Ukuru highlands, but most of them were unsuccessful in extending or even maintaining their power. Whatever the precise reason, in famine, disease, or a decline in human or cattle production, the failure was ideologically interpreted as the failure of kingship: "the tooth of the kingship becomes cold"; and "another comes and the other gets cold" (Southall 1956:205–10). This small-scale kingship was thus a highly flexible, proliferating, and exportable commodity.

It might or might not work, but by this time, when Alur society was already crystallized, it was regarded as a capacity restricted exclusively to rulers and their sons.[4]

Acoliland was ecologically somewhat like the Alur midlands but of vaster extent. It seems to have been the scene of immigration by a large number of relatively independent Lwo groups from the north. They developed small polities, which sometimes replaced one another through the incorporation of previous inhabitants and diverse later arrivals. They were influenced by groups from the more pastoral environment to the east and by the return of groups from the Bunyoro sphere (after their earlier migration there), with more advanced ideas of politico-ritual organization. According to Girling (1960:126), "there are good grounds for stating that each Acholi ruler enjoyed a degree of relative independence. And although there was never any close or formal political control exercised by the Banyoro over the Acholi, nevertheless many of them regarded the Bakama [kings] as their suzerains in some sense. Also it seems that the Payera, in a similar way, enjoyed the respect of most other Acholi groups." However, it is likely that the special influence of Bunyoro and Payera was due to the mid-nineteenth century advent of slave traders and guns, which tended to polarize large, powerful groups and small, weak groups into those that could resist and win greater power and centralization and those that had to succumb and seek protection. As Girling observed, "the best watered and most fertile part of the country lies in the area between the rivers Unyama and Aswa which run parallel for a part of their course. This is the area in which there is the heaviest rainfall and it is the home of the Payera who formed one of the largest of the Acholi domains. Being situated centrally in the country they were in a position to exert their influence over a great part of it" (1960:15).

The Alur highlands seem to have offered both economic and hygienic conditions that stimulated population growth and polity expansion far greater than in the midlands or lowlands, or indeed anywhere in the much larger adjacent area of Acoliland. This expressed itself in territorially larger and demographically denser[5] polities of the segmentary state type (Southall 1988). Here, in these highlands west of the Nile, Alur society achieved its greatest and most distinctive development. There was lush grass for pasture, which was extended as the forests were cut, and there was rich soil for cultivation. But here too were other populations, especially Lendu and Okebo, who were incorporated by the Lwo as they pushed westwards through the generations. This interaction and incorporation not only led to larger, ethnically mixed, and gradually integrating populations, but, I now assume, to the necessary elaboration of kingship out of previous Lwo leadership roles and to the emergence of segmentary states. The name Alur symbolically stands for these processes and their results.

As we have seen, it is possible to compare the settlement patterns of the Alur Junam and the Col, both of whom occupied the riverine zone in different parts of the Nile Valley. It is also illuminating to compare the Col state with Ukuru, the largest segmentary state developed by the Alur in the highlands, as these seem to be the largest states known to have been developed by the Lwo. It is noteworthy that they occupy the northeastern and southwestern extremities of their dispersed area of occupation.

The Col occupied the west bank because the ridges suitable for occupation above the flood level were there. There were none near the east bank, consequently occupied by the Jieng' in their transhumant system. It was probably this ecological contrast that kept the Col and the northern Jieng' ethnically distinct (see Note 9). Interestingly, the Nath, who are geographically more distant from the Col than are the Northern Jieng' (Padang), profess a greater sense of psychic affinity with the Col than with the Jieng' (Sharon Hutchinson, personal communication, 1986). This affinity, however, apparently has nothing to do with historical or genetic connections and is perhaps rather an expression of that generation of points of likeness that occurs between contrasted neighbors (Southall 1972:91). The Col were able to live permanently in their village while exploiting the complementary ecological resources on either side of the Nile. They fished in the river, cultivated land near their villages, and grazed their cattle during the wet season on the western side of their settlements and during the dry season on the eastern margins of the river, on the islands, and even across on the east bank of the Nile (Lienhardt 1954:149). This type of agricultural and riverine production yielded a settlement pattern similar to that of the Alur Junam.

We might ask why the Col developed a clearly bounded and relatively centralized state, while the Junam established a series of small, independent polities, in spite of the fact that they both occupied a similar ecological zone. Did other factors come into play? Did the presence of a single ethnic or descent group among the Col lay the groundwork for a unified settlement and thus for a unified state? Can we be sure that a single descent group was the cause and not the result of a centralized polity?

The part of the Nile valley occupied by the Junam did not have the same imperatives as that inhabited by the Col. The Junam settlement pattern was similar to the Col, but the parallel strips running along the river were wider and more irregular. Unlike the Col, who were restricted to the west bank because the ridges were located there, the Junam faced no critical difference between the east and west banks. Although focused on the west bank, the Junam exploited the agricultural, riverine, and hunting resources of both banks in rotation. The Junam did not have dry season pastures, in the sense of having land that had been inundated, as the Col, Jieng', and Nath had. The Junam were not affected to the same degree as the Col by limitations on the east-west extent of their productive territories.

Col territory was clearly bounded by the desert on the west, the river and the Jieng' on the east, the Jieng' and Nath on the south, and the bushy, overgrown river banks on the north, which provided the Col with a convenient no-man's-land cover for their raids against the Funj and, later, the Arabs and Turks. In addition, the Col were bordered on the south by acephalous societies, whereas the Junam were bounded on the south by the more centralized Nyoro states, whose wars of succession and factions frequently precipitated the emigration of potential rulers across Lake Albert and north down the Nile toward Junam territory. Indeed, some Junam chiefdoms owe their existence to this process.

The Col territory was settled by a fairly homogeneous group of immigrants, whose recognition of a single source of leadership provided a basis for unity. This was accented by their need to defend themselves against the outposts of Funj power. Such influences favored the development and maintenance of a single focus of ritual leadership, which in a later period was pushed by external pressures in the direction of a more centralized polity. The Junam had no such influences to propel overall ritual or political unity. Their system of economic exploitation was less sharply marked off from their neighbors on either side, while their cultural links with the Bito dynasty of Bunyoro enabled refugees, dissidents, and adventurers from the latter to establish numerous small polities independent of one another in Junam.

The Col seem to have become more politically unified and centralized only during the seventeenth century in reaction to increased pressure on all sides, from Baggara in the west, Jieng' in the south and east, and Funj in the north (Mercer 1971:410). The threats were more serious than any the early Ukuru Alur had to face from outsiders. This factor, together with the ecological situation, probably made the Col state more centralized and less segmentary than Ukuru. Nevertheless, many common processes are discernible.

It is therefore necessary at this point to examine the changing status of Col kingship, as a basis for comparison with political institutions in other Nilotic societies. Arens recently concluded that the *reth* (*king*) "functioned as a sacred symbol of the nation in every quarter, he also had absolute power and authority to command in a restricted territory of Shillukland, from which he was born, drew his initial political support and then maintained his personal capital" (1984:357). I would interpret the evidence a little differently, mainly by paying more attention to the time period in question, but it is certainly true that a ruler of this type had much greater authority in the small core area of his realm (Southall 1988).

Until the seventeenth century, the *reth* was probably an inconsequential political figure who reigned but did not govern (Southall 1988). The capital was not fixed but moved at least once in every reign. The political constitution was undoubtedly that of a segmentary state. After the seventeenth century, increasing external pressure, and perhaps internal pressure from population growth during periods of famine caused by excessive flooding or extreme drought, produced a situation that demanded more effective and more militant leadership from the *reth*. Successful raids were mounted in all directions, although some serious defeats were suffered. The Col always had to trade for salt and iron. Gradually there was an increase in the demand for ivory by the merchants further north for the luxurious classes of Sudan, Egypt, and ultimately Europe. The *reth* was able to make it his monopoly. He could also exert monopolistic strategic control of river traffic. For the first time, he acquired a personal army—war captives—which he could maintain and keep loyal with booty and profits from ivory. In the mid-nineteenth century, with the availability of guns and the addition of slave trading to the ivory monopoly, the *reth* must have been able to impose his authority over most of the state. Col tradition and royal ritual was probably elaborated and adapted at this time to strengthen and legitimize the kingship[6] by emphasizing the uniqueness of Nyikang' as royal ancestor and supernatural being, reincarnated in every *reth* (Lienhardt 1954:150). This was the peak of Col centralization and state power, but Egypt's traders and military administration were quickly closing in and the Col capital was invaded and eventually destroyed in 1861. Although Col external aggression was curtailed, the king's internal power continued until the British colonial takeover. Thus the nineteenth-century *reth* was political head of a centralized, military state, while the sixteenth- and early seventeenth-century *reth* was probably the ritual figurehead of a segmentary state.

Col tradition reports that Nyikang' and his successors for several generations disappeared at the end of their lives and were not buried (Lienhardt 1954:150), just as the Anuak nobles' ancestor Ukiro and his son Gilo both disappeared back into the river (Lienhardt 1955:37), and as the Ukuru kings' ancestor Ucak vanished again into the cloud from which he had come (Vanneste 1949:34–35). These metaphors seem to indicate a mythical period before or outside the historical era. There are two implications. Nyikang', Dak, and their immediate successors cannot be dated as historical personages, let alone as kingly rulers. On the other hand, the Lwo forerunners may well have reached the land of the Col long before the sixteenth century, a date only arrived at by wrongly treating mythical figures as historical generations. We cannot therefore suppose that Nyikang' "created a kingdom."

It seems reasonable to conclude that Col centralization was not the product of some special Nilotic, let alone Hamitic genius, but the rational reaction of people in a tightly constrained ecological niche to increasing external threat, which compelled them to exploit the corresponding opportunities of increased trade and new technology, especially firearms. The centralized state and its autocratic kingship was a rather late and brief phenomenon, uncharacteristic of Col history as a whole. This may now seem obvious, but it is a revolutionary change from the idea that nobility is something inherent, and that, for example, the Kenya Luo had no state because they had no nobles or because they lacked Hamitic influence (Wright 1952:87).

Material factors go far to explain the general shape and structure of the Col state as well as the trajectory of its development when combined with external historical factors. Ecological constraints and the presence of other peoples, in other ecological niches, forced the Col polity and settlement pattern into a straight line along the river, with its component settlements running at right angles. This compact and precise, clearly bounded shape and structure, in combination with already available Col cultural potentialities, strongly favored the development of a clear-cut, single state (and also precipitated binary oppositions more sharply than in Alur) (Evans-Pritchard 1962 [1948]:70, 81–82; Lienhardt 1955:29).

It is at first sight surprising that the Kenya Luo did not develop more specialized political institutions and offices, in view of the fact that they could not have arrived and settled where they did without coming in contact with either the Nyoro state itself, which had been taken over by their ethnic kinsfolk, or the powerful outlying states of the Nyoro complex, such as Bugabula and Bulamogi (in the present Busoga), which also show some Lwo influence.[7] One cannot say that the Kenya Luo environment inhibited the development of a specialized political office, nor that it was particularly required. Though mainly acephalous and segmentary the Kenya Luo polities became large and populous,[8] larger than those of Acoli, which were more centralized and hierarchical although smaller in scale.[9] Perhaps this resulted from the fact that in Kenya the incoming Lwo occupied their new country by pushing out the equally acephalous, segmentary Bantu groups[10] (Wagner 1949:24–26), rather than by incorporating them (although there was some Luo incorporation of Bantu and some Bantu incorporation of Luo and certainly a great deal of cultural interpenetration).[11] Some of the longest settled Luo polities, which also included diverse descent groups, developed further in the direction of specialized, hereditary, politico-ritual office. Ogot plausibly attributes this process to the change from a seminomadic pastoral to a more agrarian sedentary existence, combined with the exigencies of warfare with Bantu and pastoral Eastern Nilotes, which required the incorporation of non-Luo elements (1967:173), but it seems to have occurred rather recently, possibly in the nineteenth century.

While the Col formed a single large polity, the Alur formed many small polities, by a highly proliferating process that induced me to call them segmentary states. Ukuru was the largest although others in the highlands, such as Panduru, War, Ang'al and Mukambo were also quite large (Southall 1956:349–350). Ukuru tradition claims that Panduru, War, and many other smaller polities (but not Ang'al or Mukambo) were offshoots of its own ruling line. The claim seems convincing although Panduru became a bitter enemy of Ukuru and would reject its claims of supremacy, insisting on its total independence but not rejecting the common genealogy. In any case, the links that existed between the polities spawned by Ukuru segmentation were of a ritual and occasional nature.

The Polities of Alur-Ukuru and Col

I shall take the example of the Ukuru Alur polity to explore the degree of similarity in structure and process between it and the Col. First of all, there is some similarity in the structure and composition of ethnic identity. Both Col and Ukuru are ruled by royal lines calling themselves Lwo, Nyilwo, or Nyalwo. The lineages descended from past rulers form a substantial part of the population. All such agnatic descendants claim to be Lwo, or alternatively *rwodhi* (sing. *rwoth,* king, chief); thus, "royals" or "nobles." Lwo is an ancient ethnic identity and does not itself in any way connote royal or noble. Lineages whose link with the ruling line is very remote have become de facto commoners, like the *jowatong'* (Evans-Pritchard 1940b:34), and, to a lesser extent, the *tung' dwong'* among the Anuak (Lienhardt, 1958b:25). The Alur nobles became extremely numerous, although the designation "noble" is not as misleading as the translation of the Nath *dil* as aristocrat.[12] Royal polygyny accounts for much of the Lwo numerical preponderance, while the proportion of commoners has also been reduced because colonial administrations separated commoners whom they perceived as ethnically different in new settlements of their own, to remove what they felt to be a kind of serfdom. The distinction seemed to imply that all Lwo were royal and all non-royals were foreigners, absorbed from other ethnic groups. This in turn might imply that Alur society did not exist until such absorption of foreigners had taken place. In fact, it was only by absorbing foreigners that the Lwo became royal and their polity developed towards statehood.

In Col this status of lapsed noble is precisely defined as *ororo* and the reason for their demotion is given a traditional explanation, whereas in Alur they simply merge with the general population and are generally called *lwak* (pl. *lwaga*), which seems here to connote the mass of the ordinary commoner subject population. Somewhat similar is the Anuak usage of *lwak* to denote the band of young men forming the manpower force of a village (Lienhardt 1957:347). However, in Anuak and Col, as well as Jieng' and Nath, *lwak* has the more concrete meaning of cattle byre, the building in which cattle are kept at night, or in which they are protected from insects by the smoky fire burned in the byre, but it also means by extension the communal solidarity of the men who gather and socialize there as in a guest house or club (Pumphrey 1941). It is also, of course, the name of the southern, and original, Col territorial moiety. The case of *lwak* is consistent with the derivation of abstract concepts from pre-existing concrete meanings. Jieng' and Nath have primarily the concrete meaning. The more hierarchical Anuak and Col have both the concrete and abstract meanings. The Alur have only the abstract. Their loss of the concrete could simply reflect their movement into a different environment where the specialized cattle byre lost its importance.

Col is more particularly the term for free commoners, whom the Alur call *lwak*. In both cases it seems that most, if not all, of these commoner lineages are of foreign origin. Col tradition suggests the incorporation of many foreign elements at the period when the Lwo were moving into and establishing themselves in Col territory. The same is true of the Alur. The process of incorporation continued right into the twentieth century, on a more massive scale than was possible for the Col, because the Alur had a hinterland of acephalous peoples further west, among whom they were able to infiltrate in the process of incorporation. The Col ethnic environment did not provide this opportunity.

Although Col in the strict sense refers to the commoners only, it has come to stand for the people as a whole, in exactly the same way as has the term Alur. It would seem that, in both cases, their more comprehensive localized ethnic identity came into existence as an aspect of the process whereby ruling lines incorporated foreign elements into their following as they completed their migratory journey and "crossed the last river," as it were, to form a definitive settlement and create a new society (Lienhardt 1954:148–49). This was more definite in the Col case, as their territory seems to have remained rather stable for centuries, and was more clearly demarcated both ecologically and ethnically. By contrast, the Ukuru rulers and their following, after crossing the Nile to the west, continued gradually moving further up into the highlands for three or four generations, and although the core area of the kingdom has been stable since then, its territory and that of its segmentary offshoots continued to expand westward. Both Col and Alur are therefore names of newly composite ethnic identities which came into existence as a result of the incorporation of foreigners by Lwo. Indeed, it was only this incorporation of foreigners that made the Lwo royal. As Ogot remarked, "perhaps chiefship or kingship and plural societies go together" (1964:300). Indeed, incorporation marks the beginning of political rule and state formation, while the association of different groups occurs within the context of stateless society.

In the absence of such a process of incorporation, leading in the direction of state formation, the Lwo are known and know themselves simply as Lwo, as in the case of the Kenya Luo, or by names of the ancestral type. Thus the Anuak are properly called Kwar Nyigiilo, the descendants of Giilo (Evans-Pritchard 1940b:9) and it is interesting that from the Anuak perspective the Col are Kwar Nyikang'o, the descendants of Nyikang', although in fact the Col (apart from the ruling clan) are precisely not the descendants of Nyikang' but strictly speaking the commoners. We see here the extent to which the structure of ethnic identity is determined by political economy.

The Col also use the term *dil* (pl. *dyil*), not known to the Alur, for resident members of the descent group to which a settlement is held to belong, or to whose ancestors Nyikang' is believed to have allotted it, while immigrants are called *wedh,* which may be cognate with the Anuak *welle* (Lienhardt 1958b:24) and the Alur and Kenya Luo *welo* (guest, immigrant), used in the same sense. The first sense of *dil* is the same as in Nath, where its translation as aristocrat seems inappropriate. Col and Alur both use *bang'* (pl. *bong'*) for the non-free population, which in Col was attached to the king as *bang'reth,* whereas the Anuak nobles use *bang'* for all commoners (Evans-Pritchard 1940b:51), as do the Acoli (*lobong'*). Col *reth,* Anuak *rath,* and Alur *rwoth* (Acoli *rwot,* Kenya Luo *ruoth*) are cognates. The Anuak also seem to have used *rath* for their kings and nobles (Evans-Pritchard 1940b:51). The Col use *kwareth* (kings' descendants) for all Lwo, as the Alur use the plural *rwodhi*. The Anuak use *warath* (son of noble) but usually call nobles *nyiye*. The Kenya Luo use *ruoth* for any leader, such as a lineage head, but not for any whole category. Thus, to a large extent, the conceptual systems of all these people are variations of a single set.

A Gradient of State Formation Processes

The most fascinating and difficult part of any comparison such as this is the analysis of process. The Col, Alur, Anuak, Kenya Luo, Jieng', and Nath provide almost a gradient of state formation processes. I assume that basic Nilotic culture carried certain latent potentialities, not wholly determined by forces and relations of production (letter from F. Engels to J. Bloch, dated September 21–22, 1890, in Tucker 1978:760–65), which could at times lie dormant and in other circumstances could be developed in various directions, or further suppressed (Southall 1970). It is to be expected that likenesses between the Col and Alur would be greatest when external influences and the adaptation to them had changed the Col least, in other words, before the eighteenth century.

The *reth*'s council is said to have contained the heads of only neighboring settlements (Mercer 1971:423), as was the case with the Ukuru *rwoth*. According to Pumphrey (1941:12), whenever one settlement (*podh*) fought against another and refused to obey the *reth*'s orders, he called upon settlements neighboring the disputants to join him in raiding the culprits, burning their villages, and driving off their cattle. This was exactly the sanction employed in Ukuru. It represents the most elementary form of political authority and is diagnostic of the segmentary state. It is almost self-activating, because it legitimates raiding and plunder, whereby the king's subjects prove their loyalty and reap the benefits in a single operation (Southall 1988:64). "Each settlement contains, in microcosm, the administrative difficulties of the tribe" (Pumphrey 1941:7), another characteristic of the segmentary state, which was equally the case in Ukuru.

Lienhardt has explored recurring similarities in the relations between Nilotic kings and their mothers' kin (1955:29–42), suggesting that close mother's kin are usually supportive, while distant classificatory kin may be hostile. As he recognized, this is to some extent an inevitable feature of a patrilineage system, for if the normative solidarity and support of agnates breaks down in rivalry and jealousy, the mother's kin are bound to be the next resort. They were the natural major support of rival agnates claiming the kingship in Col, Anuak, and Alur. In a similar way, they are said to be sometimes closer than agnates in Nath feuds.

The *reth* of Col was selected by some ritual process in which the Nuba, to whom Nyikang' had given his daughter in marriage, played a part (Lienhardt 1954:151; 1955:35). The Ukuru *rwoth* was selected through being the rival lucky enough to find the bead placed in his porridge, or able to place a bead in the deceased king's mouth (Southall 1956:359), a process which the inside elders could presumably manipulate. The Anuak *rath* was selected simply by superior force. It is significant that selection by a superior force was associated with an office that had minimal state power and no wide ritual influence, while the ritual process of selection in Col and Alur was associated with considerably greater institutionalized state power and wide-ranging ritual influence. Lack of ritual institutionalization in the Anuak case strongly suggests a temporary phase. Offices without state power or wide ritual influence may not require any sacred mystification, whereas in Jieng' the Spear Masters provided vital ritual leadership and coordination, which required the strong backing of sacral and supernatural powers, since the Jieng' did not generally develop institutionalized political authority.

The interaction of culture with political economy in the case of the Anuak provides an especially interesting supplement to the Col and Ukuru cases. Anuakland seems to have received a number of diverse Nilotic descent groups, some Lwo, some Jieng', some Nath, who mingled and intermarried as they took possession of the country and adapted themselves to the limitations and possibilities of its environment (Evans-Pritchard 1940b:31–34). The ecological imperatives were very clear. Given the basic Nilotic technology and familiarity with cultivation, fishing, herding, and hunting, the flood plain of western Anuakland seems to have offered little choice as to settlement pattern. They had to settle on isolated mounds and other limited ridges of high ground near the numerous water courses. This precipitated a society consisting of quite separate and politically autonomous villages, each under the authority of the head of its dominant or first settling lineage, to which members of various other lineages were attached. There was no need for an extensive and wide-ranging transhumant pattern of the Jieng' or Nath type, which would have enforced larger-scale social coordination, no tightly constricting ecological niche of the Col kind to enforce densely related contiguous settlements and encourage integration and unity, and no sparse hinterland of fertile territory and weak acephalous populations to encourage infiltration, expansion, and political elaboration as in the case of Ukuru.

But the Anuak did have a shorter transhumant movement between their permanent wet season villages on the ridges at the edge of the flood and their dry season camps on large mounds dotted here and there within it (Evans-Pritchard 1940b: 16). This system irresistibly recalls that of the Lozi in Zambia, as noted long ago by Gluckman (1968 [1941]: 1, 87). The two share extraordinary features in common, but, strangely enough, Gluckman chose to make a comparison with the obviously contrasted Nath (and Ila) rather than with the Anuak (1968 [1948]: 102), perhaps because Evans-Pritchard's visit to the latter was so brief and fraught with difficulties that he could not possibly collect much of the data desirable for such a comparison. Both Anuak and Lozi have mixed economies based on productive flood plain agriculture, fishing, and limited cattle keeping. Neither use cattle for bridewealth, despite the apparently strong pastoral tradition of the Anuak. Both move their residence annually between ridges on the margin and mounds within the plain, although the main villages of the Lozi are on the latter and those of the Anuak on the former.

With a relatively specific ecological adaptation such as this, how were the cultural heritage and ideological presuppositions of the two people affected? Did such similar processes of appropriation of nature determine equally similar superstructures, or was this prevented by differing historical circumstances and differing interactions with neighbors? Or did differing ideological equipment itself have the capacity to bend the process of appropriation into supporting different superstructures in each case?

Gluckman speculates (1968 [1941]: 89–91) that the Lozi "reached the Plain probably under a small female chief, with weak authority," but that there was a change from matriliny to patriliny and from female to male chiefship, brought about by ecological conditions in which some mounds were richer than others, producing inequality and demanding a more political, male kingship, relating to rights of property in plain resources and the necessity for coordination of economic activities and defense against neighboring peoples.

It would seem that Anuak and Lozi arrived in their respective habitats with major differences in cultural and ideological heritage. The Anuak probably had an extensive agnatic lineage system and a strong pastoral orientation; the Lozi had a weak pastoral orientation and a matrilineage system. Anuak settled without the kind of chiefship the Lozi apparently brought with them, while the Lozi arrived without agnation. As we have noted, material factors condition in the *longue durée* and do not quickly obliterate all cultural differences. Lozi kingship was based on the river. Could the Anuak have used the river in this way—as the colonial gunboats did? Gluckman's "female chief" speculation may not be correct. It gives expression to Murdock's view that cognatic systems may derive from a blend of matrilineal and patrilineal factors—not convincingly applicable to Southeast Asia or the Anglo-Saxon world.

In the course of time, the processes of appropriation brought both peoples to a remarkably similar kinship organization, both having villages dominated by an agnatic core (Gluckman 1968 [1941]:26; Evans-Pritchard 1940b:27). The Anuak clans and larger and more distant lineages lost their rule of exogamy, which was likewise absent in Lozi. They differed somewhat in that the Anuak dominant lineages probably (see Note 7) formed a larger part of the village population than in Lozi and the rest of the population consisted of sections of other lineages attached to the dominant lineage by affinal and cognatic ties, whereas the attached population of Lozi villages probably did not consist of lineage sections but of small groups of matrilineal and affinal kin. This was a slight difference in practice and it is likely that the *de facto* composition of Lozi and Anuak villages was very similar in kinship properties. It is remarkable that matrilineal kin who stayed in a Lozi village could be assimilated to the agnatic core by treating a mother's brother as a father in the genealogy, or treating a mother as a man, exactly as occurred among the Nath, Col, and very probably among the Anuak also.

The basic idiom of agnatic core with attachments is thus similar in both cases, but the two kin terminologies are very different, suggesting that we have here an element of superstructure which is not completely determined by the infrastructure, not at any rate unless in the very long term.

The two big differences between Lozi and Anuak, which are no doubt interlocked, are the much higher mobility between mounds and far greater political centralization in the Lozi mounds, but there is no data to prove this conclusively (there seems no doubt that Anuak villages were much further apart). The interaccessibility of the Lozi villages facilitated and perhaps demanded greater coordination between them, out of which eventually developed the powerful Lozi state, with its hierarchy of titles and named positions, to which land rights were attached. The king's conferring of titles and names, making promotions and allocating land to clients greatly accentuated population mobility and the continuous mixing of the composition of each village.

In the Anuak case it was the higher banks of the upper reaches of the rivers further to the east that made possible a form of ritual coordination between the more closely spaced villages, but before the arrival of firearms it never achieved any significant political centralization.

The phenomenon of the nobles and the kingship (*rath*) in eastern Anuakland appears at first sight like a striking cultural deviation, but Evans-Pritchard does conclude that the headmanship throughout Anuakland contains the essential principle of the kingship (1940b:137). In the earliest period the kingship seems to have been no more than a glorified headmanship, and in no case was a noble more than a village chieftain, without authority over neighboring villages until the introduction of rifles at the end of the last century (Evans-Pritchard 1940b:52). In other words there were only relative differences between the system of headmen and the system of nobles and a slight shift of circumstances could turn the one into the other. Eastern Anuakland provided such a shift because the flood plains gave way to forest and the river banks were higher, so that for these reasons a denser settlement of villages much closer to one another was possible. The early kingship differed from headmanship only in that members of the royal clan dispersed to found other villages, in which they became dominant as headmen, while recognizing the purely ritual supremacy of the king (*rath*) (a process that seems basically similar to that whereby the early Alur kingdom of Ukuru spread and proliferated). This introduced at least a tenuous network of relationships between villages that had not existed before. But it was the greater proximity of villages in eastern Anuakland that made such a network possible, thus transforming headmen into nobles and their clan head into a king. Evans-Pritchard insists that the nobles' villages of the east were just as autonomous politically as the headmen's villages of the west, but that they were not isolated politically because they shared the common value of the kingship, for which they all competed, and this made them a polity. He actually compares the spread of Anuak kingship to the possible diffusion of Col kingship from the southern half of the country (gol Nyikang) to the north (Evans-Pritchard 1962 [1948]: 80).

We are thus able to show that the common set of concepts possessed by spatially divergent groups of similar or common origin diverges in the course of adaptation to differing local ecological and historical factors, while on the other hand, totally unrelated groups, thousands of miles apart, but at a similar level in their modes of production, converge and develop similar features when they move from quite contrasted natural environments into very similar ones.

Regicide

The village-based autonomous power of numerous Anuak nobles, linked together in the same lineage, seems to have been the factor which induced them to compete for kingship by winning possession of the royal emblems through killing the incumbent. Tradition suggests that early kings held office for life, or at least for long periods, and it was only in the mid-nineteenth century, and probably in response to external influence from Galla and Amhara "to the east," that king killing increased in frequency, enabling the royal emblems to circulate faster and faster, thus multiplying the numbers of kings' sons eligible to succeed and creating a vicious circle. Although the introduction of rifles is placed by Evans-Pritchard at the end of the century, Turkish raiders reached the Sobat by 1830, so it is entirely possible that odd guns came into the hands of Anuak nobles much earlier and precipitated the practice of regicide. The fascination of Anuak regicide is that it was purely political and secular. Although the office was ritual, the Anuak king was not in the least divine, notwithstanding the exaggerated respect displayed in greeting him (Evans-Pritchard 1940b: 62–64). There was no ritual cycle nor any set of beliefs requiring that kings be put to death. The process of investiture seems, from the ritual point of view, almost perfunctory (Evans-Pritchard 1940b: 76, 90, 95). All this may suggest that the elaboration of ritual and belief develops to bolster an office whose incumbents have some success in winning stability and dominance for it, rather than the other way around. The Anuak case therefore throws an interesting light on divine king killing in Col and Jieng'.

Why did ritual regicide develop in the relatively centralized Col system, secular regicide in the highly uncentralized Anuak system, and no regicide in the Alur segmentary state system which stood between the two in the degree of centralization? And why did an approximation of ritual regicide occur among the Jieng' who were even less centralized than the Anuak? Surely these are instances in which the ritualization of the polity cannot be related in any consistent fashion to its political economy. Perhaps these are good examples of cultural choices and logic not materially determined. However, a possible explanation is as follows. The Col kingship was defined as unique and clearly bounded by the interaction and adaptation of the people with their particular ecology. Therefore, the aspirations of the many qualified aspirants to kingship could only be satisfied by eliminating the incumbent, whereas in Alur there was an easy alternative in aspirants going to found new petty realms of their own on the periphery. This process was explicitly formulated and encouraged by the Ukuru kings who said to their troublesome sons, "go and break the country over there," and provided them with the wives, cattle, and following to do it. On the other hand, in Anuak, while investment with the royal emblems conferred no significant increase in political power or wealth, there were no weak, acephalous neighboring peoples to confer on nobles as an alternative avenue of advancement as in the Alur case, so their only avenue of advancement was to eliminate the present holder of the emblems. In this sense, the Col system was closed, Anuak relatively closed, and Ukuru open. As we have noted, Anuak king killing may not have occurred in the earliest period when holders of the emblems seem to have remained ritual kings for life, or at least for long periods, and the process of regicide may only have begun, or become habitual, when rival nobles began to acquire guns.

Regicide among the Jieng' took the form of voluntary death by aged and distinguished Masters of the Fishing Spear (Lienhardt 1961:298–312). Clearly they were not kings in any accepted sense of the term, nor were they contenders for the golden bough in the grove at Nemi. The Jieng' practice does illustrate a significant point in the continuum of regicide. The evidence for regicide is often ambiguous, but there is a clear distinction between the asserted duty of social leaders to snuff out the life of a deficient king in Col or Rwanda, the voluntary serene death of aged Masters of the Fishing Spear, and the involuntary, violent death of the Anuak *rath,* or of the King of the Wood (Frazer 1950 [1922]: 1). The contrast accurately represents the difference between egalitarian and more hierarchical societies.[13]

If Nath and Jieng' are so closely related to one another, why did the latter have an egalitarian voluntary form of regicide and the former not? The Nath were generally lacking in ritual elaboration; much of their ritual and religion was derived from the Jieng'. The distinction may be exaggerated by the circumstance that our knowledge of Nath is drawn mainly from their recent eastern expansion, which brought new processes into play. The Jieng' Masters of the Fishing Spear correspond in many ways to the Nath Leopard Skin Priests. If we knew more about the latter among the Western Nath the correspondence might be even greater. From the ethnography we have, the Jieng' Spear Masters were essential to local solidarity because of agnatic heterogeneity, which resulted from the dislocations caused by Nath raiding. The Eastern Nath, to whom most of our knowledge relates, seem not to have needed the Spear Master role in its full form because they were, in recent times, entirely occupied in conquering and incorporating Jieng'. Correspondingly their disputes were settled mainly by force of arms, with the additional arbitration provided by the Leopard Skin Priest (*Kuaar muon*) (who corresponded closely to the Jieng' Spear Master). It has taken a further step with the current practice of the Eastern Nath purifying *themselves* from the contamination of homicide (Sharon Hutchinson, personal communication, 1986).

In Seligman's account, probably in this passage referring to Western Nath, the eldest son of the primal Nath couple, Gau and Kwong, was both Leopard Skin Chief and Land Chief, "the most important man in the tribe" (1932:207). Beidelman also concluded that the Leopard Skin Chief, Land Chief, and prophet could all be the same person (1971:375), and Evans-Pritchard found that among Western Nath the control of age sets, which he normally ascribed to the Man of Cattle, could be in the hands of a prophet (1940a:250), who might be Man of Cattle at the same time. One can only conclude that, despite the obvious variation and the divergence of Eastern from Western Nath in a number of respects, a role of central ritual authority seemingly identical to that of the Jieng' Spear Master could be found among the Western Nath, who were regarded as the original or "home" Nath (Evans-Pritchard 1940a:5).

The Nath Leopard Skin Priest further identifies himself with the Jieng' Spear Masters through their special divinity *ring* (flesh) when in his sacrifice for incest he addresses *kwoth ring gwari,* "the spirit of the Flesh of my fathers" (Evans-Pritchard 1935:40). We must therefore envisage a pre-nineteenth century (or earlier) situation in which the Nath and Jieng' had similar ritual leadership roles that developed in divergent directions to produce the relatively powerless Leopard Skin Priests of Eastern Nath and the much more influential Spear Masters of Western Jieng'. However, the ritual leaders of the Western "home" Nath may have retained much more of their essential similarity with the ritual leaders of their neighboring Jieng'. Swazi and Zulu had evolved more centralized political systems than the Nath and Jieng', partly because their ecologically rich environment did not impose a transhumant existence, and partly in reaction to the increasing intensity of the threat from white capitalist penetration, which only hit Nath and Jieng' a hundred years later.

It would seem that Eastern Nath were still led by the type of secular war leaders who had guided their recent expansion. They were in no mood to recognize ritual leadership, but they did recognize the ultimate practical need for ritual arbitration of homicide in the very limited manner described by Evans-Pritchard in his account of the Leopard Skin Priests. On the other hand, the Jieng', especially the Western Jieng' of whom we know most from Lienhardt's account, had their agnatic structure fragmented by Nath raiding and needed an alternative focus of solidarity, which their Spear Masters provided. On the average, the Jieng' had far more cattle than the Nath, and their material interests were better served by endeavoring to protect them and escape with them rather than by indulging in the type of aggressive raiding to which the Nath had been conditioned by their original need to break out of their confinement in the Jebel-Ghazal triangle (Southall 1976:474–76). The Jieng' were no less capable fighters but their larger herds demanded protection and strategic withdrawal rather than aggressive raiding. Nath had originally been the center people who had to fight to get out of their limited territory. Jieng' by this process had become peripheral people for whom it was more advantageous to withdraw with their large herds and expand outwards rather than fight and lose them. We must remember how few the Nath must have been. They doubled their population by the incorporation of Jieng' in their eastward expansion of the nineteenth century. Before then, they had probably fewer than 50,000 members and the Jieng' had ten to twenty times as many.

The Jieng' concentration on the preservation of cattle rather than aggressive fighting was consistent with the development of ritual leadership to replace agnatic solidarity broken up by Nath raiding, providing the focus and legitimation for the local association of unrelated lineage segments. The geopolitical situation of the Jieng' thus meant that they could neither do without ritual leadership as a focus of solidarity, nor could they provide it with any possibility of centralization, in view of their extensive transhumant pastoral economy. The result was that their ritual leaders possessed extreme sanctity, with many of the characteristics of divine kings but none of their political powers.

The interpretation that I have given of the Col regicide, if it has any validity, could be seen as one from the perspective of ecology and political economy, which is entirely compatible with, and complementary to, Evans-Pritchard's brilliant structuralist interpretation. He concluded that divine kingship is typical of, though not restricted to, societies with pronounced lineage systems in which political segments are parts of a loosely organized structure without governmental functions—that is to say, the wider political organization takes a largely ritual and symbolic form. The moral density (which I would take as a reflection of the ecological constraints) was great enough for segments to be represented by common symbols in the kingship, but not great enough to eliminate the fissive tendencies of the structure, which are expressed in the circulation of the king, or of the kingship, and in the attachment of the kingship, through the king, to particular localities with sectional interests, so that other sections assert rights in the kingship against the king, in the name of the Col. This culminates in rebellions against the king, not the kingship, with the killing of the king. The kingship embodies a contradiction between dogma and social facts, between the office and the incumbent, between agnates and mothers' kin, and between centripetal and centrifugal tendencies, which are solved by customary regicide.

Gluckman has argued that rituals of rebellion openly express social tensions and allow the acting out of a symbolic dominance by those who are in fact subordinate, thus bringing about catharsis (1963 [1954]: 112). They are an instituted process demanded by sacred tradition, seemingly against the established order, yet aimed at blessing that order to achieve prosperity (1963 [1954]: 114). Gluckman considered that rituals of rebellion may be confined to situations where strong tensions are aroused by conflict between different structural principles which are not controlled in distinct secular institutions (1963 [1954]: 136). Spiro thinks it is pointless to symbolize something which exists already (1972: 601), missing the point that participation in ritual generates orectic forces and is therefore strengthening (Turner 1974: 55). He thus wrongly accuses Gluckman's theory of being merely expressive while his is instrumental. If we follow Spiro's theory (1972) that these are culturally constituted defense mechanisms, which allow for disguised gratification of a forbidden motive, reducing the likelihood of its undisguised gratification and therefore protecting society from its disruptive consequences, it reinforces but otherwise hardly affects our interpretation, however different the source of the theory.

Where rituals of rebellion heighten the solidarity of the component units that, either in unison or in opposition to one another, express symbolic opposition to central institutions of the group to which all belong, they may be seen as an extension of the principle of complementary opposition, carried on from acephalous societies to a higher level in societies with central institutions. In the Col case they channel segmentary oppositions into a single binary opposition. But Anuak village rebellions are not ritual but real, and they may heighten the solidarity of the fighting groups involved, but in the ordinary secular, segmentary sense of complementary opposition.

Evans-Pritchard states that all kingship is sacral or sacerdotal. In deference to Frazer, he suggests that divine kingship *is* distinct from other kingship, although all kingship has some features of divine kingship. This is not entirely satisfactory, unless one regards a definition as a lucid statement of a central tendency (polythetic), rather than an attempt to give fixed boundaries to meaning. This is probably what we should do, although of course centrality itself is relative.

Evans-Pritchard definitely includes the Anuak in his final discussion of divine kingship, concluding in their case that "moral density is great enough for the segments to be represented by a common symbol in the kingship but not great enough to eliminate the powerful tendencies towards fission in the structure they compose" (1962 [1948] : 85). The Anuak emblems and the status of *rath* attached to them circulate in less than half of Anuakland, vaguely defined only to a certain extent by the forest zone as opposed to the open savannah. Although the emblems are essentially symbolic objects, they seem to carry no ritual, let alone any secular, powers with them. If a noble who was eligible by virtue of his father's incumbency could muster sufficient support to topple the incumbent, kill him, and seize the emblems, he obviously also had the support to dominate his own village and exercise some influence beyond it. But the struggle for the emblems was in itself purely secular, not ritual. There was no moral maxim stating that the *rath* holding the emblems should be killed if he grew sick or ineffective. We could only argue for the symbolic coincidence that if the incumbent was toppled and killed, that in itself proved he was weak and deserved it.

The case of the Jieng' expresses a very interesting shift in the ordering of the model in the direction opposite from the Anuak, for no secular struggle for emblems or royal office is reported, but the Masters of the Fishing Spear had considerable supernatural power, were held to be of divine origin, and were believed to crown the attainment of great sanctity in old age by calling voluntarily for their followers to bury them alive. Their emblems were not in any way distinctive. Everyone had a fishing spear. Some spears were sacred and potent because of their special owners, not the other way around. The great Master of the Fishing Spear, who approximated to a divine king, owed his position to achievement rather than ascription. He had to belong to a fishing spear clan, and would be helped by being a respected leader of a significant lineage segment, but of the many who might qualify in this way, the ones of preeminent renown must have emerged through personal qualities.

The Masters of the Fishing Spear tremble when their clan divinity, Flesh, enters their bodies, as the successor to the Col kingship trembles when the spirit of his ancestor Nyikang' enters him (Evans-Pritchard 1962 [1948]:79). Burton compares the mock battle for the power of Flesh, which occurred during the dance at the live burial of an Atuot Master of the Fishing Spear (*gwan ring*) to the civil war at the installation of the Col *reth* (1981:18). Thus again similar historical ecologies produce similar superstructural institutions among widely separated peoples, while the basically similar superstructures of neighbors assume differing forms from differential adaptation to constraining environments. The bewildering array of manifestations which are involved in any consideration of divine kingship clearly renders attempts at classification meaningless and precise definition misplaced. They are a signal demonstration of the imaginative creativity of power.

It would be easy to conclude that king killing, as opposed to the universal belief in its occurrence, only actually occurred in the context of succession wars (here one must distinguish between wars aimed at succession before and after the fact of the death of an incumbent). However, where regicide is a culturally defined occurrence, embedded in an elaborately detailed context of ritual, one must entertain the possibility that it did in fact occur. Similar considerations apply to the ritual, symbolic, or historical truth of the dying god, whether Christ, Osiris, Tammuz, or the Emperor of China (where "voluntary death" became suicide).

Vaughan (1980:135–41) puts divine kingship in the universal human problem of succession from one generation to another. It is an interesting insight that divine kingship raises this problem symbolically to the highest level of society. But surely only as an adjunct to the central concern. The powers of divine kingship were dangerous to the king himself, but they were also dangerous to society at large. They were benign and beneficial if kept in proper balance, but if out of balance, destructive and evil, as the Nyakyusa case shows (Wilson 1959:21–29).

Divine kingship represents the ambiguous and controversial pivot between egalitarian and hierarchical society, between the monopoly of the imaginary and the material means of production (Godelier 1978:766), the birth of exploitation. Divine kings were loved, but they were also feared. The office itself was feared so much that eligible candidates refused it, or had to be kidnapped and forced into it. From one instance to another, the fear varied from mystical to political, for the office was both mystically and politically dangerous. The king might be killed by the overwhelming force of the mystical powers conferred upon him, or simply slain by the rival aspirant for the golden bough. Deng squares the circle when he informs us that "chieftainship (sc. divine kingship) began with Jok (Divinity) . . . from the Byre of Creation," while on the other hand every father is the divine leader of the family (Deng 1978:115–117). As Lienhardt shows, the fundamental theme is life not death (1961:318–19).

It has long been debated whether divine kings were killed. In Nkore where it was previously stated that kings were poisoned when ailing or senile (Roscoe 1923:50), Karugire seems to prove conclusively that this was not the case (1971:92–93). There were ample reasons for the people to believe that it occurred. The cases of Rwanda, Burundi, and other interlacustrine kingdoms are similar and rest on no more conclusive evidence. Vaughan has produced a case where kings were really killed. No one has doubted that the Anuak kings were killed, but here they were hardly divine and no ritual was involved so it is an exception which further disproves the supposed rule.

It now seems more pertinent to note that what really matters is not whether kings were killed, but that kingship mediates between humanity and divinity, life and death, youth and age, weakness and power, sowing and reaping, creation and destruction. It mediates metaphysically at all times, but dramatically at times of death and succession, which are often marked by orgiastic rites characteristic of such liminal occasions. The circumstances were frequently such that it was universally believed that kings should not, could not, and therefore did not die natural deaths, (Wilson 1959:121–22) but so far from requiring that this actually occurred, it is more likely that almost every possible combination of these factors was played out in the varied sociocultural circumstances of kings, all of whom as Evans-Pritchard argued were in some sense sacred. Other exceptional beings, such as semidivine and royal ancestors, are frequently believed not to have died but mysteriously to have disappeared, as in the celebrated case of the Bacwezi (Roscoe 1923:21; Crazzolara 1950:92–93), or the early kings of Col, Anuak, and Alur, as already noted. The interesting question of divine queens has hardly been explored.

There were many alternative possibilities. If the king could be rendered immortal, prolonging his life into the other world through mummification and lavish material provision, the need to kill the king to preserve the potency of kingship did not arise. Or the death of others might be made to replenish the king's life force. Hinduism separated the royal role from the priestly role, ranking the latter above the former, so that the king was shielded from the dangers of divinity. Japan's unique arrangement of placing the king at the peak of society, but depriving him of political power for a millennium, reverses the usual situation. Yamaguchi shows how kingship "incorporates marginality as well as centrality . . . as a realization of the mythical scene and of the marginal situation," in the roles of hero-trickster, exile, wandering god and victim-scapegoat (1977: 165–74). With the axial revolution, there was a polarization between humanity and divinity, this world and the other world, so that kings lost their divinity but retained divine rights and attributes. In feudalism the king became more *primus inter pares* with a diminished gap between the monarch and the rest of the aristocratic hierarchy, but the European society of Western Christendom generated the extraordinary dialectic of Holy Roman Emperor and Pope, each vying for qualities of the other, Pope for political power, Emperor for ritual sanctity, even to the point of imitating one another's ceremonial dress and regalia. Simply to say, with Evans-Pritchard, "rex est mixta persona cum sacerdote" (1962 [1948]: 36) is to miss the unfolding dialectic of kingship and mode of production.

Conclusion

I have examined, in an almost functionalist manner, but within a different theoretical perspective, how far all the other social institutions of a number of related peoples covary with their own past and present efforts at working in, on, through, and with their environments to secure their subsistence and to ensure the maintenance and reproduction of themselves and their system whereby they do so. Their environment includes all neighboring groups with or against whom they react. Although covariation cannot amount to a proof of determination, it can demonstrate the possible extent of determinism. Given our limited knowledge, such an exercise can only show a certain degree of plausibility, which can be increased if it is repeated with other bodies of material and not effectively demolished by counter-argument.[14]

This study has suffered from gaps in information for the present and recent past, but even more from the inherent lack of historical time depth for oral societies, despite the good studies of Johnson, Mercer, and others. The older, more modest ethnographies frequently expressed the hope that their deficiencies would be overcome by subsequent studies, but we may have to face the fact that this will never happen. Nothing has amplified Evans-Pritchard's ethnographic researches on the Nath of the 1930s, or Lienhardt's on the Jieng' of the 1940s. Current projects which might have been expected to assist, such as the Jonglei scheme (now for the moment abandoned, because of the resurgent civil war), do not desire empirical data on local social conditions. We still do not know, and may never know, exactly what part Nath and Jieng' men, women, and children played in the traditional productive process and who controlled and disposed of the product.

In considering the relation between superstructural and infrastructural elements, from whatever arbitrary point in the past, we face the fact that at that point the people already carried with them a cultural heritage. We might speculate from Evans-Pritchard's hint that the basic agnatic predisposition of the Nath, and the Jieng', and perhaps also the Lwo, was derived from, or reinforced by, the productive system they developed in the Upper Nile basin habitat (1937:211, 215). The full potentialities of such dispositions can never be discerned from study of contemporary culture alone, for they are latent as far as the observer is concerned.

I have explored the development of leadership positions in the context of the varied natural and social environments of Nath, Jieng', Col, Anuak, Alur, Acoli and, to a lesser degree, Kenya Luo. In the Nath and Jieng' environment, the development of political authority was inhibited, but stimulated in that of the Col, and, in a segmentary form, in that of the highland Alur. Evans-Pritchard builds up an interpretive explanation for the appearance of regicide in the compact, circumscribed conditions of the Col, and documents a totally different form of it among the Anuak. On this basis, we can see why it did not develop in Alur or Acoli and why it assumed yet another voluntary form in Jieng'. The dispersed environmental exploitation of the Nath and Jieng', with two moves for the former and three for the latter (Lienhardt 1958a:132), the compactly localized exploitation of Col local groups, the contrast between the isolated mounds of the western Anuak in the treeless flood plain and the interconnected villages on the higher river banks of the forested regions of eastern Anuak, the contrasted environmental and political conditions of Alur settlement in their very different section of the upper Nile valley, the intermediate conditions of the Alur midlands and the special ecological, demographic, and political opportunities of the Alur highlands, the relatively homogeneous spread of small scale polities in Acoliland and the expansion of huge, acephalous, territorial lineages in Kenya Luo—all these make a certain amount of consistent if far from conclusive sense when viewed as the outcome of groups with a certain common cultural baggage struggling to subsist and survive in this range of ecological and political contexts.

An enquiry into the degree of infrastructural determinism involved in the social systems of what were until recently comparatively autonomous and relatively small societies is of the greatest significance, for, despite the inadequacy of the data, the problem is somewhat easier to study within a small compass than it is in the context of a highly interconnected, huge, and complex world system.

We have made a very tentative and inconclusive commentary on the social organization of a number of Western Nilotic peoples. We have seen this as the interaction between peoples who necessarily already possessed a certain cultural and sociological equipment and heritage, which cannot be traced back to any ultimate *terminus a quo*. Consequently, the extent to which their social and cultural heritage can be traced to their interaction with their total environment as it can now be comprehended is limited. But nonetheless a considerable part of it can be seen as arising from the necessities of appropriating nature to obtain a livelihood and securing the reproduction of the system and of themselves.[15]

Notes

1. I endeavor as far as possible to use the peoples' real names rather than their fabricated and corrupted colonial names. For Nath and Jieng' see Southall (1976: 463–64); Collo or Col see Westermann (1912b:xx) and Lienhardt (1954:142); Acoli see Girling (1960:1–2). Acoli is derived from Shuli, the form used in the early colonial days, and Shuli can only have arisen from the various ways in which the Arab slave traders communicated to themselves and to the early European explorers, administrators, and their interpreters the fact that these people of North Uganda spoke a language closely related to the Col or Collo, whom they also called Shuli (*ibid.*) and whom they all knew five hundred miles further down the Nile Valley. The recurrence of the ancient root Col thus shows the link be-

tween these two widely separated groups, as Luo (Lwo) shows the link between the Luo in Kenya, Uganda, Zaire, and the Sudan.

The use of 'c' for English 'ch' (church) is now very well established in African and other ethnography and will be used here in the case of Acoli and Col. The aim is not pedantic perfection of phonetic representation. But as I am referring to African peoples by the designations which are their own, rather than by the names invented and foisted upon them by colonial powers and other foreigners ignorant of their languages and cultures, somewhat deplorably picked up and perpetuated even by anthropologists, it is no bad thing to mark the change of ethnic names by this simple economy of spelling.

2. Ogot 1964, 1967; F. M. Deng 1971, 1972, 1973, 1978, 1980; L. A. Deng 1984.

3. The inhabitants are called: *ocholo,* a Shilluk, (pl. *wate chol,* children of Shilluk, Shilluks); the country is called *fote chol,* country of the Shilluks. The word *chol* perhaps means "black," vide below. A second name of the people is *okano,* descendants of *kano;* this name is connected with Nyikang, the national hero of the Shilluks. The name Shilluk (sing. Shilkawi) is given to them by the Arabs, and has now become their common designation; it is, of course, derived from *ocholo.* The Shilluks call themselves: *ocholo,* a Shilluk man, (pl. *chol*), or *wate chol:* children of *chol;* their country: *fote chol;* their language: *do chonians.* Shilluks are called by the Arabs: Shilluk; by the Dinkas: Pa*lal;* by the Abyssinians: Jambo. The Dinkas call themselves: Jane; they are called by the Shilluks: *ojano* (pl. j*am*); by the Arabs: Dinka, or Denka. The Nuers call themselves: ganat, a Nuer man (pl. k*ega*nat); their language: *tok* nat; they are called by the Shilluks: Nuer; by the Dinkas: Nuar; by the Arabs: Nuer or Nawar' (Westermann 1912:xx). According to Westermann (1912:63): "*lojo,* (to be) black"; "Black, to be *lojo*" (p. 69).

4. As I have no ingenious or well–founded interpretation of why what I here call "stagnation" of petty ruling lines in the Nebi midlands should have occurred there repeatedly, but not, apparently, in the lowlands, where conditions appear no more favorable, the question arises (perhaps beyond proof) as to whether it was in fact not so much stagnation, as over-availability of potential petty rulers from the more important and expanding Ukuru polity in the highlands above, where the fanning out of new ruling lines from the central polity became sufficiently frequent as to be regarded as virtually institutionalized. On the other hand, I may have attached insufficient weight to the ecological possibilities of the lowlands. In precolonial times, the combination of fishing and hunting hippo and crocodile in the Nile, and fishing and farming on both sides of the river may have made the riverine zone more productive and stable than the midlands, which may also have been more subject to occasional drought and famine.

5. In 1948 the population density per square mile in Alurland was 112 in the highlands, 71 in the midlands, and 64 in the lowlands (Southall 1956:12–13) compared with the Acoli average of 20 (Girling 1960:15). However different these may be from the precolonial densities, the contrast certainly holds.

6. In Madagascar, as Imerina emerged as a centralized state, its rulers appropriated from local groups their sacred emblems to construct a national *palladium* reinforcing their power (Berg 1985).

7. Soga is another fairly recent ethnic designation, which probably means island, referring to the territory between the Nile, Lake Victoria, the Mpologoma River, and Lake Kyoga. It is also possible that Kyoga and Soga are cognates.

8. Southall (1952:14–15) shows this for the Luo of South Nyanza. Densities were higher still in the main Luo settlement area of Central Nyanza.

9. Parker Shipton (1984) has usefully drawn attention to the fact that in this region segmentary populations (Luo, Luyia, Gusii, Gisu, Kiga) seem to have built up higher densities than the monarchical states (Ganda, Nyoro, Nkore, Sukuma, Nyamwezi) contrary to what some might expect. Whether this was due to the fact that, on the whole, these segmentary peoples occupied highland areas of higher rainfall and fertility, or that they developed different descent and marriage systems, or to other factors, and in what causal sequence, calls for further investigation.

10. Clearly this is a case to be added to the further exploration of Sahlins' idea of predatory expansion (Sahlins 1961).

11. This is interestingly documented for Busoga by Cohen (1977:28–29, 86–87, 161 and 1978).

12. Evans-Pritchard's selection of the term aristocrat as a complementary opposite of stranger in the DIL-RUL polarity (1940a:214–23) is very awkward, as he disclaims any difference of *rank* for an aristocrat. The *dil* has "prestige rather than rank and influence rather than power" (1940a:215). It is the (first) settler—stranger, or host/owner—guest/immigrant relationship which arises inevitably from the combination of descent, land, and mobility in African societies. It is paralleled by the Jopiny-Jodak distinction in Kenya Luo (Southall 1952:21), whereas in the more hierarchical societies of Alur and Col the parallel distinctions do involve differences of rank. The status of *dil* is so hedged about with qualifications and exceptions in Evans-Pritchard's meticulous account of the concept, and in practice the distinctive status of *dil* is so uncertain or virtually non-existent in all the empirical data on Nath local communities supplied by Evans-Pritchard (Southall 1976) that instead of the term aristocrat I shall distinguish between owners and immigrants in these parallel cases.

13. However, among the Northern Jieng' of whom we know very little, ritual leadership was more elaborate and perhaps more hierarchical and centralized (Bedri 1948). Lienhardt comments "it appears to me that the formal aspect of priest-chieftainship is more developed there than among the Western Dinka, and some of its regalia and ceremonies are reminiscent of the neighboring Shilluk" (1961:257, 312).

To judge from Deng's account the Ngok Jieng, north of the Bahr-el-Arab, had more powerful and formally hereditary chiefs. This may reflect a reaction to Arab influence in fairly recent times.

In both these instances we are dealing with the possible influence of diffusion rather than independent endogenous change. This is not to suggest the Northern Jieng' copied the Shilluk or the Ngok copied the Arabs, but that the proximity of more powerfully centralized polities may have focused reactive changes upon them.

14. It is none other than the process of guessing and validation or falsification,

which has been dignified as the "hermeneutic circle" (Ricoeur 1979:91).

15. See the discussion of these issues in the contexts of differing accounts of the Nath in Karp and Maynard (1982).

References

Arens, William

1984 The Demise of Kings and the Meaning of Kingship: Royal Funerary Ceremony in the Contemporary Southern Sudan and Renaissance France. Anthropos 19:355–67.

Bedri, G. E.

1939 Notes on Dinka Religious Beliefs in Their Hereditary Chiefs and Rainmakers. Sudan Notes and Records 22.

1948 More Notes on Padang. Sudan Notes and Records 29.

Beidelman, T. O.

1971 The Translation of Culture; Essays to E. E. Evans-Pritchard. London: Tavistock.

Bere, R. M.

1947 An Outline of Acholi History. Uganda Journal 11:1–8.

Berg, Gerald

1985 Royal Authority and the Protector System in Nineteenth Century Imerina. *In* Madagascar: Society and History. C. Kottak, J.-A Rakotoarisoa, A. Southall and P. Verin, eds. Durham, N.C.: Carolina Academic Press.

Burton, John W.

1981 Ethnicity on the Hoof. Ethnology 20:157–62.

Butt, Audrey

1952 The Nilotes of the Sudan and Uganda. London: International African Institute.

Cohen, David William

1977 Womunafu's Bunafu. A Study of Authority in a Nineteenth Century African Community. Princeton: Princeton University Press.

1978 Lwo Camps in Seventeenth Century Eastern Uganda. *In* Proceedings of the Third International Congress of Africanists. B. A. Ogot, ed. Evanston: Northwestern University Press.

Crazzolara, J. P.

1950 The Lwoo. Part I. Lwoo Migrations. Verona: Missioni Africane.

1951 The Lwoo. Part 2. Lwoo Traditions. Verona: Missioni Africane.

1954 The Lwoo. Part 3. Clans. Verona: Missioni Africane.

Dean, Virginia Lee
1978 Illness, Beliefs, and Social Change: A Study of the Lugbara of Northwest Uganda. Ann Arbor, Michigan: University Microfilms International.

Deng, Francis Mading
1971 Tradition and Modernization: A Challenge for Law Among the Dinka of the Sudan. New Haven: Yale University Press.
1972 The Dinka of the Sudan. New York: Holt, Rinehart and Winston.
1973 The Dinka and Their Songs. Oxford: Clarendon.
1978 Africans of Two Worlds: The Dinka in Afro-Arab Sudan. New Haven: Yale University Press.
1980 Dinka Cosmology. London: Ithaca Press.

Deng, Lual Acuek Lual
1984 The Abyei Development Project: A Case Study of Cattle Herders in the Sudan. Ph.D. dissertation, Anthropology Department, University of Wisconsin-Madison.

Durkheim, Emile
1915 The Elementary Forms of the Religious Life. London: George Allen and Unwin.

Ehret, Christopher
1982 Population Movement and Culture Contact in the Southern Sudan, ca. 3000 B.C. to A.D. 1000: A Preliminary Linguistic Overview. *In* Culture History in the Southern Sudan, Archeology, Linguistics and Ethnohistory. John Mack and Peter Robertshaw, eds. pp. 19–48. Nairobi: British Institute in Eastern Africa, Memoir No. 8.

Evans-Pritchard, E. E.
1935 The Nuer: Tribe and Clan. Sudan Notes and Records 18:37–87.
1937 Economic Life of the Nuer: Cattle. Sudan Notes and Records 20(3):209–45.
1940a The Nuer. Oxford: Clarendon.
1940b The Political System of the Anuak of the Anglo-Egyptian Sudan. London: Lund Humphries for the London School of Economics and Political Science. Monographs on Social Anthropology, No. 4.
1962 [1948] The Divine Kingship of the Shilluk of the Nilotic Sudan. The Frazer Lecture, 1948. Reprinted in Essays in Social Anthropology. London: Faber.

Frazer, Sir James
1950 [1922] The Golden Bough. One Volume Abridged Edition. New York: Macmillan.

Girling, F. K.
1960 The Acholi of Uganda. Colonial Research Studies No. 3. London: Her Majesty's Stationery Office.

Godelier, M.
1978 Infrastructures, Society and History. Current Anthropology 19(4): 763–71.

Gluckman, H. M.
1968 [1941] Economy of the Central Barotse Plain. The Rhodes Livingstone Papers No. 7. Manchester: Manchester University Press.
1963 [1954] Rituals of Rebellion in South-East Africa. Reprinted in Order and Rebellion in Tribal Africa. London: Cohen and West.

Karugire, S. R.
1971 A History of the Kingdom of Nkore in Western Uganda to 1896. Oxford: Clarendon.

Karp, Ivan and Kent Maynard
1982 Reading the Nuer. Current Anthropology 23:481–503.

Lienhardt, Godfrey
1954 The Shilluk of the Upper Nile. *In* African Worlds. Studies in the Cosmological Ideas and Social Values of African Peoples. Daryll Forde, ed. pp. 138–63. London: Oxford University Press for International African Institute.
1955 Nilotic Kings and Their Mother's Kin. Africa 25(1):29–41.
1957 Anuak Village Headmen. Africa 27(4):341–55.
1958a The Western Dinka. *In* Tribes Without Rulers: Studies in African Segmentary Systems. John Middleton and David Tait, eds. pp. 97–135. London: Routledge and Kegan Paul.
1958b Anuak Village Headmen II. Africa 28(1):23–35.
1961 Divinity and Experience: The Religion of the Dinka: Oxford: Clarendon.

Marx, Karl and Friedrich Engels
1975 Collected Works, Vol. 4. Moscow: Progress Publishers.

Middleton, Dorothy, editor
1969 The Diary of A. J. Mounteney Jephson. Emin Pasha Relief Expedition 1887–1889. Cambridge University Press for Hakluyt Society.

Middleton, John
1960 Lugbara Religion. London: Oxford University Press for International African Institute.

Mercer, P.
1971 Shilluk Trade and Politics from the Mid-17th Century to 1861. Journal of African History 12(3):407–26.

Ogot, Bethwell A.
1964 Kingship and Statelessness Among the Nilotes. *In* The Historian in Tropical Africa. J. Vansina, R. Thomas, and L. V. Thomas, eds. pp. 284–304. London: Oxford University Press for International African Institute.

1967 History of the Southern Luo. Nairobi: East African Publishing House.

Pumphrey, M. E.
1941 The Shilluk Tribe. Sudan Notes and Records: 1–45.

Ricoeur, Paul
1979 The Model of the Text: Meaningful Action Considered as a Text. *In* Interpretive Social Science: A Reader. Paul Rabinow and William Sullivan, eds. pp. 73–101. Berkeley: University of California Press.

Roscoe, John
1923 The Banyankole. Cambridge: Cambridge University Press.

Sahlins, Marshall
1961 The Segmentary Lineage: An Organisation of Predatory Expansion. American Anthropologist 63:322–44.
1976 Culture and Practical Reason. Chicago: University of Chicago Press.

Santandrea, Stefano
1968 The Luo of the Bahr El Ghazal. Bologna: Editrice Nigrizia.

Schweinfurth, G., F. Ratzel, R. W. Felkin, and G. Hartlaub, editors
1883 Emin Pasha in Central Africa. Best Collection of His Letters and Journals. London: George Philip & Son.

Seligman, C. G.
1932 Pagan Tribes of the Nilotic Sudan. London: Routledge et al.

Shipton, P. M.
1984 Lineage and Locality in East African Systems of Land Tenure. Ethnology 23:117–32.

Shiroya, Okete J. E.
1970 The Lugbara of Northwestern Uganda: Migration and Early Settlement. MSP/15/70/71, Department of History, Makerere University, Kampala.
1971 Inter-ethnic Relations in Pre-Colonial Northwestern Uganda: The Lugbara and Alur as Assimilators. MSP/15/71/72, Department of History, Makerere University, Kampala.

Spiro, Melford E.
1972 An Overview and a Suggested Reorientation. *In* Psychological Anthropology. Francis L. K. Hsu, ed. pp. 573–607. Cambridge: Schenkman.

Southall, Aidan W.
1952 Lineage Formation Among the Luo. International African Institute Memorandum 24. London: Oxford University Press.
1954 Alur Tradition and Its Historical Significance. Uganda Journal 18:2.

1956 Alur Society, A Study in Processes and Types of Domination. Cambridge: Heffer.

1970 Cross Cultural Meanings and Multilingualism. *In* Language Use and Social Change. W. H. Whiteley, ed. pp. 376–96. London: Oxford University Press.

1972 Twinship and Symbolic Structure. *In* The Interpretation of Ritual: Essays in Honour of A. I. Richards. J. S. La Fontaine, ed. pp. 73–114. London: Tavistock.

1976 Nuer and Dinka Are People: Ecology, Ethnicity and Logical Possibility. Man 11(4):463–91.

1988 The Segmentary State in Africa and Asia. Comparative Studies in Society and History 30(1):52–82.

Tucker, Robert C., editor

1978 The Marx-Engels Reader. Second Edition. New York: W. W. Norton.

Turner, V. W.

1974 Dramas, Fields and Metaphors: Symbolic Action in Human Society. Ithaca: Cornell University Press.

Vanneste, M.

1949 Legenden geschiedenis en gebruiken van een Nilotisch Volk. Alur teksten (Mahagi, Belgisch-Kongo). Institut Royal Colonial Belge, Section des Sciences Morales et Politiques. Memoires 18(1).

Vaughan, James

1980 A Reconsideration of Divine Kingship. *In* Explorations in African Systems of Thought. Ivan Karp and Charles S. Bird, eds. pp. 120–42. Bloomington: Indiana University Press.

Wagner, Gunter

1949 The Bantu of North Kavirondo. Vol. 1. London: Oxford University Press for the International African Institute.

Westermann, Diedrich

1912 The Shilluk. Philadelphia: The Board of Foreign Missions of the United Presbyterian Church of North America.

Wilson, Monica

1959 Communal Rituals of the Nyakyusa. London: Oxford University Press for the International African Institute.

Wright, A. C. A.

1952 Lwoo Migrations—A Review. Uganda Journal 16(1):82–88.

Yamaguchi, Masao

1977 Kingship, Theatricality, and Marginal Reality in Japan. In Text and Context: The Social Anthropology of Tradition. Ravindra K. Jain, ed. pp. 151–79. Philadelphia: Institute for the Study of Human Issues.

Part Three

Circulating Centers of Power

Dan Bauer

The Sacred and the Secret: Order and Chaos in Tigray Medicine and Politics

Introduction

The following case is pieced together from several informants, including the victim of the event, which had occurred fifteen years before my arrival among the Tigray in the Inderta region of Ethiopia.[1]

> It was an undoubtedly tired Gebre Yesus who made his way up the steep trail to the village of H'areyna and paused, as travelers do today, to look out from the cliff from which one can see for many miles. He had traveled two days from Tembien in order to discover the cause of his summoner's problems and was now almost at the village. His services had been called for by 'Atsbih'a Melles, the son of a prosperous man and a wealthy man himself, who bore the title of *re-isa debri* (monastery head), the kind of title given to persons who gave large contributions to the church. 'Atsbih'a was convinced that someone in his village was trying to do him harm and he had asked Gebre Yesus, a well-known diviner (*deftera*), to find out who it was. It is likely that all Gebre Yesus knew was that

his summoner had lost most of his cattle to disease, and so naturally feared for the safety of himself and his family.

Upon reaching the house of the *re-isa debri,* the great diviner, noting the impressive rectangular limestone blocks and dome of the prestigious *h'idmo* style, probably surmised that his new client had possessed some means when he was still a young man setting up his household, as anyone who knew the wealth of the father would have expected in any case. It was the house of a man of means and ambition. As the diviner approached the compound he would have likely seen his client's beautiful (and to this day still famous) mule, another sign that the client was a man of some resources. It was quite possible, given these signs of affluence, that someone envied the *re-isa debri* and was doing him harm—perhaps a poorer sibling, as so often is the case.

An individual generally summons a diviner from outside a village when one cannot rely on local diviners, any of whom might be in the hands of one's village enemies. The *re-isa debri* reportedly explained to Gebre Yesus that he was sure that someone was using medicines (*medih' anit*) against him. What he wanted to know was by whom? The diviner might have guessed this much simply by the fact that he had been called in from outside.

Gebre Yesus apparently did not have to check very far to discover that few people shared his client's view of the cause of his misfortune. Many people thought it was God's retribution for 'Atsbih'a excessive pride. He was said to have been in the habit of riding his mule through the center of the village, rather than of dismounting and proceeding on foot, as a modest man would have done. While others went hungry, he washed his mules in whey. He acted like "a man of a thousand cattle"—and he had not even earned the wealth himself. It was all inherited from his father.

The case was unclear. Was it a mother of *mu'* (hubris) and therefore a theological problem, or was it a case of *medih'anit* (medicines) and therefore a question of calculating enemies? To answer this, the diviner had to perform several tests.

As it is reported today, the great diviner found the case of 'Atsbih'a to be one of hubris, of God's displeasure. 'Atsbih'a had placed himself above others unjustifiably, just as the fallen angel had placed himself above God. The village accepted Gebre Yesus's "findings." While 'Atsbih'a never accepted the diviner's findings, he did not seek a second opinion, nor ask a diviner to see if it were spirit possession. The problem showed none of the signs. No one could remember him suggesting that the cause of his misfortunes was witchcraft, although that remained a possibility. He always maintained that his downfall, which began with these misfortunes, was the result of *medih'anit,* that is to say of the conscious efforts of his enemies.

(Years later when I met him, the *re-isa debri* was a poor man working as a plowman for his son-in-law.)

This case demonstrates that the Tigray have several competing belief systems to explain affliction. These systems involve three semiautonomous conceptions of sources of misfortune, each with a high degree of internal consistency but, at the same time, in contradiction with one another. These sources are the theological (God's will), the secular (generally the actions of fellow humans), and spirit possession (the effects of uncontrolled forces). These systems relate directly to Tigray concerns about power and authority, and chaos and order. The system that prevails in a specific situation is largely the result of the interests of various actors. For example, while few individuals would readily accept the charge of hubris for themselves, many communities prefer that the mighty fall, especially when they apparently have achieved a height unjustifiably. Although their clients may not like their finding, few diviners want to appear as being seduced by gold. To understand why a person chooses a particular explanation, one needs to develop an empathetic perspective in the sense used by Weber (1958). Just as Weber found that in order to understand feudal belief one had to consider the perspectives and interests of those occupying positions within a feudal structure, one can understand Tigray beliefs about the cause of affliction by considering the position of the victim or community and asking what they would want the outcome to be.

In this paper, I want to relate the available choices, *i.e.,* the competing systems of belief (sin, sorcery, spirit possession, etc.), to Tigray concerns about power and authority. The explanations fall into distinct classes, with each contradicting the other in significant ways. For example, spirit possession as a cause of misfortune is thought to be antithetical to theological explanation. Secular explanations, such as the use of "medicines," are outside the realm of religious orthodoxy. Yet, these respective, logically contradictory forms of explanation, when combined, constitute a coherent system of symbolic relations that provide an analogue to Tigray political ideology, which is equally composed of apparently contradictory idioms.

The Tigray find themselves surrounded by three irksome and sometimes fearsome political dangers: the chaos that comes from power unrestrained by authority, the constraints imposed by authority itself, and the machinations of personal competitors. The analogues in the domain of affliction are: the unrestrained power of possessing spirits, God's retribution for religious failures, and the use of sorcery or witchcraft by enemies.

I will address three concerns in this paper: (1) the nature of integration in belief systems, (2) the relation of what is "officially" denied in belief, or of what Karp (1980) following Goffman has called the "underlife," to systems of belief, and (3) the basis of legitimacy in actions as well as in belief.

To have legitimizing effects, symbols must demonstrate a meaningful relationship to a system of belief. The cultural unit of analysis in this case is not, as with Turner (1964) or Beidelman (1973), the ritual setting, but Tigray medical beliefs, which categorize afflictions and actors. The internal complexity of some belief systems, in this case the domain of Tigray medicine, allows for strategic selection of appropriate affliction categories (sin, witchcraft, sorcery, etc.) by appropriate actors (victims, diviners, the community, etc.).

The Setting

The Tigray are plow agriculturalists who have practiced their own form of Christianity since the fourth century. They number some two million people and are the co-inheritors with the Amhara of the Axumite Empire, having provided several emperors. Tigiñña[2] is a Semitic language closely related to Amharic and the liturgical language, Gi-iz.

The semi-arid Tigray landscapes are reminiscent of the American Southwest. Depending on the region, the cliffs and valleys are dotted with small hamlets of three to six houses or nucleated villages of one to five thousand people. Each village (*hagare seb*) is an administratively separate religious and political entity, with its own church and headman (*ĉika ŝum*). In the Inderta region, villages form compact, nucleated settlements of homesteads composed of a compound divided between houses and a cattle byre. Compounds are bounded by stone walls or thornbush fences. The compounds abut one another forming an almost "urban" mass, cut through by paths. The byres display individual wealth and are used for entertaining when the number of guests exceeds the capacity of the house. Houses vary in type from thatched wattle-and-daub huts to elaborate stone dwellings with dome-like, lime-covered roofs. The parish church, generally a rectangular building with a row of stone columns, reminiscent of the Acropolis facing the direction of the setting sun, lies a short, but tortuous walk outside the village. The church is served by local men.

Priests often number up to 10 percent of the household heads and are generally outnumbered by deacons.

The village lands consist of a commons area and agricultural holdings (see Bauer 1973, 1985 [1977], and 1987). Villages have one of two systems for distributing agricultural lands, one based on an elaborate system of inheritance and omnilineal descent (*risti*) (Hoben 1972; Bauer 1973, 1985, 1987) and the other based on common ownership by residents (*chigurafgoses*) (Bauer 1973, 1985, 1987). Both arrangements involve intense competition for land, particularly among siblings and other close relatives under the *risti* system.

Power, Authority, and Medical Belief

Tigray cosmology embodies a Hobbesian view of human nature. In this view society presents an inherent "problem of order," explicated by political beliefs and theology. In their simplest form, the problem and the solution can be explained as follows: men are inherently aggressive; if they are left unchecked, their desires will inevitably lead to disorder. The solution therefore lies in having authorities who will control men. The chaotic potential of nature is portrayed metaphorically in the Tigray view of the spirit world, a world inhabited by *zars*, which are "foreign" entities that attack their victims capriciously. An otherworldly solution is pictured in their image of the all-knowing, all-seeing, and just God, the ultimate source of authority. Yet such a view, by its own logic, denies the very existence of such uncontrollable beings as *zars*. It is God-sanctioned authority which prevents Hobbesian chaos in this world. Those who would exercise their will are brought under control by persons of authority within the political hierarchy, in which God is at the head and controls even the emperor.

Interestingly, Tigray medical beliefs depict both the Hobbesian spirit world and its opposite, God, as sources of affliction. Thus misfortune can have its source in either of two worlds: one controlled by forces unintelligible to the ordinary person, and one where human motives hold sway. Fortes' distinction (1966) between the "patent" and the "occult" applies here. The patent can be understood as a cause-and-effect relationship; the relationship between occult forces and human action, on the other hand, is one of influence. Even priest-directed atonement cannot cause God to change the course of events, although it might influence

Him. At the other pole, the *zar* spirits are beyond any direct human agency. Spirit mediums can only bring spirits under some kind of control by attempting to influence their own possession spirits to rein in the offending *zar.*

Tigray divination and curing thus reflect highland Ethiopian concerns about human nature and social order, *i.e.,* concerns of human political relations. Allan Hoben's statement (1970) that, if the Amhara hold any illusions about mankind they are negative, holds equally true for the neighboring and culturally related Tigray. Both groups believe, and the Tigray say, that "the satisfied person is the aggressive person." Thus fasting helps people to be moral. By contrast, eating allows people to achieve their natural potential—aggression. (This differs sharply with our own beliefs on the subject, in which people are naturally quiescent if their needs are satisfied.) The Tigray view of natural aggressiveness is reflected in their concerns for power and authority. As one informant put it, "if it were not for headmen, villagers would constantly fight one another, and these headmen themselves would organize their villages to fight one another, if it were not for the existence of governors above them." The informant recounted the political hierarchy in this manner, finally noting that the emperor, who controlled the level below him, also submitted to the authority of God. In short, the Tigray believe that if people do not submit themselves to a chain of authority, ultimately sanctioned by God, they are subject to a Hobbesian grasping for sheer power, which would inevitably lead to chaos. They believe that human nature, by itself, does not allow people to live with one another peacefully. Instead, a fundamental premise of Tigray social belief is that agencies external to the individual, preferably sanctioned by God, are required if men are to live in harmony.

Power and Space

The same dimensions of power and God-sanctioned authority are reflected in the order of the universe as symbolized by the spatial layout of churches. In a small room in the center of the church lies a ritually activated replica of the ark of the covenant, a direct link to the Holy Spirit. Only priests and deacons in good standing and in a state of purity may enter this room. Outside the room lie a series of concentric zones of diminishing holiness. Beyond the covenant chamber inside the church is a spirit-free zone that requires purification in the form of confession and postcoital bathing before it may be entered. Outside the church but within the churchyard is a zone that requires less purity. Beyond the yard is a wilderness zone, a grove of trees that may not be cut. Like the center of the church, which is imbued by the Holy Spirit, the grove is inhabited by spirits. These spirits (*zars* and others), however, are aggressive and unruly, and represent a heightened version of nature and chaos.

Space is both a symbol and resource of power. The center of the church, which is occupied exclusively by priests and deacons during mass, clearly signals to the congregation that only certain individuals may mediate with the Holy Spirit. The mediation takes place in the ark room itself, which is hidden from view and where the actual mediatory devices are kept. From their seats, however, members of the congregation can see who enters the holy chamber and thus who has the power to mediate. This invisible performance contrasts with a highly visible action. Biblical incantation can take place anywhere. Although holy books are read in prescribed areas of the church and churchyard during mass, an individual with appropriate knowledge can perform the incantations anywhere, even in the privacy of his house (as occurred in the case of Zenawi Melles described below). By contrast, the creation of powerful substances, such as holy water, can be accomplished only through contact with the ark and, therefore, the space in which it is enclosed. The socially visible right to this holy space, held by priests and deacons, indicates that one also has the right of access to the powerful controlling and enabling potential of the ark. Entering the ark chamber brings one directly in contact with God's power itself.

Ethiopian tradition explains the presence of an ark in each church as being tied to the founding of the nation itself, which resulted from the liaison between King Solomon and Queen Sheba described in the Bible. According to the story, their son Menelik I, the first emperor of Ethiopia, wanted to meet his famous father and crossed the Red Sea with his retainers to visit him in the Holy Land. On his trip back to Ethiopia, his retainers revealed that they had stolen the sacred ark from Solomon. Since that time, the ark has rested in the church at Axum. The replicas that are found in local churches have been ritually blessed with the power of the original ark. Although Menelik was innocent of the theft, it was his journey from the "Hamitic and damned" land of Sheba to the "blessed" land of Solomon that brought sacred and secular order together in Ethiopia, through the presence of the ark.

Ethiopians, like the rest of us, live in an imperfect world. In spite of the secular order brought by Menelik's state and the presence of the ark, disorder, in many forms, including personal affliction, exists in day-to-day life. Tigray have, as already noted, several systems of ideas to account for it. Each system of ideas, although internally coherent, contradicts the other systems in important ways. Diviners of various kinds mediate some of the contradictions and at the same time mediate Tigray fears of both chaos and of excessive order (see Bauer and Hinnant 1980).

According to one Tigray belief system, affliction comes from the ultimate symbol of order, God. Indeed, from a strictly theological perspective this is the only possible source. Since God is omnipotent and omniscient, misfortune is seen as the result of God's will. The only logical and theologically correct recourse is to submit oneself to God's authority through his agents, the priests (qaŝi), who through their contact with the ark and scripture can cleanse and prescribe penance. My informants agreed on the relationship between God's disfavor, affliction, and cure, and found it an appealing explanation of other people's problems. They did not, however, use it to explain their own misfortunes, because of its implication that the victim was somehow at fault. (See also Evans-Pritchard's 1937 account of Azande oracles.)

The secular explanation suggests that suffering is the result of human action. Problems may be caused by sorcery, witchcraft, contagion, or, though not of human action, simple bad luck. The virtue of this line of reasoning is that one can blame misfortune on one's enemies. The problem can be solved by discovery and redress rather than by atonement and sacrifice. When the problem cannot be resolved by common sense, one must seek a person with "theoretical" knowledge (see Horton 1967).

Diviners and Secular Explanations

Because they possess theoretical knowledge, priests would seem to be likely candidates to perform secular diagnoses or cures. But because they fall directly under the authority of God, they are committed to theologically correct explanations. Diviners (*deftera*), on the other hand, have theoretical knowledge but do not come under the control of God. They have been trained as priests, but because of physical imperfections or personal failures, such as a missing limb or adultery, they are disqualified from celebrating mass. They have come into contact with the Holy Spirit through the medium of the ark. Unlike priests, *deftera* do not possess the institutionalized charisma needed to perform the mass nor the capacity for casuistry and the prescription of penance. However, they share some of the liabilities of priests. They are not as separate from ordinary men as Catholic priests are, since they are generally local farmers and family men with local kin and genealogies. They are not as common as local priests, who may represent up to 10 percent of household heads in a village. There may be only one *deftera* of note in an area encompassing several villages. The position of one *deftera* I knew illustrates their powers in general.

Zenawi Melles of the village of H'areyna was known widely for his ability to use medicines (*medih'anit*). Like all young men setting out on a priestly career, he had begged for food and had studied with a master. Then he had entered a monastery in Gojjam, attaining the title of liturgical master (*mergieta*). His progress toward priesthood ended when he lost his sight and was thus "disfigured." His career was ended. Blindness disqualified him from becoming a priest or even celebrating the mass as a deacon (*diakon*) because, from a theological view, such an affliction was a sign of God's disfavor. Zenawi now leads the church music and coordinates the liturgy during mass. He earns most of his livelihood from teaching the Bible to would-be deacons and priests, an impressive feat given his particular disability.

In his own village and in the surrounding area, Zenawi was well-known for his ability to use theoretical knowledge for secular purposes. He could do many things that people using common sense knowledge could neither do nor fully explain. This included burning down the houses of enemies from a distance of half a mile by using biblical incantation. His ability to perform such feats, at least at the level at which informants explain it, derived from knowledge, rather than from special grace or possession. One of my assistants, himself a deacon who had learned "love magic" from Zenawi, was afraid to use it because of the possible facial disfigurement or blindness that might result from a mistake while in contact with such powerful forces.

The power of *deftera* derives, at one level, from their knowledge of the use of powerful forces not available to others. In this sense, they are more like scientists than faith healers. At another level, however, diviners gain power and charisma from their contact with powerful forces. Within the secular system of thought, Zenawi's blindness represents a badge of contact with potent powers. But his charisma stems not only from contact with "natural" forces but from contact with the ark of the covenant and the Holy Spirit, which all diviners, as former deacons, have had. The importance of the spiritual element is suggested by the fact that diviners are referred to by the same term as practicing deacons. Both are *deftera*.

Indeed, it might be argued that deacons themselves gain a measure of legitimacy from their association with diviners. Deacons could refer to themselves by a term which differentiates them from diviners, namely *diakon,* but usually do not. Another suggestive element is that informants believe that some actual priests secretly practice divination and curing "on the side" and that they are in fact more powerful than *deftera*. (This is a variation on the Azande who believe effective diviners are secretly witches, as reported by Evans-Pritchard 1937.[4])

Thus *deftera* cross over from the everyday world of ordinary men, through both training and ritual processes, into the occult world of religion (*haymanot*) and return with special knowledge that can be used for solving problems in the mundane world. While priests use this knowledge for the higher purpose of curing souls, their failed compatriots, the *deftera,* use it for practical purposes, such as curing the body or burning down the houses of enemies. It could be argued that the possibility of religious legitimacy of their activities adds to their reputation for efficacy. They can be seen as having crossed the boundary between the sacred and the profane in much the same way that Menelik crossed the Red Sea. He brought back the sacred ark; they bring back sacred knowledge. Both have come into contact with the sacred ark and thus are mediators.

In contrast to a rigid theological doctrine, *deftera* are much more flexible in identifying the cause of misfortune. They may ascribe misfortune to a wide variety of sources, most of them secular. They may attribute personal affliction to excessive pride, an offense against God (as well as to the community in general), much as a priest would. Alternatively, they may attribute it to the use of medicines by the victim's enemies. They may ascribe misfortune to contact with contagious materials that are left along pathways by people who are sick, so that they might be relieved from illness,[5] or to the machinations of a witch (*buda*).[6] *Deftera* use certain procedures, which usually involve biblical incantations and incense readings, to discover the source of affliction. In most cases, they also prescribe cures, which usually have strong biblical references, most notably in the form of incantations based on biblical passages.

Spirit Mediums

The solutions that *deftera* find to resolve secular problems are nearly universally accepted as valid. Although particular findings may come into dispute, most are accepted, even by priests who go to *deftera* for secular cures. The solutions of another type of mediator and curer, the spirit medium, however, enjoy much less popular acceptance. If the *deftera,* by virtue of his training and ordination, stands symbolically with one foot inside the inner ark room and the other foot in the spirit-free zone of the church, the spirit medium stands at the other extreme, with one foot in the churchyard and the other in the grove. The spirit medium mediates between the secular world and the realm of the wild, voracious, and pagan spirits that reside in the wilderness zone.

Victims possessed by spirits may suffer from a variety of problems but they are always characterized by bizarre, trance-like behavior. According to the logic of spirit possession, the spirits have strong appetites and search for suitable human vehicles through whom they can make their wishes known. Those affected are not at fault, but are merely the victims of some unfortunate accident; they are simply "captured." (Our own view of medicine usually has a similar amoral quality.) This is in contrast to the Holy Spirit, which inflicts injury in response to a moral transgression. With spirit possession there is no authority, no orderliness. The spirits simply want things, such as silver rings and fancy dresses for their material abodes or a ride in the anthropologist's Land Rover. There is no authority to keep them in line; they dwell in the realm of pure, power–hungry *id.* (For a parallel, see Karp in this volume.)

One does not appeal to the orderliness of God's justice or resort to the formulaic procedures of a *deftera* to confront these spirits. They understand only coercion and, therefore, must be handled with power. The spirit medium can deal with the spirit that possesses a victim only because she herself is possessed by a more powerful spirit. After she determines what the victim's spirit wants, she negotiates an agreement and the victim finds relief. The victim's illness recedes and her trance behavior disappears, except on certain prescribed occasions.

The recruitment of a spirit medium also reflects the contrast between authority (*mebti*) and power (*haile*). It differs from priests who follow a set procedure to achieve a status within a well-prescribed institution, or from *deftera* who gain a position by learning to use complicated formulas. By contrast, the spirit medium is chosen randomly. She is "overpowered" by a passing spirit. Although mediums can theoretically be male or female, significantly all of them are female, maintaining the often-noted association between women and nature.

The victims are overwhelmingly women. Most women—and a few afflicted men—accept the concept of possession by non-Christian spirits (*zars*), such as these. Men, however, generally regard their wives' possession as a charade designed to gain favors from them, and view spirit mediums as profit–seeking charlatans. In other words, both adherents and unbelievers describe spirit possession in an idiom of coercive power.[7]

To her followers, a spirit medium possesses true charismatic powers and has the right to make rather onerous demands on victims for both recompensation and deviant public behavior. Male victims, for example, must wear their hair in long, buttered ringlets. Although this "wild" hair style reflects the disorderliness of spirits, it also exposes the victims to negative, public criticism because Tigray men normally keep their hair short through periodic shaving.

Holy Men

One final figure deserves mention: the holy man. Holy men do not fit neatly into any one of the three systems of belief. They are wild and possessed, like victims of spirit possession. However, they are possessed not by wild spirits but the Holy Spirit itself. Thus they bridge the two extremes, that of spirit possession and the authority of God. Holy men are extremely rare, although one suspects that their number increases at critical points in Ethiopian history. They tend to be hermitic, living underground in caves, which are made "cultural" by cutting out squared-off windows. They have the disorderly appearance of individuals suffering from possession. The difference is that they are possessed by the Holy Spirit. These figures assert their special position by violating the rules of etiquette (nudity, etc.) and exhort politically important men to undertake good deeds, such as the construction of churches (Allan Hoben, personal communication). They symbolically unite disorder with order under a single banner, while intervening in the day-to-day realm of politics. Their symbolic importance is such that, even if they did not exist as real persons, the native belief in their existence would nonetheless be of great significance.[8] However, as mediators among three worlds—the holy, the mundane, and the wild—they fail to sort out the issues as clearly as do their counterparts, the diviner–priests and spirit mediums.

Conclusions

This overview of Tigray cosmology allows us to draw some conclusions in three important areas of concern: (1) the nature of the integration of belief systems, (2) the relation of the "underlife," as Karp (1980) used the concept, to belief, and (3) the relation of legitimacy to action as well as belief.

The contradictions that I found in what the Tigray regard as officially religion (*haymanot*) with divination and curing can be overcome for the most part by situational applicability. These are the kinds of contradictions that informants rarely notice but that they cannot explain when such discrepancies are pointed out. Spirit possession presents the most serious conceptual problem, because it suggests the existence of entities that are the product of neither man nor God. When informants notice these contradictions, they either express disbelief or take a pragmatic stance, citing circumstantial evidence and using phrases equivalent to "I don't know how it works, but this is what happened."[9]

The three systems of belief are perfectly integrated on a symbolic rather than a literal or logical level. If religion, and by extension ritual, constitute "models of" and "models for" society (Geertz 1977), then the three systems together form a model of the Tigray individual and society. This model bears an interesting resemblance to that of Freud (1960). The "wild" spirits have obvious id-like qualities with their unquenchable appetites. The mundane world, which is portrayed as populated with rational, self-seeking people, reflects the realm of ego "interests." The world of religion, which is conceived of as a moral one, represents the super-ego. The model, of course, differs substantially from Freud's in that forces and sanctions are perceived as external to individuals. Neither are regarded as being part of the mind. As *Mergieta* Zenawi explained, "men do what is good out of fear, fear of what other men will do to them and fear of what God will do to them." In his view, no principle, such as that of the conscience, could influence human behavior.

The existence of the kind of human nature represented by the image of the wild spirit world explains, metaphorically, the antisocial behavior of enemies in the everyday world. The existence of the world of the Holy Spirit explains a person's good behavior. Tigray views to the contrary, such beliefs presumably do have some effect in constraining behavior.

The concept of the "underlife" is useful in this analysis. If we were to examine only what the Tigray believed officially, we would have to ignore the wild spirits. The Tigray not only regard them as "foreign" in origin but most Tigray assert that they do not exist. Yet if they were neglected, the rest of Tigray social philosophy would seem less cohesive and less compelling. Their status is not quite the same as Turner's "blocked exegesis" (1964), in which an informant cannot explain some phenomena because the examination itself would destroy its ritual effectiveness. The underlife expressed in the wild spirits is fully open to Tigray intellectual examination. However, the Tigray must deny the validity of the wild spirits; otherwise, they would have to reject the essential qualities of the moral order expressed in the concept of God and the Holy Spirit.

Turner (1964:32) dealt with a related notion when he attempted to demonstrate the mechanism through which the "obligatory" becomes the "desirable" and concluded that ideas were coupled with emotions through rituals. Here, I suggest that medical practice by its very nature does the same thing—symbolically it amalgamates ideas and emotions.

For the Tigray, as well as for ourselves, it takes an act of faith to entrust our health, life, or fortune to a medical practitioner. For example, when I go to a doctor I accept his diagnosis and prescription only insofar as I believe they are based on sound reasoning, *i.e.,* on science. Although he is not a scientist in the strict sense of the term, the doctor clothes his hunches in scientific language. He describes my upset stomach as "gastroenteritis." My belief in his diagnosis stems from the scientific symbols he uses. Just as the doctor is not a scientist, a *deftera* is not a priest. The linguistic confusion of M.D. and Ph.D. under the term "doctor" parallels that of diviner and deacon under *deftera.* The diviner uses the symbols of religion to validate his hunches.

Turning to the other side of the coin, we may ask why the Tigray find religion compelling. Part of the answer lies, of course, in what we have already said. Some form of authority is, in a sense, logically necessary given the Tigray view of human nature, characterized as it is by a voracious appetite for power. The important question is what makes religion emotionally compelling, and how is faith sustained on a continuing basis?

Part of the answer lies in Tigray divination and curing. Tigray religion is not just a theory, as Euclidian geometry might be; it is the source of symbols used to cure the human body. While the failure of Euclidian geometry would probably not threaten my life, the failure of religion would expose the Tigray's life to risk. Religious symbols are thus revitalized by being brought into contexts of great personal concern. They take on a true life and death meaning. The *deftera* is more powerful for having borrowed sacred symbols; the Church is enhanced for having lent them.

The third and final topic I want to explore is the relationship between legitimacy and action. With Weber's work (1958), scholars began to accept the notion that politics depend on ideas. Actors use ideas to formulate action in accordance with their perceived interests, which in turn influence the form of their ideas. Barth (1966) also explores some of the mechanisms through which ideas, action, and interests mutually influence one another. Like Weber, Barth insists that an analysis should consider the actor's perspective. In his study of herring fishermen, for example, he interpreted the stereotypical behavior of skippers and net bosses as stemming from their strategic action under a variety of material and ideal incentives and constraints (Barth 1966). The Tigray medical and political world views allow both the afflicted and the diviners choices in diagnoses, which may be negotiated. Victims and diviners try to reach an accord as to diagnosis: is it witchcraft or is it sorcery? Such negotiation feeds back upon the ideas themselves. Victims follow a hierarchy of options, as discussed below.

When one is afflicted, one's friends suggest going to the priest. The afflicted is likely to resist this action because the priest has no option, given the premises to which he must adhere, except to find the victim guilty of committing some affront to God. The victim prefers to be diagnosed as being afflicted by sorcery, that is to say, having been ensorcelled by one's enemies. This not only removes the onus of being guilty oneself but gives the victim leverage over his foes. If suspicion falls on a poorer sibling, who might otherwise be due some charity, the victim can cut him off, or at least decrease his demands. Diseases do not always obey human action, and should they prove intractable other options must be explored.

For the Tigray, spirit possession is a "marginal" belief, chosen when established belief fails (see Bauer and Hinnant 1980). Women may use it to redress marital relations. Men resist it when it is applied to their wives and they seem to find it an acceptable option for themselves only when all else fails. For a man, spirit possession is probably worse than being guilty of offending God because of its high social cost, *e.g.,* odd clothing and hair style and a mendicant way of life. For a woman, spirit possession involves less cost, in that it does not demand a complete change in daily life. Indeed, it may result in some gains, such as legitimized demands in the domestic setting and membership in a community of afflicted women. For women, spirit possession, once under control, is a periodic and momentary inconvenience.

Diviners, too, are subject to the influence of various interests in making their diagnoses. Patrons may wish to have particular suspicions validated. Communities may have already reached their own "verdicts." If they are to retain credibility, diviners must steer between these often contradictory convictions. The Church, diviners, spirit mediums, and the afflicted victim each form constituencies with specific interests in defining affliction. Ideas about enemies, authority, and chaotic power are the materials out of which Tigray beliefs about affliction are forged. A selective attention to logical fit among the components of a belief "system" tempered by interests yet finding coherence at a looser symbolic level is not a unique quality of Tigray thought but applies equally to most systems, including, no doubt, our own.

Notes

1. The research on which this paper is based was carried out over a 17-month period during 1968–70 in the Inderta region of Tigray Province and was supported by a predoctoral research grant from the National Institute of Mental Health. I would like to thank Larry Taylor, Ivan Karp, and Bill Arens for reading earlier drafts of this paper and making valuable suggestions. They have contributed greatly to the improvement of the paper. The errors are, of course, my own.

2. The orthography used in this paper are as follows: ~ over an *n* indicates a sound similar to that marked in this manner in Spanish; /\ over a *c* indicates the English *ch,* as in "Charles"; and /\ over an *s* indicates the English *sh,* as in "shun."

3. By "theoretical knowledge" I mean the knowledge that goes beyond the ordinary person's view of understandable cause and effect and generally involves interpretation of the world through the use of abstraction about invisible "forces" and relationships (see Horton 1967).

4. The cases are parallel in that the diviner, who from the perspective of "official" ideology, performs on the basis of knowledge, is suspected of enhancing his power through mystical means. This seems to be a quite general principle. A "gift for diagnosis" is what separates "good" doctors from ordinary physicians. Where mystical forces are available within the cosmology they take the form of a "gift."

5. The principle here, in a sense, is the reverse of Foster's "limited good" (1965). Certain categories of affliction are thought to be in constant supply. To get rid of an ailment one must give it to another. To rid a village of the contamination associated with a stillbirth, the collected women of a village must fling the fetus over the border into the territory of the neighboring village. At all times some village will be contaminated until the offending object reaches the ocean. Individuals can rid themselves of a disease, such as measles, by putting contaminated food along a trail so that a passerby will become afflicted and relieve them of the ailment (Bauer and Hinnant 1980), much as the ancient Hebrews believed.

6. Tigray witches (*buda*), like those in many cultures, do not know that they have this potential, except by the accusations made against them. The capacity for witchcraft is ascribed to artisans (*t'ebib*). Thus, while the diagnosis of witchcraft does imply human agency, it does not necessarily denote conscious human

intent to harm. Witches indulge in such uncultured behavior as the eating of food not permitted to Christians, including the organs of living persons, and nocturnal escapades, such as riding on hyenas or even turning into them. H'areyna has no artisans and witchcraft plays a small part in the explanation of affliction.

7. The term "idiom" increasingly takes on a precise meaning in social anthropology. It refers to a set of concepts and images used to describe and account for social relationships (Evans-Pritchard 1940; Taylor 1981, 1983). Even in the same society, the logical principles that organize idioms may be used as separate domains of action. Thus, Karp and Maynard (1983) show that the Nuer use the principle of *opposition* to organize both territoriality and the age system, even though they do not invoke the two sets of relationships in the same contexts. Karp and Maynard's distinction between logical principles, cultural idioms, and patterns of action enables anthropologists to distinguish the form of local discourse from its content.

8. This parallels Willis' observation of a "disease," which his informants postulated existed for reasons of conceptual necessity but which was never diagnosed in actual cases (1972).

9. The contradiction is more than an unexplainable discrepancy. Tigray witchcraft is discrepant but presents its practitioners as inverters of Christian principles and practice. One of the damning features of spirit possession as a belief is its disregard for Christianity, which is completely irrelevant from a possession perspective. Believers in possession do not seem to care if it is related to Christianity or not. Witches, by contrast, invert and pervert Christian practice. Those accused of witchcraft vigorously deny it. Thus, unlike spirit possession, it is part of Christian discourse.

References

Barth, Fredrik

1966 Models of Social Organization. Royal Anthropological Institute Occasional Paper, No. 23.

Bauer, Dan F.

1973 Land, Leadership and Legitimacy Among the Inderta Tigre of Ethiopia. Ph.D. Dissertation, University of Rochester. Ann Arbor: University Microfilms.

1985 Household and Society in Ethiopia. 2d ed. East Lansing: African Studies Center, Michigan State University.

1987 The Dynamics of Communal and Hereditary Land Tenure Among the Tigray of Ethiopia. *In* The Question of the Commons: The Culture and Ecology of Communal Resources. Bonnie McCay and James Acheson, eds. pp. 217–30. Tucson: University of Arizona Press.

Bauer, Dan F. and John Hinnant

1980 Normal and Revolutionary Divination: A Kuhnian Approach to

African Traditional Systems of Thought. *In* Explorations in African Systems of Thought. Ivan Karp and Charles Bird, eds. pp. 213–36. Bloomington: Indiana University Press.

Beidelman, T. O.
1973 Swazi Royal Ritual. Africa 36(4):373–405.

Evans-Pritchard, E. E.
1937 Witchcraft, Oracles and Magic Among the Azande. Oxford: Clarendon Press.
1940 The Nuer. Oxford: Clarendon Press.

Fortes, Meyer
1966 Religious Premises and Logical Techniques in Divinatory Ritual. Transactions of the Royal Society of London, Series B, Vol. 251: 409–22.

Foster, George
1965 Peasant Society and the Image of Limited Good. American Anthropologist 67(2):293–315.

Freud, Sigmund
1960 The Ego and the Id. Joan Riviere, transl. James Strachey, ed. New York: Norton and Company.

Geertz, Clifford
1977 Centers, Kings, and Charisma: Reflections on the Symbolics of Power. *In* Culture and Its Creators; Essays in Honor of Edward Shils. Joseph Ben-David and Terry Nichols, eds. pp. 150–71. Chicago: University of Chicago Press.

Hoben, Allan
1970 Social Stratification in Traditional Amhara Society. *In* Social Stratification in Africa. Arthur Tuden and Leonard Plotnicov, eds. pp. 187–224. New York: The Free Press.

Horton, R.
1967 African Traditional Thought and Western Science. Part 1. Africa 37(1):50–71; Part 2. Africa 37(2):155–87.

Karp, Ivan
1980 Beer Drinking and Social Experience in an African Society: An Essay in Formal Sociology. *In* Explorations in African Systems of Thought. Ivan Karp and Charles Bird, eds. pp. 83–119. Bloomington: Indiana University Press.

Karp, Ivan and Maynard, Kent
1983 Reading the Nuer. Current Anthropology 24(2):481–502.

Taylor, Lawrence
1981 Man the Fisher: Salmon Fishing and the Expression of Community in Rural Ireland. American Ethnologist 8:744–88.

1983 Dutchmen of the Bay. Philadelphia: University of Pennsylvania Press.

Turner, Victor
1964 Symbols in Ndembo Ritual. *In* Closed Systems and Open Minds. Max Gluckman, ed. pp. 20–51. Chicago: Aldine.

Weber, Max
1947 The Theory of Social and Economic Organization. A. M. Henderson and Talcott Parsons, transl. Glencoe, Illinois: The Free Press. (Original: Wirschaft and Gesellschaft, Part 1, Tubingen, 1922)
1958 The Protestant Ethic and the Spirit of Capitalism. Talcott Parsons, transl. New York: Schribner.

Willis, R. G.
1972 Pollution and Paradigms. Man 7(3):368–78.

Alma Gottlieb

Witches, Kings, and the Sacrifice of Identity or *The Power of Paradox and the Paradox of Power among the Beng of Ivory Coast*

While living among the Beng in Ivory Coast, I became acquainted with a young woman named Affoué.[1] A friendly, good-humored, and very intelligent woman, she was more willing than many women her age to discuss serious questions of Beng society with me. I was shocked one day when her cousin Aia, who had introduced us, said to me, "You know she's a witch, don't you?" I asked Aia how she knew this. Aia responded, "Haven't you noticed that she's totally flat-chested? And she's never menstruated, so she'll never have children. She sold her menstrual cycle to the witches so she could buy witchcraft with it." My first reaction—as a Westerner rather than an anthropologist—was to mention to Aia that there are Western drugs, probably available at the dispensary thirty miles away, that could very possibly cure Affoué's condition. Aia responded, "But they wouldn't work for Affoué. Don't you understand? She *sold* her menstrual cycle. She will *never* menstruate."

On another occasion, my friend Aia surprised me again with information about witchcraft. Aia had been educated in Ivoirian schools but had been obliged to return to the village after her father's death, which left her no base of emotional and financial support. She revealed to me that her father had died from being bewitched by his elder brother, who was now the regional king and had bewitched her father soon after taking office. She explained that it was the duty of every new king to bewitch three relatives within a year of assuming office, and Aia's father had merely been one of the victims of that rule.

What do these two types of witchcraft—one seemingly very personal, the other apparently political—have to do with one another? In the following pages I will suggest that both these kinds of Beng witchcraft indicate the witch's willful sacrifice of a crucial component or aspect of identity. The discussion will thereby explore how the Beng notion of identity is wide enough to include certain kinspeople in some circumstances (*cf.* Fortes 1973:289; Mauss 1938; Zahan 1979:9). The general power of the Beng witch, I argue, is based not on *external* symbols and techniques, as it seems to be in many other societies, but, in its most potent and archetypical form, on the sacrifice of identity. The power of the witch and the power of the king, though used for opposite ends, nevertheless make use of the same symbolic repertoire and hence are closely allied.

The Beng

Before analyzing Beng notions of witchcraft, I will summarize the relevant aspects of Beng society. There are about 10,000 Beng living in the prefecture of M'Bahiakro in Ivory Coast and an undetermined number living in the neighboring subprefecture of Prikro. They speak one of the Southern Mande family of languages whose other speakers all live farther to the west and southwest in Ivory Coast. The Beng's immediate neighbors are the Baule to the south and west, the Ando to the east and southeast (both Akan groups), and the Djimini and Diammala (Senufo groups) to the north and northwest. In the precolonial era the Beng enjoyed trade relations, especially through their famous kola nut production, with these and other local ethnic groups.

Beng say that until the colonial era, the men hunted regularly in addition to farming (primarily yams and fruit and nut trees, including the kola trees), but with the introduction of cash crops by the French (especially coffee and cocoa), hunting has taken a secondary place to farming. Women continue to farm and gather (primarily vegetal products), as before. Beng social structure is based on double descent: there are matriclans and patriclans, each type having its own functions and symbolic associations (Gottlieb 1988b). Patriclans have less to do with witchcraft and politics and more to do with the transmission of food and other taboos, funeral ritual styles, the mechanics of marriage negotiations, and the afterlife, and for this reason they figure little into the present discussion.

The Beng area in the prefecture of M'Bahiakro is divided into two political regions called the Forest and Savanna (these designations are more symbolic than they are strictly descriptive of the actual ecology of the two regions), each containing localized matriclans and nonlocalized patriclans. Each of the two regions has a king and a queen presiding over it. Although the king is more visible in political affairs, he is said to consult the queen on all major decisions. She serves as his stand-in if he is sick or otherwise indisposed, helps choose an heir to the kingship if she survives her coruler, and is a co-owner of the mystically powerful objects that come with the offices of king and queen. The king and queen are always members of a single matriclan and are classified as siblings (though they may be cousins).

Going down the political scale, there are several villages in each of the two political regions. Each village has a male and female chief (though nowadays the female chief's post is sometimes left empty). As with the regional king and queen, the male and female chief are viewed as corulers of their village and are "siblings" (or cousins) belonging to a single matriclan. In the discussion that follows, I will discuss primarily kings, but it should be borne in mind that queens and male and female village chiefs hold much the same types of power as does the king, but in scaled-down form.

Each of the two kings is viewed as the sovereign ruler of the region over which he has jurisdiction; hence he has important legal powers. His court was traditionally the highest appeals court after a clan or village trial (there is now the possibility of using a nearby Ivoirian town court, but the Beng resort to this most infrequently). The king tries cases in the first instance involving problematic situations that transcend a single village, such as certain disputes or the violation of certain grave taboos. In addition to this judicial role, the king nowadays holds region-wide meetings to deal with affairs of modernization, such as proposals to build a new dispensary in the region or to admit loggers in to cut down forest trees for timber.

As with many African peoples, politics for the Beng are intimately tied to religion; indeed it is hard to distinguish the two as separate realms at all. For in the Beng view, the king holds authority by virtue of his relationship to what anthropologists call mystical notions. Every king is viewed as an owner of the Earth, which is the primary focus for worship among the Beng. The Earth itself is seen both as a unity, and as refracted into several smaller, bounded Earths contained within the Beng region. In each of these forms, the Earth is said to hold great mystic powers over human life. Each village is associated with at least one named Earth, each of which has two Masters of the Earth (one primary and one deputy Master of the Earth) who offer sacrifices and prayers to that Earth on behalf of all who either wish to or are required to worship it. These Masters of the Earth are said to "own" the Earths that they are entitled to worship. Ultimately, however, the king "owns" all the Earths associated with the villages in his region as indeed he "owns" *everything* in his region. Hence ultimately he has jurisdiction over all the activities that occur in his region having to do with worship of the Earth.

The Earth shapes the daily lives of the Beng in intimate and far-reaching ways. In particular, it lays down a large array of taboos that must never be violated. Violations of the most important "taboos" concerning the Earth automatically result in punishment and atonement (via sacrifice) approved by the king of the transgressor's region. Such sins would include a couple who illicitly have sexual relations in an area allied to an Earth shrine (see Gottlieb 1988a), or any individual who directly transgresses an Earth shrine—for instance by talking to, staring at, or touching it. These violations are considered to endanger the entire region, and therefore must be dealt with by the king of that region.

The king has other mystic abilities not directly linked to his custodianship of the Earth. For instance, he is said to have visionary powers—he will foresee dire "natural" calamities before they befall the region, if such calamities are interpreted as punishment for sins committed, and will warn the region of such calamities. About once a month he sends a representative to consult with a distant diviner who will reveal any immoral activities that may have occurred in the king's region and need to be ritually rectified. Furthermore, the king of one region inherits with his office the knowledge of how to stop a baby from choking. I interpret this as a symbol of his responsibility for ensuring the well-being of his people, as represented by an infant (the epitome of fertility) literally gasping for life. Additionally, the king may offer occasional sacrifices to "bush spirits" or to spirits of ancestors causing misfortunes such as droughts or excessive infant and child mortality in the villages. In general, then, the king is responsible not only for the legal but also the moral and spiritual well-being of the people living in his region.

All this is in direct contrast to the power of witches. Beng witches, like their counterparts elsewhere in Africa, are viewed as immoral: in the Beng case, they "consume" their relatives with whom they have the most in common symbolically and emotionally—that is, their uterine kin—to assuage their personal "hunger" for "meat."[2] In so doing, they threaten to undermine the symbolic foundation of a significant component of the Beng descent system. For the matriclan system is based on what I term a fund of shared "identity" (Gottlieb 1988b). Uterine kin are viewed as emotionally close, to the point of symbolic equivalence and sociological interchangeability (see below). Bewitching a matrikinsperson is, then, an act of ultimate immorality.

One is inevitably led to the question of motivation. I often asked informants why a given witch had killed a particular matrikinsperson. Sometimes my informant would offer a trivial excuse as a motivation—the victim had borrowed a dish the week before and hadn't yet returned it to the witch, the victim had refused to lend the witch money until two months hence, at harvest time—but invariably my informant explained that these "reasons" were merely pretexts. Ultimately, no one can really know what lies in a witch's heart, my informants explained, what motivates him or her to bewitch a matrikinsperson. This feature underscores the immorality of witchcraft for the Beng: not only does a witch kill a matrikinsperson—with whom one has so much in common symbolically and sociologically—but there is no knowable reason for the act. In times past, witches were killed if proven guilty by an ordeal.

At least two kinds of ordeals existed. First, suspected witches might have a mixture of pounded chili peppers smeared all over their faces and then be chased into the forest. If they returned to the village, they were considered innocent; if not, they were presumed guilty. A second method was more indirect. A sacrifice was performed using a chicken. As in all Beng animal sacrifices, after being killed, the chicken was opened up and the officiating priest inspected the ovaries or testicles. If they were white, it indicated the good intentions (*i.e.*, innocence) of the person donating the chicken (the suspected witch), but if black, it indicated that the chicken donor was lying about his or her innocence and was indeed a witch. In this case, the now-convicted witch would be escorted to a spot in the forest. Here, at least in one village, a certain Djimini man (see Beidelman 1982) would beat the witch lightly with a wooden club and then toss him or her into a pit in which there was a boa snake that would consume the witch. To my knowledge, neither of these ordeals has been practiced for some time, because of modern Ivoirian law. Nowadays, witches are socially ostracized to varying degrees—they often have few friends and are generally shunned while walking through the village.

In the remainder of the article, I will discuss aspects of witchcraft as they emerge in both the personal and political spheres, basing the latter discussion on the brief sketch of the Beng sociopolitical structure provided above. I will begin by treating the personal type of witchcraft carried out by private citizens and then move on to the political type brought about by office-holders. I will conclude by suggesting that both types of witchcraft partake of the same symbolic structure and constitute the two extreme and opposite versions of a single symbolic mode, which has to do with the Beng philosophy of identity.

In this discussion I will not refer directly to the notion of "power," because for the Beng, power itself is in many ways defined by what I term "identity." As many recent writers have argued for West Africa and elsewhere (*e.g.*, Etienne 1987; Bledsoe 1980), power in this small-scale society rests ultimately in people. This view of "wealth [or power]-in-people," as it has been called, has been taken to mean that people represent the economic potential of their labor. However, people also represent the *sociological* potential of role replacement. The notion of "perpetual kinship," introduced some time ago in African studies (see Cunnison 1956), is relevant here. As Cunnison understood it for the Luapula of Zambia, however, "perpetual kinship" was based on a further notion of "positional succession," in which, as Poewe (1981) has written of the same people: "Upon death every individual must be succeeded by a living matrikin. The successor is said to assume the identity, names, titles, and relationships of the deceased. According to Luapula philosophy, he is the deceased. Relationships of the past are therefore lived in the present and perpetuated into the future" (p. 54). This view of perpetual kinship thus rests on an idea of collapsed time: past social roles are recreated in the present and into the future, and individuals are considered nothing more than transitory occupiers of those roles. (For a similar view of time among the Avatip of Papua New Guinea, see Harrison 1988.)

For the Beng, I suggest that the situation is related, but not identical. The emphasis here is not so much on given individuals occupying permanent, atemporal sociological roles as on a group of (matrilineally related) individuals sharing symbolic attributes, or what Schneider (1968:52 and *passim*) would call "substance," by virtue of membership in the particular group. In other words, I stress the symbolic underpinnings of the sociological situation, whereas Cunnison stressed the sociological underpinnings of the symbolic situation, perhaps because of differences in both the ethnography and our own theoretical predilections.

In short, I suggest that for the Beng, political power is based ultimately on a notion of identity, and identity in turn is based on a certain understanding of symbolic "substance" as it is shared by uterine kin. How such "substance" or "identity" is manipulated for both personal and political gain is explored below.

Personal Witchcraft

Some Beng are "born" witches, but others must acquire their knowledge themselves (although unlike the Azande and others, the Beng make no terminological distinction between these two types of witches: both are called *brunã*).[3] All born witches inherit their witchcraft talents from the matriline, generally from the mother. (See below how this is relevant to the political use of witchcraft.) For the nonhereditary witches, there are two means to acquire knowledge of witchcraft: one may either be taught witchcraft, again by the mother; or one may buy the knowledge of the craft. But the price of buying this knowledge from another witch is quite high: one informant estimated its cost as perhaps 500,000 CFA, which is anywhere from 2½ to 5 times the average annual salary of a Beng villager (the exchange rate fluctuates from about 200–400 CFA to the dollar). It would clearly be unusual for a villager to have this amount of money available. But there are other means to purchase witchcraft, using even more valuable resources as currency: one may purchase the knowledge of witchcraft by selling either a vital spiritual or physical part of a human being. The victim may either be the person who is buying the witchcraft or any member of that person's matriclan (usually a close relative such as a child or sibling).

A prospective witch may sell a matriclan member's name (*to*) or soul or spirit (*niniŋ/wru*) (see Note 15); or may sell his or her own arm or, if a woman, her menstrual cycle and breasts. If the witch chooses the first method, as soon as the victim is deprived of either name or spirit, he or she immediately starts dying a physical death if the spirit was stolen or a mental death—that is, madness—if the name was stolen. The latter is illustrated in the following case:

> T went mad suddenly. The day he went mad, he publicly announced the cause. He said it was his own mother, A, who had bewitched him. A wanted to be rich and so she "took" her son's name and "carried" it up to some Muslim witches in a northern village who bought the name and then later sacrificed it. In return, they guaranteed A that she would be rich: all her crops would always be abundant. The minute they sacrificed the name, T immediately went mad, while his mother started getting rich.
>
> Every three months for a period of about a month he would hit anyone for no reason, or walk around naked and try, unsuccessfully, to seduce or rape women he encountered, or enter a woman's kitchen and eat everything in sight while she tried to chase him out. At times he would have to be tied up for a few weeks in his house, being fed there and using a chamber pot. Once he wounded a man with a machete and a village elder called in the police, who took him to be cured at a psychiatric hospital; but when he was released and returned to the village, he was still mad.

In this case the woman, A, merely sold her son's name in exchange for economic advantage. Apparently she committed no further acts of witchcraft against other matrikin, although it is uncertain whether she could have if she had wanted to.

But some other would-be witches sell their matrikin victim's spirit to practicing witches, and in these cases the victim immediately falls sick and later dies bodily. As they have spiritually killed the victim, however, it is said that such witches—along with the witches to whom the victim was sold—may immediately begin "eating" the victim's *body,* even if the sick victim is not ostensibly dead to the world (see Note 15). The witches and the prospective witch feast invisibly on the victim's body, or "meat" (*soŋ*), together, and within three to four months at most, the victim's external body indeed dies. With this method, the prospective witch always gains some techniques for committing future acts of witchcraft against his or her matrikin, such as receiving invisible poisonous leaves to put in a victim's wash water or invisible poison to put in a victim's food.

It is significant that in both forms of buying witchcraft—selling the victim's name and selling the victim's spirit—the victim is always a close matrikinsperson of the prospective witch—generally a parent, child, or sibling.[4] I suggest that such close matrikin comprise on one level a portion of an individual's own identity, so that by selling an aspect of a close matrikinsperson, a prospective witch sells part of his or her own identity.

The second mode of buying witchcraft consists of a prospective witch selling a central aspect of his or her own bodily identity. One may sell the use of an arm/hand,[5] which is essential to performing all kinds of physical labor (especially if it is the right arm/hand, used more than the left in physical labor). The result of "selling" the arm/hand is that the body part becomes totally and permanently limp, making it effectively useless. As in any labor-intensive society, the arm/hand is a primary source of individual self-esteem, economic self-sufficiency, and general social status, in addition to its direct social and economic value to those to whom one owes a certain amount of yearly labor (especially one's parents, spouse, and elder siblings). This perceived value is evident in linguistic usage. One of the euphemisms for menstruation is the expression *a wɔ trɔ,* literally "her arm/hand is low." When a woman works in the forest (chopping wood) or in the fields (farming), her arm/hand is constantly "raised," that is, in motion. When she is menstruating, she is forbidden to perform work in any area connected to an Earth shrine, which includes all the fields and the forest (see Gottlieb 1988a). So a menstruating woman cannot perform any work other than cooking and cleaning inside the village. The expression "her arm/hand is low," referring to incapacity for labor while menstruating, highlights the Beng view of the arm/hand as symbolizing the human capacity for labor. "Selling" the use of one's arm/hand in exchange for the power to perform witchcraft is tantamount to renouncing the ability to perform some or all forms of labor. Apparently, the labor power that one thus renounces is more than made up for by the different sort of power that one gains: the power to bewitch other matrikin with the ultimate goal of eating their "meat," thereby avoiding hunger despite the lack of a good working arm.[6]

Prospective female witches may also buy witchcraft by selling their menstrual cycle and breasts. In this case, the woman will never again menstruate, develop breasts, or have children, as with Affoué. My informant on this subject assured me that there were many other women who chose this route to acquiring witchcraft. Here the woman sacrifices a central part of her identity as a female—her potential maternity, and all the symbolic, social, and economic power that this implies—in exchange for the power of bewitching others, again to eat their "meat."[7] (For another perspective on the Beng view of the female body, see Gottlieb n.d.)

In both the above cases, the would-be witch sells an essential component of his or her own personal identity—the ability to perform labor, or to be fertile though producing children—in exchange for acquiring a destructive power over others in his or her own matriclan. The next section will explore a type of *political* witchcraft that also requires a willful sacrifice of a component of identity, in the form of matriclan members.

Witch-Kings

Many others working in Africa have noted that political authority is sometimes closely allied to what might be called the "dark side" of power. De Heusch (1982) and Adler (1982), for instance, have both shown how African kings sometimes reveal two contrasting sides to their image and their behavior: they may appear as benevolent protectors of their land and people, but they are also capable of despotic acts of terror. Art sometimes reveals this ambiguity. For example, of the king of Benin, Fraser (1972a), citing Dark, *et al.* (1960:35), has written about "the depiction of the Oba [king] holding the tails of a pair of crocodiles or leopards, one on either side of his head. . . . This motif, known as the 'Animal Master' or *dompteur* . . . express[es] graphically the idea of a leader's control over various forces, good as well as evil. In Benin, the design serves in part to underscore the Oba's own power, because the leopards he holds are symbolic of himself" (p. 263). The forms such "dark powers" take vary considerably. In some societies, the malevolent aspect of a king's power may be confined to periodic public ritual, as Smith (1982) has argued is the case among the Swazi. Elsewhere, the immoral side to power may take the form of privileged royal incest and "endocannibalism," as Muller (1980) has described among the Rukuba of Nigeria. Of Benin, Ben-Amos has written (1976), "The right to kill is *the* defining characteristic of leadership" (p. 246). This model approaches the Beng case; the Beng are pacifists in that, with rare exceptions, it is taboo to kill people outright, but as I have shown, they do "kill" people through witchcraft. In Beng society, "royal transgression" takes the form of witchcraft practiced systematically by newly installed kings.[8] (For another case of witch-leaders, see Douglas 1975:24 on the Lele of Zaire.)

When a man accedes to the kingship, he and his subjects know that he has one year within which to live up to the challenge of his office and bewitch three close relatives. One relative may be anyone in his matriclan; another relative must be someone in his immediate uterine family (often a sibling); and the third relative must be either his own child (see Note 4) or his sister's child. There are similar requirements for newly installed queens and male and female village chiefs.[9] My informant assured me that the rule is carried out in every case.[10] I was told of only one case in which a newly installed office-holder had "defaulted" on the requirements of the office, leading to dire consequences:

> A newly installed female village chief of village R tried to kill her own son by witchcraft but she couldn't bring herself to complete the act. [It may be significant, my informant mentioned, that this village chief had only two children.] Finally, she said that she herself would rather die than have to kill her own son. So the male chief of village R [with whom she jointly ruled] obligingly bewitched her, and she soon died.

Thus the new office-holder takes the obligation to bewitch close matrikin very seriously; default on the requirement is made at the cost of his or her own life.

I heard of a related incident on another level, concerning a particular village matriclan. In village P, there is a revolving village chiefship, in which each of four matriclans is supposed to contribute alternately the village male and female chiefs. Earlier in Beng history, however, one of these four matriclans decided to withdraw from the revolving chiefship.

> Long ago, when it came matriclan X's time to contribute a member to be the chief of village P, the clan elders refused to do so because they did not want to have other clan members killed in witchcraft by the new chief. One clan elder said, "Before taking someone from our clan they'll have to make a tree in the forest into the village chief!" A long and bitter dispute resulted between clan X and the rest of village P, but to this day X has not contributed a member to the village chiefship.
>
> Recently some moves have been made to remedy the situation. Thus some elders in village P preliminarily sacrificed a cow to the founder of village P to apologize for clan X having removed itself from the chiefship rotation cycle. But at the time I left the field about four months after this first cow sacrifice, none of the necessary follow-up sacrifices had yet been done. The king of the region in which village P is located commented to me that P "could not be a good village" until clan X reinstated itself back into the village chiefship rotation cycle.

For our purposes, the significance of this situation lies in the king's statement that P cannot be a "good village" until matriclan X is brought back into the village chiefship cycle—and, by implication, permits clan members to be killed through witchcraft by the new chief. Thus there is a conflict between what we might term a pan-human valuing of life and the official ideology of Beng chiefship (which requires certain deaths), which has not yet been resolved. To this, the king views only one solution as satisfactory: reinstating clan X into the revolving chiefship and permitting the new village chief from clan X to bewitch specified matrikin.

One should not assume that this conflict between "pan-human" and cultural values is by any means universal among individual Beng, who seem to take it for granted that matrikin will be killed within a year of a king assuming office. My friend Aia, for instance, as mentioned earlier, had a father who had been killed in witchcraft by his brother when the latter became king. Aia seemed to harbor little resentment toward the king for having killed her father, because, as she told me, she recognized his action as an obligation of office. She and I regularly visited the king, and she served as my translator/assistant on these occasions.

In addition to the new king's own witchcraft, when a king or queen accedes to the position, every village chief is required within a year's time to bewitch one uterine kinsperson and "send over" the spirit to the new king or queen for the latter to "eat." In this case, the required category of matrikinsperson is not specified: any one will do. This obligation is a clear symbol of the chiefs' political loyalty to the new king or queen; that they can sacrifice an aspect of their own uterine identity demonstrates that they are willing to cooperate in putting the interests of the state, and its new head, above their own narrow kinship interests.

Before I analyze why matrikin alone must be bewitched by the newly installed king or chief, it should be noted that there is also some witchcraft activity at the other end of the king/chiefship cycle: at the funeral. Here, one notices a similarity to kingship systems elsewhere in Africa that have been described as exhibiting a certain kind of chaos—even to the point of civil war—at a king's death, and possibly during the entire period of interregnum (Gluckman 1954b, 1956; Goody 1966; Uzoigwe 1973). In the Beng situation, such "chaos" is confined to the king's or chief's funeral, and it again takes the form of witchcraft. At a Beng king's funeral, all mourners are considered especially vulnerable to witchcraft, which is easiest to perform on these occasions. Although witches are normally restricted to bewitching a fellow matriclansperson, at a king's funeral, they may bewitch people in *any* matriclan so long as a witch from the intended victim's matriclan is present. Thus the bewitchings at a king's funeral take on a certain random quality. (Mourners at a king's funeral invariably include people from virtually all villages and all matriclans, not just members of the king's village and matriclan.) Many parents do not bring their children to such funerals, as children are considered especially vulnerable to witchcraft. Many adults do not go to a king's funeral unless they can obtain adequate protection against witchcraft, in one of two forms: either by bringing certain plants to carry around, which are said to repel witchcraft;[11] or by coming accompanied by a "good witch" (*brunã gɛŋ*) who could personally ward off witchcraft attempts. Thus at the end of a king's reign there is let loose a kind of free-for-all witchcraft to which anyone present at the funeral is vulnerable. Such a period of malevolent license might be seen as a metaphor for the political situation, also a period of malevolent license: the onset of the interregnum period (generally one year) with no king to lead the state.[12]

This is in direct contrast to the kind of witchcraft deaths that take place at the beginning of a king's reign.[13] As I have mentioned, these deaths are conducted only at the hands of the king himself, and two of the three victims must be in specified kinship relationships to the king. Although death, especially by witchcraft, disrupts the attempt of society to create order, the form of witchcraft killings by the newly installed king is a relatively orderly version of death, as it specifies both who the witch is and, to some extent, who the victims must be.

But as "orderly" as the required acts of witchcraft by a king might seem on one level, a basic paradox is inherent. Unlike some other African societies in which a new king must kill his rival predecessor to obtain office (*e.g.*, Vaughan 1980), the new Beng king must kill his potential future supporters, those in his matriclan, some of them quite close. Why should this be an obligation of each new king? The answer has to do with what the matriclan represents to an individual Beng in general, and to a Beng king in particular. In certain crucial ways, matrikin are viewed as a sociological component of an individual's own identity, and the sacrifice of a matrikinsperson is a sacrifice of part of oneself.

Identity and the Matriclan

On a sociological level, matriclan members are considered interchangeable in many contexts. Four examples will be given, although many others might be added. The first concerns beliefs about infant development. If a baby is born with teeth, or if an infant cuts its upper teeth first, these are anomalies and considered bad omens. In the old days, such babies were killed.[14] If the baby was not killed, someone else in the baby's matriclan would soon die, in replacement of the infant.

A similar situation has to do with a certain kind of sacrifice to the Earth. If one is desirous of obtaining something (either material or social), one can offer a sacrifice to the Earth, called *dolɛ ló,* to request it. In this case, one is obliged to offer a second sacrifice to the Earth, called *tõ bolɛ,* three years later to thank the Earth (whether or not the Earth in fact granted the request). If the petitioner neglects to thank the Earth three years later with the second sacrifice, someone else in the petitioner's matriclan will be killed by the Earth. If the second sacrifice is still not done, another matriclan member will be killed by the Earth, and so on, until the petitioner finally offers the required second sacrifice to the Earth. Any person in the matriclan is eligible as an unwilling victim of the Earth, so long as the original petitioner refrains from offering the Earth its due sacrifice.

One may ask why the Earth does not simply kill the delinquent petitioner directly as a punishment. In this case, the Earth would not obtain the required sacrifice (*tõ bolɛ*) and thus would only succeed in gaining punishment but not, as it were, restitution. By killing a matrikinsperson of the negligent petitioner, I suggest, the Earth gains both punishment—by killing an aspect of the petitioner's identity, a matrikinsperson—and, presumably, restitution—in the form of guilt and/or fear now instilled in the sinner, which will finally lead him or her to offer the second sacrifice to the Earth. (The petitioner would know of his or her responsibility for the matrikinsperson's death because diviners determine the causes of all deaths.)

Matrikin are vulnerable to being killed by an angry Earth in a related circumstance. The most sinful activity in Beng cosmology is for a couple to have intercourse outside the village, where no kapok tree has been planted ritually to legitimate human sexual activity (see Gottlieb 1988a). Should a couple transgress this rule, they must first confess, then are semipublicly punished, and then must offer a sacrifice (*pɔ gba*) to apologize to the Earth for having polluted it by their action. But if the couple does not confess, they may not be punished; even so, the Earth has been polluted and demands restitution. In this case it is said that the Earth may make the couple ill, but if they continue to avoid confessing and expiating their sin, it is said that the Earth may kill relatives of the guilty couple, especially any of their matrikin, until the couple finally confess, are punished, and, by their sacrifice, apologize to the Earth. Again, I suggest that the couple themselves are not said to be killed by the Earth for the same reason as was offered in the case of the *tõ bolɛ* sacrificer above. Killing the guilty party would rule out obtaining the necessary apologetic sacrifice, but killing matrikin results in both punishment and, some time later, the required sacrifice.

Lastly, a similar principle operates in the sphere of funerals. A range of kinspeople is required to contribute different items as sacrifices (*sraka*) to the cadaver, depending on their kinship relationship to the deceased. In some cases, only the eldest of a uterine group of terminologically identical kin is held responsible for the contribution. For instance, an old woman, A, died, leaving behind only an adoptive son and a co-wife's son. The co-wife's son, K, was required to contribute in his dead father's name: one hand-woven cloth—for burial with the cadaver; one chicken—for sacrifice and eating; and one goat—for sacrifice and eating. However, K had an "elder brother," T—really, a matrilateral parallel cousin—and so this man, although he was not *genealogically* related to the dead woman as her co-wife's son, was *terminologically* the eldest in this position, and thus he contributed the most expensive item on the list, the goat. In this case, then, two men shared one kinship role as they shared one kinship category via the shared symbolic "substance" of matriclan "identity." Thus in the four circumstances discussed (as well as several other cases)—baby teething anomaly, Earth sacrifice default, sexual pollution of the Earth, and funeral donations—matrikin are viewed as sociologically interchangeable as well as symbolically identical, and one may be punished or killed instead of another by mystical means.

Concerning symbolic "substance," a more positive attribute shared by matrikin has to do with an inherited mystical or spiritual property. Each human being is born with a soul (*niniŋ*), present from the moment of conception. It is significant that the soul is always inherited through the matriline. This soul, as we have seen, is essential to maintaining life; if it is killed through witchcraft, the victim soon dies in body as well, for the spiritual soul is deemed necessary to physical human life.[15] Because the soul is inherited through the matriclan, all matriclan members may be seen as sharing a type of "mystical substance" with one another. In contrast, patriclan members share no such "mystical substance."[16]

A more trivial and pejoratively viewed attribute that may be inherited through the matriline is body odor (*mia gbiŋ*). Not all individuals have body odor, but those who do invariably inherit it from the matriline; this form of "substance," too, may be shared only by matrikin and not by patrikin.

Another level of social relations relevant here is friendship. An informant told me that one cannot be friends (*gwe*) with a fellow matriclan member—one's friends are either unrelated to one or they are fellow patriclan members. My own informal observations of friendship patterns certainly bore out this observation. My informant expressed a combination of amusement and shock at the idea of being friends with a matrikinsperson. The reason for this is clear: for two people to be friends implies some structural and psychological distance between the two people that is bridged by the friendship (*cf.* Brain 1976:15–16). But there is no such distance between *matriclan* members, who are viewed as sociologically interchangeable at many levels, and so the possibility of friendship between them is precluded.

There are certain political implications of this situation. All kings, queens, and village chiefs are chosen by reference to matriclans. That is, a particular matriclan may have a monopoly on a given political office (chiefship of a certain village or the regional kingship), or, alternatively, the office may be filled from two or more given matriclans, as with village P, above. There is no competition for such positions, I was told often, as the jobs themselves are dangerous and therefore undesirable. Only "strong" people would even consider holding such positions, for they would need the powers of witchcraft to protect both themselves and their constituents from witchcraft attempts, but also to carry out the necessary acts of installation witchcraft; and they would need moral rectitude to render judgments fairly without being tempted by bribes, which would anger the Earth (which "likes the truth") and leave themselves vulnerable to being killed by the Earth as a punishment. Potential heirs to a newly vacated throne must be ritually begged to accept the position by a formal delegation (*cf.* Gilbert 1987:314 on a parallel custom among the Akuropon of Ghana). Lesser candidates who do not feel up to the job, though selected, may pass it over for these reasons. The Beng insist that this rules out any rivalry among matrikin for the position.

Accordingly, Beng political succession rules are quite explicit and allow no scope for competing candidates, unlike many matrilineal regimes of succession (Douglas 1969:129). With all Beng political offices, succession operates laterally: the next younger classificatory brother/sister (or, if this generation is exhausted, nephew/niece) of the previous office-holder is chosen, according to complex rules concerning alternation between lineal groups. The significant point is that all heirs are designated according to quite specific rules, permitting no institutionalized rivalry among a group of potential candidates.

These political factors, combined with the symbolic and social attributes of matriclanship enumerated above, indicate that a king's, queen's, and village chief's own identity is combined with his or her matrikinspeople's identities even more than is true for non-officeholders.

For all these reasons, when a king bewitches a matrikinsperson, I suggest, he is sacrificing an aspect of his own socio-symbolic identity.

Witches and Witch-Kings, Identity and Power

In discussing African kingship, many writers have explored the nature and extent of divine kings' powers (*e.g.*, Arens 1979). Specifically, recent authors have demonstrated how kings rely on and manipulate publicly recognized external symbols, such as stools, umbrellas, and drums, as well as rituals, to legitimate and even enhance their own positions (Beidelman 1966; Beier 1982; Ben-Amos 1976; Brain 1980; Crowley 1972; Fagg 1970; Fraser 1972b; Gluckman 1954a; Kyerematen 1969; Lebeuf 1969:135–67, 261–81, 295–312; Rudy 1972; Smith 1982; Thompson 1972; Vansina 1972; Willett 1972; also *cf.* Geertz 1977, 1980). This new emphasis on the primacy of symbolic objects and actions in legitimizing political authority is a welcome development in political theory. The present article has provided a variation on this theme. Rather than examining individual symbolic objects or actions, I have explored what might be termed an indigenous *ideology* of kingship. In particular, I have focused on a type of apparent disorder—witchcraft—that is practiced normatively by a newly installed king. But I have emphasized that the power of such witchcraft constitutes not so much a material symbol as an ideological one, that of "identity." In the Beng view, power appears to devolve from relations between certain categories of persons, as they are conceived symbolically. The nature of this symbolically based power has been the subject of this article.

It may be argued that a king's sacrifice of uterine kin after he takes office is a symbolically expedient means for him to demonstrate his commitment to the office. That is, by willingly sacrificing three uterine kin, he demonstrates to the polity that he agrees to do what is necessary for the state to prosper, even to the point of harming those he personally holds most dear. His action might be seen as the ultimate sacrifice. As with the bewitching of uterine kin by village chiefs for the benefit of a new king or queen, the king shows by his own action that he is capable of holding the needs of the kingdom above his own family interests. As an Akuropon of Ghana explained his society's traditional custom of anointing the new stools of newly installed kings with the blood of a sacrificed matrikinsperson, "Something which is valuable is used, not something useless . . . someone from the family is more valuable than anyone else" (Gilbert 1987:308). Moreover, on a functionalist level, one might argue—as Bohannan (1958) has done for a similar situation—that this action demonstrates to the citizenry how powerful the king is: he commits the ultimate act of destruction, the sacrifice of identity, and yet the polity not only does not fall apart, it prospers. As Douglas (1975) has suggested for the Lele of Zaire, witch-chiefs demonstrate through acts of witchcraft their transcendence of ordinary notions and standards of morality, "giving sinister power to the idea of chiefship" (p. 24). As such, witchcraft committed by a king can convince even a native cynic of the king's powers and thus enhance his prestige.

But once this is accepted, another issue concerning the question of identity as it pertains to Beng political thought must be broached. On the one hand, the king's bewitching of uterine kin shows that he can be *independent* of those kin, and thus rule fairly. On the other hand, the same act also demonstrates that he has ultimate *control* over those kin. As uterine kin comprise an aspect of one's identity and as kings owe their position to membership in the matriclan, it is logical that they should be obliged to demonstrate their power over the uterine aspect of identity by the ultimate mystical means: witchcraft. In sum, there seems to be a certain dialectical relationship between these two models of witch-kings. In fulfilling their duty to practice witchcraft, kings show both their *control over and independence from* their uterine kin, who constitute a sociosymbolic aspect of their own identity. These opposite models of a king's witchcraft underline the paradoxical foundation of a king's power, as revealed by the requirement for him to bewitch three uterine kin: he must demonstrate simultaneously by this act that he controls uterine kin, but for the ultimate purpose of destroying a select group of them. A king thereby represents the potential of encompassing all: protection and destruction, kinship and its denial, devotion and disloyalty. As Gilbert (1987) has written of the Akuropon, the king has "the characteristics of all men" (p. 328); similarly, Bloch (1987) has shown how Merina kings of Madagascar resolved all contradictions caused by ideology and oppositions.

In the Beng case, the king's embodiment of all oppositions is even more dramatic than I have indicated thus far. Not only must he bewitch three matrikin, but it is said that he is the owner of everything in the kingdom. When he accedes to the throne, he is "given the country," and because of the weightiness of this responsibility, he ritually weeps at his installation. Henceforward he has responsibility over not only all material objects, all domestic animals, and all people, but also over abstract concepts such as causality. This makes him ultimately responsible for all illness and misfortune, all crimes and sins—and all acts of witchcraft. If a witch wishes to kill someone, he or she first must gain the approval of the king. If he agrees—which is rare—the intended victim will soon die. If the king refuses, he must provide a substitute, who must be a member of the king's own matriclan. Once again, the principle of identity lies at the heart of political power.

As mentioned above, a new king's three victims must be: (1) a real or classificatory (uterine) sibling; (2) a real or classificatory (uterine) child; and (3) anyone in the matriclan. The first two victims constitute the whole range of significant relationships within the matriclan: siblingship, for one's own generation, and the MB-ZS or the parent-child relationship, for two adjacent generations. The third victim is not specified and thus leaves any other person in the matriclan available for the role of victim. That the king should be required to engage in the bewitching of this set of people—which represents the entire possible set of matrikin—reveals the wide scope of his potential for violence. Paradoxically, such violence is dramatically limited: the three required victims are *metaphors* for a larger set of people, but they are also only three individuals. That the king is limited to three, and only three, victims thus constitutes yet another paradox—it reveals both the enormity of his potential for violence and, simultaneously, a certain limitation on his actual practice of that violence. Likewise, the king's "ownership" of everything in his kingdom, including all acts of witchcraft, is premised on a paradox. He is pledged to protect his subjects from witchcraft, but the king may save a potential victim only at the expense of one of his own matrikin. Once again, it is identity that forms the basis of the paradox. (For other paradoxes and contradictory values evident in Beng society, see Gottlieb 1986b, 1989.)

It should now be clear that private witches and witch-kings comprise two ends of the Beng dialectic that defines symbolic power. For the Beng, power is based on the use and sacrifice not so much of material techniques and objects as of an aspect of one's own sociosymbolic identity. A private witch benefits in personal power and in mystical "meat" consumption but loses in public status; a king comes out even further ahead by benefitting politically as well. It is the sacrifice of identity that gives both private witches and, even more so, kings—who by Beng definition are witches—their power.

I will conclude this discussion by briefly comparing the Beng case with the Amba of Uganda, with whom on the surface the Beng seem to have much in common. Winter (1963), in an impressive and subtle article, has analyzed Amba beliefs about witchcraft. The Amba bewitch only covillagers, who represent the extent of the moral universe. Bewitching a covillager is, therefore, a symbol of the most immoral action imaginable, and this explains why witches are viewed as immorality incarnate.

This view of witchcraft as absolute evil is typical in Africa. But the Beng replicate the Amba case in more specific ways: both define witchcraft as an "endogamous" activity (although the Amba use residence and the Beng use descent as the criterion for inclusiveness), which is the reason that witchcraft is the epitome of immorality in both societies. Yet the Beng have refined the Amba view of witchcraft considerably. The highest Beng officials make use of the power of witchcraft; indeed, the legitimacy of their rule depends on their obligatory (though circumscribed) practice of witchcraft. But other witches, who do not hold political office, are reviled and were at one time killed. Witchcraft for the Beng does represent the height of immorality, but it is not only practiced by immoral people, for all that. Kings as well as witches use this power, but witches use it unrestrictedly for their own benefit, whereas kings use it only for the political "good"—to demonstrate control over, and independence from, their own socio-symbolic uterine identity. Ultimately, political authority is based on such control over identity. Put another way, kings gain their *legitimacy* from their use of uterine identity, while witches gain their *illegitimacy* from the same source; it is the context—political versus personal—that determines which type of power shall prevail, as Weber observed long ago (1947). Unlike many other centralized African societies, the creative source of power among the Beng is not so much external symbolic objects and actions as the psychosocial fund of uterine identity that underlies Beng social relations.

Acknowledgments

I conducted field research in 1979–80 among the Beng of M'Bahiakro in Ivory Coast, with the generous support of a doctoral grant from the U.S. Social Science Research Council, which I gratefully acknowledge. I had the privilege of receiving inspired comments on earlier versions of this article from Monni Adams, Mona Etienne, Eric Gable, Philip Graham, Ivan Karp, Aidan Southall, Constance Sutton, and Annette Weiner, none of whom, of course, is responsible for my responses to their suggestions.

Notes

1. Names of all Beng individuals, villages, and clans in this article are changed or otherwise coded to impede identification of those who may not wish to be identified publicly.

2. Beng phrase the goal of witchcraft in the food idiom of "meat" (*soŋ*), but this does not appear to be a metaphor for other, more mystical types of "substance," per se.

3. For this reason, following the Beng lead, I use the word *witch* simply to refer to both types of practitioners, those born with the knowledge of witchcraft and those who acquire it later in life. Rather than making much of this distinction, Beng instead emphasize another dichotomy that for them is more significant: that between "good witches" (*brunã geŋ*) and "bad witches" (simply, *brunã*). Most "bad witches" have been taught by their mothers, though some are born with the power, and some buy it; in contrast, most "good witches" are born with their power, though some buy it (none is taught it). (See below for details.) Unless otherwise indicated, when I refer to "witches" in this article, I am discussing "bad witches"; this follows Beng usage, in which *brunã* ("bad witch") is the unmarked category and *brunã geŋ* ("good witch") the marked category.

4. The individual witches of a given matriclan are said to be in league with one another and feast jointly on their victims' bodies. To bewitch an individual of a matriclan other than one's own is difficult and thus very rarely done. To do so, the aspiring witch would first have to gain the permission of the witches of the potential victim's matriclan, who would agree to share the "meat" of the victim with the witch outside their matriclan. Such permission is generally not granted, which explains for the Beng why witchcraft is almost always aimed against matrikin.

For these reasons, a male witch might bewitch his own child only if he has married a woman within his own matriclan, in a matriclan-endogamous marriage. (For other reasons, however, matriclan-endogamous marriages are considered one of the ideal types of marriage; see Gottlieb 1986a). Similarly, one may bewitch his or her father only if he has married a kinswoman.

5. The Beng word *wɔ* refers both to the arm and the hand; as with many African languages, there is no handy linguistic way to distinguish what English speakers regard as two distinct parts.

6. For a similar though more cosmologically oriented view of the hand, see Willis (1972 : 375) on the Fipa of Tanzania.

7. Amba women of Uganda are also reported to "bewitch" themselves by making themselves barren, but in that patrilineal society, it is said to be done as revenge against a husband to avoid bearing children for his patrilineage (Winter n.d. : 58–60). As the Beng have a system of dual descent, this motive would not be relevant for them.

8. The idea that the power of witchcraft itself may be ambivalent is not new in anthropology. Monica Wilson (1959) explored the possibilities of such ambivalence in her subtle discussion of the Nyakyusa and Ngonde of South Africa—the same word describes both the nefarious type of witchcraft practiced solely to ex-

press jealousy and to eat "meat," and the more productive type of witchcraft used to express one's justified anger and/or desire for revenge. Wilson pointed out that this double aspect of witchcraft reveals how the same kind of "energy" can be used for both legitimate and illegitimate ends.

9. Newly installed queens must also kill three victims. Male village chiefs must bewitch two kinspeople—the first, a sister's child and the second, any other matriclansperson. A female village chief must bewitch only one person—either a child of her own or a sister's child. In the remainder of the article, for the sake of brevity and because kings represent the extreme version of this subject, I will refer simply to kings when discussing this type of witchcraft; but such references also apply to queens and to male and female village chiefs, in what might be called a "political office-holder/witchcraft complex."

10. That such deaths should actually occur in every instance and not merely be an ideal rule followed only occasionally, should not be surprising. Cannon (1942) broadly outlined the physiological mechanisms of how fear causes death, without external physical-biological provocation. In the Beng case, one might postulate that because it is commonly known that three victims within the matriclan must die within a year of a new king assuming office, anyone in the king's matriclan—and particularly anyone fitting the two specified kinship statuses—who falls ill during the king's first year is bound to be convinced that he or she has been chosen as the king's victim, and will become worried; such anxiety will worsen the illness, which perpetuates the worry, and so on, until he or she finally dies—in Cannon's term—of "fright." Likewise, any matrikinsperson with whom the king was not on good terms would consider him or herself to be a particularly likely victim and might fall sick from worry and eventually die, as above.

It is also possible that this process may work in ex post facto. A diviner (who always pronounces upon the cause of death) will say that any member of the king's matriclan who dies within a year of his accession was one of the king's victims.

11. One such item is a lemon stick (*lomlɛ pléplé*) that is chewed on during the funeral. The lemon leaf from the same tree, which is used for medicinal purposes exclusively, is also used to protect against a disease called "mouth" to which new crops and new infants are both vulnerable. If an admirer compliments either a field of new crops or a new infant, the crop or the infant immediately begins shrinking and, unless treated soon with other medicines, will soon die. Lemon leaves are also burnt in a corpse room to absorb the odor of the cadaver, which is considered to harbor a potentially fatal disease called, metonymically, "corpse." Another item used to protect against witchcraft at kings' funerals is the leaf called *nonu pléplé lánà,* which has an aroma similar to that of the lemon leaf. During a king's funeral, a mourner may put some *nonu pléplé* leaves behind the ear or (for a woman) tie them up in a knot tucked into the waist of her skirt fabric. This leaf is also burnt in the corpse room, along with lemon leaves, also to protect against "corpse." Thus the various parts of the lemon tree, as well as similar-smelling *nonu pléplé* leaves, are all used to guard against mystically activated diseases, of which witchcraft unleashed at a king's funeral is but one example.

A third item used by cautious mourners at a king's funeral is the *vowlo baŋ*, a liana. Before taking her children to the funeral, a concerned mother bathes them in a rinse made with the leaves from this liana.

12. However, during the interregnum period, a deputy is chosen until the real heir is selected a year after the king's death and later installed. Because of this, the interregnum period itself, apart from the king's funeral, which marks its beginning, it not as disorderly as it might be (*cf.* Goody 1966:10–12).

13. Fortes has aptly observed (1968:6) that a king's installation and funeral ceremonies are often in symbolic opposition to each other, which is certainly true of the Beng.

14. The Ivory Coast government now prohibits such killings, but an informant mentioned cautiously that they may still take place occasionally. The practice is done elsewhere in Africa—for example among the Venda (cited in Zahan 1979:9, 159).

15. The soul that is formed in a fetus from the moment of conception is called *niniŋ*. At death, the *niniŋ* goes somewhere—my informants did not know where—and the *wru* of the dead person—which might be translated as its spirit—goes off to *wrugbe,* or "spirit village," where all but a few spirits go in the afterlife. Informants did not rule out the *possibility* that the *niniŋ* becomes the *wru* at death, but they seemed skeptical of it.

When discussing witchcraft, most informants said that the witches eat the victim's *wru* (spirit), but one informant said that they eat the victim's *niniŋ* (soul) (see Note 17).

16. Two other "mystical" attributes are inherited: "blood" (*waŋ*), and "character" or "personality" (*sié*). But "blood" is inherited from *both* the mother and the father; in contrast, one's "character" or "personality" is inherited from *either* the mother or the father. Thus unlike the "soul," neither "blood" nor "personality" constitutes a source of "substance" that is necessarily shared among only one type of clan member (patrikin or matrikin). It is true that patriclan members share a food and/or other taboo item, and that this might be construed as a source of shared "mystical substance." However, I would contend that among the Beng, these food taboos in fact do not produce among patrikin anything like the feeling of "shared substance" that the notion of the matrilineally inherited soul does among uterine kin. (See Gottlieb 1983, 1988b for more on the differences between matriclans and patriclans.)

17. Moreover, as in Note 15, if it is the matrilineally inherited *niniŋ* (soul) that the witch eats (and not the *wru* [spirit] which is created at death), the system would be even more self-referential: a witch gains knowledge via the matriclan, and then consumes the matrilineally transmitted substance (*niniŋ*) of fellow matrikin.

References

Adler, Alfred

1982 The Ritual Doubling of the Person of the King. *In* Between Belief and Transgression, Structuralist Essays in Religion, History, and

Myth. John Leavitt, transl. Michel Izard and Pierre Smith, eds. Pp. 180–92. Chicago: University of Chicago Press.

Arens, W.
1979 The Divine Kingship of the Shilluk: A Contemporary Evaluation. Ethnos 44(3–4):167–81.

Beidelman, T. O.
1966 Swazi Royal Ritual. Africa 36(4):373–405.
1971 Nuer Priests and Prophets: Charisma, Authority, and Power among the Nuer. *In* The Translation of Culture. T. O. Beidelman, ed. London: Tavistock Publications.
1982 Comments on Panelists of Restructuring Power Session. Paper presented at the Annual Meeting of the Northeastern Anthropological Association, Princeton.

Beier, Ulli
1982 Yoruba Beaded Crowns: Sacred Regalia of the Olokuku of Okoku. London: Ethnographica.

Ben-Amos, Paula
1976 Men and Animals in Benin Art. Man 11:243–52.

Bledsoe, Caroline
1980 Women and Marriage in Kpelle Society. Stanford: Stanford University Press.

Bloch, Maurice
1987 The Ritual of the Royal Bath in Madagascar: The Dissolution of Death, Birth and Fertility into Authority. *In* Rituals of Royalty: Power and Ceremonial in Traditional Societies. David Cannadine and Simon Price, eds. Cambridge: Cambridge University Press.

Bohannan, Paul
1958 Extra-processual Events in Tiv Political Institutions. American Anthropologist LX:1–11.

Brain, Robert
1976 Friends and Lovers. New York: Basic Books.
1980 Palace Art. *In* Art and Society in Africa. London: Longman.

Cannon, Walter B.
1942 "Voodoo" Death. American Anthropologist XLIV:169–81.

Crowley, Daniel J.
1972 Chokwe: Political Art in a Plebeian Society. *In* African Art and Leadership. Douglas Fraser and Herbert Cole, eds. Madison: University of Wisconsin Press.

Cunnison, Ian
1956 Perpetual Kinship: A Political Institution of the Luapula. Rhodes-Livingstone Journal XX:28–48.

Dark, Philip C., with W. Forman and B. Forman
1960 Benin Art. London: Routledge and Kegan Paul.

de Heusch, Luc
1982 The Drunken King, or the Origin of the State. Roy Willis, transl. Bloomington: Indiana University Press.

Douglas, Mary
1969 Is Matriliny Doomed in Africa? *In* Man in Africa. Mary Douglas and Phyllis M. Kaberry, eds. London: Tavistock.
1975 Social and Religious Symbolism of the Lele. *In* Implicit Meanings: Essays in Anthropology. London: Routledge & Kegan Paul. Originally published in Zaire 9 [April], 1955).

Etienne, Mona
1987 Contradictions, Constraints and Choices: Widow Remarriage among the Baule of Ivory Coast. *In* Widows in African Societies: Choices and Constraints. Betty Potash, ed. Stanford: Stanford University Press.

Fagg, William B.
1970 Divine Kingship in Africa. London: British Museum.

Fortes, Meyer
1968 On Installation Ceremonies. Presidential Address, Proceedings of the Royal Anthropological Institute of Great Britain and Ireland for 1967.
1973 On the Concept of the Person among the Tallensi. *In* La Notion de Personne en Afrique Noire. Actes du colloque internationale du C.N.R.S. organisé par Germaine Dieterlen. Germaine Dieterlen, ed. Paris: C.N.R.S.

Fraser, Douglas
1972a The Fish-Legged Figure in Benin and Yoruba Art. *In* African Art and Leadership. Douglas Fraser and Herbert Cole, eds. Madison: University of Wisconsin Press.
1972b The Symbols of Ashanti Kingship. *In* African Art and Leadership. Douglas Fraser and Herbert Cole, eds. Madison: University of Wisconsin Press.

Geertz, Clifford
1977 Centers, Kings, and Charisma: Reflections on the Symbolics of Power. *In* Culture and Its Creators: Essays in Honor of Edward Shils. Joseph Ben-David and Terry Nichols, eds. Chicago: University of Chicago Press.
1980 Negara. Princeton: Princeton University Press.

Gilbert, Michelle
1987 The Person of the King: Ritual and Power in a Ghanaian State. *In* Rituals of Royalty: Power and Ceremonial in Traditional Societies.

David Cannadine and Simon Price, eds. Cambridge: Cambridge University Press.

Gluckman, Max

1954a Rituals of Rebellion in South-East Africa. The Frazer Lecture for 1952. Manchester: Manchester University. *Reprinted in* Order and Rebellion in Tribal Africa: Collected Essays with an Autobiographical Introduction. New York: Free Press, 1963.

1954b Succession and civil war among the Bemba. Human Problems in British Central Africa XVI. *Reprinted in* Order and Rebellion in Tribal Africa: Collected Essays with an Autobiographical Introduction. New York: Free Press, 1963.

1956 The Frailty in Authority. *In* Custom and Conflict in Africa. London: Basil Blackwell.

Goody, Jack R.

1966 Introduction. *In* Succession to High Office. Jack Goody, ed. Cambridge: Cambridge University Press.

Gottlieb, Alma

1983 Village Kapok, Forest Kapok: Notions of Separation, Identity and Gender among the Beng of Ivory Coast. Ph.D. dissertation, University of Virginia.

1986a Cousin Marriage, Birth Order and Gender: Alliance Models among the Beng of Ivory Coast. Man 21(4):697–722.

1986b Dog: Ally or Traitor? Mythology, Cosmology and Society among the Beng of Ivory Coast. American Ethnologist 13(3):477–88.

1988a Menstrual Cosmology among the Beng of Ivory Coast. *In* Blood Magic: The Anthropology of Menstruation. Thomas Buckley and Alma Gottlieb, eds. Berkeley, Los Angeles, London: University of California Press.

1988b Rethinking Double Descent: A Beng Perspective. Paper presented at the Annual Meeting of the American Anthropological Association, Phoenix (1988).

1989 Hyenas and Heteroglossia: Myth and Ritual among the Beng of Côte d'Ivoire. American Ethnologist 16(3).

n.d. Reflections on Female Pollution among the Beng of Ivory Coast. *In* Beyond the Second Sex: Essays in the Anthropology of Gender. Peggy Sanday and Ruth Goodenough, eds. Philadelphia: University of Pennsylvania Press. In press.

Harrison, Simon

1988 Magical Exchange of the Preconditions of Production in a Sepik River Village. Man 23(2):319–33.

Kyerematen, A.

1969 The Royal Stools of the Ashanti. Africa XXXIX(1):1–10.

Lebeuf, Annie M. D.

1969 Les principautés kotoko. Essai sur le caractère sacré de l'autorité.

Etudes et Documents de l'Institut d'Ethnologie, Université de Paris. Paris: C.N.R.S.

Mauss, M.
1938 Une catégorie de l'esprit humain: la notion de personne, celle de "Moi." Journal of the Royal Anthropological Institute LXVIII: 263–81. *Reprinted in* Sociologie et Anthropologie. Paris: Presses Universitaires de France, 4th ed., 1968.

Muller, Jean-Claude
1980 Le Roi Bouc Émissaire. Quebec: S. Fleury.

Poewe, Karla O.
1981 Matrilineal Ideology: Male-female Dynamics in Luapula, Zambia. London: Academic Press.

Rudy, Suzanne
1972 Royal Sculpture in the Cameroons Grasslands. *In* African Art and Leadership. Douglas Fraser and Herbert Cole, eds. Madison: University of Wisconsin Press.

Schneider, David M.
1968 American Kinship: A Cultural Account. Englewood Cliffs: Prentice-Hall.

Smith, Pierre
1982 Aspects of the Organization of Rites. *In* Between Belief and Transgression: Structuralist Essays in Religion, History and Myth. John Leavitt, transl. Michel Izard and Pierre Smith, eds. Chicago: University of Chicago Press.

Thompson, R. F.
1972 The Sign of the Divine King: An Essay on Yoruba Beaded Crowns with Veil and Bird Decorations. *In* African Art and Leadership. Douglas Fraser and Herbert Cole, eds. Madison: University of Wisconsin Press.

Uzoigwe, Godfrey N.
1973 Succession and Civil War in Eunyoro-Kitara. The International Journal of African Historical Studies VI(1):49–71.

Vansina, Jan
1972 Ndop: Royal Statues among the Kuba. *In* African Art and Leadership. Douglas Fraser and Herbert Cole, eds. Madison: University of Wisconsin Press.

Vaughan, James H.
1980 A Reconsideration of Divine Kingship. *In* Explorations in African Systems of Thought. Ivan Karp and Charles S. Bird, eds. Bloomington: Indiana University Press.

Weber, Max

1947 The Theory of Social and Economic Organization. A. M. Henderson and Talcott Parsons, trans. Glencoe, Illinois: The Free Press. (Original: Wirschaft und Gesellschaft, Part 1, Tubingen, 1922.)

Willett, Frank

1972 Ife, the Art of an Ancient Nigerian Aristocracy. *In* African Art and Leadership. Douglas Fraser and Herbert Cole, eds. Madison: University of Wisconsin Press.

Willis, R. G.

1972 Pollution and Paradigms. Man 7(3):369–78.

Wilson, Monica

1959 Divine Kingship and the "Breath of Men." The Frazer Lecture for 1959. Cambridge: Cambridge University Press.

Winter, E. H.

1963 The Enemy Within: Amba Witchcraft and Sociological Theory. *In* Witchcraft and Sorcery in East Africa. John Middleton and E. H. Winter, eds. London: Routledge & Kegan Paul.

n.d. Bwamba: A Structural-Functional Analysis of a Patrilineal Society. Cambridge: W. Heffer.

Zahan, Dominique

1979 The Religion, Spirituality, and Thought of Traditional Africa. Kate Ezra and Lawrence M. Martin, transl. Chicago: University of Chicago.

Victoria Ebin

Transfers of Power: The King and the Secret Society in a Time of Crisis

Beyond Hierarchy

Anthropologists' studies of hierarchical societies in Africa have tended to focus on formal authority structures, categorizing levels of power as either political or religious. However, the use of these categories creates rigid dichotomies that bear little resemblance to the way in which real societies exist on an everyday level. As Leach (1977) has noted, conceptual models are necessarily models of equilibrium systems, and real societies can never exist in equilibrium.

These studies have ignored the internal dynamic of societies in which authority is diffused throughout the community and the exercise of authority is never either wholly political or religious in nature; in fact, chieftaincy usually has aspects of religious power, and priesthood is a position of considerable political influence. Such broad distinctions between types of authority become useless when one considers individuals whose power is only occasional and who have little or no formal ties to political or religious leaders.

I would like to look at the internal dynamic of a community when individuals not associated with institutionalized authority step forward to play a crucial role. At these times, power shifts to individuals who perform more effectively in specific situations than the office-holders and usual figures of authority. Such shifts often occur in crisis situations—in the present example, during a time of heightened community anxiety about witchcraft.

The subject of witchcraft in Africa has been studied from many different angles. Evans-Pritchard, in *Witchcraft, Oracles and Magic* (1937), saw witchcraft accusations as highlighting areas of tension and ambiguity in social relationships, providing an X-ray of fragile points in community life. The population's fear of being accused of witchcraft was seen as a way to maintain normative behavior; envy, for example, was supposedly characteristic of witches, and people were warned that jealousy of their neighbors could cause them to act unknowingly as witches (Evans-Pritchard 1937:111).

Witchcraft as a way to vent otherwise unacceptable hostility supported the "homeostatic" theory of society, in which witchcraft was a safety valve that allowed members to cope with conflict (Douglas 1970:xix). Following this line of reasoning, Field (1960) and Ward (1956) regarded an increase in witch-finding cults as an indication of increasing stress and predicted that it would occur in times of rapid social change. J. R. Goody (1957), however, challenged the notion that an increase in witch-finding cults provided an easy index to social stress and, moreover, questioned the idea that rapid change inevitably led to increased social unrest.

Witchcraft and the Dou

In this paper I will examine a community's reaction to a dramatic increase in witchcraft activities. In an Akan community of southwest Ghana, in the mid-1970s, a series of disasters, culminating in the deaths of several children, proved too great for the powers of the authorities—the king (*omanhene*) and the spirit mediums (*ahoimea*)—to protect the community. At this time, a new group of actors, the members of a secret society known as the *dou,* stepped forward to confront the witches thought to be responsible for the crisis.

The *dou* society is found in communities along the border between

Ghana and Ivory Coast. Descriptions of its activities vary considerably, and many different sorts of masked dances bear the group's name. In this particular community, the *dou* functions mainly as a witch-finding cult and bears little resemblance to the *dou* described by Bravmann (1974). The central activity of this *dou* group is the performance of a masked dance to identify the member of the community who has been practicing witchcraft and to weaken the powers of potential witches.

Only men can belong to the *dou* society, and members describe themselves as *kontiri* (real men). The initiation rites are said to be rigorous, and only the initiated can wear the masks. The head of the secret society, who gives offerings to the *dou* spirits, is referred to as a *kɔmea,* the same word used for a spirit medium, but unlike the spirit mediums, the *dou kɔmea* is not possessed by the spirits.

Masked dances are not an Akan tradition and, according to informants, the Akan peoples imported the *dou* from the north. Although secret societies are said to contradict the ideology of the centralized Akan state (McLeod 1981:67), evidence of their existence, particularly in the westernmost Akan regions, dates at least as far back as the nineteenth century (McLeod 1975:108).

Mystical Power Roles

Why does a community that emphasizes centralized control over the spirit world and the king's sovereignty in the political realm tolerate the potentially disruptive activities of a powerful men's secret society? To examine this question, I will look at the performances of male and female masked spirits in terms of specific Akan notions of the appropriate use of mystical power by men and women.

Like other Akan groups, this community has a hierarchical political organization in which political authority is focused on the office of the king and branches out to the chiefs and subchiefs of the outlying villages. A complex organization of court officials and counselors has diverse responsibilities as palace servants and functionaries.

The model of centralized authority also extends to the spirit world. The gods (*abosom*), who are said to inhabit the rivers and trees in the forest surrounding the village, form a hierarchy that reflects the political organization of the state; the chief god Tano—associated with the river Tano, which flows through the Akan region—is surrounded by his court of lesser gods. Throughout the Akan region, the river Tano is associated with royal authority, and many village chiefs have their own Tano god, who is served by a spirit medium.

The gods have power to possess people and speak through them, and the women spirit mediums (*ahoimea*)—who are part of the king's court—act as their mouthpieces. The head spirit medium (who descends from a former slave lineage that has special responsibilities toward the Tano god) serves the powerful god Tano, and when he possesses her, she wears the royal regalia ordinarily reserved for the king. The king is forbidden to see the medium at this time and he must rely on reports from a member of his court.

Among the spirit mediums, allegiance to the king and to the community are important themes. The king often supervises their apprenticeships and appoints their teachers, and at the end of the initiation rites, when the new mediums normally "place" their gods in the shrine, they swear an oath of allegiance to the king. This initiation rite for new spirit mediums serves to integrate new gods and spirits into the community. The head medium tries to persuade the new gods, with promises of regular offerings, to leave the forest and come settle in the town to protect the community.

Spirit mediumship is a potential threat to the status quo in a highly centralized society. The mediums function as the mouthpieces of the gods who figure in oral traditions of the founding of the state and, while possessed by these spirits, the words of the spirit medium resonate with the powers of the spirit world. Although their incorporation into the court structure acts as a sort of control over their activities and somewhat limits the potentially disruptive nature of spirit mediumship, the women, on occasion, have stepped beyond their role as the servants of the king, and used their powers to demand major reforms.

Other practices also represent a departure from this ideal of centralized control over the spirit world as well. In fact, the herbalists (*dninzinea*)—the male competitors of the spirit mediums—use magical objects in ways strikingly different from the prescribed practices outlined above. These men have no official role in the court and, though they are sometimes close to the king, acting as his diviners and providing him with protective amulets, they are not part of the political hierarchy. Their use of magical objects is outside the king's control and the spirits they call upon are not part of the hierarchy of gods and spirits mentioned above. The herbalists practice their skills as individuals, and no official organization binds them together or obliges them to follow a set of common practices or procedures.

Their mystical powers depend on the use of magical objects, known as *amoa,* whose powers are generally said to be lesser than those of the gods, but nevertheless are potent. The head spirit medium—the official specialist in this realm and the representative of the king—claims the right to judge the appropriateness of the *amoa* for community use, but the herbalists, who sometimes travel great distances to acquire reputedly powerful magical objects, do not always rigidly obey her demands.

Unlike the spirit mediums, the herbalists do not publicly name their spirits or perform a public rite of incorporating them into the community. Nor do they swear an oath of allegiance to the *omanhene,* promising to use their powers to protect the community from harm.

The *amoa* used by the herbalists are either man-made or natural objects imbued with spirit power and, unlike the gods, they can be bought and sold, and they rarely possess their owners. Whereas the *abosom* are incorporated into the political framework and are served by recognized spirit mediums who are part of the court hierarchy, the *amoa* are out of reach of political control. They are obtained by individuals, often in times of crisis, during a perceived need for special mystical protection from, for example, witchcraft.

Fear of witches is a dominant theme in community life. During the period of my fieldwork, members of the community attributed many sorts of disasters to the witches, who were said to meet at night in the tall trees on the outskirts of town. In particular, the spirit mediums, to whom people came for an explanation of the disasters, held the witches responsible for a series of illnesses and deaths in one lineage, the many road accidents of a lorry driver, and the epidemics—particularly affecting children—that swept through the area.

Witchcraft is effective only between matrikin and people claim that elderly women are most likely to be witches. The central activity of a witch is the destruction of her matrilineal kin. Often described as a barren or elderly woman, the witch devours children instead of bearing them. McLeod (1975: 111) has noted that the image of a witch represents an inversion of social values. A witch goes naked at night, eats not with her mouth but with her anus, and meets at night with other witches in the tops of trees on the outskirts of town.

The Akan people believe that every individual needs some mystical powers simply in order to survive the ordinary strains of life. Everyone is born with a personal spirit, known as a *sunsum,* which provides protection from everyday hazards, but one can deliberately develop and strengthen this power through the use of "medicines" and magical objects. While this power is necessary to protect oneself and family against the attacks of destructive witches, a person who has a strong *sunsum* can unknowingly use this power to make mystical attacks on others. In effect, he can become a witch.

Holders of political office, the *omanhene,* and chiefs—as well as the herbalists and spirit mediums—require special mystical powers to carry out the demands of their roles and to protect those under their care. The Akan people believe that these political and spiritual leaders cannot carry out their roles if they are not themselves powerful witches (E. Goody 1970:212). They deliberately acquire witchcraft by bathing in infusions believed to have magical powers and by the use of magical objects. Though it is well known that they possess special powers, the community does not generally suspect them of using those powers destructively—although accounts do exist of chiefs being accused of witchcraft (Terray 1979:153).

Despite their reputation as possessors of powerful witchcraft powers, the king and the spirit mediums cannot combat witches in the community who use their powers destructively. Even Tano, the most powerful Akan god, is said to be helpless against them. When people perceive an increase in witchcraft, they must rely on outside sources to confront witches.

Although the king personally can do nothing against witchcraft attack, he can take measures to protect the community. Early accounts of witch-finding techniques emphasize the king's central role. In the last decades of the nineteenth century, an Abron chief in the western Akan region, for example, organized the performance of a masked dance known as Sakrobundi to detect witches. The dance was located almost exclusively in royal capitals and was actively supported by the chiefs (Terray 1979:156, 164). Another accepted Akan technique to deal with witches was the poison ordeal (*odum*) in which the accused proved his innocence by vomiting. Village chiefs who wanted to use the poison to test a suspected witch had to send word to the king, who kept the poison in the palace. The poison was then delivered by a servant of the king, who prepared the solution. The goods of a suspect who was found guilty became the property of the chief (McLeod 1975:110; Terray 1979:153). Corpse carrying, another witch-detecting method, was also controlled by the chiefs. According to this practice, bearers carried the corpse through the village, and it became agitated when it approached the witch responsible for its death. In all of these examples, it is noteworthy that the witch-detecting forces come, in one way or another, from outside the community—Sakrobundi is a spirit from the North, the cadaver is no longer in the world of the living—and their external origins are an important aspect of their reputations.

Witch-finding cults increased at the beginning of the twentieth century when the colonial government's suppression of former methods to combat witches, such as corpse carrying, masked dances, and the poison ordeal, forced people to seek out new techniques (McLeod 1975:110). Until this time, the chiefs apparently limited the spread of witch-finding cults and controlled their entry into the community, but by the late nineteenth century, when Asante defeat by the British weakened the chiefs' political control, antiwitchcraft shrines seem to have proliferated among the population.

While antiwitchcraft shrines are popular in the Akan region, they are sometimes a source of unease to the chiefs. The *dou* has long had ambiguous relations with political authority. According to local reports, it has existed in the Akan region since at least the 1930s, and in the late 1950s the king reportedly asked the local government authority to ban the *dou* because two men had died during its performance. However, according to informants, the *dou* members took it upon themselves to acquire masks again in the late 1960s because they believed there was an increase in witchcraft activity.

In the mid-1970s, the *dou* society decided to perform its masked dance again. The *dou* members came to discuss the coming event with the *omanhene,* who offered to keep the masks in his house, but the *dou* priest refused. Subchiefs in surrounding villages also emphasized at this time their reliance on the *dou* society as a means to control witchcraft; a chief of a nearby village claimed responsibility for bringing the *dou* to his community, and another mentioned his wish to obtain the masks for his community. In another example, members of the royal family of one village sold their masks to the royals of another village.

Although the king and chiefs have little choice but to rely on the *dou,* they are clearly aware of its potential dangers. The king's offer to house the masks may have been partly an expression of help, but it also seems to have been an attempt to acquire greater control over their use. According to informants, if the king and chiefs were to see the *dou* masks, the consequences would be the same for them as for women who see the *dou* figures—their skin would be covered with scratches and sores.

The Dou *Performance*

Once members of the *dou* decided to perform the witch-detecting dance, a member of the *omanhene*'s court walked through the town announcing the coming event. The following morning the women were up early to carry out their communal ritual purification of the town, known as the *momomɛ*. The women gathered at the king's house and swept the streets of the town, depositing the refuse on the very edge of the town. Their songs emphasized that they were cleaning the town, not only of its litter but also of mystical pollution (*efeya, monzue*) identified with the state of danger and death brought on by witchcraft. Then the women outlined the borders of the town with white clay, defining the spatial limits of the town against the dangers of the forest, which is seen as the source of mystical power.

While the women were carrying out their purification, the *dou* members were preparing for the evening's performance by clearing a space in the forest. At the end of the day, men began to arrive from town, and by nightfall a large crowd had gathered to watch the performance when members of the *dou* society would dance, wearing the *dou* masks. It is said that only *dou* members can accept a masked figure's invitation to join the dance, and *dou* members give a special greeting to the masked dancers.

The drummers started to play a special rhythm to call the spirits from the forest. The female masked spirit was the first to appear, wearing a flat mask of what appeared to be cardboard painted red and white with facial features outlined roughly in charcoal, and a long raffia gown. The female spirit is the least powerful of the *dou* spirits, and her role is to prepare the way for the two male masks. As the female figure danced, she made sweeping movements, bending low and moving from side to side as the men stood around her in a circle and hovered over her. She invited to dance with her a man reputed to be a powerful witch and to possess dangerous medicine. Then she danced alone, sweeping as she danced, and finally disappeared into the forest.

The next figure to appear represented a male *dou* spirit known as Amoa Bensua, wearing a wood mask with horns. This masked spirit possesses powers to detect those who have deliberately caused harm; it danced briefly and was then joined by the female mask. The two of them danced together, and then the male masked figure crouched in the center of the space as the female danced around him in circling movements said simultaneously to contain and reinforce the male's powers. The drummers paused for a rest; when they began again, the female mask danced around the space first in order, it was said, to look for evil. Next, a member of the *dou* society appeared, carrying a flaming torch, and he ran about the clearing chasing, it was said, after the witches to point them out to the gods. The male and female figures danced briefly, which the spectators took as a sign that the case must be serious indeed, as the third, and most powerful mask, was left to make the accusation.

The third mask, like the preceding one, represented a horned creature, usually described as a bush cow. The name of this mask is Efie Anoa, which translates literally as "home trap," and refers to a proverb about a man who is bitten by insects in his cloth; the special task of this particular spirit is to identify a witch who belongs to the royal family.

Efie Anoa swept out of the darkness with his eyes glowing and the full raffia dress billowing out behind him, and brandishing a piece of burning wood. He danced in the center of the clearing, weaving in and out of the circle of men and waving the piece of flaming wood at the spectators. As he danced, he swooped low, close to the ground, and began to spin around very quickly. Suddenly, he broke the spin, jumped in front of a man, and threw a handful of burning raffia at him.

The accused was a member of the king's court and a chief's linguist in a neighboring village. The masked spirit accused him of being the unwitting cause of the epidemic by bringing the illness back with him from a recent trip to a large coastal town. Though he was said to be a powerful witch, he was not accused of deliberately using his powers aggressively. However, Efie Anoa singled him out, reprimanded him publicly, and made him pay a heavy fine.

The accusation highlights the potentially adversarial nature of the relationship between the *dou* and the king. The presence of a masked spirit whose sole purpose is to accuse a member of the royal family of witchcraft is bound to be a source of unease for the king. But it is clear that the king must rely on the *dou* as the most effective means of protection from witchcraft. The incidence of witchcraft is proof that neither the king's powers nor those of the head spirit medium are sufficient to combat it; the main god, Tano, is explicitly said to be helpless against witches.

The king's role in the *dou* rites further reveals the ambiguity of his relations with the secret society. The use of court linguists to announce the performance of the *dou* demonstrates the royal family's involvement with the *dou* secret society. However, the *omanhene* was not even allowed to watch the performance—he had to remain inside for a week, and when he next appeared publicly, he wore the war dress, covered with mystical charms that he puts on only in times of great mystical danger.

Men's Power, Women's Power

To understand how the potentially disruptive *dou* has become incorporated into the community's arsenal against witches, it is useful to look in detail at how the accusation of witchcraft was made—in particular, how the activities of the male and female masked spirits correspond to general ways men and women in the community use mystical power acceptably. I will look first at the role of women in the masked dance. Although the women of the community are not directly involved with the *dou* dance, they play an important role in preparing for the evening's performance. In the *momomɛ* ritual, they cleanse the town by sweeping away rubish, and they also banish the mystical pollution which can cause illness and death. This rite demonstrates complementary aspects of men's and women's use of mystical power. In the past, in times of war when the men were off fighting, the women, who remained behind, swept the streets to rid the area of the mystical pollution said to arise from the nearby scene of bloodshed and death.[1]

In the women's performance of the *momomɛ,* as in the female mask's role in the *dou,* the women sweep. Although the broom is an object of everyday practical use, it also has mystical properties. Every spirit medium counts among her ritual possessions a small broom, which she uses in her healing rites to drive away illness. However, even an Ordinary broom has special status. At certain times, the word for *broom* cannot be uttered, and the Akan refer to it by the term *amoding,* "that which cannot be said"; this same term also refers to women's sexual organs. This object, so identified with women's domestic tasks, cannot be used as a weapon. As Esther Goody (1970) has described, among the Gonja of northern Ghana aggression in the domestic realm is forbidden—if a woman hits a man with a stirring stick, he will become impotent. In the Akan community, striking a person with a broom creates a state of mystical danger, *monzue,* and can cause a man to become impotent or die. A woman may use a broom to cleanse her compound, to sweep away mystical pollution as well as the everyday rubbish, but she cannot use it aggressively.[2]

In the *momomɛ* rite, the women define the area where social interaction can safely take place by circumscribing the spatial categories of the town against the dangers of the forest. Using their mystical powers, women transform the town from a state of illness, death, and witchcraft attacks to one of safety. By defining and rendering safe this designated social space, women create conditions where social life can flourish.

This theme of control over space emerges particularly clearly in the spirit mediums' rituals of integration for new spirits, such as *amoa*. The mediums' rites of spirit integration emphasize the division between the town—the place for all essentially human activities—and the hot, dangerous disorder of the forest—the abode of the gods and the source of magical objects (McLeod 1981:20). Their rites, like the women's *momomɛ,* focus on the purification of the circumscribed area of the town and the individuals and objects within it. On one occasion, when a group of spirit mediums was performing a purificatory rite in the town, they discovered that a well-known herbalist was in the audience, with some magical objects (*amoa*). The women decided that he had intended to disrupt their ritual and they punished him by making him sit on a stool in the center of their "stage" inside a circle of white clay that they drew around him. Within the circle, the mediums contained and neutralized his malevolent powers, a striking example of the spirit mediums' concern with controlling unacceptable mystical forces. The female mask was to repeat this same gesture in the *dou* performance when she danced around the crouching male figure. Though in these two examples, the aims are different—the spirit medium draws a circle around the male to neutralize his power, and the *dou* female figure dances around the crouched male figure to reinforce his power—the circumscribing and "containing" movements are the same.

The rites to integrate new magical objects into the town further demonstrate the spirit mediums' control over space. On one occasion, a hunter found in the forest an object believed to have mystical powers. He brought it to the head medium who, along with a member of the *omanhene*'s court, performed rites to discover the nature of the object's spirit; they decided it was benevolent and gave it a name. The hunter kept it as his own personal spirit and gave it offerings during the annual yam festival.

Men do not follow the same practices in their use of mystical power. The male herbalists are said to work at night, secretly, whereas the women spirit mediums make public performances; the men perform the *dou* in the forest at night, and the women's *momomɛ* rite takes place during the day in the center of town. The herbalists use their mystical powers aggressively and boast openly of their ability to send mystical misfortune (*monzue*) to others. On public occasions, they challenge each other to dance before the crowd—a risk to which only those who are very confident of their powers will expose themselves. To stumble or fall during the performance brings an immediate and irreparable loss of face. When the spirit mediums perform publicly, the herbalists gather around them and are said to use their powers to make the women trip. The fear of such an attack, according to the mediums, may keep a woman from performing publicly. The one spirit medium who does dance frequently and with confidence is married to a lineage head who is reputed to be a powerful witch. He is always conspicuously present at her public divining sessions and, before the performance, he ostentatiously places magical objects around the area where she will dance.

Like the spirit mediums, the herbalists acquire their mystical power deliberately, but unlike the women, the use of their powers is unrestrained by the demands of the king. They send *monzue* (mystical danger) to their enemies and to the enemies of those who come to consult them. Many of the herbalists display prominently in their rooms an object known as a "night gun," which is made of quills and which they claim to shoot at night. Despite their aggressive and often showy use of mystical power, none of the herbalists were accused of witchcraft during the period of my fieldwork.

Dou *Masks and Everyday Life*

Within this Akan community, the dominant ideology stresses the centralization of power in the office of the king, but the men's secret society and the activities of the herbalists contradict this ideal. Nevertheless, an examination of the male and female *dou* masks reveals parallel uses of mystical power by men and women in everyday life in the society.

The female mask is the first to appear, and she prepares the space where the two male masks will dance. Just as the women in the town purify the streets by dancing and sweeping in the *momomɛ*, the female mask cleanses the space where the central act of the masquerade—the accusation of a witch—will take place. She transforms the clearing in the forest into a space which has the "cool" properties appropriate to a social gathering. The female mask is painted red and white, two colors which have a particular significance in women's purificatory rituals. White is associated with peace, harmony and "cool,"[3] ideal qualities for the town and its inhabitants.

Red represents objects and individuals associated with the mystical powers of the forest. Gold, believed to possess mystical power, is described as red; the clay used to make cooking hearths is "red" in its natural state but, once brought to town and made into a hearth, it is painted white. Other examples of potentially dangerous objects represented as red are the forest monster with flowing red hair who causes men to become lost in the forest, and witches, who are recognizable by the red smoke rising from the tops of their heads and by the quantities of red palm oil they consume. The spirit mediums, when possessed by their gods of the forest, sing "Our eyes are as red as possible," referring to their ability to see into the spirit world. The king, sometimes known as Red Foot because of his heavy gold bangles, possesses special mystical powers. Such mystical powers are necessary to his ability to rule, but they are also a potential source of danger. On ritual occasions, the king and spirit mediums, as well as other members of the community who have special powers, such as twins, dress in white cloth and cover their bodies with white clay; they also wear bracelets of alternating red and white beads, a visual representation of the "cooling" of their powers, now made appropriate and safe for the town. Before major rituals, the king orders the palace to be painted white, and the spirit mediums coat the gods' shrines on the edge of town with white clay, and the large tree in the center of town, whose shade provides a place for social gatherings, receives a coat of white paint around its base.

The red and white paint on the female mask seems to refer to the spirit's origins in the forest and its associations with potent mystical power, as well as its "cool" positive properties. The alternating colors proclaim the spirit's power to protect the community and to transform a dangerous state of being into one suitable for social life. Using her power, she creates a space where the male mask can perform.

The male masks represent fantastic creatures—a bush cow with a maw like a crocodile, burning red coals for eyes, and large crossed horns. The second and more powerful of the male masks is painted mostly black, except for the teeth in the long rectangular snout, which are red and white. Black is significant here; the Akan often associate black with the transition state between the world of the living and the world of the spirits (McLeod 1981:173).[4]

As noted above, witchcraft accusations come from someone outside the Akan community—and what could be more distant than the *dou* spirit from the north, represented as a melange of forest creatures painted mostly black? Such an assemblage of features, all emphasizing the spirit's distance from everyday life, is appropriate to a mask which will accuse a member of the royal family of practicing witchcraft.

Using a male spirit mask for this task is significant. Armed with their secret knowledge and magical objects, men use their powers aggressively. The male mask which accuses a member of the royal family reflects the behavior of the male herbalists, while the female mask, like women in their mystical activities, uses its powers to define and transform space into an area free of evil power.

The *dou* is not indigenous to the Akan region, but it has become an important source of protection against witches. Though the presence of a secret society in a community that stresses the centralization of political and religious authority seems a potential threat to the status quo, the structure of the witch-accusing performance conforms to the ways men and women use mystical power in the community. The masked dance reflects the community's conflicting attitudes toward the use of mystical power and illustrates the dichotomy between the ideal of controlled mystical power and the use of mystical power by individuals acting independently and often aggressively.

Notes

1. A surveyor with the Boundary Commission of 1893 noted that in a village along the present-day Ghana and Ivory Coast border the women had just performed a rite of communal purification in preparation for the *dou* masquerade (Vroom, no date provided). Perrot (1982:31–32) has provided a similar description of the *momomɛ* among the Ndenye in Ivory Coast. Here, too, the rite is performed in times of war, when a woman dies in childbirth or when the community is perceived to be in danger—for example, when a rainbow appears in the western part of the sky.

Delafosse, too, (1913:266–268) has given a colorful account of a *momomɛ* performance among the Akan in Ivory Coast performed when the men were off at battle. He described the women dancing up and down the village singing bawdy songs in which they insult the enemy leader's virility and make unfavorable comments on his sexual prowess. Throughout the ceremony, the women call each other by their husband's or male kinsmen's names, they pass around a calabash from which they take swigs of water, which they pretend is palm wine, and they recount their exploits in war and love.

2. Esther Goody (1970) has discussed the use of legitimate and illegitimate ag-

gression by men and women in the Gonja state of northern Ghana, and explored the ways in which the use of mystical aggression by men and women is interpreted according to their different needs for aggression in daily activities. Women, whose realm is the domestic sphere, have less need to use aggression than men, who are the protectors of their lineages, hunters, warriors, and candidates for political office. Women are more likely to be accused of practicing witchcraft than men because they have less valid reason to use aggression on a mystical and physical level; their realm is the domestic sphere, and, in this context, any aggression is said to create a state of mystical danger.

3. This contrast between the "cool" of the town and the dangers of the forest corresponds to R. F. Thompson's discussion of "cool" as the incarnation of purity (1973:4).

4. The stools, which are the focus of the ancestor cult and the channel to the ancestors who are in the "other world," are black. The *akua'ba* dolls carried by women who want to conceive are also black, a reference to the belief that the spirits of the ancestors are waiting in the other world to be reborn.

References

Bravmann, R. A.

1974 Islam and Tribal Art in West Africa. Cambridge: Cambridge University Press.

Delafosse, M.

1913 Coutumes observées par les femmes en temps de guerre chez les Agni de la Côte d'Ivoire. Revue d'Ethnographie et de Sociologie IV:266–68.

Douglas, M.

1970 Witchcraft Confessions and Accusations. ASA Monograph 9, London.

Evans-Pritchard, E. E.

1937 Witchcraft, Oracles and Magic among the Azande. Oxford: Oxford University Press.

Field, M. J.

1960 Search for Security. Evanston: Northwestern University Press.

Goody, E. N.

1970 Legitimate and Illegitimate Aggression in a West African State. *In* Witchcraft Confessions and Accusations. Mary Douglas, ed. ASA Monograph 9, London.

Goody, J. R.

1957 Anomie in Ashanti. Africa, 27:356–63.

Leach, Edmund

1977 Political Systems in Highland Burma: A Study of Kachin Social Structure. London: The Athlone Press.

McLeod, M. D.

1975 On the Spread of Anti-Witchcraft Cults in Modern Asante. *In* Changing Social Structure in Ghana. J. R. Goody, ed. London: International African Institute.

1981 The Asante. London: Published for the Trustees of the British Museum by British Museum Publications Ltd.

Perrot, C. H.

1982 Les Anyi-Ndenye et le Pouvoir aux 18ᵉ et 19ᵉ siècles. CEDA Abidjan, Paris Sorbonne.

Terray, E.

1979 Un mouvement de reforme religieuse dans le royaume abron precolonial: le culte de Sakrobundi. Cahiers d'Etudes Africaines, 73–76, xix(1–4): 143–76.

Thompson, R. F.

1973 An Aesthetic of the Cool. African Arts VII(1):41–43, 64–67, 89–91.

Vroom, H.

n.d. Unpublished papers. Cape Coast, Ghana.

Ward, B.

1956 Some Observations on Religious Cults in Ashanti. *Africa,* 56: 47–61.

Nancy J. Fairley

Ritual Rivalry among the Ben'Ekie

Introduction

Students of African political history are now well aware that state formation, even if set in motion by external forces, is still a complex, drawn-out process. In the reconstruction and analysis of such cases, attention has been increasingly directed toward internal forces, which were also crucial factors in the process of political centralization. Recent studies of political history have focused on indigenous sociocultural factors, such as religion, marriage alliances, rituals, inheritance rules, the exploitation of natural resources, trade, and the means of production, providing greater insight into the process of state formation (Feierman 1974; Vansina 1978; Reefe 1981; Willis 1981; and Fairley 1987).

In a similar vein, this study will unravel the peculiarities of the political culture of the Ben'Ekie of central Zaire. Rather than restricting itself to the kingship that emerged as a new center of political power, it will also focus on the shifting fortunes of other loci of political power and ideology that existed during the pre-state era. In doing so, the study will examine the innovative and successful responses of these groups to the centralization of authority. Over time, the traditional power centers that opposed political centralization generated new social forms and ideas to counteract the emergent authority of the kingship. The dual approach will document a complex political reality in which competing centers of power pursued their own political strategies and evoked their own notions of cultural legitimacy.

The political centralization of the Ben'Ekie, a Kisongye-speaking group, began as a response to the expansion of the Luba Kingdom in southern Zaire at the beginning of the eighteenth century (Fairley 1987; 1978). According to oral traditions, the Ben'Ekie, who lacked the necessary strength to halt Luba imperialism, invited the foreign warriors to settle inside their territory in the late seventeenth century. Except for the collection of tribute, the first group of migrant warriors remained detached from local affairs, leaving the Ben'Ekie politically autonomous and their traditional organization intact. A subsequent migration of Luba intruders in the early eighteenth century, however, set in motion a series of gradual organizational changes within the small host society. By far, the most profound was the initiation of a process of political centralization (Fairley 1987).

The Ekie kingship that eventually emerged was an externally based innovation, effective in organizing the society against external aggression. This development also transformed local patterns of authority from those based on "gerontocratic principles" to those based on "patrimonial principles" (Bradbury 1971). This organizational shift generated an internally based response in the form of a secret society called the *bukishi*. Efforts by this association posed a challenge to the king's monopolization of authority. Because the *bukishi* gained support throughout Ekieland, power in this small state soon emanated from two centers: the innovative kingship and the equally innovative, though traditionally oriented, *bukishi*. Consequently, the dual nature of authority in Ekie society produced a context in which political power radiated from two competing centers, which were organizationally distinct rather than hierarchically linked.

Until recently, this seemingly unique aspect of precolonial Ekie society represented an enigma for students of African political history. Because of insufficient data on Songye peoples, many scholars, such as Vansina (1966), were reluctant to speculate on the origin of this dualistic political structure. However, as the result of recently compiled data on Ekie history, it is possible to describe how one Songye state emerged and functioned in this fashion (Fairley 1978). In this paper, I will identify the major forces that contributed to the creation of a state characterized by dual authority. In addition, I will examine the effectiveness of a kingship in a society in which political institutions were not regulated in a cooperative relationship.

Ben'Ekie of Central Zaire

Systematic contact between the Ben'Ekie and non-Africans began in the latter decades of the nineteenth century.[1] Consequently, there are few written documents that pertain to the precolonial Ben'Ekie. In addition, existing sources describe the society during a period of major social dislocations, resulting from slave raiding and the European-Arab conflicts. Thus, the reconstruction of Ekie political history depends primarily on oral tradition, interpreted in the light of archeological and linguistic data, and on a few written documents.

The Ben'Ekie are a subgroup of the Songye people, located in the Kasai-Oriental region of the present Republic of Zaire. Divided into politically autonomous kingdoms or chiefdoms, the Songye groups inhabit a savannah region that lies between 5° and 6° south and 24° and 27° east. Situated in the southwestern part of Songyeland, Ekie territory is characterized by patches of moist forest surrounded by stretches of tall grass. The fertile forests are limited in number so that most cultivation lies in the savannah region. The Ben'Ekie have always lived in large permanent villages, generally located on a plateau near a stream or rivulet. A typical village is divided into recognized wards with different patriclan members living in each section. The Ben'Ekie practice bridewealth, and the ideal is for women to live in the villages of their husbands after marriage.

A majority of the population, which numbered slightly over 35,000 in 1960 (Boone 1961), is engaged in subsistence hoe agriculture. In fields located short distances from their villages, the Ben'Ekie cultivate cassava, corn, rice, groundnuts, plantains, black-eyed peas, and a variety of leafy vegetables and squashes. They also grow a variety of tree crops, including oil and raffia palms, oranges, mangoes, pineapples and lemons. In addition, they plant tomatoes, onions, red peppers, bananas, a variety of leafy vegetables, calabashes, and tobacco in fertile plots of land adjacent to their homesteads.

The Ben'Ekie also engage in limited animal husbandry, including the raising of goats, pigs, sheep, and a variety of fowl. As in the past, however, they got a large part of their protein from hunting and fishing products, such as small rodents, monkeys, boars, buffalo, and fish. They use domesticated animals mainly for ritual purposes and for the payment of legal fines, bridewealth, and today, to raise cash in emergency situations.

In addition to full–time farming, Ekie adults still pursue a wide range of craft and occupational activities. Ekie men classify as fishermen, hunters, builders, carpenters, tailors, blacksmiths, weavers, woodcarvers, basketmakers, and specialists in herbal medicine. Ekie women specialize in the production of palm oil, whiskey, sleeping mats, pots, calabash utensils, and baskets.

Gerontocracy: Prior to 1700

During the period preceding kingship, authority in both inter– and intravillage affairs was based on gerontocratic principles in conjunction with the descent system. Superimposed on this structure was a centralized ritual system, which reinforced gerontocracy and served as a powerful integrative cultural mechanism, binding one Ekie community to another.

The Ben'Ekie were organized into autonomous villages, which were grouped into territorial units called *mavumbu* (sing. *evumbu*). Each village group (*evumba*) recognized one village as the parent community with ritual precedence over its fellow members. In a similar vein, relations between separate *mavumbu* were also determined by seniority, with the earliest established village-group holding ritual precedence over the others. Lastly, the village group that traced its history back to the original founding father of the society held ritual precedence over all others. Two of the village groups were the residence of distinct title holders (*batu-mukulu*), who were direct descendants of the founding ancestor of Ekie society. Their functions were primarily ritual but they were given certain privileges in political affairs, such as being the first to speak on the village council.

The authority in these autonomous political units was vested primarily in lineage heads and recognized peace officers, who were referred to as the *mwana-nkana* (pl. *bana-nakana*). Although all adult men in the village could attend meetings of the council, a council of elders made the final decisions. These were implemented by the *mwana-nkana,* the holder of the *kibangu* staff, which embodies the authority of elders over their juniors and ancestors over the living. As the symbol of the social and supernatural order, the *kibangu* was a crucial element in the maintenance of social order.

The sanction to use the *kibangu* was derived from the priest and highest ritual authority in Ekie society, called the *tshite*. The *tshite* controlled the investiture of the *bana–nkana,* who acted as his representatives in village affairs. The *tshite* interacted with the general public only in specific ritual contexts by making the necessary sacrificial offerings to the ancestors to ensure the general fertility and prosperity of the Ben'Ekie as a people. Thus, the office served as a link between the Ben'Ekie collectively and their common ancestors.

While the office of the *tshite* was vested in one particular lineage, several lineages owned the title *mwana–nkana*. However, not every village was host to a holder of the *kibangu*. Villages lacking a *mwana–nkana* had to request the services of a title holder in a nearby village. The *bana–nkana* also mediated intervillage conflicts that arose over boundary and water resource disputes.

Thus, during the period preceding political centralization, Ekie villages were bound together by a set of commonly held religious beliefs and practices, which revolved around the *tshite* and his representatives, the *bana–nkana*. In addition, villages were ranked according to seniority and accorded ritual precedence on that basis in various types of social interaction.

Gerontocratic principles defined the distribution and implementation of authority. Women and young men were excluded, while elderly men representing the concerned social unit had the right to exercise authority. At this juncture of Ekie history, the society exemplified Weber's concept of a gerontocracy (1947). The governors and governed shared equal membership in the corporate group whose authority extended over a defined area. Since the right to exercise authority was based on relative seniority, all members of the society were potential successors to those who governed. No individual owned specific rights to a position of authority; instead the right to exercise authority was transmitted to members of the society by personal longevity. Such an arrangement apparently served the Ekie well in an era of political decentralization and community autonomy.

Waves of Warriors: ca. 1700

Although the traditional Ekie political system ensured internal tranquility, it was not as effective in the face of external encroachment. The increasingly powerful Luba Kingdom, situated to the south in the present-day Shaba Region of Zaire, was a constant threat to Ekie integrity. Shortly before the eighteenth century, the Luba began to encroach on neighboring groups and successfully reduced them to tributary status (Reefe 1981). The Ben'Ekie were no exception to the process. The Luba subjugated them during the reign of King Kadilo in the beginning of the eighteenth century and established a settlement of Luba warriors within Ekie territory. The Bena Totue, as these warriors were known, resided in a separate village under the leadership of Mpibue Builu. Their sole concern was the collection of tribute, which they in turn remitted to the Luba royal court. There is no elaboration in Ekie oral tradition of the circumstances that led to the settling of Luba warriors in their land. Luba history, however, provides an insight into the circumstances that led to their presence in Ekie territory.

In the eighteenth century, the Luba began to expand their tributary base to encompass other Bantu troops that participated in the long-distance salt and iron trade. The Ben'Ekie, as well as other Kisongye-speaking groups located in Kasai-Oriental, became the targets of the Luba expansion northward, which was the consequence of a lack of salt resources within their own territory. The Ben'Ekie and other Kasai groups participated in this trade by traveling through the heartland of the Luba kingdom to reach the source of salt and iron in Shaba (Reefe 1981:97–98). According to Luba oral traditions, King Kadilo, who reigned during the early quarter of the eighteenth century, initiated a series of attacks against several western Songye groups. Individually too weak to ward off Luba aggression, the Ben'Ekie and another Songye neighbor, the Beekalebue, formed an alliance. Surprisingly, the two groups defeated the powerful Luba king. In his retreat, Kadilo was forced to leave behind his injured warriors. Abandoned in enemy territory, the Luba warriors were taken in by the Ben'Ekie and became known as the Bena Totue (Verhupen 1936:100).

Although the historical circumstances that led to the presence of Luba warriors in Ekie territory are outlined in Luba oral traditions, the reasons why the Ben'Ekie chose to provide hospitality to their defeated enemies are not explained. A consideration of Luba military tactics yields a possible insight. According to Reefe (1981:197–98), the Luba successfully conquered their enemies by conducting a series of attacks that wore down their foe's resistance over a period of years. In effect, the Luba posed a periodic and continuous threat to their neighbors. Aware of these military tactics, the Ben'Ekie may have thought themselves incapable of repelling subsequent attacks by the more powerful Luba. In this context, the less populous and less powerful Ben'Ekie would have been in a better position to compromise with the Luba at a moment of strength and independence. Therefore, one might argue, the Ben'Ekie offered the Luba warriors an accommodation as a means of averting further Luba aggression. In spite of this, the Ben'Ekie did not avoid the inevitable. Eventually they became tributaries of the powerful Luba, although in a more peaceful manner. On the other hand, the Luba allowed the Ekie to continue to trade for the essential commodity, salt.

Although Luba oral tradition contains no subsequent reference to military conflict with the Ben'Ekie, there are additional references to Luba attacks against other Songye groups, such as the Beekalebue, Bena Milambue, and the Belande, in the same region (Verhupen 1936). Apparently the Luba and the Ben'Ekie coexisted peacefully as a result of the settlement of the Bena Totue in Ekie territory. However, they were never integrated into Ekie society and, to this day, they are referred to as Luba and retain a separate cultural identity.

With the death of the Bena Totue's first leader, Mpibue Builu, the Luba court sent an envoy of soldiers led by Mpibue Lubamba to investigate the situation. According to tradition, Lubamba's investigation concluded that Builu's death was the result of natural causes. In light of Ekie hospitality and the strong encouragement of Ekie elders, Lubamba decided to stay in Ekieland. As before, the Ekie offered a potentially dangerous group land on which to settle within their own borders. They gave Lubamba and his men a site apart from the Bena Totue, and offered him an Ekie woman as a wife.

Unlike Builu, Lubamba became involved in local political affairs by providing numerous services for the Ben'Ekie. Depicted as a skilled hunter, generous, just, and wise, Lubamba settled their disputes, which they brought to him instead of referring them to their own elders. Soon Lubamba attracted a loyal following of Ben'Ekie, who relocated in his village, Bala Bala. Because he was a foreigner, he could not be given the Ekie title, *mwana-nkana,* but instead was referred to as *mfuabana,* a title partially derived from the Luba language, which translates as "chief of the children."

According to Ekie oral tradition, Lubamba had been not only a warrior but an individual of royal stature in Luba. Why would Lubamba, as a member of the powerful Luba court, abandon this status for land, a wife, and a title in a smaller and weaker society? According to Reefe (1981), during the eighteenth century Luba society was marked by succession problems. The internal strife may have encouraged a member of the Luba royal family, apprehensive of his own future, to seek a power base outside the Kingdom. Thus, he may have been eager to take any opportunity to set up his own "small kingdom" and establish his independence from the troubled Luba court.

At Bala Bala, authority was vested in Lubamba, as *mfuabana,* and the village council, which functioned in an advisory capacity. Since they had close and regular contact with Lubamba, the Ben'Ekie were well aware of the difference between their village government and that of Bala Bala. Nevertheless, the indigenous pattern of authority, vested in Ekie elders, remained unaltered in the remaining regions of Ekieland. The lack of gerontocratic principles in Bala Bala had no apparent effect on the larger society at this point in Ekie history.

However, at the death of Lubamba his only descendant, Nkole, introduced a series of innovations which profoundly affected local patterns of authority. During Nkole's lifetime the kingship was introduced into Ekie society, ushering in new principles of authority based on the inheritance of high office.

Formative Years of the Ekie State

By the end of the eighteenth century, Lubamba's successor, Nkole, began to attack neighboring Songye and Luba–Kasai groups. Their eventual subjugation not only provided Nkole with a tribute base but also increased his stature among the Ben'Ekie. According to tradition, Nkole was as generous as his father and, as the young conqueror's success increased, he attracted larger numbers of Ben'Ekie willing to participate in his military campaigns. As the boundaries expanded, Nkole encouraged the Ben'Ekie to spread out and establish new villages. These villages came under Nkole's direct authority when he personally appointed loyal followers to the chiefly position of *mfumu* (pl. *bafumu*).

Under Nkole's leadership, Ekie society, which had previously coopted foreign warriors, now produced warriors from within its own ranks. Cutting across lineage and regional ties, these warriors formed a new social group, whose wealth and position derived from services rendered to Nkole. Outstanding warriors received the title of *kipazula,* war chief, or the position of village chief.

Under Nkole, the Ben'Ekie not only defended themselves against external aggression, but they also became the aggressors. The new spirit of militarism not only secured Ekie society as a whole, but also generated new means of personal wealth. Ekie males who served as warriors gained materially, enhancing their prestige. Thus the oral tradition concerned with this period of Ekie history emphasizes the stability and prosperity that Nkole brought to Ekieland.

Once Ekieland was secure from external threats, Nkole focused his organizational skills internally. In order to extend his authority beyond the villages within his domain, the young conqueror introduced two important ideological changes. The first involved the incorporation of the high priest (*tshite*) into Nkole's small bureaucracy at Bala Bala as a political advisor. Other members of the particular lineage that held exclusive rights to this title disapproved of this subordination, and in response established a separate village in the western region of Ekieland.

As Nkole's principal advisor and confidante, the *tshite* was forced out of ritual seclusion and into the political arena. This change meant that the *tshite* was no longer the highest ranking religious leader in the society, but only the second highest ranking political official. With his ritual duties redefined and directed toward the kingship rather than society as a whole, the *tshite* became responsible for the king's investiture, ritual purity, and burial. Although he continued to control the installation of the *bana-nkana,* these peace officers were placed under the direct authority of Nkole. As the king's representatives, the *bana-nkana* could use their authority only with his permission or at his request.

Once the *tshite* was integrated into the small bureaucracy, Nkole became the chief intermediary between the Ben'Ekie and their ancestors. Thus the highest political and religious positions in the society were fused into a single office with both sacred and secular overtones. An indigenous description of the *tshite*'s new role often employs conjugal terms: "*Tshite ena mukaji wa Nkole.*" ("Tshite is the wife of Nkole.")

This description of the *tshite*'s new role indicates not only his subordinate status to Nkole but also the interdependence established between the two highest ranking offices in the land. Symbolically speaking, Nkole and the *tshite* are the parents of Ekie society. As a result of their cooperation, the society flourishes.

The second ideological innovation introduced by Nkole involved a series of sacrificial offerings at Lake Mbebe, the burial site of the first leader of the Bena Totue, Mpibue Builu. (According to Ekie oral traditions, Builu's burial site later turned into a lake.) Seeking the approval of his Luba ancestor, Nkole offered food items, as well as eight men and eight women, to Builu's spirit, the Lake Mbebe. The Bena Totue interpreted the floating of the food and the drowning of the humans as a sign of Builu's approval of Nkole's leadership.

Nkole's two ideological innovations represent a key ritual manipulation on his part. A crucial factor in the centralization of Ekie political system, his reorganization of the religious and ritual realms integrated various social groups into the new state. By simultaneously linking with and subordinating the office of the *tshite,* who had indisputable and legitimate ties to Ekie ancestors, Nkole established the office of kingship as the primary intermediary between the Ben'Ekie and their ancestors—the ultimate source of social welfare. However, Nkole's legitimacy and success also emanated from a new Luba ancestor. The sacrificial offerings at Lake Mbebe provided Nkole with a ritual link to the powerful Luba empire. This foreign connection protected him against potential subversion by local chiefs and served to integrate the Bena Totue into the newly-founded state. The Bena Totue, who had served as tax collectors for the powerful Luba court, now played a key role in the confirmation of Ekie kings. Symbolically, they chose the Ekie kings, since the sacred Lake Mbebe was situated within their territorial domain. The appointment of all Ekie kings during the precolonial period was validated at Lake Mbebe.

Accompanying this political centralization was a change in the local pattern of authority from one based on age to one based on inheritance of office. Prior to state formation, authority was vested in councils of elders, whose authority was derived from their chronological closeness to the ancestors. The ritual sanction of the *tshite,* represented in the *bana-nkana,* was crucial in the implementation of decisions made by the councils of elders. However, once the kingship replaced the *tshite* as the highest ranking intermediary between the Ben'Ekie and their ancestors, authority was held to be derived from Nkole himself. Thus, the system of authority emanated from the king to those members of the society linked to him. Seniority, which had formally been the most important criterion for determining the allocation and implementation of authority, no longer had a legitimizing value.

In summary, Nkole fused the ritual and political spheres of society into a single office by linking and subordinating the *tshite* to himself. This fusion, which created the highest office in the land, was soon duplicated in village political affairs. Ritual and political sanction were no longer separate on the village level. Chiefs, in consultation with village councils, were able to implement political decisions in their own right, as representatives of the king.

Bukishi: *Gerontocracy Reinstated at the Village Level*

In the beginning of the nineteenth century a secret religious society (*bukishi*) emerged among the Ben'Ekie in response to political centralization. By the end of the century the *bukishi* had permeated almost all levels of the society, in some instances playing a dominant role in village affairs. The *bukishi* consisted of three inner grades.[2] Although membership was said to be universal and voluntary, in practice all persons aspiring to chiefly rank were compelled to join the first grade. The second grade, *bukishi bua nkula,* consisted of both men and women who were responsible for operating the society's initiation schools, implementing the rules laid down by the elders, and enforcing social norms. The *bakula ba bukishi,* the third and highest grade, consisted of elderly men who held legislative and judicial powers.

Every ten to twelve years during precolonial times, children of both sexes who had reached puberty were taken from their homes to spend twenty-four to thirty months in sexually segregated *bukishi* schools. During this seclusion period, the neophytes learned the skills, crafts, and behavior appropriate to adults. Because self-sufficiency was stressed, food allotments provided by the neophytes' families were gradually decreased. By the second year of seclusion, the children were able to produce their own crops for consumption. More importantly, they received instructions concerning the moral behavior expected of a *bukishi* member (*nganga;* pl. *banganga*). Such behavior was believed to guarantee the blessings of the ancestors, and thus enrich the *nganga*'s life. At the end of the seclusion period, an elaborate ceremony, symbolizing the rebirth of the neophytes, was held. Afterwards, the newly initiated members returned to their villages. Shortly thereafter, *bukishi* elders in various villages conducted a sorcery-burning ceremony. During this ceremony, all persons who possessed antisocial magical objects were encouraged to publicly burn them in a large hole dug for the occasion and a dead dog was strung up above the hole to remind villagers of their fate if they refused to do this. The entire village was expected to participate in this ceremony, which was intended to cleanse and revitalize the community. The ceremony was also conducted during the intervals between the initiation schools, when the *bukishi* elders felt there was an unusual amount of strife and hardship in the community.

Thus the *bukishi* provided a moral guide for its members, who were expected to uphold the strictures for the duration of their lives. If a *nganga* broke a *bukishi* rule, he or she was expected to confess to the elders, who would then arrange for a cleansing ceremony that was believed to purge the offender as well as appease the ancestors. Failure to follow this procedure threatened to invoke ancestral wrath, which could be extended to the offender's family and kinsmen. Violation of *bukishi* strictures was believed to defile the earth, which in turn brought undue hardship and infertility to all.

The organization represented the moral center of Ekie society, and the elders were considered to be ethical guardians. Juxtaposed between the *banganga* and the ancestors, the elders were charged with the task of maintaining a social order based on traditional ancestral customs. As long as they fulfilled their task, the *banganga* were guaranteed the benevolence of the ancestors—the ultimate source of prosperity and fertility.

The elders held tremendous power as moral guardians. This power was put into use when the *bukishi* aided village chiefs in their duties. Thus if a chief was unable to determine the culprit in a criminal case, he asked the elders to administer the ordeal by poison. If he wanted to forestall theft, a chief would request the elders to place the concerned property under their protection and put the *bukishi* emblem, a knotted palm frond, on the property; it was believed that the emblem would bring death to anyone who disregarded it. In addition, *bukishi* strictures deterred physical violence and murder by forbidding the shedding of human blood. A *nganga* guilty of homicide was viewed as impure and ostracized until ritually cleansed by the elders. It could take the offender several years to accumulate the fee for the expensive and drawn-out ceremony, placing himself and his family under the extended threat of supernatural sanction.

Despite its concern for the social and moral orders, the *bukishi* functioned as an alternative, rather than a support, for the kingship and its administrative structure. It subverted the power of the village chiefs and, in the process, indirectly diminished the power of the kingship in a variety of ways. First, *bukishi* strictures which forbade the shedding of human blood prevented the recruitment of warriors from among the *banganga* population, which effectively limited the king's ability to recruit for warfare. Second, certain *bukishi* rituals associated with the prosperity and revitalization of the society replicated rituals conducted by the king and the *tshite*. Third, *bukishi* elders considered themselves to be the earthly representatives of the ancestors, which diminished the role of chiefs in this capacity at the village level. Fourth, the *bukishi* tribunal undermined the validity of the chief's court. Finally, the *bukishi* provided a separate avenue for the achievement of authority and prestige in the society. The role of the *bukishi* in the daily life of Ekie villagers suggests that the secret society successfully competed with the formal political structure for the loyalty and allegiance of the general population, which leads us to a series of questions concerning the circumstances surrounding its creation.

Origins of the Bukishi

Questions concerning the origins of the *bukishi* elicited an array of responses from Ekie historians and persons of chiefly rank. The general consensus is that the society was founded by some unspecified elders long after the Ben'Ekie settled into their present homeland. In addition, it is agreed that the *bukishi* did not exist during the period of state formation. Persistent questions concerning its founding elicited one consistent response from interviewers: "*Kala kala, takubadi bukishi, nya, Anka kibangu.*" ("In ancient times, there was no *bukishi,* only *kibangu.*").

This statement reveals that the *bukishi* postdates the *bana-nkana,* holders of the symbolic staff (*kibangu*). More importantly, it suggests that the Ben'Ekie view the *bukishi* and the holders of the *kibangu* in a similar vein, implying that the *bukishi* served a role similar to the holders of the *kibangu.* Thus, as a duplication of the *bana-nkana,* the *bukishi* elders seem to have replaced these peace officers as the guardians of Ekie morality, after the *bana-nkana* were incorporated into the central administrative structure. The oral tradition specifies that the role of the *bana-nkana,* as well as the *tshite,* changed after the founding of the kingship. Once the *tshite* was incorporated into the king's bureaucracy, the *bana-nkana* were placed under the supervision of the king. Their role was diverted away from village affairs, since they no longer enforced the rulings of the village councils, and was limited to the settling of intervillage disputes.

During the initial stages of political centralization, Nkole successfully assumed the role of intermediary between the Ben'Ekie and the ancestors by linking himself to a subordinated *tshite* and the *bana-nkana*. His new sacred role depended on his monopolization of direct access to Ekie spiritual beings. As the *tshite*'s ritual duties were diverted away from the interests of the general populace and directed toward maintaining the sacred nature of the kingship, the kingship became the highest moral agent in the society, while the *tshite* and the *bana-nkana* became extensions of the kingship.

Although the Bena Kavungoi lineage, which held exclusive rights to the *tshite* title, voiced opposition to this change, there is no indication in the oral traditions that other groups opposed it. The absence of peace officers on the village councils would have diminished the power of the elders in village affairs, since they would no longer possess the ritual sanction necessary to implement their decisions.

Prior to kingship, the council of elders constituted the most powerful group in the secular realm. Nkole's introduction of a warrior class and chiefs, who tended to be composed of younger males, however, substantially weakened the status of elderly men in local affairs. This new social group gradually replaced the elders' influence in village affairs. Councils of elders, which had previously held legislative and judicial authority, became mere advisory bodies to chiefs without the legitimacy to enforce decisions. Their status declined further as service to the king replaced seniority as the new criteria for achieving power and prestige. As warriors, the young could augment the king's wealth, and were rewarded accordingly.

The *bukishi* society, which was founded and controlled by elders, aimed at reversing the diminishing role of elders in the political, economic, and ritual spheres. The *bukishi* gave the elders control over the *banganga* population, thus reinstating some of their authority in village affairs. Furthermore, they rechanneled some wealth into the hands of the elders through fees derived from the initiation schools, payments required for the assumption of various offices, and fines levied against offenders of *bukishi* strictures. Finally, the elders got a key role in maintaining the social order and the general welfare of the society through rituals, such as the sorcery-burning ceremony.

Therefore, the *bukishi* can best be interpreted as a movement initiated by elders in an attempt to reclaim their previous authority, at least on a village level. As part of the process, the *bukishi* elders reinstated gerontocratic principles that had existed prior to state formation. The overall effect of this movement was the prevention of complete domination by groups representing an alien political and cultural order. D'Azevedo (1962:516) offers a similar explanation for the emergence of the Poro, a secret society analogous to the *bukishi,* among the Kwa-speaking peoples of Sierra Leone and Liberia. He suggests that the Poro represented an indigenous response to foreign warlords and migrant groups who had been incorporated into Kwa society at an earlier time.

If the Ekie elders were the group most likely to have created the *bukishi,* it is worthwhile to examine the circumstances that allowed them the opportunity to reintroduce gerontocratic principles, particularly in light of the fact that political centralization had brought stability to the society by eliminating the threat of external aggression.

This may have occurred during a period of social chaos, especially soon after the founding of the kingship. This time span is crucial, since the state was founded in about the mid-eighteenth century, and the *bukishi* was probably created in the early decades of the nineteenth century. The assumption is that a discontented group, in this case the Ekie elders, used the opportunity of social turbulence to seize local power for its own interest.

According to oral tradition, the country experienced a period of social disruption after the death of Nkole. Consequently, the king's council reformulated the succession rules pertaining to the kingship, resulting in a prolonged span of time between the naming of the king's heir and his assumption to the office. The *bukishi* may have emerged during one of these intervals when the kingship was inactive.

Nkole fell ill and died during a military expedition against a neighboring group. One of his prized warriors, Madimba, declared himself king. Refusing to return to the capital with the army, Madimba installed himself among the neighboring Bena Nkoshi with the intent of ruling the Ekie people from outside their boundaries. In response the king's council, headed by the *tshite,* asked Nkole's rightful heir, Kabangu, to wage war against the usurper. Because Madimba controlled the royal army, Kabangu considered the mission suicidal and refused to comply with the request. However, Nkole's second son Kibambe, the blacksmith, accepted the mission. After supervising the forging of new weapons and the training of volunteer soldiers, he defeated Madimba and the well-trained royal army in a victorious battle.

When Kibambe returned to Ekieland, the state council dethroned Kabangu, the rightful heir, and installed Kibambe as king. They ordered Kabangu and his followers to leave Bala Bala so that the new king could rule effectively. In order to avoid additional social chaos, the council asked one of its members who possessed the *kibangu* staff to announce the decision to the general public. The state council also proclaimed that in the future no king would have the exclusive right to choose his own heir; instead, the king's choice would have to be confirmed by the council, with the stipulation that the eldest son could not be the successor.

Thus, subsequent Ekie kings could name an heir only from their junior sons. The result was that the nominated successor was often too young to assume the duties of the office. In such a case, the state council reserved the right to appoint a regent, who served until the heir was considered mature. Thus, the principle of gerontocracy was also confirmed on a national level as an aspect of legitimizing ideology. If he did not already possess it, the candidate was also expected to purchase the *mfuabana* title before receiving the title of *nkole,* supreme ruler. After the state council allowed him to make the prescribed sacrificial offering at Lake Mbebe, he became the king.

The succession rules regularly produced a period in which the office of kingship was vacant for all practical political purposes. For example, in the 1970s, the current heir to the throne, Mwana Mbo, who was in his early forties, still had not been granted permission to take the throne! The state council, in concurrence with public opinion, considered Mwana Mbo not wise enough to assume the duties of the kingship because "he was too young a man." According to the Ben'Ekie, only older men have the wisdom and fortitude that the office of *nkole* demands.

If the contemporary situation is any indication of the past, the heir's future claim may have been challenged during those periods when the kingship was inactive. During fieldwork, I was often told by informants that Mwana Mbo was not the rightful heir. In fact, the inhabitants of the Bakua Lubo village group often claimed that their chief was the real supreme ruler of the land. Their argument was based on the chief's descent from the individual who had led the Ekie migration out of Shaba in the distant past.

Although the challenges against the current claimant are only verbal, they suggest that some degree of political opposition to the claimant may have arisen in precolonial times. Thus, it is indeed possible that Ekie elders created the *bukishi* during one of these intervals. Although the exact amount of time for an inactive kingship is difficult to calculate, it is safe to estimate that it may have ranged between ten and twenty years. As of 1980, Mwana Mbo still had not been given permission to assume the duties of the kingship. He had been the official heir for ten years, although he had not had a regent. Although the government of Zaire recognizes Mwana Mbo as supreme leader of the Ben'Ekie, his own people consider him as merely an unconfirmed claimant to the throne.

Dual Nature of Power and Authority in Ekie Society

In precolonial times, the *bukishi* and kingship dominated two distinct spheres of influence within the society. The *bukishi* controlled internal affairs pertaining to the daily life of villagers, and the kingship dominated external affairs concerned with the sovereignty of the kingdom.

While the *bukishi* played an important role in village affairs and held enough power to force chiefs to recognize its presence, it also served as a powerful integrative mechanism and stabilizing force in Ekie society. It created fraternal bonds between members of different kin groups, as well as members of different villages. *Bukishi* members were able to move about freely between different territorial units because *bukishi* hospitality rules regulated interaction between members. On the local level, it linked chiefs to commoners, preventing the development of rigid social stratification. All members were equal in the eyes of Ekie ancestors. The governors and the governed were subject to the same rules. As guardians of Ekie values and morality, *bukishi* officials instructed the society in the ways of the ancestors, and in turn ritually cleansed offenders in order to maintain the benevolence of the ancestors—the society's ultimate source of fertility, prosperity, and peace.

In spite of these important contributions to the general welfare of the society, the *bukishi* represented a competitive economic force in local affairs. Chiefs who were representatives of the formal political system stood to lose revenues from their *bukishi* subjects. For example, members who committed offenses such as theft or incest were judged and fined by *bukishi* officials, rather than chiefs. Such revenues were a substantial loss for Ekie chiefs, since they were not allowed by the state to impose taxes directly on their subjects.

The *bukishi* also provided an alternative avenue for achieving prestige and status. Although the *bukishi* conferred power and prestige primarily on elderly men and women, members initiated into the two higher grades of the association were guaranteed a share of the wealth accumulated from initiation fees and various fines. Thus the *bukishi* also attracted potential candidates for positions and titles associated with the formal political system. The fact that chiefs had to be initiated into the first grade of the *bukishi* provided a means of checking the abuse of chiefly power. Since all *banganga* were expected to uphold the strictures of the association, the *bukishi* helped to define the behavior of chiefs vis-à-vis their subjects.

The rules indicate that the impact of the kingship on the village level was diminished as a result of the power of the *bukishi*. This is confirmed by the observations of others (Wauters 1949; Timmerman 1962; Wissmann 1891). Vansina (1966) describes the power of the *bukishi* in Songye societies in the following manner:

> Yet another type of political structure is provided by the Songye. Here the town was directed by a king with titleholders, as in most kingdoms, but political decisions were often made, it seems, not by this government but a religious association, the *bukishi*. Songye towns could be tributary to other Songye towns . . . Yet the *bukishi* of every town seems to have been independent of those in other cities and the structure is therefore certainly not a typical chiefdom or kingdom. (pp. 29–30)

Because of insufficient data on Songye groups, Vansina (1966) was unwilling to speculate on how this type of political structure emerged and functioned.

An important question remains. If the *bukishi* diminished the power of the kingship on the village level, why was it tolerated? Although it apparently did not pose a direct threat to the authority of the kingship, it did reduce the power of the king's representatives, the chiefs. In a way, this actually helped to preserve the kingship. *Bukishi* rules forbid its members, chiefs and commoners alike, from becoming involved in armed conflict against the king. For example, during periods of inactive kingship, the *bukishi* precepts circumvented anarchy, as well as armed rebellion. However, the rules did not apply to people who did not belong to the *bukishi;* those people in *mavumbu* established after the kingship were less involved in the *bukishi*. However, since the chiefs were initiated into the first grade of the *bukishi,* they would have also been compelled to follow the group's moral strictures.

Armed rebellions challenging the power of a claimant to the throne would have been virtually impossible to mount in light of the *bukishi* rule that forbids murder and the shedding of human blood. Even if a chief dared to ignore this stricture by contemplating rebellion, he would have found it difficult to rally support from his subjects. Evidence for this is found in the account of an attempted rebellion in the second half of the nineteenth century. At the death of Kasongo IV, his heir, Kankieza, was deemed too young to take on the responsibilities of the kingship. The state council chose Budia, Kankieza's older half-brother, as regent. However, after several years, Budia announced that he had no intention of relinquishing power to Kankieza, and instead named his own son to succeed him. The state council did not concur and informed Kankieza. Budia's unsuccessful attempt to assassinate the young heir eventually led to a civil war. As regent, Budia controlled the state army which consisted of slaves. Kankieza was unable to rally support from among the Ben'Ekie as the majority of the people abided by *bukishi* strictures. Thus, Kankieza's followers were fewer in number and less equipped than those of Budia's.

At this juncture, Kankieza was forced to appeal to his powerful neighbors, the Beekalebue, whose king, Lumpungu, headed a well-organized army equipped with firearms obtained from Zanzibari slave merchants. Pressured by the merchants to provide them with a regular quota of slaves, Lumpungu agreed to aid Kankieza on the condition that all of Budia's warriors captured in battle could be sold into slavery. Lumpungu defeated Budia, and Kankieza gained control of the Ekie kingship. His coronation, however, was the result, not of stirring the conscience of the general populace, but of creating an alliance with a powerful neighboring king who helped him destroy his opposition.

The Kankieza incident reveals additional information on the relationship between the *bukishi* and the kingship. Since the *bukishi* forbade the shedding of human blood, regardless of the ethnic affiliation of the victim, Ekie kings had to man their armies primarily with foreign slaves. Thus, by the second half of the nineteenth century, royal slaves lived in numerous villages near the capital. Although the slaves possessed essentially the same rights as free-born Ekie, they had to be prepared to abandon their work in response to a royal command for military duty.

Unlike slaves owned by Ekie commoners, royal slaves could not marry free-born Ekie nor could they join the *bukishi*. Their offspring inherited their slave status, providing Ekie kings with a stable source of warriors. By contrast, the offspring of slaves owned by Ekie commoners could intermarry within their master's kin group, and their descendants were free born and consequently absorbed into Ekie society. As a result, chiefs were unable to accumulate enough followers, whether free-born or slave, to seriously threaten the authority of the kings through a revolt. Thus, Ekie kings tolerated the *bukishi* because, through its control over the general populace, it checked the power of chiefs and rivals to the kingship during the drawn-out interregnum period.

On the whole, Ekie kings demanded very little from their subjects in terms of taxes. The Ekie court supported itself economically by exploiting its tributaries and receiving agricultural produce from royal slave villages. The king and *evumbu* chiefs were relatively unaffected by the diversion of revenues away from formal political officials to the *bukishi*. In the nineteenth century, the main sources of a chief's wealth were the slaves he received from the king and the raffia cloth that he traded with neighboring groups. Poor village chiefs, however, stood to lose economically when their subjects were largely *bukishi* members, although they could circumvent this financial loss by joining the higher grades of *bukishi* and sharing in the wealth of its officials. Such a move enhanced both their authority and wealth. Again, rather than adversely affecting the kingship, a strong association between a chief and the *bukishi* seems to have strengthened, or rather secured, the office.

Conclusions

In this study, I have demonstrated how two institutions, based on distinct principles of power and authority, emerged and coexisted in precolonial Ekie society. The fact that power emanated from both centers indicates that the *bukishi* and the kingship coexisted on relatively harmonious terms. Although the *bukishi* reinstated village elders in positions of authority, it did not threaten the existence of the kingship. Indeed, because of the important role it played in maintaining the social order, the *bukishi* served to preserve the kingship. The presence of the *bukishi* diminished the power of the chiefs, making it difficult for them to conspire against the kingship and to rally support from the ranks of the villagers. This fact was particularly crucial in maintaining the kingship when it was inactive and when challenges to its authority were likely to occur. The *bukishi* helped to maintain the social order, allowing the kings to focus their attention on expansion and conquest outside Ekieland. The *bukishi* also prevented the growth of a free-born warrior class, which benefitted the kingship in the long run, especially during the long interregnum period.

The relationship that existed between these two institutions is best characterized by mutual respect for each other's locus of power in Ekie society. The kingship was recognized as well equipped for managing external affairs, although its legitimate monopoly on physical force was limited to purposes of defense and aggression. Its primary role was to protect the sovereignty of Ekieland from external aggression. The king had at his disposal an army of slaves that was prepared to serve him at all times. This standing army made the king economically independent of the general populace. The Ekie king was able to support his court primarily with tribute acquired from conquered enemies. As a result, the king did not demand high revenues from the Ekie populace and was relatively uninvolved in the daily affairs of the village.

On the other hand, the *bukishi* was recognized as best suited for managing internal affairs and played a dominant role in village-level politics. Its primary role was to uphold Ekie morality, which in turn guaranteed the benevolence of ancestral spirits. As earthly representatives of the ancestors, *bukishi* elders monopolized the manipulation of ritual sanction, which was instrumental in maintaining social order on a village level.

The dual nature of authority in Ekie society is not necessarily unique. Brown's study (1950) of secret societies in West Africa demonstrates their tremendous power in state societies. Thus, it is possible that a dual pattern of authority also existed in these societies during precolonial times. However, what is important in the case of the Ben'Ekie is that historical data provide an insight into the social conditions under which these quasi–political institutions may have emerged. Although anthropologists have long agreed that secret societies functioned primarily to check the abuse of chiefly power, these institutions have not been examined in historical terms.

This study also provides an insight into an indigenous response to the process of state formation, which was instigated by a migration of warriors from another area. Although the historical significance of the hunter-king myth of genesis has been challenged (Reefe 1977), there is substantial evidence supporting the historical role of Luba migrants in Ekie society. It seems unlikely that the Ben'Ekie invented fictitious connections to Luba royalty as Reefe (1977) suggests is the case with other groups in eastern Zaire. A reexamination of the historicity of hunter-king origin myths may reveal that the emergence of secret societies such as the *bukishi* represents a relatively common indigenous response to the process of secondary state formation.

Notes

1. Prior to colonization in 1892, the Ben'Ekie had limited interaction with both Arabs and Europeans, including twelve years of contact with the former and ten years of contact with the latter.

2. Wauters (1947) and Van Hamme (1952) describe the *bukishi* as having two rather than three inner grades. However, my informants consistently spoke of three inner grades, the white *bukishi,* the red *bukishi,* and *bukishi* elders, specifying distinct duties and authority for each grade.

3. Data were collected during fourteen months of fieldwork conducted in Zaire between January 1976 and April 1977 under the auspices of the State University of New York, Stony Brook.

References

Boone, Olga
1961 Carte ethnique du Congo; Quart sud-est. Tervuren: Musée Royal de L'Afrique Centrale, Science Humaine, No. 37.

Bradbury, R. E.
1971 Patrimonialism and Gerontocracy in Benin Political Culture. *In* Man in Africa. Mary Douglas and Phyllis M. Kaberry, eds. pp. 17–37. New York: Doubleday and Co.

Brown, Paula
1950 Patterns of Authority in West Africa. Africa 31(4):261–78.

D'Azevedo, Warren L.
1962 Some Historical Problems in the Delineation of a Central Atlantic Region. Annals of the New York Academy of Science 96:512–38.

Fairley, Nancy J.
1978 Mianda ya Ben'Ekie: A History of the Ben'Ekie. Ph.D. dissertation, Anthropology Department, State University of New York, Stony Brook.
1987 Ideology and State Formation: Case of the Ben'Ekie. *In* The African Frontier. Igor Kopytoff, ed. pp. 91–100. Bloomington: Indiana University Press.

Feierman, Steven
1974 The Shambaa Kingdom. Madison: University of Wisconsin Press.

Overbergh, C. Van
1908 Les Basongye. Bruxelles: Albert de Wit Collection de Monographie Ethnographie.

Reefe, Thomas Q.
1977 Traditions of Genesis and the Luba Diaspora. History in Africa 4: 183–205.
1981 The Rainbow and Kings: A History of the Luba Empire to 1891. Berkeley: University of California.

Packard, Randall M.
1981 Chiefship and Cosmology: An Historical Study of Political Competition. Bloomington: Indiana University Press.

Schrader, F.
1883 Wissmann & Pogge au Travers de L'Afrique. Revue Geographique Internationale 8:81–84.

Timmerman, P.
1962 Les Sapo Sapo prés de Luluabourg. Africa Tervuren 8(2):29–53.

Van Hamme, P. E.
1952 Enquête sur le droit coutumier des Bakwa Lubo. Bulletin des Juri-

dictions Indigènes et du Droit Coutumier Congolais 20:313–24; 337–51.

Vansina, Jan

1966 Kingdoms of the Savanna. Madison: University of Wisconsin Press.

1978 The Children of Woot: A History of the Kuba People. Madison: University of Wisconsin Press.

Verhupen, Edmond

1936 Baluba et Balubaïsés du Katanga, Anvers: L'avenir Belge.

Wauters, G.

1947 L'Estorérie des noirs de voilée. Bruxelles: Editions Européenes.

Weber, Max

1947 The Theory of Social and Economic Organization. London: Hodge.

Willis, Roy

1981 A State in the Making: Myth, History and Social Transformation in Pre-Colonial Ufipa. Bloomington: Indiana University Press.

Wissmann, Hermann Von

1888 On the Influence of Arab Traders in West Central Africa. Proceedings of the Royal Geographical Society 10:525–31.

1891 My Second Journey through Equatorial Africa from the Congo to the Zambesi in the Years 1886–1888. Minna J. Bergmann, transl. London: Chattos & Windus.

Contributors

W. Arens received his Ph.D. from the University of Virginia in 1970 and is currently professor of anthropology at the State University of New York at Stony Brook. He is the author of *On the Frontier of Change, The Man-Eating Myth,* and *The Original Sin,* as well as various articles on the Shilluk and Nilotic ethnography in general.

Dan Bauer is associate professor of anthropology at Lafayette College where he heads the Department of Anthropology and Sociology. He has conducted research among the Tigray of Ethiopia and the Chinantec of Mexico. He is the author of *Household and Society in Ethiopia* and numerous articles ranging in subject matter from ecology to systems of thought. His current interests focus on the subject of power and its dramatization.

Donald Cosentino teaches African folklore and mythology at the University of California, Los Angeles. He has worked in eastern and northern Nigeria and among the Mende and Krio people of Sierra Leone in

1973–74 and 1983. He is the author of *Defiant Maids and Stubborn Farmers* and has published widely on African popular cultures in many journals and magazines. At the present time, he is researching the myths and popular traditions of Haitian Vodoun.

Victoria Ebin received her Ph.D. in social anthropology from the University of Cambridge in 1979. She has held positions at the Musée de l'Homme in Paris, Cambridge University Museum, and the Brooklyn Museum. At the present time, she is conducting comparative research on Senegalese immigrants in New York City and France, where she is currently associated with the Ecole des Hautes Etudes en Sciences Sociales.

Ronald K. Engard received his Ph.D. from Indiana University in 1986 and is currently assistant professor of anthropology at the College of William and Mary. He has conducted field research on the oral traditions, art, and social organization of the Bafut of the Northwest Province of Cameroon. His recent research focuses on the use of "constitutional symbols" in African art and on questions of art and power generally.

Nancy J. Fairley is a social anthropologist and assistant professor of Black Studies at Lehman College, City University of New York. She has conducted field work in Zaire and in the American South. Currently she is completing a research project on a black evangelical movement in the early twentieth century. Her primary research focus has been on the ways in which diverse black societies manipulate ritual power.

Michelle Gilbert received her Ph.D. from the University of London in 1982. She is currently a Mellon Fellow at the Metropolitan Museum of Art in New York, completing a book on Akwapim royal rituals. She has conducted ethnographic field work in Ghana in the kingdom of Akwapim among the Akan, Okere Buan, and the Anlo Ewe in 1976–78 and 1986–88. She is continuing research on ethnohistory, micro-politics, ideology, and spirit possession in Ghana.

Alma Gottlieb is assistant professor of anthropology at the University of Illinois, Champaign-Urbana. She has conducted field research among the Beng in the Ivory Coast in 1979–80 and again in 1985. She is coeditor (with Thomas Buckley) of *Blood Magic: The Anthropology of Menstruation* and has published numerous articles in anthropology journals. Her research interests lie in the cultural construction of knowledge, gender symbolism, theoretical issues in field work, and cultural models of social organization.

Ivan Karp is curator of African ethnography at the Smithsonian Institution's National Museum of Natural History, Department of Anthropology. A social anthropologist, he has written on the peoples of Africa, especially the Iteso of Kenya and is the author of *Fields of Change among the Iteso of Kenya* and co-editor of *Explorations in African Systems of Thought* and *Exhibiting Cultures: The Poetics and Politics of Museum Display,* as well as various articles on social organization, systems of thought, social theory, and the image of the other in Western forms of discourse.

John Middleton is professor of anthropology and religious studies at Yale University. He has done research in Uganda, Zanzibar, Nigeria, Ghana, and Kenya, and has held positions at London, Northwestern, and New York Universities. He is the author of *Lugbara Religion, The Lugbara of Uganda, The Study of the Lugbara, Land Tenure in Zanzibar, The Effects of Economic Change on Traditional Political System in Africa,* and of many papers on various topics in African anthropology.

Aidan Southall is professor of anthropology at the University of Wisconsin at Madison. He is the author of *Alur Society, Townsmen in the Making,* and the editor of *Social Change in Modern Africa* and *Urban Anthropology,* as well as many articles on social organization, ethnicity, symbolic processes, and modes of production. Currently he is writing a book on the segmentary state.

Roy Willis was born in London in 1927. After working in commerce and journalism, he studied social anthropology under Evans-Pritchard at Oxford University and conducted field research among the Fipa in 1962–64, 1966, and 1977. He is the author of *Man and Beast, There Was a Certain Man, A State in the Making,* and numerous other scholarly publications. With Signe Howell, he is joint editor of a forthcoming volume entitled *Societies at Peace.*

Bonnie L. Wright is a social anthropologist who has conducted extensive research in Senegal on stratification, the distribution of power, and concepts of personhood among the Wolof. She is currently writing a thesis in anthropology at Indiana University.